"十三五"国家重点图书

湖北省学术著作 出版专项资金
Hubei Special Funds for
Academic Publications

海上共同开发国际案例与实践研究丛书／总主编　杨泽伟

海上共同开发协定续编

杨泽伟　主编

WUHAN UNIVERSITY PRESS
武汉大学出版社

图书在版编目(CIP)数据

海上共同开发协定续编/杨泽伟主编. —武汉:武汉大学出版社,
2018.11

海上共同开发国际案例与实践研究丛书/杨泽伟总主编

"十三五"国家重点图书　湖北省学术著作出版专项资金资助项目

ISBN 978-7-307-20607-6

Ⅰ.海…　Ⅱ.杨…　Ⅲ.海洋资源—资源开发—国际合作—海洋
法—文件—汇编　Ⅳ.D993.5

中国版本图书馆 CIP 数据核字(2018)第 254408 号

责任编辑:张　欣　　　责任校对:汪欣怡　　　版式设计:汪冰滢

出版发行:**武汉大学出版社**　　(430072　武昌　珞珈山)

　　　　　(电子邮件:cbs22@whu.edu.cn　网址:www.wdp.com.cn)

印刷:武汉中远印务有限公司

开本:720×1000　1/16　印张:31.75　字数:518 千字　插页:2

版次:2018 年 11 月第 1 版　　2018 年 11 月第 1 次印刷

ISBN 978-7-307-20607-6　　定价:88.00 元

本书得到了 2017 年度教育部人文社会科学重点研究基地重大项目"维护中国国家权益的国际法问题研究"（项目编号 17JJD820006）、2016年度教育部哲学社会科学研究重大课题攻关项目"世界海洋大国的海洋发展战略研究"（项目批准号 16JZD029）、教育部哲学社会科学研究重大课题攻关项目"海上共同开发国际案例与实践研究"的资助，特致谢忱。

总　序

　　一般认为，海上共同开发是指两国或两国以上的政府在协议的基础上，共同勘探开发跨界或争议海域的自然资源。例如，德国教授雷纳·拉戈尼（Rainer Lagoni）认为，海上共同开发是建立在协议的基础上，对一块有争议海域的非生物资源进行以开发为目的的国家间经济合作方式。[①]日本学者三好正弘（Masahiro Miyoshi）强调："共同开发是一种临时性质的政府间安排，以功能性目的旨在共同勘探和（或）开发领海之外海床的碳氢化合物资源。"[②] 中国学者高之国博士也指出："共同开发是指两个或两个以上的国家达成政府间的协议，其目的是为开发和分配尚未划界的领土争议重叠区的潜在自然资源，而共同行使在此区域内的主权和管辖权。"[③]

　　从国际法角度来看，海上共同开发是和平解决国际争端原则的具体化。按照《联合国海洋法公约》第 74 条和第 83 条的规定，在达成划界协议前，"有关各国应基于谅解和合作的精神，尽一切努力作出实际性的临时安排，并在此过渡期间内，不危害或阻碍最后协议的达成。这种安排应不妨碍最后界限的划定"。此外，国际法院在 1969 年 "北海大陆架案"（the North Sea Continental Shelf Cases）的判决中也确认，大陆架划界可通过协议解决，或达不成协议时通过公平划分重叠区域，或通过共同开发

---

　　① 参见 Rainer Lagoni, Oil and Gas Deposits Across National Frontiers, American Journal of International Law, Vol. 73, 1979, p. 215。

　　② Masahiro Miyoshi, The Joint Development of Offshore Oil and Gas in Relation to Maritime Boundary Delimitation, Maritime Briefing (International Boundaries Research Unit), Vol. 2, No. 5, 1999, p. 3.

　　③ Zhiguo Gao, The Legal Concept and Aspects of Joint Development in International Law, in Ocean Yearbook , Vol. 13, the University of Chicago Press 1998, p. 112.

的协议解决。① 可见，无论是国际条约还是国际司法实践，都把海上共同开发看做相关海域划界前的一种临时性安排。

自 1958 年巴林与沙特阿拉伯签订《巴林—沙特阿拉伯边界协定》、实施海上共同开发以来，共同开发跨界或争议海域资源的国家实践已成为一种较为普遍的现象，迄今海上共同开发的国际案例也有近 30 例。回顾海上共同开发 60 年左右的发展历程，海上共同开发可以分为以下四个阶段：第一，海上共同开发的产生阶段（1958—1969 年），在波斯湾和西欧一共出现了 5 例海上共同开发案。第二，海上共同开发的发展阶段（1970—1993 年），一共出现了 14 例海上共同开发案，涉及 26 个国家，包括亚洲国家 11 个，欧洲国家 5 个，非洲国家 7 个，美洲国家 2 个及大洋洲的澳大利亚。第三，海上共同开发的回落阶段（1994—2000 年），只有一例海上共同开发案，即 1995 年 9 月英国与阿根廷签订的《关于在西南大西洋近海活动进行合作的联合声明》。第四，海上共同开发的平稳阶段（2001 年至今），进入 21 世纪以来，海上共同开发活动又渐趋增多，产生了近 10 例的海上共同开发实践。

就中国而言，中国拥有约 1.8 万千米的大陆海岸线，海上与 8 个国家相邻或相向。中国与一些周边海上邻国存在岛屿主权争议和海域划界争端。早在 20 世纪 70 年代末，中国政府就提出了"主权属我、搁置争议、共同开发"原则，试图解决中国与周边海上邻国间的岛屿主权和海洋权益争端。然而，30 多年过去了，从中国整体的周边海域来看，海上共同开发举步维艰，迄今尚未得到真正实现。

值得注意的是，2013 年 10 月，中国、文莱两国发表了《中华人民共和国和文莱达鲁萨兰国联合声明》，双方决定进一步深化两国关系，并一致同意支持两国相关企业开展海上共同开发、勘探和开采海上油气资源。紧接着，中国、越南两国发表了《新时期深化中越全面战略合作的联合声

---

① 杰塞普（Jessup）法官在该案的个别意见中也强调，在有争议但尚未划界而又有部分领土重叠的大陆架区域，共同开发的方法更合适。参见 North Sea Continental Shelf Cases（Federal Republic of Germany/Denmark, Federal Republic of Germany/ Netherlands），Judgments, I. C. J. Reports 1969, available at http：//www.icj-cij.org/docket/ files/52/5561.pdf，最后访问日期 2017 年 11 月 29 日。

明》，双方同意积极研究和商谈共同开发问题，在政府边界谈判代表团框架下成立中越海上共同开发磋商工作组；本着先易后难、循序渐进的原则，稳步推进湾口外海域划界谈判并积极推进该海域的共同开发。① 2014年11月，中国国家主席习近平分别会见前来参加亚太经合组织第22次领导人非正式会议的文莱苏丹哈桑纳尔、马来西亚总理纳吉布时也指出："中方愿意同文方加强海上合作，推动南海共同开发尽早取得实质进展"；中、马"双方要推进海上合作和共同开发，促进地区和平、稳定、繁荣"。2015年11月，《中越联合声明》再次强调："双方将稳步推进北部湾湾口外海域划界谈判并积极推进该海域的共同开发，同意加大湾口外海域工作组谈判力度，继续推进海上共同开发磋商工作组工作，加强低敏感领域合作。"可以预见，海上共同开发问题将成为未来中国对外关系的重要内容之一。因此，全面深入研究"海上共同开发国际案例与实践"，无疑具有重要的理论价值与现实意义。

为了进一步推动海上共同开发的国际法理论与实践研究，2013年10月，在武汉大学中国边界与海洋研究院和国际法研究所的鼎力支持下，特别是在武汉大学资深教授胡德坤老师的鼓励和帮助下，我以首席专家的身份，联合国内外20多家教研机构和实务部门的专家，成功申报了教育部哲学社会科学研究重大课题攻关项目——"海上共同开发国际案例与实践研究"，并被批准立项。经过几年的悉心研究，我们逐步推出了一些研究成果。"海上共同开发国际案例与实践研究丛书"就是其中之一。

"海上共同开发国际案例与实践研究丛书"的出版，具有以下学术价值和现实意义。

第一，它将开拓海洋法理论的新视野。传统海洋法研究是以《联合国海洋法公约》中的相关制度为主，而在"和平、发展、合作"的新时代背景下，"中国梦"的实现、中国海洋权益的维护给我们提出了许多新问题。"海上共同开发国际案例与实践研究丛书"从海上共同开发国际案例的分析入手，着眼于海上共同开发在"和平、发展、合作"的时代背景下面临

---

① 早在2005年10月，中国海洋石油总公司和越南石油总公司就在越南河内签署了《关于北部湾油气合作的框架协议》。

的重大挑战，对海上共同开发的相关法律问题进行深入细致的研究，同时总结归纳出海上共同开发的优势、不足、经验、教训及启示，指出中国与周边海上邻国进行海上共同开发的困境与出路，具有十分重要的现实性和前瞻性。因此，"海上共同开发国际案例与实践研究丛书"可以拓新海洋法理论研究的视野，扩大中国在该领域的国际话语权。

第二，它有利于进一步促进国际法与国内法的互动、多学科的交叉。海上共同开发问题，涉及国际公法、国际私法、国际经济法、国际投资法、国际环境法、民商法以及国际关系、国际政治和外交学等内容。"海上共同开发国际案例与实践研究丛书"对海上共同开发合同进行研究，将扩大特殊国际民商事合同的范畴，丰富国际民商事合同法的内容；对海上共同开发中的投资保护、投资保险等内容的研究，是对特殊领域的国际投资法的完善；对海上共同开发争端解决机制的研究，有利于促进对国际民商事争议解决理论的研究；对海上共同开发优势、局限及其影响因素等方面的总结，将进一步推动国际法与国际关系的相互交融。同时，海上共同开发活动的复杂性和挑战性将促使我们采用以问题为中心、多学科方向共同研究一个问题的理论研究方法，这有利于扩展研究的视角，丰富研究内容和研究方法。

第三，它有助于进一步推动能源安全问题的研究。早在1993年中国就成为了石油净进口国，到目前中国石油对外依存度已达到60%左右。因此，中国学术界一直在关注能源安全问题，这方面的研究成果也比较多。然而，已有的研究成果主要是从能源安全保障的宏观角度出发，涉及能源安全的战略、政策和法律体系的构建等问题，或对能源领域的合作做一些整体研究，并局限于一国领域内资源的合作开发。"海上共同开发国际案例与实践研究丛书"则从微观上对维护能源安全的一个具体措施——海上油气资源共同开发问题进行研究，对海上油气资源共同开发涉及的基本问题、公私法问题、争端解决机制等都进行了详细的论述，有利于进一步发展和完善有关能源安全以及海上石油资源共同开发的理论。

第四，它将为中国与周边邻国进行海上共同开发提供理论支撑。"海上共同开发国际案例与实践研究丛书"在深入研究海上共同开发基本理论问题的基础上，重点剖析已有的海上共同开发的国际案例和协定文本，详细探讨海上共同开发所涉及的第三方权利的处理、共同开发区块的划定、管理模式、税收制度、收益分配、海洋环境保护、管辖权以及争端解决程序等问题，并总结归纳出海上共同开发的优势、局限、经验、教训与启示等。"海上共同开发国际案例与实践研究丛书"的上述研究内容，无疑将为中国与周边邻国进行海上共同开发提供智力支持。同时，探讨海上共同开发周边近海资源的可行性和相关制度，为中国今后对外合作做好理论准备，也是十分必要的。

第五，它将为中国与周边邻国实现海上共同开发的突破提供法律政策建议。"海上共同开发国际案例与实践研究丛书"的出发点是分析国际社会已有的海上共同开发案例和协定文本，落脚点是中国与周边邻国海上共同开发的实践。因此，"海上共同开发国际案例与实践研究丛书"将在研究海上共同开发典型案例和协定文本的基础上，通过回顾中国与周边邻国海上共同开发的有关实践，深刻剖析中国与周边邻国的海上共同开发究竟存在哪些困境，产生这些困境的原因又是什么；最后为中国与周边邻国海上共同开发的突破提供一些具有操作性的法律政策建议。

第六，它将为维护中国岛屿主权和海洋权益提供法律解决参考方案。中国可主张的管辖海域面积约为 300 万平方千米。由于历史和现实的复杂原因，在属于中国主张管辖的 300 万平方千米的海域中，近一半存在争议，海域被分割、岛礁被占领、资源被掠夺的情况较普遍。中国的 8 个海上邻国，对中国的一些岛屿主权和海洋权益均提出不同程度的无理要求。然而，已有的海上共同开发的国际案例均表明，海上共同开发与海域划界存在着密切的关系。因此，"海上共同开发国际案例与实践研究丛书"的研究成果将为中国国家领导人、国家机关、政府部门在制定和实施中国海洋维权措施的过程中、在中国合理解决与邻国海洋权益争端的问题上，提供国际法方面的智讯，从而为中国合理解决岛屿主权和海洋权益争议提供参考方案。

"海上共同开发国际案例与实践研究丛书"的顺利出版，离不开武汉大学出版社的大力支持，特别是策划编辑张欣老师的鼎力相助，在此特致谢忱；同时，也很感谢"2017 年度湖北省学术著作出版专项资金"的资助。此外，"海上共同开发国际案例与实践研究丛书"存在的错讹之处，恳请读者不吝指正。

杨泽伟①

2017 年 11 月 29 日

于武汉大学珞珈山

①　武汉大学"珞珈杰出学者"、二级教授、法学博士、武汉大学国际法研究所和中国边界与海洋研究院博士生导师，国家社科基金重大招标项目和教育部哲学社会科学研究重大课题攻关项目首席专家。

目　　录

上篇：海上共同开发协定

一、1960 年捷克斯洛伐克与奥地利共同开发案 ················· 3
　　Agreement between the Government of the Czechoslovakia
　　Republic and the Austria Federal Government Concerning
　　the Working of Common Deposits of Natural Gas and
　　Petroleum ················· 3

二、1969 年卡塔尔与阿布扎比酋长国共同开发案 ················· 8
　　Agreement between Qatar and Abu Dhabi on Settlement
　　of Marine Boundaries and Ownership of Islands ················· 8

三、1971 年伊朗与沙迦共同开发案 ················· 11
　　1. Memorandum of Understanding between Iran and Sharjah ······ 11
　　2. 《伊朗与沙迦间谅解备忘录》 ················· 12

四、1974 年苏丹和沙特阿拉伯共同开发案 ················· 13
　　Sudan and Saudi Arabia Agreement relating to the Joint
　　Exploitation of the Natural Resources of the Sea-bed and
　　Subsoil of the Red Sea in the Common Zone ················· 13

五、1976 年英国与挪威共同开发弗里格天然气案 ················· 18
　　1. Framework Agreement between the Government of the United
　　Kingdom of Great Britain and Northern Ireland and the
　　Government of the Kingdom of Norway concerning
　　Cross-Boundary Petroleum Co-operation ················· 18

2. 《大不列颠及北爱尔兰联合王国政府与挪威王国政府间
关于跨界石油合作的框架协定》 ………………………… 54

六、1979 年泰国湾共同开发案 ……………………………… 79

1. Statement of the Territorial Sea, the Contiguous Zone,
the Exclusive Economic Zone, and the Continental
Shelf of Vietnam, 12 May 1977 ……………………… 79

2. Statement of 12 November 1982 by the Government
of the Socialist Republic of VietNam on the Territorial
Sea Baseline of VietNam …………………………… 82

3. Statement Issued by the Spokesman of the Ministry
of Foreign Affairs of 15 January 1978 ……………… 83

4. Cambodian Council of State Decree on Territorial Waters …… 85

5. The Brévié Line, 31 January 1939 …………………… 89

6. Agreement on Historic Waters of Vietnam and
Kampuchea ………………………………………… 91

7. Declaration of the Office of the Prime Minister Concerning the
Inner Part of the Gulf of Thailand, 22 September 1959 ……… 94

8. Proclamation Establishing the Breadth of the Territorial
Waters ……………………………………………… 94

9. Announcement of the Office of the Prime Minister Concerning
the Straight Baselines and Internal Waters of Thailand ……… 95

10. Proclamation on Demarcation of the Continental Shelf of
Thailand in the Gulf of Thailand, 18 May 1973 …………… 96

11. Royal Proclamation Establishing the Exclusive
Economic Zone of the Kingdom of Thailand,
23 February 1981 ………………………………… 98

12. Announcement of the Office of the Prime Minister Concerning
Straight Baselines and Internal Waters of Thailand Area 4,
17 August 1992 …………………………………… 99

13. Royal Proclamation Establishing the Contiguous Zone
of the Kingdom of Thailand, 14 August 1995 ………… 100

14. Agreement between the Government of the Kingdom
    of Thailand and the Government of the Socialist
    Republic of Viet Nam on the Delimitation of the
    Maritime Boundary between the Two Countries
    in the Gulf of Thailand, 9 August 1997 ·············· 101
15. Treaty between the Kingdom of Thailand and Malaysia
    Relating to the Delimitation of the Territorial Seas of the
    Two Countries, 24 October 1979 ···················· 104
16. Memorandum of Understanding between Malaysia and the
    Kingdom of Thailand on the Delimitation of the Continental
    Shelf Boundary between the Two Countries in the Gulf of
    Thailand, 24 October 1979 ························· 107
17. Franco-Siamese Boundary Treaty, 23 March 1907 ·········· 110
18. Continental Shelf Act 1966-Act No. 57 of 28 July 1966,
    as Amended by Act No. 83 of 1972 ···················· 114
19. Exclusive Economic Zone Act, 1984, Act No. 311 ·········· 120

七、1981 年冰岛与挪威扬马延岛共同开发案 ··············· 145
    1. Agreement between Norway and Iceland on Fishery
       and Continental Shelf Questions ···················· 145
    2. 《挪威与冰岛间关于渔业和大陆架问题的协定》 ················ 150
    3. Additional Protocol to the Agreement of 28 May 1980 between
       Norway and Iceland concerning Fishery and Continental
       Shelf Questions and the Agreement derived therefrom
       of 22 October 1981 on the Continental Shelf between
       Jan Mayen and Iceland ························· 154
    4. 《1980 年 5 月 28 日挪威和冰岛关于渔业与大陆架问题的
       协定以及 1981 年 10 月 22 日由此衍生的扬马延岛和
       冰岛间关于大陆架协定之附加议定书》 ················ 155
    5. Agreement between Iceland and Norway concerning
       Transboundary Hydrocarbon Deposits ················ 156

6.《冰岛与挪威间关于跨界油气矿藏的协定》 …………………… 163

八、**1989 年阿拉伯也门共和国与也门民主人民共和国共同开发案** ……… 168
Aden Summit Agreement between the Yemen Arab Republic and
the People's Democratic Republic of Yemen …………………… 168

九、**1995 年英国与阿根廷共同开发案** …………………………… 172
1. Joint Statement of 15 February 1990 Re-establishing
Diplomatic Relations between Britain and Argentina ………… 172
2.《1990 年 2 月 15 日英国和阿根廷恢复外交关系的
共同声明》 ……………………………………………………… 176
3. UK-Argentina Joint Statement on the Conservation
of Fisheries ……………………………………………………… 178
4.《联合王国和阿根廷关于渔业保护的共同声明》 …………… 182
5. Joint Declaration of 27 September 1995 Cooperation
Over Offshore Activities in the South West Atlantic ………… 184
6.《1995 年 9 月 27 日关于西南大西洋近海活动合作的
共同宣言》 ……………………………………………………… 189
7. Declaration of the British Government with regard to the
Joint Declaration signed by the British and Argentine
Foreign Ministers on Cooperation over Offshore Activities
in the South West Atlantic ……………………………………… 193
8.《英国政府关于〈英国与阿根廷外交部长签订有关在
西南大西洋近海活动合作的共同宣言〉之宣言》 …………… 194
9. Statement by the Argentine Government with regard to
the Joint Declaration signed by the Foreign Ministers
of Argentina and the United Kingdom on Exploration
and Exploitation of Hydrocarbons …………………………… 195
10.《阿根廷政府关于〈阿根廷外交部长与英国签订有关
油气勘探与开发共同宣言〉之声明》 ………………………… 196

十、1995 年丹麦与挪威共同开发案 ┄┄┄┄┄┄┄┄┄┄┄ 198

Agreement between the Kingdom of Denmark and the Kingdom
of Norway Concerning the Delimitation of the Continental
Shelf in the Area Between Jan Mayen and Greenland and
Concerning the Boundary Between the Fishery Zones
in the Area. 18 December 1995 ┄┄┄┄┄┄┄┄┄┄┄┄ 198

十一、1997 年丹麦与冰岛共同开发案 ┄┄┄┄┄┄┄┄┄┄ 201

Agreement between the Government of the Kingdom of
Denmark along with the Local Government of Greenland
on the one hand, and the Government of the Republic
of Iceland on the other hand on the Delimitation of
the Continental Shelf and the Fishery Zone in the Area
between Greenland and Iceland, 11 November 1997 ┄┄┄┄ 201

十二、2000 年尼日利亚与赤道几内亚共同开发案 ┄┄┄┄┄┄ 204

Treaty between the Federal Republic of Nigeria and the Republic
of Equatorial Guinea concerning Their Maritime Boundary,
23 September 2000 ┄┄┄┄┄┄┄┄┄┄┄┄┄┄┄┄ 204

十三、2010 年挪威与俄罗斯共同开发案 ┄┄┄┄┄┄┄┄┄ 208

1. Joint Statement on Maritime Delimitation and Cooperation
   in the Barents Sea and the Arctic Ocean ┄┄┄┄┄┄┄ 208
2. 《关于在巴伦支海和北冰洋海域划界与合作的
   联合声明》 ┄┄┄┄┄┄┄┄┄┄┄┄┄┄┄┄┄┄ 210

十四、2001 年东帝汶与澳大利亚共同开发案 ┄┄┄┄┄┄┄ 212

1. Timor Sea Designated Authority for the Joint Petroleum
   Development Area "Guidelines for Applications for
   Production Sharing Contracts and Criteria for Assessment
   of Applications" ┄┄┄┄┄┄┄┄┄┄┄┄┄┄┄┄ 212

2. Timor Sea Designated Authority for the Joint Petroleum
   Development Area "Interim Directions Issued under Article
   37 of the Interim Petroleum Mining Code Specific Requirements
   as to Petroleum Exploration and Exploitation in the Joint
   Petroleum Development Area" ……………………………… 218
3. Timor Sea Designated Authority for the Joint Petroleum
   Development Area "Interim Administrative Guidelines
   for the Joint Petroleum Development Area" ……………… 254
4. Timor Sea Treaty Designated Authority (Privileges and
   Immunities) Regulations 2003 ………………………… 289
5. Petroleum Mining Code for the Joint Petroleum
   Development Area ……………………………………… 291
6. Taxation of Bayu-Undan Contractors Act ……………… 316
7. Greater Sunrise Unitisation Agreement Implementation
   Act 2004, No. 47, 2004 ………………………………… 348
8. Petroleum (Timor Sea Treaty) (Consequential Amendments)
   Acts 2003 ………………………………………………… 377

十五、2006 年密克罗尼西亚与马歇尔群岛共同开发案 ……………… 394
Treaty between the Federated States of Micronesia and
the Republic of the Marshall Islands concerning Maritime
Boundaries and Cooperation on Related Matters …………… 394

十六、2006 年密克罗尼西亚与帕劳共同开发案 …………………… 400
Treaty between the Federated States of Micronesia and
the Republic of Paul concerning Maritime Boundaries
and Cooperation on Related Matters ……………………… 400

十七、2006 年法罗群岛、挪威与冰岛共同开发案 ………………… 408
Agreed Minutes on the Delimitation of the Continental
Shelf beyond 200 Nautical Miles between the Faroe
Islands, Iceland and Norway in the Southern Part
of the Banana Hole of the Northeast Atlantic ……………… 408

十八、2007 年特立尼达和多巴哥与委内瑞拉玻利瓦尔共和国

共同开发案 ·· 416

Framework Treaty Relating to the Unitisation of Hydrocarbon

Reservoirs That Extend Across the Delimitation Line between

the Republic of Trinidad and Tobago and the Bolivarian

Republic of Venezuela ·································· 416

下篇：与中国有关的海上共同开发的法律文件

一、2000 年中越关于北部湾划界协定和渔业协定 ············· 437

1. 《中华人民共和国和越南社会主义共和国关于两国在

北部湾领海、专属经济区和大陆架的划界协定》 ········· 437

2. 《中华人民共和国政府和越南社会主义共和国政府

北部湾渔业合作协定》 ···························· 440

二、2002 年《南海各方行为宣言》 ························· 449

Declaration on the Conduct of Parties in the South

China Sea ·· 449

《南海各方行为宣言》 ································ 452

三、2005 年中菲越《在南中国海协议区三方联合海洋地震

工作协议》 ·· 454

A Tripartite Agreement for Joint Marine Scientific Research

in Certain Areas in the South China Sea By and Among China

National Offshore Oil Corporation, Vietnam Oil and Gas

Corporation, Philippine National Oil Company ············ 454

四、2008 年《中日东海问题原则共识》 ··················· 463

China-Japan Principled Consensus on the East China

Sea Issue ··· 463

《中日东海问题原则共识》 ·························· 465

五、2011 年《落实〈南海各方行为宣言〉指导方针》 ·············· 468

Guidelines for the Implementation of the DOC ·············· 468

《落实〈南海各方行为宣言〉指导方针》 ·············· 469

六、中国与东盟部分国家的联合声明 ·············· 471

1. 2013 年《中华人民共和国和文莱达鲁萨兰国联合声明》 ······ 471

2. 2013 年《新时期深化中越全面战略合作的联合声明》 ········ 473

3. 2015 年《中越联合声明》 ·············· 477

4. 2016 年《中华人民共和国与菲律宾共和国联合声明》 ········ 481

七、2015 年中国外交部声明《中国东海油气开发活动正当合法》 ······ 487

《中国东海油气开发活动正当合法》 ·············· 487

后记 ·············· 489

上篇：海上共同开发协定

一、1960 年捷克斯洛伐克与奥地利共同开发案

Agreement between the Government of the Czechoslovakia Republic and the Austria Federal Government Concerning the Working of Common Deposits of Natural Gas and Petroleum

Signed at Prague, on 23 January 1960

Official texts: Czech and German

Registered by Czechoslovakia on 13 May 1964

The Government of the Czechoslovak Republic and the Austrian Federal Government,

Having regard to the fact that in the frontier sector of Vysoká-Zwerndorf there is a natural gas deposit which extends into both Czechoslovak and Austrian State territory,

Being aware of the economic significance of this deposit and similar common deposits, and

Recognizing the utility and necessity of co-operation and co-ordination in working this deposit and similar common deposits,

Have decided to conclude this Agreement in order to settle the conditions for working the common deposit of natural gas referred to above and similar common deposits of natural gas or petroleum.

Article 1

（1）As soon as the Contracting Parties discover a common workable deposit to which the provisions of this Agreement will apply under article 6 of the Agreement signed this day concerning the principles of geological co-operation between the Czechoslovak Republic and the Republic of Austria, they shall endeavour to have the said common deposit outlined within a period to be fixed by agreement.

（2）The Contracting Parties shall make arrangements for outlining the existing natural gas deposit in the Vysoká-Zwerndorf area immediately after the entry into force of this Agreement.

Article 2

（1）A Mixed Commission composed of representatives of both Contracting Parties shall be established and shall meet alternately at Prague and at Vienna in September of each year or, at the request of either Contracting Party, at any time not later than one month after such request is submitted by one of the two Contracting Parties.

（2）The task of the Mixed Commission shall be to calculate the reserves in each individual deposit and determine the share therein accruing to each Contracting Party; to lay down the conditions for working the deposits and, in particular, to prepare long-term extraction programmes; and to remove any difficulties that may arise in giving effect to this Agreement.

（3）If no objection is raised by either Contracting Party, within one month after the conclusion of a session of the Mixed Commission, to the application of the decisions reached at that session, the consent of both Contracting Parties shall be deemed *ipso facto* to have been given.

Article 3

（1）With a view to calculating the reserves in each individual deposit, the Mixed Commission shall determine at its meeting the method to be used and the scope of the necessary documentation. On the basis of such method, the Mixed Commission shall calculate the reserves in each individual common deposit. The reserves determined in this manner shall be verified or revised annually at the regular meetings of the Mixed Commission.

(2) In order to determine the method of calculating the reserves in the natural gas deposit in the Vysoká-Zwerndorf area, to calculate the reserves in that deposit and to determine the share accruing to each Contracting Party, the Mixed Commission shall meet not later than one month after the entry into force of this Agreement.

Article 4

(1) For the purpose of calculating the reserves in each individual deposit, the Contracting Parties shall provide the Mixed Commission with the necessary geological and technical documentation within a period to be fixed by the said Commission.

(2) The Contracting Parties shall keep each other informed of newly acquired data concerning each individual deposit and shall, in particular, immediately inform each other of the emergence of any special circumstances requiring instant action, for example abnormal water encroachment in places or throughout the deposit, or of circumstances which may affect the calculation of the reserves in the deposit.

Article 5

(1) The Contracting Parties shall work their proportionate shares of the total reserves in each individual common deposit. Current conditions in the deposit must be taken into account for this purpose.

(2) The details of the working of each individual deposit and, in particular, the preparation of extraction plans shall be agreed upon by the Mixed Commission. Work on the details of the extraction operations shall begin not later than six months from the date on which the consent of both Contracting Parties is deemed to have been given under article 2,

paragraph (3), of this Agreement.

(3) With respect to the Vysoká-Zwerndorf natural gas deposit, the Mixed Committee shall perform the tasks prescribed in paragraph (2) of this article at the meeting to be held pursuant to article 3, paragraph (2).

Article 6

After the extraction operations thus agreed upon have begun, the two Contracting Parties shall exchange regularly, not later than the end of each month, particulars of the previous month's output and of conditions in the deposit.

Article 7

If, in a particular year, either Contracting Party's output falls short of the quantity provided for in the extraction plan, it shall be entitled, after agreement has been reached, to make up the shortfall in the succeeding years. If, in a particular year, either Contracting Party's output exceeds the quantity provided for in the extraction plan, it must reduce its aggregate output over the next three years by the . quantity over-extracted.

Article 8

(1) If, in giving effect to this Agreement, any difference of opinion arises as to the interpretation or application of its provisions and such difference of opinion cannot be settled by the Mixed Commission, the Contracting Parties shall endeavour to settle it through the diplomatic channel.

(2) If their efforts are not successful within six months from the date on which one Contracting Party requests the other Party to deal with the matter through the diplomatic channel, the difference of opinion shall be referred for settlement to an arbitration board which shall be appointed by agreement between the two Contracting Parties.

Article 9

(1) This Agreement shall enter into force on the date of signature and shall remain in force until denounced by one of the Contracting Parties.

(2) If either Contracting Party exercises the option of denunciation under paragraph of this article at a tune when extraction is in progress at any common deposit pursuant to this Agreement, the provision of this Agreement shall apply to such deposit until its reserves are completely worked out.

IN WITNESS WHEREOF the undersigned, being duly authorized for the purpose by their Governments, have signed this Agreement and have thereto affixed their seals.

DONE at Prague on 23 January 1960 in two original copies, each in the Czech and German languages, both texts being equally authentic.

For the Government	For the Austrian
of the Czechoslovak Republic:	Federal Government;
V. DAVID	Rudolf ENDER

资料来源：Agreement concerning the working of common deposits of natural gas and petroleum. 23 January 1960, CZECHOSLOVAKIA-AUSTRIA, U. N. T. S. Vol. 495, pp. 134-140; https://treaties. un. org/doc/Publication/UNTS/Volume%20495/volume-495-I-7241-English. pdf。

二、1969年卡塔尔与阿布扎比酋长国共同开发案

Agreement between Qatar and Abu Dhabi on Settlement of Marine Boundaries and Ownership of Islands

Expressing their friendly and fraternal feelings, acting in the common interest of the two brotherly Arab States, and desiring to settle maritime boundaries and ownership of islands between them, the two parties have agreed as follows:

(1) That the island of al-Dayyina is part of the territory of Abu Dhabi;

(2) That the islands of al-Ashat and Shara iwa are part of the territory of Qatar;

(3) That neither State shall have any further territorial claim against the other to islands or waters falling outside the agreed-upon maritime boundaries;

(4) That the maritime boundaries referred to in the paragraph 3 above are as follows:

(i) A straight line from point "A", whose coordinates are as follows:

Latitude North 25° 39′ 50″

Longitude East 53° 02′ 05″

to point B, the site of al-Bunduq oil well No. 1, whose coordinates are as follows:

Latitude North 25° 05′ 54. 79″

Longitude East 52° 36′ 50. 98″

(ⅱ) A straight line from point "B" as described above to point C, whose coordinates are as follows:

Latitude North 24° 48′ 40″

Longitude East 52° 16′ 20″

(ⅲ) A straight line from point C above to point D, the mouth of the Khawral-Udayd waterway at the territorial sea boundary whose coordinates are as follows:

Latitude North 24° 38′ 20″

Longitude East 51° 28′ 05″

(5) That the points described above and the boundary lines connecting them shall as soon possible be marked on an accurate map in two copies to be signed by the two Parties showing the definitive maritime boundaries between the two countries in accordance with this Agreement;

(6) That ownership of al-Bunduq field shall be divided equally between the two Parties, who agree to consult with respect to all matters relating to said field and its exploitation in order to exercise their rights thereto on the basis of equality;

(7) That the al-Bunauq field shall be exploited by the Abu Dhabi Marine Areas (ADMA) Company in accordance with the terms of its agreements with the Ruler of Abu Dhabi, and that all revenues, profits and other benefits derived by the Government from said field shall be included in accordance with the aforementioned agreements between the Governments of Qatar and Abu Dhabi.

This Agreement and the original annexed map on which the relevant border points mentioned above have been approximately marked were signed on 1 Muharram A. H. 1389, corresponding to 20 March 1969.

(*Signed*) Zayed bin Sultan Al-Nahyan

Ruler of Abu Dhabi

Witness：

(*Signed*) Ahmad bin Ali Al Thani

Ruler of Qatar

Witness：

资料来源：http：//www. un. org/depts/los/LEGISLATIONANDTREATIES/PDFFILES/TREATIES/QAT-ARE1969MB. PDF。

三、1971 年伊朗与沙迦共同开发案

1. Memorandum of Understanding between Iran and Sharjah

November 1971

Neither Iran nor Sharjah will give up its claim to Abu Musa nor recognize the other's claim. Against this background the following arrangements will be made：

(1) Iranian troops will arrive in Abu Musa. They will occupy areas the extent of which have been agreed on the map attached to this memorandum.

(2) (a) Within the agreed areas occupied by Iranian troops, Iran will have full jurisdiction and the Iranian flag will fly.

(b) Sharjah will retain full jurisdiction over the remainder of the island. The Sharjah flag will continue to fly over the Sharjah police post on the same basis as the Iranian flag will fly over the Iranian military quarters.

(3) Iran and Sharjah recognize the breadth of the island's territorial sea as twelve nautical miles.

(4) Exploitation of the petroleum resources of Abu Musa and the sea bed and subsoil beneath its territorial sea will be conducted by Buttes Gas & Oil Company under the existing agreement, which must be acceptable to Iran. Half the governmental oil resources hereafter attributable to the said exploitation shall be paid direct by the Company to Iran and half to

Sharjah.

(5) The nationals of Iran and Sharjah shall have equal rights to fish in the territorial sea of Abu Musa.

(6) A financial assistance agreement will be signed between Iran and Sharjah.

资料来源：Memorandum of Understanding between Iran and Sharjah ［EB/OL］，http：//www. parstimes. com/history/iran_sharjah. html。

2.《伊朗与沙迦间谅解备忘录》

伊朗与沙迦既不放弃各自对阿布·穆萨岛的主权要求，也不承认对方的主权要求。鉴于这种背景而作出以下安排：

(1)伊朗军队将进驻阿布·穆萨岛，他们将占领一些区域，双方已同意这些区域标示于附在备忘录中的地图上。

(2)(a)在伊朗军队占领区域，伊朗将拥有全面的管辖权力，而且将悬挂伊朗国旗。

(b)沙迦将对该岛屿的剩余部分拥有全面的管辖权，和伊朗国旗飘扬在伊朗军营上一样，沙迦的国旗将继续悬挂在沙迦警察署的上空。

(3)伊朗与沙迦承认该岛领海宽度为 12 海里。

(4)开采阿布·穆萨岛及其邻海之下的海床底土中的石油将由巴梯斯天然气和石油公司根据现存协定来进行，这些协定必须为伊朗所接受。今后，由这种开采所获得的政府石油收入中的一半应由该公司直接支付给伊朗，而另一半则支付给沙迦。

(5)伊朗与沙迦两国国民应在阿布·穆萨岛领海享有同等的捕鱼权。

(6)一项财政协定将在伊朗与沙迦之间签订。

1971 年 11 月

资料来源：黎巴嫩《中东经济调研》1972 年 5 月 5 日，转引自蔡鸿鹏：《争议海域共同开发的管理模式：比较研究》，上海社会科学院出版社 1998 年版，第 196 页。

四、1974年苏丹和沙特阿拉伯共同开发案

Sudan and Saudi Arabia Agreement relating to the Joint Exploitation of the Natural Resources of the Sea-bed and Subsoil of the Red Sea in the Common Zone

Signed at Khartoum on 16 May 1974

Authentic text: Arabic

Registered by the Sudan on 31 October 1974

The Government of the Democratic Republic of the Sudan and the Government of the Kingdom of Saudi Arabia,

Desiring to confirm the existing bonds of friendship between the people of the two countries, and

Desiring to exploit the natural resources of the sea-bed and subsoil of the Red Sea,

Have agreed as follows:

Article I. For the purposes of the present Agreement the following expressions shall have the meanings hereunder assigned to them:

(1)"Sea-bed" includes the sea-bed and subsoil of the Red Sea.

(2)"Natural resources" comprise the non-living substances including the hydrocarbon and the mineral resources.

(3)"Territorial Sea" means the Territorial Sea as defined in the laws of the two Governments.

(4)"The Competent Minister" means the Minister appointed by the Government of the Kingdom of Saudi Arabia and the Minister appointed by the Government of the Democratic Republic of the Sudan to represent each of them in the Joint Commission.

Article II. The two Governments covenant to co-operate through all ways and means to explore and exploit the natural resources of the sea-bed of the Red Sea.

Article III. The Government of the Kingdom of Saudi Arabia recognises that the Government of the Democratic Republic of the Sudan has exclusive sovereign rights in the area of the sea-bed adjacent to the Sudanese coast and extending eastwards to a line where the depth of the superjacent waters is uninterruptedly one thousand metres. The Government of the Kingdom of Saudi Arabia claims no rights in this area.

Article IV. The Government of the Democratic Republic of the Sudan recognises that the Government of the Kingdom of Saudi Arabia has exclusive sovereign rights in the area of the sea-bed adjacent to the Saudi Arabian coast and extending westwards to a line where the depth of the superjacent waters is uninterruptedly one thousand metres. The Government of the Democratic Republic of the Sudan claims no rights in this area.

Article V. The two Governments recognise that the area of the sea-bed lying between the two areas defined in articles III and IV above is common to both Governments and shall hereafter be known as the Common Zone. The two Governments have equal sovereign rights in all the natural resources of the Common Zone which rights are exclusive to them. No part of the territorial sea of either Government shall be included in the Common Zone.

Article VI. The two Governments confirm that their equal sovereign rights in the Common Zone embrace all the natural resources therein and that they alone have the right to exploit such resources. The two Governments undertake to protect their sovereign rights and defend them against third parties.

Article VII. To ensure the prompt and efficient exploitation of the natural resources of the Common Zone there shall be established a

Commission referred to hereafter as the Joint Commission. The Joint Commission shall be charged with the following functions:

(a) to survey, delimit and demarcate the boundaries of the Common Zone;

(b) to undertake the studies concerning the exploration and the exploitation of the natural resources of the Common Zone;

(c) to encourage the specialised bodies to undertake operations for the exploration of the natural resources of the Common Zone;

(d) to consider and decide, in accordance with the conditions it prescribes, on the applications for licences and concessions concerning exploration and exploitation;

(e) to take the steps necessary to expedite the exploitation of the natural resources of the sea-bed in the Common Zone;

(f) to organise the supervision of the exploitation at the production stage;

(g) to make such regulations as may be necessary for the discharge of the functions assigned to it;

(h) to prepare the estimates for all the expenses of the Joint Commission;

(i) to undertake any other functions or duties that may be entrusted to it by the two Governments.

Article VIII. The Joint Commission established under article VII of this Agreement shall be a body corporate enjoying in the Kingdom of Saudi Arabia and the Democratic Republic of the Sudan such legal capacity as may be necessary for the exercise of all the functions assigned to it.

Article IX. The Joint Commission shall consist of an equal number of representatives from each of the two countries and each side in the Joint Commission shall be headed by the competent Minister. The Regulations shall lay down the Joint Commission's rules of procedure.

Article X. The Joint Commission shall have a sufficient number of officials. The Joint Commission shall determine their number and terms of service.

Article XI. The seat of the Joint Commission shall be the city of Jeddah in the Kingdom of Saudi Arabia. The Joint Commission may, however, hold meetings at any other place it decides upon.

Article XII. The Government of the Kingdom of Saudi Arabia shall provide such funds as would enable the Joint Commission to discharge effectively the functions entrusted to it. The Government of the Kingdom of Saudi Arabia shall recover such funds from the returns of the production of the Common Zone and in a manner to be agreed upon between the two countries.

Article XIII. Whereas the Government of the Democratic Republic of the Sudan has concluded on May 15th, 1973, an agreement whereby it has given exploration licences to Sudanese Minerals Limited and the West German Company of Preussag which agreement has created legal obligations on the Government of the Democratic Republic of the Sudan, the two Governments have agreed that the Joint Commission shall decide on this matter in such a manner as to preserve the rights of the Government of the Democratic Republic of the Sudan and in the context of the regime established by this Agreement for the Common Zone.

Article XIV. In the event that any accumulation or deposit of a natural resource extends across the boundary of the exclusive sovereign rights area of either Government and the Common Zone, the Joint Commission shall determine the manner in which it is to be exploited provided that any decision taken shall guarantee for the Government involved an equitable share in the proceeds of the exploitation of such accumulation or deposit.

Article XV. The application of this Agreement shall not affect the status of the high seas or obstruct navigation therein within the limits provided for by the established rules of public international law.

Article XVI. If a dispute arises respecting the interpretation or implementation of this Agreement or the rights and obligations it creates, the two Governments shall seek to settle such dispute by amicable means.

If the settlement of the dispute through amicable means fails, the dispute shall be submitted to the International Court of Justice. The Parties accept the compulsory jurisdiction of the International Court of Justice in this respect.

If one of the two Governments takes a measure which is objected to by the other, the objecting Government may ask the International Court of Justice to indicate interim measures to be taken to stop the measure objected to or to allow its continuance pending the final decision.

Article XVII. This Agreement is subject to ratification in accordance with the constitutional requirements of each Government and shall enter into force on the day on which the instruments of ratification are exchanged.

DONE in the City of Khartoum on this day, the twenty fourth of Rabi Thani 1394 Hijra, corresponding to the sixteenth of May, 1974, in two original texts in Arabic, both of which are authentic.

For the Government	For the Government
of the Kingdom	of the Democratic Republic
of Saudi Arabia:	of the Sudan:
AHMED ZAKI YAMANI	MANSOUR KHALID
Minister of Petroleum	Minister for Foreign Affairs
and Mineral Resources	

资料来源: Agreement relating to the joint exploitation of the natural resources of the sea-bed and subsoil of the Red Sea in the common zone, 16 May 1974, SUDAN-SAUDI ARABIA, UNTS. Vol. 952, p. 193, https://treaties. un. org/doc/Publication/UNTS/Volume% 20952/volume-952-I-13605-English. pdf。

五、1976年英国与挪威共同开发
弗里格天然气案

1. Framework Agreement between the Government of the United Kingdom of Great Britain and Northern Ireland and the Government of the Kingdom of Norway concerning Cross-Boundary Petroleum Co-operation

The Government of the United Kingdom of Great Britain and Northern Ireland（hereinafter referred to as "the United Kingdom Government"）and the Government of the Kingdom of Norway（hereinafter referred to as "the Norwegian Government"）；

Referring to the Agreement of 10 March 1965① between the two Governments relating to the Delimitation of the Continental Shelf between the two Countries and the Protocol supplementary to it of 22 December 1978②；

Having regard to Article 4 of the said Agreement under which the two Governments have undertaken, in consultation with the licensees, to seek to reach agreement as to the manner in which trans-boundary reservoirs shall be most effectively exploited and the manner in which the proceeds deriving therefrom shall be apportioned；

① Treaty Series No. 71（1965）Cmnd 2757.
② Treaty Series No. 31（1980）Cmnd 7853.

Having regard also to the existing Agreements entered into between the two Governments relating to the joint exploitation of trans-boundary reservoirs and to the laying and operation of pipelines for transportation of petroleum produced from one side of the Delimitation Line to a destination on the other side of that line, listed in Annex E;

Mindful that submarine pipelines may be subject to special arrangements which may or may not contain provisions identical with relevant rules of general international law;

Affirming that the provisions of this Agreement will not prejudice the views of the Parties in the negotiation and conclusion of any future treaty;

Mindful of the initiative taken by Energy Ministers at the end of 2001 and the Pilot-Konkraft recommendations made in August 2002 in their report 'Unlocking Value Through Closer Relationships' to strengthen co-operation between the Kingdom of Norway and the United Kingdom in petroleum developments across the continental shelves appertaining to the two States;

Recognising that neither Government will impede the transportation of petroleum from one side of the Delimitation Line to the market on the other side of the Delimitation Line by means of any unfair, non transparent or discriminatory charge or in any other way, nor impose any requirements which have the practical effect of hampering such transportation;

Desiring to deepen further their co-operation with respect to petroleum cross-boundary projects and to achieve optimal exploitation of the petroleum resources on the continental shelves appertaining to the two States;

Recognising that to this end there is a need to secure proper sharing of information between the two Governments;

Have agreed as follows:

Chapter 1　General Principles

Article 1. 1　Scope

This Agreement shall apply to cross-boundary co-operation between the United Kingdom Government and the Norwegian Government with regard to Petroleum activities.

Article 1. 2　Definitions

For the purposes of this Agreement:

"Authorisation" means any authorisation, consent, approval, Licence or permit issued under the law of either State, relating to the exploration and/or the Exploitation of Petroleum and/or the Construction and Operation of Installations and/or Pipelines;

"Construction and Operation" includes the design, fabrication, installation, laying, use, maintenance, repair and decommissioning of Installations and/or Pipelines but does not include access to Pipelines in accordance with Articles 2. 4 to 2. 7;

"Cross-Boundary Pipeline" means:

(a) a Pipeline crossing the Delimitation Line transporting Petroleum from the continental shelf of one State to the continental shelf or the territory of the other State; or

(b) a Pipeline transporting Petroleum and which is associated with a Trans-Boundary Reservoir, whether crossing the Delimitation Line or not, and where Licensees of both States of that Trans-Boundary Reservoir have a participating interest in that Pipeline;

but shall not include a Pipeline covered by an Agreement listed in Annex E;

"Cross-Boundary Project" means any of the following projects which are not covered by an Agreement listed in Annex E:

（a）the Construction and Operation of a Cross-Boundary Pipeline；

（b）the exploration for and/or the Exploitation of a Trans-Boundary Reservoir, including the Construction and Operation of an Installation for that purpose; and

（c）a project making use of a Host Facility；

"Delimitation Line" means the line defined in the Agreement of 10 March 1965 between the two Governments relating to the Delimitation of the Continental Shelf between the two Countries and the Protocol supplementary to that Agreement of 22 December 1978；

"Exploitation" includes the appraisal, production, treatment and processing of gas or liquids from a reservoir and/or the injection, reinjection or storage of any substance used for or derived from the appraisal, production, treatment and processing of those gases or liquids；

"First Dry Gas Link" means the Pipeline which is the first one authorised to be constructed after the date of signature of this Agreement and which transports dry gas originating from the Norwegian regulated dry gas system into United Kingdom offshore Infrastructure, whether or not that Pipeline is an "inter-connecting pipeline" under the Framework Agreement signed at Stavanger on 25 August 1998；①

"Host Facility" means：

（a）an Installation on one side of the Delimitation Line used for the exploration and/or Exploitation of a reservoir which is wholly on the other side of the Delimitation Line; and/or

（b）an Installation used for the exploration and/or Exploitation of a Trans-Boundary Reservoir if the Installation is placed outside the Unit Area of that Trans-Boundary Reservoir; and/or

（c）an Installation within a Unit Area which is used for the exploration and/or Exploitation of a reservoir outside that Unit Area；

"Infrastructure" means Installations and Pipelines；

"Inspector" means any person authorised by the competent authority

---

① Treaty Series No. 9 （2003）Cm 5762.

of either State to carry out inspection activities relating to:

(a) the Construction and Operation of any Infrastructure relating to a Cross-Boundary Project; or

(b) any metering system relating to a Cross-Boundary Project;

"Installation" means any artificial island, structure or other facility for Petroleum activity, including drilling rigs, floating production units, storage units, flotels, well heads, intrafield Pipelines and intrafield cables, but excluding supply and support vessels, ships that transport Petroleum in bulk, other Pipelines and cables;

"Langeled South" means the part of the Langeled Pipeline starting at the downstream tie-in weld on the downstream expansion spool connected to the Langeled sub-sea valve station located at the Sleipner field on the Norwegian continental shelf and terminating immediately downstream of the Langeled pig receiving facilities at the terminal at Easington in Yorkshire in the United Kingdom;

"Licence" means a permit issued by one of the Governments to carry out exploration for and/or Exploitation of Petroleum in a given area or, if applicable, for the Construction and Operation of a Pipeline;

"Licensee" means the individual or body corporate, holding a Licence;

"Licensees' Agreement" means an agreement between the Licensees of the United Kingdom Government and the Licensees of the Norwegian Government, entered into in accordance with this Agreement, relating to a Cross-Boundary Project, and any supplementary agreement to such agreement, including any amendment or modification to or any waiver of or departure from any provision of such agreement;

"Petroleum" means all liquid and gaseous hydrocarbons existing in or derived from natural strata, as well as other substances produced in association with such hydrocarbons;

"Pipeline" includes any connection point and/or associated valve or pig trap to that Pipeline;

"Trans-Boundary Reservoir" means any single geological Petroleum structure or Petroleum field which extends across the Delimitation Line; and

"Unit Area" means the area for joint exploration and/or Exploitation of a Trans-Boundary Reservoir, as set out in the Licensees' Agreement as approved by the two Governments.

Article 1. 3   Jurisdiction

(1) Nothing in this Agreement shall be interpreted as affecting the sovereign rights and the jurisdiction which each State has under international law over the continental shelf which appertains to it.

(2) All Installations on the continental shelf appertaining to the United Kingdom shall be under the jurisdiction of the United Kingdom and all Installations on the continental shelf appertaining to the Kingdom of Norway shall be under the jurisdiction of the Kingdom of Norway.

Article 1. 4   Authorisation

(1) The two Governments shall use their best efforts to facilitate Cross-Boundary Projects and shall not prevent or impede such projects by unreasonably withholding Authorisations.

(2) The two Governments shall co-ordinate their relevant Authorisation procedures and where both Governments issue Authorisations they shall be given simultaneously, unless agreed otherwise, and shall be compatible with each other.

(3) A Government shall not alter or modify any Authorisation for Cross-Boundary Projects nor grant the like rights to any other person nor consent to any assignment of any rights or obligations under such Authorisation where such changes are likely to affect materially the interests of the other Government, without prior consultation with that Government and having taken due account of all relevant matters raised by it.

(4) In particular, a Government shall not grant any Authorisation or alter or modify an Authorisation for a Pipeline referred to in Chapter 2, so

as to prevent there being joint or unified ownership of the whole length of the Pipeline, unless the two Governments agree otherwise.

(5) A copy of an Authorisation granted by one of the Governments shall be made available on request to the other Government.

Article 1. 5   Health, Safety and Environment: Standards

(1) The health, safety and environmental standards and/or requirements of the Government issuing the Authorisations relating to Cross-Boundary Projects shall be met. Both Governments recognise that, where there is an agreement pursuant to Article 2. 4 (5), that agreement shall not affect the application by the receiving coastal State of its own health, safety, environmental and other requirements for the Pipeline in question.

(2) To facilitate Cross-Boundary Projects, the two Governments shall encourage, where possible, the adoption of common health, safety and environmental standards and requirements. In any event, the two Governments shall seek to ensure that their respective standards and requirements are compatible. There shall be full consultation between the two Governments to this end.

(3) Having regard to the fact that:

(a) the Government with responsibility for the Host Facility may have an interest in health, safety and environmental issues concerning the reservoir being exploited and any associated facilities on the other State's continental shelf, and

(b) the Government with responsibility for the reservoir being exploited and any associated facilities may have a similar interest in such issues concerning the Host Facility,

the competent authorities of the two Governments shall consult with a view to putting in place appropriate procedures to safeguard the said interests of each Government.

(4) The two Governments undertake to make every endeavour, jointly and severally, after consultations, to ensure that:

(a) the Construction and Operation of any Installation or Pipeline shall not cause pollution of the marine environment or damage by pollution to the coastline, shore facilities or amenities, or damage to sensitive habitats or damage to vessels or fishing gear of any country; and

(b) appropriate procedures are in place for the safety and health of personnel.

(5) The competent authorities of the two Governments shall develop procedures for the implementation of this Article, including measures to be taken in an emergency.

Article 1. 6   Health, Safety and Environment: Physical Access and Inspection

(1) To enable Inspectors from each State to safeguard the interests of their Government in respect of health, safety and environmental matters, the competent authorities of the two Governments shall consult in order to agree on procedures for:

(a) consultation;

(b) access to all relevant information;

(c) physical access, at all stages, to any Infrastructure relating to a Cross-Boundary Project; and

(d) physical access in the territory of either State to terminals which are relevant to a Cross-Boundary Project.

(2) The Inspectors of each Government shall act in co-operation and consult with Inspectors of the other Government with a view to achieving compliance with the health, safety and environmental standards and/or requirements applicable to a Cross-Boundary Project.

(3) An Inspector of one Government may, with regard to Installations located on the continental shelf appertaining to the other State, request an Inspector of the other Government to exercise his powers to ensure compliance with the standards and/or requirements referred to in paragraph (2) whenever it appears that circumstances so warrant. In the event of any disagreement between the Inspectors of the

two Governments or the refusal of the Inspector of the one Government to take action at the request of the Inspector of the other Government, the matter shall be referred to the competent authorities of the two Governments.

（4）If it appears to an Inspector of either Government to be necessary or expedient for the purpose of averting an incident involving risk to life or serious personal injury, whether the danger is immediate or not, or minimising the consequences of such an incident, and time and circumstances do not permit consultation between the Inspectors of the two Governments, that Inspector may order the immediate cessation of any or all operations in relation to a Cross-Boundary Project. Immediately thereafter, the fact of such an order and the reason therefore shall be reported to the competent authorities of the two Governments who shall then consult to consider the actions necessary for the safe and speedy resumption of operations.

Article 1.7 Metering Systems and Inspection

（1）Both Governments shall approve any metering system which is related to a Cross-Boundary Project and which is of common interest. The competent authorities of the two Governments shall establish procedures for early approval of such a system.

（2）When adopting standards for such metering systems, the two Governments shall pay particular regard to the economic impact of such standards on the Cross-Boundary Project in question, and shall ensure that the adoption of such standards shall not unfairly or unduly burden the economics of that Project. In the case of a Cross-Boundary Project making use of a Host Facility, the two Governments shall pay due regard to the prevailing standards for metering systems on that Host Facility. The two Governments shall also give due consideration as to whether new metering systems are appropriate in the light of metering arrangements already in place elsewhere on the continental shelf or in the territory of either State.

（3）The competent authorities of the two Governments shall establish arrangements so that Inspectors of both Governments have access to relevant metering systems on the continental shelf or in the territory of either State to ensure that their interests are safeguarded.

Article 1. 8　Physical Security

The competent authorities of the two Governments shall consult one another with a view to concluding such mutual arrangements as they consider appropriate in relation to the physical protection of Infrastructure.

Article 1. 9　National and International Emergency

Nothing in this Agreement shall prejudice the exercise by each Government of its powers in the case of national or international emergency. Consultations shall be held at the earliest opportunity in order that the two Governments may agree on appropriate joint measures to reconcile the urgency of the situation with their common interest in the most effective Exploitation of reservoirs or the use of Infrastructure.

Article 1. 10　Exchange of Information

（1）Subject to lawful restrictions as to disclosure and use, both Governments will ensure the proper exchange of information between them relating to Cross-Boundary Projects.

（2）Recognising that the United Kingdom and Norwegian offshore pipeline and production systems will increasingly become interlinked, there is a need for increased information flows about upstream operations which affect downstream operations, and vice versa, and for information sharing, in particular between the Governments, other regulatory authorities and the relevant system operators. The two Governments recognise that such considerations apply also to existing pipeline connections between the two States.

（3）Where one Government, in order to ensure safe, effective and stable operations of the systems, places obligations on its field, pipeline, terminal or system operators to provide information about forecast or actual production from or through their facilities, or seeks to establish voluntary arrangements for the provision of that information, the other Government will not put obstacles in the way of the provision of such information by those field, pipeline, terminal or system operators about production crossing the Delimitation Line and being landed in the territory of the first Government. Both Governments will encourage the fullest exchange of information to meet these requirements.

(4) This Article applies to Cross-Boundary Projects, as well as to any installation and/or pipeline covered by any of the Agreements listed in Annex E.

Article 1. 11   Tax

Profits arising from the use of Infrastructure relating to Cross-Boundary Projects, capital represented by such Infrastructure and capital gains arising from the disposal of such Infrastructure or an interest therein shall be taxed in accordance with the laws of the United Kingdom and the Kingdom of Norway respectively, including the Convention for the Avoidance of Double Taxation and the Prevention of Fiscal Evasion with respect to Taxes on Income and Capital signed at London on 12 October 2000[1] and any Protocol or Protocols to that Convention or any Convention replacing that Convention as may be signed in the future.

Article 1. 12   Construction of Pipelines and Use of Existing Infrastructure

(1) The two Governments shall seek to facilitate the use of existing Infrastructure capacity on fair, transparent and non-discriminatory terms including, where appropriate, the installation of connection points and/or any necessary associated valves during the construction of Pipelines to

---

[1]   Treaty Series No. 26 (2001) Cm 5136.

facilitate the process for subsequent tie-ins.

(2) In furtherance of paragraph (1), should the two Governments receive a proposal for the Construction and Operation of a Pipeline (additional to Langeled South) to land Norwegian dry gas directly in the United Kingdom in circumstances where adequate spare capacity is available in United Kingdom offshore Infrastructure, the two Governments shall consult with a view to satisfying themselves that the process for selecting the transportation solution has been open and transparent and that the best economic solution has been selected. The determination of the need for and selection of transport capacity shall follow broadly the Work Process set out in Annex A.

Article 1. 13　Continued Use and Termination

(1) Where an Authorisation which has a direct effect on a Cross-Boundary Project is about to expire, and the holder of the Authorisation seeks its renewal, the Government responsible for that Authorisation shall, subject to its law, renew it.

(2) Where an Authorisation which has a direct effect on a Cross-Boundary Project:

(a) is likely to be or has been revoked; or

(b) is due to expire or has expired without a renewal of that Authorisation being sought; or

(c) is likely to be or has been surrendered,

the Government responsible for that Authorisation shall, in consultation with the other Government, consider the economic and practical options for continued use. Provided that economic and practical options for continued use are established, the Government responsible for that Authorisation shall, in accordance with its law, issue a new Authorisation to enable the Cross-Boundary Project to continue.

Article 1. 14　Decommissioning

(1) In respect of Installations associated with Cross-Boundary

Projects, decommissioning plans are subject to the approval of the Government on whose continental shelf or in whose territorial waters the Installation is situated, after full consultation with the other Government. The aim of both Governments shall be to seek to reach agreement on decommissioning methods and standards and both Governments shall approve the timing of any such decommissioning.

(2) In respect of Cross-Boundary Pipelines:

(a) both Governments shall approve the timing of the decommissioning of a Cross-Boundary Pipeline;

(b) both Governments shall seek to reach agreement on decommissioning methods and standards; and

(c) in respect of the decommissioning of Langeled South, the two Governments shall approve the timing, methods and standards of such decommissioning.

(3) Decommissioning plans shall include:

(a) an estimate of the cost of the measures proposed in it; and

(b) details of the times at or within which the measures proposed in it are to be taken or make provision as to how those times are to be determined.

(4) In making decisions on decommissioning plans, the Government or Governments responsible shall address fully and take proper account of:

(a) applicable international requirements, standards or guidelines;

(b) safety hazards associated with decommissioning, including where relevant transport and disposal;

(c) safety of navigation;

(d) the environmental impact of the measures proposed;

(e) the impact of the measures proposed on other users of the sea;

(f) best available cost-effective techniques;

(g) economic factors;

(h) the timetable for decommissioning;

(i) the impact of the measures proposed on the continued operation or decommissioning of the Infrastructure not covered by the decommissioning plan;

(j) the views expressed by other persons having an interest; and

(k) other relevant matters raised by either Government.

(5) The Government or Governments responsible for the approval of the decommissioning plan may approve the plan with or without modifications or conditions. Before approving the plan with modifications or subject to conditions, the Government or Governments responsible for the approval of the decommissioning plan shall give the person (whether or not a Licensee) who submitted the plan an opportunity to make representations about the proposed modifications or conditions.

(6) The Government or Governments responsible for the approval of the decommissioning plan shall act without unreasonable delay in reaching a decision as to whether to approve or reject the plan and shall require the implementation of any plan so approved.

(7) If the decommissioning plan is rejected, the Government or Governments responsible for the approval of the plan shall inform the person who submitted the plan of the reasons for doing so. That person shall, in such circumstances, be required to submit a revised plan within a specific time limit acceptable to the Government or Governments.

Article 1. 15   Framework Forum

The two Governments hereby establish a Framework Forum to facilitate the implementation of this Agreement. The Framework Forum shall include representatives of each Government. The two Governments may agree to other parties attending when appropriate. The Framework Forum shall provide a means for ensuring continuous consultation and exchange of information between the two Governments and a means for resolving issues without the need to invoke the dispute settlement procedures set out in Chapter 5. The Framework Forum shall meet twice yearly or at other intervals agreed by the two Governments, and shall be subject to such further arrangements as may be agreed by the two

Governments from time to time.

Chapter 2   Construction and Operation of and Access to Pipelines

Article 2. 1   Authorisations

(1) Where the two Governments agree to the Construction and Operation of a Cross-Boundary Pipeline, they shall individually grant the Authorisations required by their respective national law.

(2) When an Authorisation referred to in paragraph (1) is required by only one Government, that Government shall consult with the other Government before granting such Authorisation.

Article 2. 2   Agreement between Pipeline Owners

(1) In respect of a Cross-Boundary Pipeline which is associated with a Trans-Boundary Reservoir and where Licensees of both States of that Trans-Boundary Reservoir have a participating interest in that Pipeline, each Government shall require its Licensees and/or its holders of an Authorisation to enter into a Licensees' Agreement. The Licensees' Agreement shall incorporate provisions to ensure that, in the event of a conflict between the Licensees' Agreement and this Agreement, the provisions of this Agreement shall prevail.

(2) The Licensees' Agreement shall be submitted to the two Governments for their approval. Such approval shall be deemed to have been granted unless the Licensees and/or the holders of an Authorisation have been notified to the contrary, by either Government, within 60 days of its receipt of the document in question.

Article 2. 3   Pipeline Operator

The appointment and any change of operator of a Cross-Boundary

Pipeline shall be subject to agreement by the two Governments.

Article 2. 4   Access System: Terms and Conditions

(1) The terms and conditions for access to a Cross-Boundary Pipeline, including the setting of entry and exit tariffs, shall be in accordance with applicable European Union law. The principles of fairness, non-discrimination, transparency and open access to spare capacity and avoidance of any abuse of a dominant position or other anti-competitive behaviour shall apply.

(2) Access to a Cross-Boundary Pipeline shall include physical access to capacity and, where appropriate, to facilities supplying technical services incidental to such access.

(3) Where a Government determines the financial terms for access to Pipelines related to a Cross-Boundary Project, those terms shall be such that they promote the optimal use of existing Pipelines and do not inhibit alternative options for using United Kingdom and Norwegian Pipelines and Pipeline systems, in whole or in part, for the transportation of Petroleum from one State to the other State.

(4) Where there are proposed changes to the regulations or guidelines relating to access to Pipelines of one State which may affect the commercial parties of the other State, there shall be the fullest consultation between the two Governments before any changes are made and due account shall be taken of any representations made.

(5) The two Governments may agree, on a case-by-case basis, to apply the access regime applicable to a Cross-Boundary Pipeline on the continental shelf of one State to the same Pipeline whilst on the continental shelf of the other State, but not in the coastal State's territorial waters.

(6) The two Governments have agreed, in conformity with paragraph (5), that the Norwegian regulated access system shall apply to Langeled South and that the Norwegian Government shall set the exit tariffs, onshore, for that Pipeline.

Article 2.5   Access System: Entry Points and Tariffs

(1) This Article applies to the setting of regulated entry points on either continental shelf and entry tariffs for Langeled South for Petroleum produced from a reservoir wholly or in part on the continental shelf appertaining to the United Kingdom.

(2) Entry points and tariffs referred to in paragraph (1) shall be agreed jointly by the two Governments. Such entry tariffs shall normally be set at zero, subject to adjustments for positive or negative effects on the throughput and provided that all costs related to the tie-in are otherwise covered.

(3) The two Governments shall, upon request, supply commercial parties with relevant information regarding the setting of new entry tariffs in such a manner as to provide predictability prior to investment decisions. Such information shall be supplied without undue delay, and, if possible, within sixteen weeks of such request. Such tariffs shall be formally determined simultaneously with the approval of the relevant project.

(4) The conditions set out in this Article may also apply to other Cross-Boundary Pipelines if so agreed by the two Governments.

Article 2.6   Access System: Exit Points and Tariffs

(1) This Article applies to the setting of regulated exit points and exit tariffs, offshore, in connection with the establishment of the First Dry Gas Link between United Kingdom and Norwegian offshore Infrastructure.

(2) Exit points and tariffs referred to in paragraph (1) shall be set by the Norwegian Government in accordance with the principles set out in Annex B, and after full consultation with the United Kingdom Government.

(3) The Norwegian Government shall provide sufficient information to the United Kingdom Government to enable that Government properly to

satisfy itself that the decision fully and properly takes into account the principles set out in Annex B.

(4) The conditions set out in this Article may also apply to other Cross-Boundary Pipelines if so agreed by the two Governments.

Article 2. 7　Access System：Dispute Settlement

(1) This Article shall apply to：

(a) any dispute between the owner or operator of Langeled South and a shipper of Petroleum originating from the continental shelf appertaining to the United Kingdom as to whether or not the owner or operator of Langeled South has fully and properly complied with the terms and conditions laid down in the applicable regulated access system；

(b) any dispute concerning a tariff between the owner or operator of a United Kingdom Pipeline to which the First Dry Gas Link is to be connected and a shipper of Petroleum originating from the Norwegian continental shelf；and

(c) any dispute with regard to access to any other Cross-Boundary Pipeline, not covered by sub-paragraph (a) or (b) above, to the extent agreed by the two Governments.

(2) As regards a dispute covered by paragraph (1) (a), the dispute shall be submitted simultaneously to both Governments who shall jointly resolve the dispute within a reasonable time frame, taking into account the need for a speedy resolution. The principles underlying the determination of the dispute by the two Governments shall be transparent and non-discriminatory and wholly in accordance with Article 2. 4 (1). The decision of the two Governments shall be binding on all the parties involved.

(3) As regards a dispute covered by paragraph (1) (b), the dispute shall be resolved by the United Kingdom Government in accordance with the principles set out in Annex C, after fully consulting the Norwegian Government. The United Kingdom Government shall provide sufficient information to the Norwegian Government to enable the latter

Government properly to satisfy itself that the decision fully and properly takes into account the principles set out in Annex C.

Chapter 3   Joint Exploitation of Trans-Boundary Reservoirs as a Unit

Article 3. 1   Unitisation and Authorisations

(1) Where the two Governments, after consultation with their respective Licensees, agree that a Petroleum reservoir is a Trans-Boundary Reservoir which should be exploited, it shall be exploited as a single unit in accordance with the terms of this Agreement, unless otherwise agreed by the two Governments.

(2) Subject to paragraph (1), the two Governments shall individually grant the Authorisations required by their respective national law.

(3) In the event that a Trans-Boundary Reservoir is to be exploited as a single unit by making use of a Host Facility, the two Governments shall agree the most appropriate procedures to exploit that Trans-Boundary Reservoir.

Article 3. 2   Agreement between the Licensees

(1) Each Government shall require its Licensees to enter into a Licensees' Agreement to regulate the Exploitation of a Trans-Boundary Reservoir in accordance with this Agreement. The Licensees' Agreement shall incorporate provisions to ensure that in the event of a conflict between the Licensees' Agreement and this Agreement, the provisions of this Agreement shall prevail.

(2) The Licensees' Agreement shall be submitted to the two Governments for their approval. Such approval shall be deemed to have been granted unless the Licensees have been notified to the contrary, by either Government, within 60 days of its receipt of the Licensees' Agreement.

Article 3.3　Determination and Apportionment of Reserves

(1) The Licensees' Agreement shall define the Trans-Boundary Reservoir to be exploited and include proposals for the determination of:

(a) the geographical and geological characteristics of the Trans-Boundary Reservoir;

(b) the total amount of the reserves and the methodology used for the calculation; and

(c) the apportionment of the reserves as between the Licensees of each Government.

(2) The Licensees' Agreement shall also specify:

(a) either the arrangements for the outcome of a determination to apply for all time to all activities connected with the Exploitation of the Trans-Boundary Reservoir, or the procedures, including a timetable, for any redetermination of the matters referred to in paragraph (1), to be carried out by the unit operator, at the request of the Licensees or of either Government; and

(b) the procedures, including a timetable, for the resolution of any dispute between the Licensees about any of the matters referred to in paragraph (1).

Article 3.4　Determination and Expert Procedure

(1) If either Government is unable to agree to a proposal for the determination or redetermination of any of the matters referred to in Article 3.3 (1), it shall so notify the other Government and the unit operator within the period provided for in Article 3.2 (2).

(2) The two Governments, having regard to the desire to reach an early resolution, shall use their best endeavours to resolve the matter in question. The unit operator may submit alternative proposals for this purpose.

(3) If, within 60 days of the notification referred to in paragraph (1) or such other period as the two Governments may agree, the two Governments remain unable to resolve the matter in question, a single expert shall be appointed to reach a timely and independent determination of that matter. The expert shall be appointed and act in accordance with the terms of Annex D.

Article 3. 5   Inclusion of Additional Licensed Area

(1) If, after a Licensees' Agreement has been approved by the two Governments, the Governments agree that the limits of the Trans-Boundary Reservoir extend into an area of the continental shelf in respect of which another party holds a production Licence, the two Governments shall require all their respective Licensees with a participating interest in the Trans-Boundary Reservoir to agree arrangements for the effective Exploitation of the Petroleum in the area. Any such arrangements shall be made within the time limit stipulated by the two Governments, be consistent with the provisions of this Agreement and be subject to the approval of the two Governments. The provisions of Article 3. 2 shall apply to any such arrangements which take the form of a Licensees' Agreement.

(2) In the event that arrangements are not made within the stipulated time limit, any further action to be taken shall be decided jointly by the two Governments.

Article 3. 6   Inclusion of Non-Licensed Area

(1) If, after a Licensees' Agreement has been approved by the two Governments, the two Governments agree that the Trans-Boundary Reservoir extends into an area of the continental shelf which is not covered by a production Licence, the Government, to which the area of the continental shelf appertains, shall, without unreasonable delay, seek to remedy the situation by offering the said area for Licence.

(2) In the event that a production Licence is granted covering the

area referred to in paragraph (1), the two Governments shall require all their respective Licensees with a participating interest in the Trans-Boundary Reservoir to agree arrangements for the effective Exploitation of the Petroleum in the area. Any such arrangements shall be made within the time limit stipulated by the two Governments, be consistent with the provisions of this Agreement and shall be subject to the approval of the two Governments. The provisions of Article 3. 2 shall apply to any such arrangements which take the form of a Licensees' Agreement.

(3) If a production Licence is not granted or if a production Licence is granted but arrangements are not made within the stipulated time limit, any further action to be taken shall be decided jointly by the two Governments.

Article 3. 7   Unit Operator

A unit operator shall be appointed by agreement between the Licensees of the two Governments as their joint agent for the purpose of exploiting a Trans-Boundary Reservoir in accordance with this Agreement. The appointment of, and any change of, the unit operator shall be subject to prior approval by the two Governments.

Article 3. 8   Appraisal Wells

Subject to its law, neither Government shall withhold a permit for the drilling of wells by, or on account of, its Licensees for purposes related to the determination of any of the issues referred to in Article 3. 3.

Article 3. 9   Development Plan: Exploitation of a Trans-Boundary Reservoir

(1) The unit operator shall submit to the two Governments for their approval a development plan for the effective Exploitation of a Trans-Boundary Reservoir and for the transportation of Petroleum therefrom.

(2) In the event that a Trans-Boundary Reservoir is to be exploited by making use of a Host Facility, the development plan referred to in

paragraph (1) shall include a description of those modifications to and operations on the Host Facility which are directly linked to the Exploitation of the Trans-Boundary Reservoir.

(3) The unit operator may at any time submit amendments to the development plan to the two Governments and may also be required to do so at the request of the two Governments. All amendments to the development plan are subject to approval by the two Governments.

Article 3. 10   Commencement of Production

Unless otherwise agreed by the two Governments, neither Government shall permit the commencement of production from a Trans-Boundary Reservoir unless the two Governments have jointly approved, in accordance with this Agreement:

(a) the Licensees' Agreement;

(b) the unit operator referred to in Article 3. 7; and

(c) the development plan referred to in Article 3. 9;

and have each granted any other necessary Authorisations.

Article 3. 11   Use of an Installation within a Unit Area for the Exploitation of another Reservoir

In the event that an Installation, which is located within a Unit Area, is to be used for the exploration and/or Exploitation of a Petroleum reservoir outside that Unit Area, any necessary amendments required to the development plan referred to in Article 3. 9 shall be submitted to the two Governments for approval. Such approval shall not be granted if such use would adversely affect the Exploitation of the Trans-Boundary Reservoir in accordance with this Agreement, unless the two Governments agree otherwise.

Article 3. 12   Cessation of Production

The two Governments shall agree on the timing of the cessation of the production from a Trans-Boundary Reservoir.

Chapter 4   Project Using a Host Facility

Article 4. 1   Authorisations

Where the two Governments and their respective Licensees agree to a project using a Host Facility, each Government shall, in addition to giving any approvals for the purposes of Articles 3. 9 and 3. 11, individually grant any Authorisations required by its respective national law.

Article 4. 2   Development Plan

Subject to Articles 3. 9 and 3. 11, each Government shall require its Licensees to submit to it for its approval a development plan or a modification to an existing development plan, covering matters relevant to a project referred to in Article 4. 1.

Article 4. 3   Governmental Decision

Subject to Chapter 3, any Governmental decision:

(a) which relates to an Installation outside a Unit Area and which is relevant to its use as a Host Facility for a reservoir on the other side of the Delimitation Line or a Trans-Boundary Reservoir; or

(b) which relates to a reservoir on one side of the Delimitation Line making use of a Host Facility on the other side of the Delimitation Line, and which is relevant to that use;

shall be made by the Government on whose side of the Delimitation Line the Host Facility is placed or the reservoir lies, in close consultation with the other Government, taking due account of all matters raised by that Government. An example of such a decision is the timing of the cessation of the relevant activities.

Article 4. 4   Operator

Subject to Article 3. 7, the appointment or change of operator of the reservoir and/or the Host Facility shall be subject to the approval of the Government on whose continental shelf the reservoir or Host Facility lies after consultation with the other Government.

Chapter 5   Dispute Settlement

Article 5   Conciliation Board

(1) Subject to paragraph (2), should the two Governments fail to reach agreement on the interpretation or application of this Agreement, including any matter to be resolved under it, the following dispute settlement procedure shall apply, unless the dispute falls within the procedures agreed under Article 3.4, or unless the two Governments agree otherwise:

(i) either Government may request that the disputed matter be submitted to a Conciliation Board;

(ii) the Conciliation Board shall consist of five members. Each Government shall designate two members, and the four members so designated shall designate the fifth (who shall not be a national of or habitually reside in the United Kingdom or in the Kingdom of Norway) who will act as the Chairman of the Conciliation Board;

(iii) if either Government fails to designate one or more members of the Conciliation Board within one month of a request to do so, either Government may request the President of the International Court of Justice to designate the required number of members;

(iv) the same procedure shall apply *mutatis mutandis* if the four Conciliation Board members fail to designate a fifth member to act as Chairman within one month of the designation of the fourth member;

(v) the Conciliation Board shall be entitled to all relevant information and may carry out any necessary consultations;

(vi) the Conciliation Board shall be required to reach a decision within a reasonable time limit (taking into account the need for a speedy resolution);

(vii) decisions of the Conciliation Board shall be taken by simple majority and shall be binding on the two Governments; and

(viii) further rules of procedure relating to decisions of the Conciliation Board may be agreed by the two Governments.

(2) Where it falls to one Government, in accordance with Article 2. 6 or Article 2. 7 (3) to determine an exit tariff, offshore, in a regulated access system or to settle a dispute over a tariff in a negotiated access system and the Framework Forum has been unable to resolve a disagreement between the two Governments on the matter in question, the Conciliation Board shall consider, at the request of either Government, whether:

(a) the information, which the Government taking the decision has provided to the other Government, was sufficient to enable that other Government properly to satisfy itself that the decision fully and properly took into account the principles in Annex B or Annex C; and

(b) the decision fully and properly took account of the relevant principles in Annex B or Annex C.

Chapter 6   Final Clauses

Article 6. 1   Amendments and Termination

The two Governments may amend or terminate this Agreement at any time by agreement. Either Government may at any time request that consultations are initiated with a view to considering amendments to this Agreement. Such consultations shall commence within two months of the request, and shall be conducted expeditiously. In such consultations the two Governments shall consider fully and take proper account of the proposals for amendment with the aim of reaching a mutually acceptable solution within the shortest possible time.

Article 6. 2　Other Petroleum Agreements

Without prejudice to Articles 1. 10 and 2. 6, this Agreement shall not affect the continued operation of the other Petroleum Agreements listed in Annex E, which shall prevail as long as they remain in force. Consequently, where the development of a Trans-Boundary Reservoir or of a project making use of a Host Facility is subject to this Agreement, a Pipeline, which is associated with such a development and which falls within the provisions of the Framework Agreement signed at Stavanger on 25 August 1998, shall be subject to the latter Agreement.

Article 6. 3　Entry into Force

This Agreement shall enter into force on the date on which the two Governments shall have informed each other that all necessary internal requirements have been fulfilled.

In witness whereof the undersigned, duly authorised by their respective Governments, have signed this Agreement.

Done in duplicate at Oslo this 4th day of April 2005 in the English and Norwegian languages, both texts being equally authoritative.

For the Government of the United Kingdom of Great Britain and NorthernIreland

MIKE O'BRIEN

For the Government of

the Kingdom of Norway

THORHILD WIDVEY

Annex A

Work Process
To Determine the Need for and Selection of Additional Transport Capacity for Dry Gas from the Kingdom of Norway to the United Kingdom

（1）The following describes the process for establishing additional capacity for dry gas transport from the Gassled dry gas system to the United Kingdom, i. e. capacity in excess of the Vesterled and the Langeled South pipelines. This work process will involve Gassco (operator of the Norwegian continental shelf dry gas infrastructure), the owners of gas infrastructure in the Kingdom of Norway and the United Kingdom, gas shippers and the authorities in both countries (the Ministry of Petroleum and Energy and the Petroleum Directorate in Norway and the Department of Trade and Industry in the United Kingdom).

（2）The annual Shipping and Transportation Plan prepared and maintained by Gassco registers the bookings and requests for future transport capacity by all companies (i. e. shippers) on the Norwegian continental shelf. The requested capacities in the Shipping and Transportation Plan are based on indicative volumes. The information provided by the shippers identifies both the entry and exit points for the different Gassled Areas (e. g. Area D-dry gas system) in the Norwegian continental shelf gas transportation system. The annual Shipping and Transportation Plan published in the second quarter of each year identifies the need for possible new transportation capacity and will determine the need for a new, dry gas connection from the Norwegian continental shelf to the United Kingdom. Timing (i. e. start up year) and the alternative Norwegian continental shelf node points to be assessed (e. g. Draupner, Sleipner, Heimdal etc.) will be included.

（3）For example, the Shipping and Transportation Plan for 2003, presented to the User Forum on 12 June 2003 showed a requirement for an aggregated future capacity for shipments of dry gas to the United Kingdom from 2008 of 120 Million Sm3/d. Based on data from the Shipping and Transportation Plan in 2003, planned capacity at that time (Vesterled + Langeled South pipelines) was 105 Million Sm3/d, indicating a need for possible new transport solutions from the Norwegian continental shelf to the United Kingdom from 2008 of up to 15 Million

Sm3/d.

(4) Financing of any new transportation connection will require, on the one hand a group of gas shippers with an interest in transporting gas from the Norwegian continental shelf, and on the other, groups of investors (United Kingdom, Norwegian or others) putting forward proposals to build new transportation capacity. These groups may, therefore, have common members. United Kingdom infrastructure owners may also be part of the investor group.

(5) Gassco will publish a Shipping and Transportation Plan every year. If such plan concludes that additional transport capacity is required and the shippers are prepared to take forward a project then they will open commercial discussions with United Kingdom infrastructure owners and potential investor groups. At the same time, the shippers and investors will initiate the commercial process with Gassco, on behalf of Gassled, for a tie-in to the Norwegian Gassled dry gas system. Exit tariffs will be determined by the Norwegian Government in accordance with Annex B. It is recognised that the potential investors and shippers must have early information on the cost of transportation in both the new and existing transportation systems to provide a basis for their investment and booking decisions.

(6) The shipper group and the potential investors, working with Gassco, will consider the technical and commercial proposals and carry out the concept selection process for the most appropriate new transportation connection. If a new connection is needed at least two years will be needed in preparation, to allow for the commercial and contractual discussions and for construction.

(7) All reasonable options for gas transportation will be developed to a similar level of technical and commercial maturity before concept selection to ensure a fair and open competition. Cost estimates and corresponding technical documentation will be open and accessible to all relevant parties.

(8) The process will be transparent but will also need to recognise

the need to maintain effective competition between the proposals. To aid transparency, the mechanism for measuring and assessing proposals against the selection criteria will also be published in advance of the evaluation. The decision on the best option, including the route, for transporting gas to the United Kingdom, should be based on clear economic principles and provide the best economic solution for the shippers. The process will be fully transparent to the Framework Forum and that body will be the final arbiter in verifying that the concept selection process is being carried out in an open, fair and non-discriminatory manner and in accordance with the predetermined process. The Framework Forum will also be responsible for keeping development of new transport infrastructure under review and for encouraging a timely commercial process.

(9) If it is agreed that the link pipeline is incorporated into Gassled then Gassco will chair the process for establishing or amending the Participants' Agreement (ownership agreement) for the new infrastructure, including decisions on the investment shares and capacity rights, and will become the operator of the connection.

(10) The two Governments recognise that changes to the way in which the offshore industry in either the United Kingdom or the Kingdom of Norway is organised and/or regulated could result in a need to revise the Work Process set out in this Annex. In such event, the two Governments will, through the Framework Forum, revise this Annex so that it continues to reflect the process for establishing additional capacity to transport Norwegian dry gas to the United Kingdom. In drawing up any revision of this Annex, the two Governments will seek to satisfy themselves that the work process for selecting the best option, including the route, for transporting gas to the United Kingdom is fair and transparent, based on clear economic principles and provides the best economic solution for the shippers.

Annex B

The Principles for Determining Exit Points and
Tariffs Offshore for the Norwegian Dry Gas System

（1）When an application to connect a Norwegian upstream system into a United Kingdom upstream system, or vice versa, is made and an exit tariff is to be determined, the Norwegian Government stipulating the tariff shall fully consult the United Kingdom Government before establishing a new exit point from the regulated system and the related tariff at such exit point.

（2）The two Governments shall apply the principles of non-discrimination, transparency and fairness for all parties concerned. The two Governments will aim to ensure optimal development and use of existing United Kingdom and Norwegian upstream transportation systems to ensure economically sound solutions and encourage the cost-efficient use of existing systems. The tariffs shall be cost-reflective.

（3）The Norwegian Government shall, when establishing an exit point and the related tariff, address fully and take proper account of the following factors：

（a）system effects in one system（capacities, pressures, temperatures, quality, etc.）as a result of offshore connection to another system. Such effects could be positive or negative；

（b）as a general principle all relevant investment costs arising from the new connection, including, where appropriate, a fair expected return to owners, shall be reimbursed by the users. Due account shall be taken of any wider benefits or costs to that system as a result of that connection；

（c）fair sharing of operating costs. The exit tariff from the Gassled system will include a fair share of the operating cost of the Gassled system；

(d) a fair expected return to owners on all basic (historic) capital costs of existing systems used to transport gas to the new exit point. This element will be well below the exit tariff at landing points.

(4) The Norwegian Government shall upon request supply commercial parties or the United Kingdom Government with relevant information regarding the stipulation of new tariffs in such a manner as to provide predictability prior to investment decisions and in any event, if possible, within sixteen weeks of such a request being made.

(5) Exit tariffs shall be formally determined simultaneously with the approval of the relevant project.

Annex C

Third Party Access to Upstream Infrastructure on the United Kingdom Continental Shelf Tariff Setting Principles

(1) The United Kingdom Government supports the principle of non-discriminatory negotiated access to upstream infrastructure on the United Kingdom continental shelf, encourages transparency and promotes fairness for all parties concerned since it is important that prospective users have fair access to infrastructure at competitive prices whilst recognising that spare capacity in upstream infrastructure has a commercial value and that, having borne the cost and risk of installing it, the owner should be entitled to derive a fair commercial consideration for that value. Any tariff imposed by the Secretary of State would, accordingly, reflect a fair payment to the owner for real costs and for opportunities forgone.

(2) If the Secretary of State's powers to require access and to set a tariff were to be used:

(i) infrastructure owners would have their consequential costs reimbursed, including indirect ones (e.g. the cost of interruption to the owner's throughput while a pipeline is modified to enable third party use);

(ii) the tariff would be set so that the third party would bear a fair share of the total running costs incurred after his entry;

(iii) unless the supply in question were marginal or the infrastructure owner had already made other sufficient arrangements to recover the full capital costs, the financial arrangements proposed would normally take account of the basic capital costs① as well as the costs arising from the entry of the third party.

(3) On occasion, prospective third party users may be competing for access to the same limited capacity in infrastructure. In such circumstances, the Secretary of State is unlikely to require the owner to make the capacity available to a prospective user who values the capacity less than other prospective users and thus does not offer a better deal for the owner.

(4) For infrastructure with insufficient ullage to accommodate a third party's requirements, given the owner's rights and existing contractual commitments, the Secretary of State is unlikely to require access to be provided. If he were to do so, the tariff would need to reflect at least the cost to the infrastructure owner of backing off their own production and/ or another party's contracted usage to accommodate the third party's (i. e. be based on the concept of opportunity cost).

Annex D

Expert Procedure

(1) This Annex shall apply where a matter is to be determined by an expert pursuant to Article 3. 4 of this Framework Agreement.

---

① In newer infrastructure or infrastructure constructed or oversized with a view to taking third party business, the tariff set by the Secretary of State would normally include an allowance for recovery of capital costs incurred in the expectation of third party business. This allowance in the tariff would be set at a level sufficient to earn the owner a reasonable return on these costs if that allowance were applied to throughput expected at the time of the decision to invest-recognising the uncertainty inherent in projections of future use.

（2）The expert shall be chosen and his mandate and employment terms settled by agreement between the two Governments. The expert shall be chosen from amongst persons or organisations who or which are recognised as experts in the relevant field and who or which can provide undertakings in respect of any conflict of interests which shall be in the form set out in the Appendix, unless otherwise agreed by the two Governments. Any contractors that the expert may employ to assist in reaching his decision must also provide undertakings in substantially similar terms. The expert and any contractor so employed will be required to safeguard the confidentiality of any information supplied to him.

（3）If no agreement has been reached on the choice of expert, the mandate and/or his employment terms within 6 weeks from the date on which either Government initiates the process provided for in this Annex, the two Governments shall ask the President of the Institut français du pétrole, or such other person or organisation if so agreed by the two Governments, to choose an expert from between two candidates, one nominated by each Government, and/or to determine the mandate and/or the terms of employment. If only one Government has nominated an expert, that expert shall be chosen.

（4）Each Government shall ensure that all information requested by the expert in order to reach a decision shall be provided promptly. The expert may only meet with one Government jointly with the other Government. All communications between one Government and the expert outside such meetings shall be conducted in writing and any such communication shall be copied to the other Government.

（5）Within 12 weeks of his appointment, the expert shall provide a preliminary decision to the two Governments together with a fully detailed explanation of how that decision has been reached. Thereafter there will be a period of 8 weeks (or such other period as the two Governments may agree) from the date that the preliminary decision is communicated to the two Governments so that they may seek clarification of that decision and/or make submissions to the expert for his consideration.

The final decision of the expert along with a fully detailed explanation for that decision shall be communicated in writing to the two Governments within 4 weeks of the end of this period. Save in the event of fraud or manifest error, the decision of the expert shall be final and binding on the two Governments who shall ensure that the decision is implemented by the unit operator acting on behalf of the relevant licensees.

(6) The expert shall apportion liability for his fees and costs between the two Governments in a way that seems to him to be just and reasonable in all the circumstances. Either Government may recover from the unit operator any amounts payable under this paragraph.

Appendix to Annex D

Model Conflict of Interest Undertakings

(1) [Name of expert] hereby warrants that he has not performed since [date], and will not perform during the course of his resolution of the matters in question, any work for either the Government of the United Kingdom or the Government of the Kingdom of Norway, or any Licensee of the [ ] Field or a Licensee of any other Field on the continental shelf appertaining to the United Kingdom or the Kingdom of Norway, which could influence his performance of, or conflict with his duties in relation to his resolution of the aforesaid matters in question. In particular, he warrants that he has not undertaken any work relating to the [ ] Field or for any of the [ ] Field Licensees within the last two years.

(2) [Name of contractor] hereby warrants that he has not performed since [date], and will not perform during the period for which he has been engaged by [name of expert] in connection with the Framework Agreement of 4 April 2005 concerning Cross-Boundary Petroleum Co-operation, any work for either the Government of the United Kingdom or the Government of the Kingdom of Norway, or any [ ] Field Licensee or a Licensee of any other Field on the continental

shelves appertaining to the United Kingdom or the Kingdom of Norway, which could influence his performance of, or conflict with his duties under his contract with [name of expert]. In particular, he warrants that he has not undertaken any work relating to the [ ] Field or for any of the [ ] Field Licensees within the last two years.

Annex E

Existing Petroleum Agreements

Agreement of 22 May 1973, ①as amended by the Exchange of Notes dated 27 July 1994②, relating to the transmission of petroleum by pipeline from the Ekofisk field and neighbouring areas to the United Kingdom

Agreement of 10 May 1976③, as amended by the Agreement of 25 August 1998④ and the Exchange of Notes dated 21 June 2001⑤ relating to the exploitation of the Frigg Field Reservoir and the transmission of gas therefrom to the United Kingdom; and the use of the installations and pipelines for the exploitation and transmission of Hydrocarbons

Agreement of 16 October 1979⑥, as amended by the Exchange of Notes dated 24 March 1995⑦, relating to the exploitation of the Statfjord Field Reservoirs and the offtake of petroleum therefrom

Agreement of 16 October 1979⑧ and Supplementary Agreements of 22

---

① Treaty Series No. 101 (1973) Cmnd 5423.
② Treaty Series No. 1 (1995) Cm 2721.
③ Treaty Series No. 113 (1977) Cmnd 7043.
④ Treaty series No. 21 (2002) Cm 5513.
⑤ Treaty series No. 43 (2001) Cm 5258.
⑥ Treaty Series No. 44 (1981) Cmnd 8282.
⑦ Treaty Series No. 57 (1995) Cm 2941.
⑧ Treaty Series No. 39 (1981) Cmnd 8270.

October 1981① and 22 June 198310,② as amended by the Exchange of Notes dated 9 August 1999③, relating to the exploitation of the Murchison Field Reservoir and the offtake of petroleum therefrom

Agreement of 21 November 1985④, amended by the Agreement of 1 November 2004, between the two Governments relating to the transmission by pipeline of Heimdal Liquids to the United Kingdom

Framework Agreement of 25 August 1998⑤ relating to the laying, operation and jurisdiction of inter-connecting submarine pipelines

资料来源：英国政府官方网站，https：//www. gov. uk/government/uploads/system/uploads/attachment_data/file/243184/7206. pdf。

2. 《大不列颠及北爱尔兰联合王国政府与挪威王国政府间关于跨界石油合作的框架协定》

陈思静 译　王阳、梅玉婕 校

大不列颠及北爱尔兰联合王国政府(后称英国政府)与挪威王国政府(后称挪威政府)；念及两国于 1965 年 3 月 10 日签订的有关大陆架划界的协议,⑥ 以及 1978 年 12 月 22 日签订的补充议定书；⑦ 考虑到两国政府依上述协定第 4 条所承担(的义务)，经与许可证持有人协商，双方同意就如何最有效地开发跨界资源、如何分配开采收益，达成协议；同样念及两国政府已达成的有关跨界油气资源开发、划界线一侧到另一侧目的地的石油

---

① Treaty Series No. 25 (1982) Cmnd 857.

② Treaty Series No. 71 (1983) Cmnd 9083.

③ Treaty Series No. 110 (2000) Cm 4857.

④ Treaty series No. 39 (1987) Cm 201.

⑤ Treaty Series No. 9 (2003) Cm 5762.

⑥ 英国政府 1965 年第 2757 号敕令书，条约集第 71 号(文件)。

⑦ 英国政府 1980 年第 7853 号敕令书，条约集第 31 号(文件)。

运输管道的铺设及运营的协定，这些协定列于附件E；顾及管理海底油气运输管道，需要特定的安排，而这些安排可能包含或不包含与一般国际法类似的相关规则；确保本协定的相关条款，不影响未来双方在谈判、缔结新条约时的观点；考虑到两国的能源部长在2001年底提出的倡议，以及"派劳特-科克拉夫克"（工作组）在2002年8月给出的建议——他们在其制作的题为"通过更紧密的关系激发价值"的报告中指出，两国应加强对分布在两国大陆架上的油气资源的开发合作；认识到两国政府既不能采取各种不公平、不透明、歧视性或任何其他方式妨害划界线一侧到另一侧市场的石油运输，也不应强加任何阻碍该运输实际效果的要求；意欲进一步加深双方在跨界油气资源项目上的合作，实现跨越两国大陆架边界的油气资源的最优开发；为达此目的，认识到确保两国适当分享信息的需要；达成以下协议：

第一章　一般原则

1.1条　范围

本协定，应适用于英国政府和挪威政府之间的与石油活动有关的跨界合作。

1.2条　定义

为本协定的目的：

"授权"是指，依据两国国内法，与石油资源勘探和（或）开发、设备、管道建设、运营相关的所有授权、同意、准许、颁发许可或授予许可行为；

"建造与运营"包括设备和（或）管道的设计、制造、安装、铺设、使用、保养、维修和拆除，但不包括依据第2.4条至第2.7条所规定的对管道的使用；

"跨界管道"是指：

（a）一条跨越两国大陆架划界线的、将一国大陆架上的石油资源，运送至另一国大陆架或领土的管道；或者：

（b）与跨界油气田相关的石油运输管道，无论该油气田是否跨越大陆架划界线，开发该矿藏的两国许可证持有人，对于该管道享有参与股权；

但是，不应包含本协定附件 E 所列明的管道；

"跨界工程"是指本协定附件 E 未列明的所有下列工程：

（a）跨界管道的建设和运营；

（b）跨界油气田的勘探和（或）开发，包括为此目的而进行的设备建造和运营；以及

（c）一项利用东道国设施的工程；

"划界线"是指两国政府于 1965 年 3 月 10 日签订的与大陆架划界有关的协定和 1978 年 12 月 22 日签订的补充议定书，所划定的界线；

"开采"包括对一矿藏中气体或液体的评估、生产、处理和加工，以及（或者）在评估、生产、处理和加工的过程中，对开发所得的气体、液体，进行注射、回注和储藏；

"第一干气链"是指，在本协定签署之后，第一条获得建造许可的、将挪威所产的干气运输至英国的海上平台的管道，无论该管道是否为 1998 年 8 月 25 日"斯塔万格框架协定"①所规定的"相互连接的管道"；

"东道国设施"是指：

（a）整体位于"划界线"一侧且用于勘探和（或）开采"划界线"另一侧油田的设备；

（b）用于勘探和（或）开采某一跨界油气田的设备，如果该设备位于跨界油气田的单元区之外；

（c）位于单元区内、用于勘探和（或）开采单元区之外的油气田的设备；

"基础设施"指设备和管道；

"监督员"是指经两国主管当局授权、对下列活动进行监督的任何人：

（a）与"跨界工程"相关的任何基础设施的建造和运营；

（b）与"跨界工程"相关的任何计量系统；

"设备"是指为油气活动而建造的人工岛屿、结构或其他设施，包括钻探设备、浮动生产单元、储藏单元、浮式住宿船、井口装置、场内管道和场内电缆，但不包括供给和后勤船只、整批运送原油的船只以及其他的管道和电缆；

---

① 英国政府 2003 年第 5762 号敕令书，条约集第 9 号（文件）。

"兰格勒德南管道"是指"兰格勒德管道"的一部分，该段的起点位于下游膨胀阀门的管段焊接处，该焊接处与挪威大陆架上的"斯莱普纳油田"的兰德格勒南阀门站相连，终点位于英国约克郡伊宁顿码头的兰格勒德收油设施的清管器阀门；

"许可证"指经由两国政府颁发的许可，许可相关企业在指定区域勘探和(或)开采石油资源，在条件允许的情况下，许可的内容包括建造与运营管道；

"许可证持有人"是指持有许可证的个人或法人团体；

"许可证持有人协定"是指，英国政府和挪威政府的许可证持有人之间，依据本协定，就跨界工程所达成的协议，或相关的补充协议，包括对协议中任何条款的修订、修改、废弃和背离；

"原油"包括天然地层中存在的、或从中开采的所有液体和气体矿藏，也包括生产出的、与此类油气资源相关的其他物质；

"管道"包括管道间的任何连接点和(或)管道阀门，或清管器接收器；

"跨界矿藏"是指，所有单一地质构造或者跨越"划界线"的油田；以及

"单元区"是指，经两国政府所批准的"许可证持有人协定"所划定的"跨界矿藏"共同开发勘探区和(或)开采区。

第 1.3 条　管辖

(1)本协定中的任何条款，不应解释为，对两国依国际法而享有的对其大陆架的主权权利与管辖权产生影响。

(2)位于英国大陆架上的所有设备，应归英国管辖；位于挪威大陆架上的所有设备，应归挪威管辖。

第 1.4 条　授权

(1)两国政府应尽它们的最大努力，便利跨界工程的实施，不得以不合理撤回授权的方式，组织或妨碍此类工程的实施。

(2)两国政府应当协调它们的相关授权程序，除非另有规定，应同时颁发许可证，许可证内容应彼此兼容。

(3)在与另一国进行商议、充分考虑另一国提出的相关因素之前，一国政府不得修改或变更跨界工程的任何授权，也不得向其他法人授予类似权利，也不得在可能对另一国政府权利造成实质影响的情况下，以授权的

形式，同意分配类似的任何权利或义务。

（4）特别地，非经两国政府另行订立协议，其中一国政府不得对第2章所指的管道进行授权，也不得修正和改变此类授权，以防共有或统一所有整个管道的情况出现。

（5）经一国政府请求，该国政府有权获取另一国政府授权书的副本。

第1.5条　健康，安全和环境：标准

（1）两国政府对跨界项目颁发的许可应当满足健康、安全、环境的标准和（或）要求。两国政府认识到，若存有依照第2.4条第5项而达成的协议，该协议不影响资源接收国对管道施加的本国健康、安全、环境（标准）和其他要求。

（2）为便利跨界工程（的实施），两国政府应尽可能地鼓励制定共同的健康、安全、环境标准和要求。无论如何，两国政府应力图确保它们各自的标准和要求相兼容。为达此目的，两国政府应进行充分的协商。

（3）考虑到下列事实：

（a）对东道国设施负有责任的政府，可能对正在开采矿藏的健康、安全和环境问题，以及位于另一国大陆架的相关设施，享有利益，并且

（b）对正在开采的矿藏和相关设施负责的政府，可能在这些问题上，对东道国设施享有相似的利益，

两国政府的主管当局，应当相互协商，建立一套合适的程序，保障两国政府的上述利益。

（4）在磋商之后，两国政府承诺，尽一切努力，共同地或独立地确保：

（a）任何设备和管道的建造、运营，不应对海洋环境造成污染，也不应对海岸线、岸上设施或康乐设施造成污染损害，不对生物敏感区以及任何国家的船只和钓鱼装置造成损害；以及

（b）确保海上人员安全和健康的适当程序。

（5）两国政府的主管当局应当为实施本条而制定适当的程序，包括紧急情况下应采取的措施。

第1.6条　健康，安全和环境：实际进出和监督

（1）为确保两国的监督员可以保障其本国政府在健康、安全和环境事项上的利益，两国政府的主管部门应相互磋商，以便达成下列程序：

（a）协商；

（b）所有相关信息的获取；

（c）在（开发）的任何阶段，实际进出与跨界项目相关的任何基础设施；

（d）实际进出位于两国领土上的、与跨界工程相关的终端。

（2）一国政府的监督员应与另一国政府的监督员相互磋商、协作，以便就适用于跨界工程的健康、安全和环境标准和（或）要求的相互兼容达成意见。

（3）若有事实依据，一国政府的监督员，可以请求另一国政府的监督员行使权力，以确保另一国大陆架上的设施，达到了第 2 款所规定的标准和要求。若两国政府的监督员意见不一致，或一国政府的监督员在收到请求后拒绝采取行动，则该争议应由两国政府的主管部门解决。

（4）若一国监督员认为，一起事故可能会带来生命危险，或对人身造成严重损害，无论危险是立即的或长期的，出于减轻损害或将事故影响最小化的目的，且当时的时间状况、具体情形不允许两国政府的监督员进行沟通，在必要和便利的情况下，该监督员可以命令某一跨界项目的特定设备或全部设备停产。之后，监督员应立即向两国政府的主管当局报告发布命令的情况及其理由，两国政府应就安全、迅速恢复运营行动的必要措施展开磋商。

第 1.7 条　计量系统和监督

（1）两国政府应批准与（双方享有）共同利益的跨界工程相关计量系统。两国政府的主管部门应就这些系统的初步审批设置程序。

（2）若要采用这些计量系统的标准，两国政府应当特别关注这些标准对跨界项目的经济影响，应当确保采用这些标准，不会不公正、不适当地加重项目的经济负担。在跨界项目使用东道国设施的情况下，两国应注意东道国设施计量系统的现行标准。若两国大陆架或两国领土的其他地方，已有计量系统，两国政府应适当考虑新计量系统的合理性。

（3）为确保两国的权益能够得到保障，两国政府的主管部门应建立适当安排，使两国的监督员可以访问两国大陆架或领土上的相关计量系统。

第 1.8 条　实体安全

两国政府的主管部门应当相互磋商，以便就基础设施的实体防护达成他们认为合适的有关共同安排。

第 1.9 条　国内和国际紧急状况

本协定中的条款，不妨碍两国政府在面临各自国内和国际的紧急状况时，行使权力。为缓解紧急状况、使矿藏和基础设施可以得到最高效的开发与利用，进而实现他们的共同利益，两国政府应尽早举行磋商，以达成适当的共同措施。

第 1.10 条　信息交换

(1)在法律限定的信息披露与使用范围内，两国政府应确保就跨界工程进行合适的信息交换。

(2)认识到英国和挪威的海上管道相互连接的程度将会提高，有必要增加上游产业运营的信息流动，(该信息流动)会影响下游产业的运营，反之亦然。特别是政府间、相关主管当局之间和相关系统运营者之间的信息分享将很有必要。两国政府认为，这样的考虑，同样适用于两国之间已连接的管道。

(3)若一国政府，为确保相关系统得以安全、高效、稳定的运行，对其油气田、管道、终端和系统营运商施以提供信息的义务，要求营运商汇报产自其设施或经由其设施运输的油气预计产量或实际产量，或者试图制定信息自愿提供制度，另一国政府，不得对油气田、管道、终端和市场的营运商加以提供信息的限制，这些信息主要涉及跨越"划界线"的产品和在前述一国接收的产品。为满足这些要求，两国政府应鼓励充分地交换信息。

(4)本条适用于跨界项目，以及附件 E 中所列明的所有设备和(或)管道。

第 1.11 条　税收

使用跨界油气田相关的基础设施而产生的利润、此类基础设施的资本盈利、处置此类基础设施的收益和利息收入，应当按照英国和挪威的法律分别征税，这些法律包括 2000 年 10 月 12 日在伦敦签订的《避免双重征税以及防止所得税和资本税逃税漏税的公约》，以及未来可能签订的该公约的修正案或者替代性公约。

第 1.12 条　管道的建设和既有基础设施的使用

(1)两国政府应当寻求既有基础设施能力的公平、透明、不歧视的使用，包括在恰当的时候，在建设管道的过程中，为便利接下来连接工程的进行，应当建造连接点和(或)必要的连接阀门。

(2)为贯彻落实第(1)款，当英国的海上基础设施出现产能、运能闲置时，如果两国政府收接收一项建造和运营管道(除"兰格勒德南管道"外)的提议，使挪威的干气可以直接运至英国本土，两国政府应相互磋商，确保选择了公开、透明、经济效益最高的运送方案。运输能力需求的确定与选择应广泛地遵循附件 A 所列出的工作程序。

第 1.13 条　续用和终止

(1)如果一项对跨界工程有直接影响的许可证即将到期，且许可证持有人试图申请给许可证续期，负责颁发许可证的政府，应当依据其国内法，给许可证续期。

(2)如果一个对跨界工程有直接影响的许可证：

(a)有可能或已经被撤销；或者

(b)有可能或已经到期，而许可证持有人并不申请给许可证续期；或者

(c)有可能或已经让与，

负责颁发旧许可证的政府，应当与另一国政府沟通，考虑选择继续使用(工程)的经济性和实用性。如果具备相应的经济性和实用性，负责颁发旧许可证的政府，应该依据其国内法，颁发一个新的许可证，确保该跨界工程得以继续(运营)。

第 1.14 条　拆除

(1)关于一国大陆架或领水内的跨界工程的设备拆除计划，应在两国政府充分协商后，由该国政府予以审批。两国政府的目标应是，寻求就拆除的方法、标准达成一致意见，两国政府亦应同意该项拆除计划的时间。

(2)对于跨界管道来说：

(a)两国政府应当共同审批跨界管道拆除的时间节点；

(b)两国政府应寻求就拆除的方法与标准达成一致意见；并且

（c）对于"兰格勒德南管道"的拆除，两国政府应审批拆除的时间节点、方法和标准。

（3）拆除计划应当包括：

（a）拟议措施的花费预估；并且

（b）在拟定的时间段内、将会采取的措施的细节，以及确定这些时间段的规则的细节。

（4）在对拆除计划作出决定时，对之负责的某国政府或两国政府，应当充分处理并适当考虑下列要素：

（a）可以适用的国际要求、标准或指南；

（b）与拆除相关的安全危害，包括因运输（拆除的废弃物）和清理而导致（的相关危害）；

（c）航行安全；

（d）拟议措施的环境影响；

（e）拟议措施对该海域其他使用者的影响；

（f）最高性价比的技术；

（g）经济因素；

（h）拆除的时间表；

（i）拟议措施对于（工程）继续运营的影响，或者对计划中未包含的基础设施的拆除的影响；

（j）其他利益相关者的观点；并且

（k）两国政府提出的其他相关问题。

（5）负责审批拆除计划的某国政府或两国政府，无论是否存在修订或附加条件，皆可审批通过拆除计划。在附有修订或附加条件的拆除计划审批通过之前，递交拆除计划的实体（无论是不是许可证持有人），有权就修订或附加条件提出交涉。

（6）负责审批拆除计划的某国政府或两国政府，应毫不迟延地就同意或拒绝拆除计划做出决定，并应要求实施已审批通过的任何计划。

（7）如果拆除计划未能通过，负责审批拆除计划的某国政府或两国政府，应告知计划申请人计划被拒绝的原因。在这种情况下，该申请人，应在某国政府或两国政府可以接受的特定时间范围内，按照要求递交经修订的计划。

第 1.15 条　框架论坛

为便利本协定的实施，两国政府据此建立框架论坛。框架论坛应包含两国政府的代表。适当的时候，两国政府可以同意其他实体的参与。框架论坛的功能在于，确保两国政府的持续磋商和信息交换；在没有必要使用第五章规定的争端解决机制时，解决问题。框架论坛应每年会晤两次，或以两国政府同意的其他频率会晤。框架论坛应符合两国政府在其他时间达成的进一步安排。

第二章　管道的建造、运营和使用

第 2.1 条　授权

（1）若两国政府同意建造与运营一条跨界管道，它们应单独依据各自国内法进行授权。

（2）若第（1）款中提及的授权只需一国政府（授予），该国在授权之前应与另一国政府协商。

第 2.2 条　管道所有者之间的协定

（1）若一条跨界管道与跨界矿藏相连接，且该矿藏的两国经营人，都对跨界管道持有参与股权，两国政府应要求，持有其许可证的经营人，和（或）获取其授权的经营人，应达成"许可证持有人协定"。"许可证持有人协定"应包含下列的类似条款：若"许可证持有人协定"与本协定相冲突，优先适用本协定的规定。

（2）"许可证持有人协定"应递交两国政府审批。除非许可证持有人和（或）授权的持有人，在某国政府收到协定文本后的 60 天内，收到来自某国政府的反对意见，则"许可证持有人协定"视为审批通过。

第 2.3 条　管道运营商

对跨界管道运营商的安排和变更，应符合两国政府达成的协定。

第2.4条　使用系统：条款和条件

(1)使用跨界管道的条款和条件，包括进口关税和出口关税的设定，应当符合可适用的欧盟法。应当适用公平原则、非歧视原则、透明和闲置运能的公开使用原则、避免滥用市场支配地位原则，以及其他的反不正当竞争行为原则。

(2)对跨界管道的使用应当包括对管道运输能力的实际使用以及在适当情况下，便利地提供与使用相一致的技术服务。

(3)若一国政府决定对跨界工程相关管道的使用设定财政条款，这些条款应当促进既有管道的最佳使用，也不妨碍选择其他方案，利用英国和挪威运输系统的部分或整体，将油气资源由一国运至另一国。

(4)当(某一国)提议对管道使用规则和指南进行改动，可能会对另一国的商事主体造成影响时，两国政府应在规则和指南发生变动之前，在充分考虑两国代表意见的情况下，进行最充分的协商。

(5)两国政府可以同意，就具体个案而言，将一国大陆架上使用跨界管道的制度，适用于另一国大陆架上的同一管道，但本款不适用于一国领海内的管道。

(6)两国政府已同意，依据第(5)款，挪威受管制的使用规则体系，应适用于"兰格勒德南管道"，且挪威政府应在岸上为该管道设立出口关税。

第2.5条　使用系统：入口点和关税

(1)本条适用于双方大陆架上受管制的入口点的设定，以及当"兰格勒德南管道"输送了英国大陆架上某一矿藏的石油产品(无论该矿藏的整体还是部分位于英国大陆架上)时入口关税的设定。

(2)第(1)款所指的入口和关税的设定，应经两国政府共同同意。入口关税应通常应设置为0，假定所有管道接头的花费已包括其中，并依据对生产力可能造成的积极影响与消极影响进行调整。

(3)在商事主体作出投资决定之前，经商事主体的请求，两国政府应当，以为商事主体作出投资决定提供可预见性的方式，向其提供与新设定的入口关税相关的信息。这些信息的提供不应有不当延误，并在可能的情况下，应当在提出请求后16周以内提供。在批准相关项目时，此类关税也应同时正式确定。

(4)若两国政府同意，本条的规定也可以适用于其他跨界管道。

第 2.6 条　使用系统：出口点和关税

(1)本条适用于受管制的出口点和关税的设定，设定方式与第一个连接两国海上设施的干气连接杆相关。

(2)挪威政府应依据附件 B 所列举的原则，在与英国政府进行充分协商之后，设定第 1 款所指的出口点和关税。

(3)挪威政府应向英国政府提供充分的信息，以使英国合理地确信，挪威政府的决定充分地、适当地考虑了附件 B 所列的原则。

(4)若两国政府同意，本条的规定也可以适用于其他跨界管道。

第 2.7 条　使用系统：争端解决

(1)本条应当适用于：

(a)"兰格勒德南管道"的所有者或运营商和起航于英国大陆架上的石油托运人之间的任何争端，无论"兰格勒德南管道"的所有者或运营商是否充分和适当地遵循了管道使用系统的条款和条件；

(b)任何将与"第一干气链"相连的英国管道的所有者或运营商，同起航于挪威大陆架的石油托运人之间，就关税发生的争端；以及

(c)上述(a)项和(b)项未涵盖的任何其他跨界管道的使用而发生的争端，(但)争端的范围以两国政府同意(的范围)为限。

(2)对于第(1)款(a)项所涉及的争端，应当同时递交给两国政府，而考虑到快速解决的需要，两国政府应在一个合理的时间范围内解决争端。两国政府对争端做出决定的基准原则，应是透明、无歧视，并且完全符合第 2.4 条第(1)款(所规定的原则)。两国政府的决定对争端的双方都具有拘束力。

(3)对于第(1)款(b)项所涉及的争端，英国政府应当与挪威政府充分协商后，依据附件 C 所列的原则加以解决。英国政府应向挪威政府提供充分的信息，以使挪威合理地确信，英国政府的决定充分地、适当地考虑了附件 C 所列的原则。

第三章　作为一个整体的跨界矿藏的共同开发

第3.1条　联合开采与授权

（1）两国政府，在与其相应的许可证持有人磋商之后，认定将要开采的油气矿藏是跨界矿藏，除非两国政府另有约定，应依据本协定所规定之条款，将该矿藏作为单一整体进行开采。

（2）依据第（1）款，两国政府应当依据各自的国内法，单独进行开发授权。

（3）若将要开采一处作为单一整体的跨界矿藏，且开采需要使用东道国设施，两国政府应就开采该矿藏商定最为合适的程序。

第3.2条　许可证持有人之间的协定

（1）两国政府应要求它们的许可证持有人达成协定，并依据该协定开采跨界油气资源。许可证持有人协定应包含（这样的）条款，以确保当许可证持有人协定与本协定发生冲突时，本协定的条款优先适用。

（2）许可证持有人之间的协定，应递交两国政府以待批准。在许可证持有人向两国政府递交协定文本后60日内，除非许可证持有人收到两国政府的相反通知，否则视为已经批准。

第3.3条　油气储量的测定与分配

（1）许可证持有人协定，应当界定有待开发的跨界油气田，并且应为下列事项的决定提供建议：

（a）跨界矿藏的地理和地质特征；

（b）该矿藏的总量和总量的计量方法；以及

（c）两国政府许可证持有人之间的矿藏分配比例。

（2）许可证持有人之间的协定也应当特别指明：

（a）任何时间段内提请的，与开采跨界矿藏相关的，所有活动决定结果的安排，或者经一方经营人或一国政府提请，对联合经营人实施的第（1）款相关事项重作安排的程序（包含时间表）。

(b)解决许可证持有人之间的、与第(1)款相关的任何争端的程序(包含时间表)。

第3.4条 决定和专家程序

(1)如果任何一国政府不同意就第3.3条第(1)款相关事项的决定或重新安排所作的建议,它应当在第3.2条第(2)款所规定的时间段内,通知另一国政府和联合经营人。

(2)两国政府,秉承尽早达成解决方案的意愿,应竭尽全力解决问题。为此目的,联合经营人可以递交替代性的建议。

(3)如果在第(1)款规定的通知发出60天内,或者在两国政府可能同意的其他时间段内,两国政府始终未能解决上述问题,它们应指定一名独立专家,就上述问题作出及时、独立的决断。独立专家的指定与行事应符合附件D的条款。

第3.5条 包含额外已获授权区域

(1)如果,在许可证持有人协定已获两国政府批准之后,两国政府审批通过的跨界矿藏的范围延伸至另一许可证持有人的矿区,两国政府应当要求其他他们所有的、对跨界矿藏持有参与股权的经营人,为实现该片区域原油的有效开采而达成安排。此类安排应在两国政府规定的时间段内完成,应符合本协定的条款,并得到两国政府批准。采用"许可证持有人协定"形式的此类安排,第3.2条对之适用。

(2)若该安排未能在规定期限内达成,则进一步的行动应由两国政府共同决定。

第3.6条 包含未获授权区域

(1)如果,在许可证持有人协定已获两国政府批准之后,两国政府认定,跨界矿藏的范围可以延伸至一块未授予开发许可的矿区,则矿区所属国政府应当毫不迟延地,以对该矿区授予许可的方式寻求补救。

(2)如果授权的开发许可包含第(1)款所指的区域,两国政府应当要求所有对跨界矿藏持有参与股权的相关经营人,为实现该片区域原油的有效开采而达成安排。任何此类安排应在两国政府规定的时间段内完成,应符合本协定的条款,并得到两国政府批准。此类安排采用"许可证持有人协定"的形式，第3.2条对之适用。

（3）如果一国政府未能授与开发许可，或者虽然该国授予了开发许可，但上述安排未能在规定的时间段内达成，则进一步的行动应由两国政府共同决定。

第3.7条　联合经营人

依据本协定，为实现对跨界矿藏的开发，两国政府授权的许可证持有人，应达成合意，指派联合经营人作为它们的共同代理人。任何联合经营人的指派与变更，应提前获得两国政府的同意。

第3.8条　评价井

两国政府不得依据其国内法，撤回某一钻井许可，或基于对第3.3条相关问题做出决定的考虑，撤销对其许可证持有人的授权。

第3.9条　发展计划：跨界矿藏的开采

（1）为有效开发和运输跨界矿藏中的资源，联合经营人应向两国政府递交发展计划，以待批准。

（2）若利用东道国设施开采跨界矿藏，则第（1）款所指的发展计划应包括对与跨界矿藏开采直接相关的东道国设施及其运营的修订，进行描述。

（3）联合经营人可以在任何时间主动向两国政府递交发展计划的修正案，两国政府也可以随时要求联合经营人递交修正案。所有发展计划的修正案应经两国政府批准。

第3.10条　开始生产

非经两国政府另行合意，在两国政府未依据本协定共同审批完成下列事项的情况下，一国政府不得授权从跨界矿藏（的一侧）开始生产：

（a）许可证持有人协定；

（b）第3.7条所指的联合经营人；并且

（c）第3.9条所指的发展计划；

并且都已进行了其他必要的授权。

第3.11条　为开发另一矿藏而使用单元区块内的设备

如果位于一个单元区块内的设备，被用于该区块外油气矿藏的勘探和开采，则第3.9条规定的、对发展计划所作的必要修订，应递交两国政府批准。依据本协定之规定，若这一设备的使用，会对跨界矿藏的开发产生不利影响，则两国政府不得批准，除非另经它们合意。

第3.12条　生产的终止

两国政府应就某一跨界矿藏生产终止的时间节点达成一致意见。

第四章　使用东道国设备的项目

第4.1条　授权

若两国政府及各自的许可证持有人，对一项使用东道国设备的项目达成一致意见，两国政府，除依据本协定第3.9条和第3.11条之目的审批通过外，应当分别依据各自国内法，单独进行授权。

第4.2条　发展计划

依据第3.9条和第3.11条，两国政府应当要求它们的许可证持有人递交发展计划或既有发展计划的修正案以待它们批准，这一发展计划和发展计划修正案应包含第4.1条所指的项目的相关问题。

第4.3条　政府决定

依据第三章，所有的政府决定：

（a）与单元区块外的设备相关，以及与使用东道国设备开发"划界线"另一侧的油气矿藏或跨界矿藏有关；或者

（b）与跨界线一侧的油气资源相关，（该油气资源）使用了划界线另一侧的东道国设施，且与该东道国设施的使用相关；

在与另一国政府紧密协商，且充分考虑了另一国政府提出的所有问题后，应由放置东道国设施或油气矿藏所在的那一侧政府作出。这方面的一个例子是相关活动终止的时间节点的决定。

第4.5条　经营者

依据第3.7条，在与另一国政府协商之后，油气矿藏和（或）东道国设

施经营人的指派或变更，应获得油气矿藏所在或放置东道国设施那一侧的政府的审批同意。

第五章 争端解决

第5条 调解委员会

(1)依据第(2)款，若两国政府不能就本协定的解释和适用，包括任何待解决的任何问题，达成一致意见，除非两国政府另行合意，或适用第3.4条规定的争端解决机制，则应适用下列争端解决机制：

(i)任何一国政府可以请求，将争端递交调解委员会。

(ii)调解委员会应由5名委员构成。每国政府任命2名委员，被任命的4名委员共同任命第5名委员(该委员不得为挪威或英国的国民，其惯常居所地也不得位于英国或挪威)。调解委员会的第5名委员将作为调解委员会的主席。

(iii)在请求提出后的一个月内，如果任何一国政府不能在一个月内指派一名或多名调解委员会的委员，则任何一国政府都可以请求国际法院的院长指派空缺的一名或多名委员。

(iv)被任命的4名委员，在第4名委员任命后一个月内，不能就第5名委员的任命达成一致意见，那么加上必要的变更，可以适用(与第(iii)款)相同的程序。

(v)调解委员会应当有权获取所有相关信息，并举行任何必要的磋商。

(vi)应当要求调解委员会在一个合理期限内做出决定(考虑快速解决争端的需要)。

(vii)调解委员会的决定以简单多数通过，决定对两国政府具有拘束力。并且

(viii)两国政府可以进一步协商确定委员会作出决定的相关程序。

(2)如果一国政府在其权限内，依据第2.6条和第2.7条第(3)款来确定一个受管制的使用系统中的海上出口关税，或处理一项经协商的使用系统中的关税争端，而"框架论坛"不能就解决两国政府之间的分歧，在收到一国政府的申请后，调解委员会应当考虑：

（a）作出决定的政府提供给另一国政府的信息，是否使另一国政府合理地确信，决定已经充分、适当地考虑了附件 B 或附件 C 所列举的原则；并且

（b）决定本身是否充分、适当地考虑了附件 B 或附件 C 所列举的原则。

第六章　最后条款

第 6.1 条　修正案与暂停适用

两国政府可以在任何时候以协议的形式，修订或终止本协定。两国政府都可以在任何时候，就本协定的修订提请磋商。在提出申请后的两个月内，两国政府应启动并迅速展开磋商。为在尽可能短的时间内达成一项双方共同接受的方案，两国政府应充分、适当地考虑修正案中的提议。

第 6.2 条　其他原油协定

在不损害第 1.10 条和第 2.6 条的情况下，本协定不影响附件 E 中所列举的其他原油协定的实施，只要这些协定保持生效状态，它们应优先适用。因此，若某一跨界矿藏的开发、某一使用东道国设施的开发项目受本协定规制，且 1998 年 8 月 25 日在斯塔万格签订的框架协定，规制与此类开发项目相关的管道，这些管道应受后者规制。

第 6.3 条　生效

两国政府在相互通知对方，已完成必要的国内法程序之日，本协定生效。

下列签署人，经其各自政府正式授权，在本协定上签字，以昭诚信。

2005 年 4 月 4 日签订于奥斯陆，以英文文本和挪威文本为作准文本，两种文本具有同等效力。

大不列颠及北爱尔兰联合王国政府：　　挪威王国政府：

麦克·奥布莱恩　　　　　　　　　　　索希尔德·魏德维

附件 A

《工作流程：确定运输挪威至英国 干气管道剩余运力的需求与管道的具体选择》

(1)下述内容详述，如何确定从"加斯勒德"干气系统至英国的运输系统，也就是"维斯特里管道"和"兰格勒德南管道"的剩余运力。该工作流程将涉及"加斯科"公司(挪威大陆架干气基础设施的运营商)，挪威和英国干气基础设施的所有者，干气托运人和两国政府的主管部门(挪威能源和石油部、挪威原油署和英国贸易和工业部)。

(2)年度"船舶运输和管道输送计划"的准备和维护、托运人对挪威大陆架各公司的未来运力使用的申请和预订，由加斯科公司负责。所请求的船舶运输和管道输送的运力，应基于参考的成交量做出。船舶所有者提供的信息，应当指明加斯科区域(例如区块 D——干气系统)的每个入口点和出口点。每年第二季度公布年度"船舶运输和管道输送计划"，该计划应指明对新运力的可能需求，并确定新的从挪威大陆架至英国大陆架的干气连接的需要。计划应当包括时间(也就是启动的那一年)和挪威大陆架上替代性的待验证节点(例如德雷普纳、斯普雷尼、海姆达尔等)。

(3)例如，于 2003 年 6 月 12 日递交给"使用者论坛"的当年度"船舶运输和管道输送计划"，就表明至 2008 年，为将干气运输至英国，总共需要 1.2 亿 Sm³/d 的运力。基于 2003 年制定的"船舶运输和管道输送计划"，那时的计划运力("维斯特里管道"和"兰格勒德南管道")是 1.05 亿 Sm³/d，这表明需要制定一些新的解决方案，以弥补 1500 万 Sm³/d 的缺口。

(4)对建设新交通枢纽的财政资助，一方面要求，对从挪威大陆架运输天然气和液化气有利益的托运人群体，对提升运输能力提出建议草案，另一方面也要求，挪威和英国的投资人群体提出此类建议草案。当然，这些群体，可能有共同的成员。英国基础设施的所有者，也可以是投资人群体的一员。

(5)"加斯科"公司将每年公布一份"船舶运输和管道输送计划"。如果该计划认定，需要提升运力，且托运人将启动一项新项目，则他们将推动

（托运人）、基础设施所有者和潜在的投资者群体进行商业探讨。同时，托运人和投资者可以代表"加斯勒德"，为与挪威"加斯科"干气系统进行衔接，同"加斯科"（公司）进行商业谈判。挪威政府依据附件B确定出口关税标准。应当认识到，潜在投资者和承运人必须尽早获取与新运输系统和既存运输系统的运输费用相关的信息，这样可以为他们作出预订和投资决定提供基础。

（6）托运人群体和潜在投资者，在同"加斯科"（公司）进行合作时，将考虑技术和商业提案，并为最合适的新运输枢纽实施概念选择进程。如果需要建设一个新枢纽，那么该枢纽需要至少提前两年进行准备，就该枢纽的修建展开商业化和合同的讨论。

（7）为确保公平、开放的竞争，在进行概念选择之前，所有合理的气体运输方案，应在技术和商业上达到相似的成熟度。花费预估和相关的技术文件，应对所有相关当事方公开，使其可以获取。

（8）选择进程是透明的，但也需要认识到，有必要使各个方案之间可以形成有效的竞争。为保证透明度，在进行评估之前，估量、评估各项方案的标准也应当公布。对最佳方案的决定，包括运输气体至英国的路线，应当基于清晰经济原则作出，并应为托运人提供最经济的方案。选择进程对"框架论坛"应是完全公开透明的，"框架论坛"作为最终的仲裁者，有权依据前置的程序，对概念选择进程的公开性、公正性、非歧视性作出决断。"框架论坛"应也应对发展受审查的新运输设施和及时推动商业化进程负责。

（9）如果双方当成一致意见，同意将连接管道接入"加斯勒德"管道系统，那么"加斯科"公司将会成为枢纽的运营商，并将主导签订或修订新基础设施的"参与者之间的协议"（所有者协议）的进程，这些协定的内容包括对投资份额、权利能力的决定。

（10）两国政府认识到，若要修改挪威或英国大陆架上相关产业的组织方式和（或）法律规范，将会导致修订本附件中的工作流程。在这种情况下，两国政府应当，通过"框架论坛"，修订本附件，以使其继续反应，确定挪威至英国额外干气运输能力的流程。在本附件任何修订版本的起草过程中，两国政府应使它们自己确信，基于清晰经济原则，选择最佳方案（包括从挪威运输干气至英国的路线）的流程，是公平和透明的，该方案对托运人而言是最为经济的方案。

附件 B

《挪威干气系统确定出口点和海上关税的原则》

（1）当一个将挪威上游系统连接至英国上游系统的方案得到运用，反之亦然，且出口关税行将确定时，挪威政府在受管制的系统中确定一个新的出口点并为之确立关税标准之前，应与英国政府就关税问题进行全面磋商。

（2）两国政府应对所有相关主体适用非歧视原则、透明原则和公平原则。为确保相关方案的经济合理性，鼓励对既有系统的合算利用，两国政府应致力于对既有商业运输系统实现最佳发展和有效利用。关税应当反映实际的支出。

（3）挪威政府在设定出口点和相关关税时，应当充分处理并考虑下列因素：

（a）因与其他海上系统相连，而对某一系统产生的影响（运力、压力、温度、质量等）。这样的影响可是正面的，也可是负面的。

（b）作为一项一般原则，因兴建新枢纽而产生的所有相关投资花费，在适当的时候，应由管道使用者公平地返还给管道所有者。同时，应当适当考虑，兴建新枢纽可能对该系统带来的更多收益或支出。

（c）公平地分担运营费用。"加斯勒德"系统的出口关税应包括对该系统的运营费用的公平分担。

（d）对于利用既有运输系统，将气体运输至新出口点而产生的基础性（历史性）资金花费，要对管道所有者进行公平返利。这一返利要远低于着陆点的出口关税。

（4）挪威政府应在收到请求后，向商事主体或英国政府提供新关税的相关信息，以便为他们作出投资决定之前提供可预测性。在任何情况下，如有可能，这一信息应在收到该请求的 16 周以内予以提供。

（5）在相关项目审批通过时，出口关税也应当同时正式确定。

附件 C

《第三方使用英国大陆架上的上游设施：关税确定原则》

（1）在（有关商事主体）就英国大陆架上上游设施的使用展开磋商时，英国政府支持非歧视原则的适用，支持（磋商过程）的透明化，提升有关当事方的公平感，因为潜在的使用者以竞争性的价格公平地使用基础设施是很重要的，同时认识到上游设施闲置能力的利用具有商业价值，而设施的所有者已经承受了安装设施的花费和商业风险，出于公平经商的考量，设施所有者应有权收费。国务大臣要求征收的所有关税，参照设备所有者的真实花费和失去的机遇，反映对设备所有者的公平收益偿还。

（2）如果国务大臣要行使权力，要求（设施所有者准许）使用并设定关税：

（i）设施所有者随之而来的费用，包括间接的费用（例如，为适用第三者的使用需求，对管道进行调整，引起所有者的生产中断，进而造成的损失），应得到补偿；

（ii）设定的关税，应使第三方公平分担其介入之后的总体经营成本；

（iii）除非供应量可以忽略不计，或者设施所有者已经为收回全部的资金花费做出了其他的充分安排，否则拟议的财政安排，通常情况下应考虑基础资本花费，① 也应考虑因第三方介入而产生的费用。

（3）有时，预期的第三方使用者，可能会为了同一有限的基础设施运力而展开竞争。在这种情况下，国务大臣不得要求设施所有者将可用的运力转让给，相比其他使用者而言，资产和能力较低的使用者，进而使所有者不能实现一笔更符合其利益的交易。

（4）如果设施的运力不足第三方的需求，考虑到所有者的权利和已有

---

① 对于考虑到运营第三方业务而更新的设施、在建的或过大的设施，国务大臣设定的关税，通常应包括一笔资金收回的津贴，以补贴因开展可预期的第三方业务而产生的资金花费。认识在预测未来的使用时，存在一些固有的不确定性，如果这项津贴针对作出投资决定时预期开展的生产情况，则这项津贴的标准，应足以使所有者可就这些花费获得合理的收益偿还。

的合同承诺，国务大臣（一般）不得要求（所有者）提供（运力）。如果国务大臣打算这么做，关税应至少反映，设施所有者减缓生产的成本，和（或）为供应该第三方而减少对已有合同相对人的供应而产生的成本（也就是说，基于机会成本的概念）。

附件 D

《专家程序》

（1）当处理本协定第3.4条所指的相关争端时，适用本附件，由一独立专家作出决断。

（2）专家的选择、职权和雇佣条款，应由两国达成的协定加以确定。除非两国另行合意，专家应当从，被公认为该领域的专业人士或者专业组织中选择，且选择的专家应当提供本附件规定的利益冲突承诺书。专家为作出决定，可雇佣承包人，但该承包人也应提供大体相同的承诺书。专家及其雇佣的承包人应对提供给他们的所有信息保密。

（3）如果两国政府未能就专家的选择、职权和（或）雇佣条款达成一致意见，在任何一国政府提起本附件的相关程序后的6周内，两国政府各提名一个候选人，并请法国石油研究院的院长，或两国政府另行合意的其他机构、个人，从候选人中确定专家人选，并且（或者）决定专家的职权范围和（或者）雇佣条款。如果只有一国政府提名了专家，则应选择这名专家。

（4）当专家为了作出决定而要求两国政府提供相关信息时，两国政府应及时提供。专家只能同时与两国政府代表会面。在会面之外，如果专家与一国政府进行沟通，则沟通应以书面形式进行，且沟通的书面副本应送交另一国政府。

（5）在专家获得认命的12周之内，专家应当为两国政府作出一个初步决定，并附上决定如何作出的详细解释。在两国政府收到初步决定之后的8周时间（或两国政府另行合意的其他时间段），两国政府可寻求专家澄清其决定，并且（或者）可以向专家提交意见供其考虑。在本阶段结束后的4周内，专家应作出最终的决定，并附上详细的解释，决定和解释应以书面形式向两国政府送达。若无欺诈或明显错误，这一决定应当构成最终决定，并对两国具有拘束力，两国政府应确保，该决定由代表相关许可证持有人的联合经营人实施。

（6）在任何情况下，专家应对其收费和政府支出，以对其而言比较公平合理的方式，承担责任。依据本款，两国政府可以向联合经营人收费。

附件 D 的附加文件：《利益冲突的承诺书范本》

（1）[专家姓名]在这此保证，在他处理相关争端期间[自某日起]，他不会为英国政府、挪威政府工作，也不会为属于英国或者挪威大陆架上的[某]油气田或其他油气田的许可证持有人工作，假如这样的工作会影响他职能的履行，或者这样的工作与他解决前述问题的职责相冲突。特别是，他保证，在作出决定后 2 年内，他将不会从事任何与[某]油田相关的工作，也不会为[某]油田的许可证持有人工作。

（2）[承包人姓名]在此保证，他自[某日]起，在参与[某专家]组织的、与 2005 年 4 月 4 日签订的框架协议相关的跨界石油合作的争端处理期间，他不会为英国政府、挪威政府工作，也不会为属于英国或者挪威大陆架上的[某]油气田或其他油气田的许可证持有人工作，假如这样的工作会影响他职能的履行，或与他同[某专家]签订的合约所规定的职责相违背。特别是，他保证，在作出决定后 2 年内，他将不会从事任何与[某]油田相关的工作，也不会为[某]油田的许可证持有人工作。

附件 E

《既存的石油协定》

1973 年 5 月 22 日签订，① 由双方于 1994 年 7 月 27 日以换文的形式加以修订，与埃科菲斯克油田及相邻区域的原油，经管道运输至英国的有关协议②

---

① 英国政府 1973 年第 5423 号敕令书，条约集第 101 号（文件）。
② 英国政府 1995 年第 2721 号敕令书，条约集第 1 号（文件）。

1976 年 5 月 10 日签订、① 以 1998 年 8 月 25 日的协定、2001 年 6 月 21 日的外交换文②修订的，关于开发弗里格气田并将开发所得产品向联合王国输送天然气的协定；③ 以及为开采和运输油气资源而使用设备和管道（的协定）

1979 年 10 月 16 日签订，④ 经由双方于 1995 年 3 月 24 日以换文形式修订的关于国家湾油田开发和资源运输的协定。⑤

1979 年 10 月 16 日签订，⑥ 于 1981 年 10 月 22 日⑦和 1983 年 6 月 22 日另行签订补充协定，⑧ 由双方于 1999 年 8 月 9 日以换文方式修订的⑨、关于默奇森油田开发和资源运输的协定。

1985 年 11 月 21 日签订，⑩ 经双方于 2004 年 11 月 1 日修订，有关（利用）海姆达尔液化气管道运输（油气资源）至英国的协定。

1998 年 8 月 25 日签订的，有关铺设、运营、管辖和相互连接海底管道的框架协定。⑪

---

① 英国政府 1977 年第 7043 号敕令书，条约集第 113 号（文件）。
② 英国政府 2002 年第 5513 号敕令书，条约集第 21 号（文件）。
③ 英国政府 2001 年第 5258 号敕令书，条约集第 43 号（文件）。
④ 英国政府 1981 年第 8282 号敕令书，条约集第 44 号（文件）。
⑤ 英国政府 1995 年第 2941 号敕令书，条约集第 57 号（文件）。
⑥ 英国政府 1981 年第 8270 号敕令书，条约集第 39 号（文件）。
⑦ 英国政府 1982 年第 8577 号敕令书，条约集第 25 号（文件）。
⑧ 英国政府 1983 年第 9083 号敕令书，条约集第 71 号（文件）。
⑨ 英国政府 2000 年第 4857 号敕令书，条约集第 110 号（文件）。
⑩ 英国政府 1987 年第 201 号敕令书，条约集第 39 号（文件）。
⑪ 英国政府 2003 年第 5762 号敕令书，条约集第 9 号（文件）。

六、1979 年泰国湾共同开发案

1. Statement of the Territorial Sea, the Contiguous Zone, the Exclusive Economic Zone, and the Continental Shelf of Vietnam, 12 May 1977(《1977 年 5 月 12 日越南关于领海、毗连区、专属经济区和大陆架的声明》)

The statement which is dated May 12, 1977, and has been approved by the Standing Committee of the SRV National Assembly, reads in full as follows:

The Government of the Socialist Republic of Vietnam,

After approval by the Standing Committee of the National Assembly of the Socialist Republic of Vietnam,

Declares that it has defined the territorial sea, the contiguous zone, the exclusive economic zone and the continental shelf of the Socialist Republic of Vietnam as follows:

(1) The territorial sea of the Socialist Republic of Vietnam has a breadth of 12 nautical miles measured from a baseline which links the furthest seaward points of the coast and the outermost points of Vietnamese offshore islands, and which is the low-water line along the coast.

The waters on the landward side of the baseline constitute internal waters of the Socialist Republic of Vietnam.

The Socialist Republic of Vietnam exercises full and complete sovereignty over its territorial sea as well as the superjacent air space and the bed and subsoil of the territorial sea.

（2）The contiguous zone of the Socialist Republic of Vietnam is a 12-nautical-mile maritime zone adjacent to and beyond the Vietnamese territorial sea, with which it forms a zone of 24 nautical miles from the baseline used to measure the breadth of the territorial sea.

The Government of the Socialist Republic of Vietnam exercises the necessary control in its contiguous zone in order to see to its security and custom and fiscal interests and to ensure respect for its sanitary, emigration and immigration regulations within the Vietnamese territory or territorial sea.

（3）The exclusive economic zone of the Socialist Republic of Vietnam is adjacent to the Vietnamese territorial sea and forms with it a 200-nautical-mile zone from the baseline used to measure the breadth of Vietnam's territorial sea.

The Socialist Republic of Vietnam has sovereign rights for the purpose of exploring, exploiting, conserving and managing all natural resources, whether living or non-living, of the waters, the bed and subsoil of the exclusive economic zone of Vietnam; it has exclusive rights and jurisdiction with regard to the establishment and use of installations and structures, artificial islands; exclusive jurisdiction with regard to other activities for the economic exploration and exploitation of the exclusive economic zone; exclusive jurisdiction with regard to scientific research in the exclusive economic zone of Vietnam; the Socialist Republic of Vietnam has jurisdiction with regard to the preservation of the marine environment, and activities for pollution control and abatement in the exclusive economic zone of Vietnam.

（4）The continental shelf of the Socialist Republic of Vietnam comprises the seabed and subsoil of the submarine areas that extend beyond the Vietnamese territorial sea throughout the natural prolongation of the Vietnamese land territory to the outer edge of the continental margin, or to a distance of 200 nautical miles from the baseline used to measure the breadth of the Vietnamese territorial sea where the outer edge of the continental margin does not extend up to that distance.

The Socialist Republic of Vietnam exercises sovereign rights over the Vietnamese continental shelf in the exploration, exploitation, preservation and management of all natural resources, consisting of mineral and other non-living resources, together with living organisms belonging to sedentary species thereon.

(5) The islands and archipelagos, forming an integral part of the Vietnamese territory and beyond the Vietnamese territorial sea mentioned in Paragraph I, have their own territorial seas, contiguous zones, exclusive economic zones and continental shelves, determined in accordance with the provisions of Paragraphs 1, 2, 3 and 4 of this statement.

(6) Proceeding from the principles of this statement, specific questions relating to the territorial sea, the contiguous zone, the exclusive economic zone, and the continental shelf of the Socialist Republic of Vietnam will be dealt with in detail in further regulations, in accordance with the principle of defending the sovereignty and interests of the Socialist Republic of Vietnam, and in keeping with international law and practices.

(7) The Government of the Socialist Republic of Vietnam will settle with the countries concerned, through negotiations on the basis of mutual respect for independence and sovereignty, in accordance with international law and practices, the matters relating to the maritime zones and the continental shelf of each country.

资料来源: http: //www. un. org/Depts/los/LEGISLATIONANDTREATIES/PDFFILES/VNM_1977_Statement. pdf。

2. Statement of 12 November 1982 by the Government of the Socialist Republic of VietNam on the Territorial Sea Baseline of VietNam (《1982 年 11 月 12 日越南社会主义共和国政府关于越南领海基线的声明》)

In implementing the provisions of paragraph 1 of the statement on the territorial sea, the contiguous zone, the exclusive economic zone and the continental shelf issued by the Government of the Socialist Republic of VietNam on 12 May 1977 after being approved by the Standing Committee of the National Assembly of the Socialist Republic of VietNam,

The Government of the Socialist Republic of VietNam makes the following statement on the baseline from which the breadth of the territorial sea of VietNam shall be measured:

(1) The baseline from which the territorial sea of the continental territory of VietNam shall be measured is constituted by straight lines connecting those points the co-ordinates of which are listed in the annex attached herewith.

(2) The territorial sea baseline of VietNam which starts from point 0-the meeting point of the two baselines for measuring the breadth of the territorial sea of the Socialist Republic of VietNam and that of the People's Republic of Kampuchea, located in the sea on the line linking the Tho Chu Archipelago with Poulo Wai Island-and which ends at Con Co Island shall be drawn following the co-ordinates listed in the attached annex on the 1/100, 000 scale charts published by the Vietnamese People's Navy prior to 1979.

(3) The Gulf of Bac Bo (Tonkin Gulf) is a gulf situated between the Socialist Republic of VietNam and the People's Republic of China; the maritime frontier in the gulf between VietNam and China is delineated according to the 26 June 1887 Convention of frontier boundary signed between France and the Qing Dynasty of China.

The part of the gulf appertaining to VietNam constitutes the historic waters and is subjected to the juridical régime of internal waters of the Socialist Republic of VietNam.

The baseline from Con Co Island to the mouth of the gulf will be defined following the settlement of the problem relating to the closing line of the gulf.

(4) The baseline for measuring the breadth of the territorial sea of the Hoang Sa and Truong Sa Archipelagos will be determined in a coming instrument in conformity with paragraph 5 of the 12 May 1977 statement of the Government of the Socialist Republic of VietNam.

(5) The sea as lying behind the baseline and facing the coast or the islands of VietNam constitutes the internal waters of the Socialist Republic of VietNam.

(6) The Government of the Socialist Republic of VietNam holds that all differences with countries concerned relating to different sea areas and the continental shelf will be settled through negotiations on the basis of mutual respect for each other's national independence and sovereignty in conformity with international law and practice.

HANOI, 12 November 1982.

资料来源: http://www. un. org/Depts/los/LEGISLATIONANDTREATIES/ PDFFILES/VNM _1982_Statement. pdf。

3. Statement Issued by the Spokesman of the Ministry of Foreign Affairs of 15 January 1978(《1978 年 1 月 15 日 (柬埔寨) 外交部 发言人 (关于领海、毗连区、专属经济区和大陆架) 的声明》)

The Ministry of Foreign Affairs of Democratic Kampuchea would like to reaffirm the stand of Democratic Kampuchea concerning the territorial sea, the contiguous zone, the exclusive economic zone and the continental shelf of Democratic Kampuchea, the stand that the Government of Democratic Kampuchea has successively stated precisely.

(1) Democratic Kampuchea exercises its full and entire sovereignty over its territorial sea, the breadth of which is established on 12 nautical miles, measured from the baselines. Democratic Kampuchea also exercises this sovereignty over the airspace over its territorial sea as well as over the bed and subsoil of its territorial sea.

(2) Democratic Kampuchea entirely exercises its rights of control over the contiguous zone which extend on 12 nautical miles from the external limit of its territorial sea.

(3) Democratic Kampuchea has exclusive sovereign rights for the purpose of exploring and exploiting, conserving and managing all the natural resources of the superjacent waters, the bed and the subsoil of its exclusive economic zone situated beyond its territorial sea and extending up to 200 nautical miles from the baselines.

Democratic Kampuchea exercises its exclusive sovereign rights over its continental shelf, comprising the sea-bed and subsoil of the submarine areas that extend beyond its territorial sea throughout the natural prolongation of its land territory. Democratic Kampuchea exercises these sovereign rights over its continental shelf for the purpose of exploring and exploiting, conserving and managing all the natural resources of the sea-bed and subsoil.

(4) All the islands of Democratic Kampuchea have their territorial seas, their contiguous zones, their exclusive economic zones and their continental shelves.

(5) The Government of Democratic Kampuchea takes appropriate steps to safeguard entirely the sovereignty, rights and interests of Democratic Kampuchea in its territorial sea, its contiguous zone, its exclusive economic zone and its continental shelf.

(6) The Government of Democratic Kampuchea will settle with parties concerned by the above maritime zones according to each specific

situation.

Phnom Penh, 15 January 1978

资料来源: http://www.un.org/Depts/los/LEGISLATIONANDTREATIES/PDFFILES/KHM_1978_Statement.pdf。

4. Cambodian Council of State Decree on Territorial Waters(《柬埔寨国会关于领水的法令》)

The chairman of the Council of State, considering that the PRK has full sovereignty and inviolable rights over its territorial waters and its continental shelf;

Considering that the PRK must watch over its sovereignty, security and national defense toward the sea and ensure the best exploitation of natural resources in its territorial waters and continental shelf in order to serve the national defense and reconstruction efforts and the improvement of the people's living standards;

Considering the Constitution of the PRK;

And the Council of Ministers having been informed;

Has decreed the following:

Article 1

The full and entire sovereignty of the PRK extends beyond its territory and internal waters to a maritime zone adjacent to its coasts and its internal waters, designated by the name of the territorial waters of the PRK.

This sovereignty also extends to the airspace above the territorial waters of the PRK as well as to the seabed and subsoil of these waters.

Article 2

The width of the territorial waters of the PRK is 12 nautical miles (1 nautical mile equaling 1,852 meters) measured from straight baselines, linking the points of the coast and the furthest points of Kampuchea's [Cambodia's] furthest islands; these baselines are traced along the low-water mark.

These straight baselines are concretely defined in Annex 1 of this decree.

The internal waters of the PRK are the waters located between the baseline of the territorial waters and the coasts of Kampuchea [Cambodia].

Article 3

The outer limit of the territorial waters of the PRK is a line each point of which is at a distance equal to the width of the territorial waters from the closest point of the baseline.

In the maritime zone between Kach Kut Island and the terminus of the land border between Kampuchea [Cambodia] and Thailand, the limit of the territorial water of the PRK follows the dividing line of the maritime waters determined by the historic border stipulated in the Franco-Siamese treaty of 23 March 1907.

Article 4

The contiguous zone of the PRK is a maritime zone located beyond and adjacent to its territorial waters, with a width of 12 nautical miles measured from the outer limit of the territorial waters of the PRK.

In its contiguous zone, the PRK exercises necessary control in order to oversee its security and to prevent and check violations of its customs, fiscal, health and emigration and immigration laws.

Article 5

The exclusive economic zone of the PRK is a maritime zone located beyond its territorial waters and adjacent to the latter. This zone extends to 200 nautical miles measured from the baseline used to measure the width of the territorial waters of the PRK.

The PRK has sovereign rights over the exploration and exploitation and the preservation and management of all organic or inorganic natural resources of the seabed, of its subsoil and of the waters above it and over other activities leading to the exploration and exploitation of its exclusive economic zone.

In its exclusive economic zone, the PRK has exclusive jurisdiction regarding the setting up and use of installations, devices and artificial islands and marine research; and has jurisdiction over the preservation of the marine environment and the control of pollution.

Without prior authorization or agreement by the PRK. foreign ships are forbidden to fish or exploit any natural resources in any form, or to undertake scientific research in the exclusive economic zone of the PRK. When they have obtained prior authorization or agreement, they must conform with the Jaws and regulations of the PRK concerning fishing, the exploitation of other natural resources and scientific research, and with other regulations relating to them decreed by the PRK, and must strictly carry out all obligations provided in the licenses or the contracts.

Article 6

The continental shelf of the PRK comprises the seabed and the subsoil of the submarine areas that extend beyond the territorial waters throughout the natural prolongation of its land territory to a distance of 200 nautical miles from the baseline used to measure the width of the territorial waters of the PRK.

The PRK exercises sovereign rights over its continental shelf for the purposes of exploration, exploitation. preservation and management of its natural resources comprising mineral resources and other inorganic or organic resources belonging to sedentary species living on the continental shelf.

The PRK has the exclusive right to regulate the setting up and use of installations, devices and artificial islands or drilling on its continental shelf for the purposes of exploration, exploitation or any other purpose.

All activities carried out by foreigners on the continental shelf of Kampuchea [Cambodia]. for whatever end, must be the object of an authorization or an agreement by the PR Government and conform with the laws and regulations of the PRK.

Article 7

The PRK will settle, by means of negotiations with interested states, all problems concerning the maritime zones and continental shelf in a fair and logical manner on the basis of mutual respect for sovereignty, independence and territorial integrity.

Article 8

The PRK will negotiate and agree with the SRV [Vietnam] on the maritime border in the historic waters zone of the two countries fixed in the agreement on the historic waters of the two countries signed on 7 July 1982 in line with the spirit and letter of the Treaty of Peace. Friendship and Cooperation between the two states signed on 18 February 1979.

Article 9

All provisions contrary to this decree are purely and simply abrogated.

Article 10

The minister of national defence, the minister of interior and the ministers concerned are charged each in his proper field, with the implementation of this decree.

The Baseline Retained for the Limitation of the Territorial Waters of the PRK.

The baseline retained for the limitation of the territorial waters of the PRK is made up of segments of a line passing successively" through the following points, the coordinates of which are expressed in degrees, minutes and tenths of a minute. the longitude being counted from the meridian of Greenwich.

ANNEX 1

Number	Geographical Place	Latitude (North)	Longitude (East)
1	Border point on low-water mark between Thailand and the PRK according to treaty of 23 March 1907	11°38′8″	102°54′3″
2	Kack Kusrovie	11°06′8″	102°47′3″
3	Kack Voar	10°14′0″	102°52′5″
4	Poulo Wai	09°55′5″	102°53′2″
5	Point 0 out at sea on the southwest limit of the historic waters of the PRK	According to the agreement of 7 July 1982	

资料来源: http: //www. un. org/Depts/los/LEGISLATIONANDTREATIES/ PDFFILES/KHM_1982_Decree. pdf。

5. The Brévié Line, 31 January 1939(《1939 年 1 月 31 日布莱维线》)

Directorate of Political Affairs

Number 867 *I* API

Hanoi, 31 January 1939

The Governor General of Indochina

Grand Officer of the Legion d'Honneur

To the Governor of Cochin China

(I Bureau) in Saigon

Subject: Islands in the Gulf of Siam

I have the honor of informing you that I have just reexamined the question of the islands of the Gulf of Siam, the possession of which is disputed between Cambodia and Cochin China.

The situation of this group of islands, scattered along the Cambodian coast and some of which are so near the coast that land filling presently being carried out will seem to fuse them to the Cambodian coast in a relatively near future, logically and geographically requires that these islands be under the jurisdiction of the Administration of Cambodia.

I believe that it is impossible to let the present state of affairs continue as it is, which is forcing the inhabitants of these islands to refer, either at the price of a long crossing, or at the price of a long detour through Cambodian territory, to the Administration of Cochin China.

As a consequence, I have decided that all the islands located north of the line perpendicular to the coast starting from the border between Cambodia and Cochin China and making a 140 grad angle with the north meridian, in accordance with the attached chart, will be from now on administered by Cambodia. The Protectorate will, in particular, take over the police of these islands.

All the islands south of this line, including the islands of Phu-Quoc, will continue to be administered by Cochin China. It is understood that the demarcation line thus made will make a line around the north of the island Phu-Quoc, passing three kilometers from the extreme ends of the north shore of this island.

Administration and police powers on these islands will thus be clearly distributed between Cochin China and Cambodia, so that all the future disputes might be avoided.

It is understood that the above pertains only to the administration and policing of these islands, and that the issue of the islands' territorial jurisdiction remains entirely reserved.

You will please make provisions so that my decision is immediately put into effect.

Please notify me of the receipt of this letter.

Signed: BREVIE

资料来源: Clive Howard Schofield, *Maritime boundary delimitation in the gulf of Thailand*, Durham: Durham University, 1999, pp. 479-480. Available at Durham E-Theses Online: http://etheses. dur. ac. uk/4351/。

6. Agreement on Historic Waters of Vietnam and Kampuchea (《越南和柬埔寨关于历史性水域的协定》)

The Government of the Socialist Republic of Vietnam and the Government of the People's Republic of Kampuchea,

DESIROUS of further consolidating and developing the special Vietnam-Kampuchea relations in the spirit of the Treaty of Peace, Friendship and Cooperation between the Socialist Republic of Vietnam and the People's Republic of Kampuchea signed on February 18, 1979.

CONSIDERING the reality that the maritime zone situated between the coast of Kien Giang Province, Phu Quoc Island, and the Tho Chu ~ rchipelago of the Socialist Republic of Vietnam on the one side, and the coast of Kampot Province and the Poulo Wai group of islands of the People's Republic of Kampuchea on the other, encompasses waters which by their special geographical conditions and their great importance for the national defence and the economy of both countries have long belonged to Vietnam and Kampuchea,

HAVE AGREED ON THE FOLLOWING:

Article 1

The waters located between the coast of Kien Giang Province, Phu Quoc Island, and the Tho Chu archipelago of the Socialist Republic of Vietnam on the one side, and the coast of Kampot Province and the Poulo

91

Wai group of islands of the People's Republic of Kampuchea on the other, form the historical waters of the two countries placed under the juridical regime of their internal waters and are delimited (according to the Greenwich east longitude) :

To the northwest by a straight line stretching from coordinates 09 degrees 54′ 2″ north latitude-102 degrees 55′ 2″ east longitude and coordinates 09 degrees 54′ 5″ north latitude-102 degrees 57′ 2″ east longitude of Poulo Wai Islands (Kampuchea) to coordinates 10 degrees 24′1″ north latitude-103 degrees 48′0″ east longitude and I 0degrees 25′6″ north latitude-103 degrees 49′ 2″ east longitude of the Koh Ses Island (Kampuchea) to coordinates 10 degrees 30′0″ north latitude-103 degrees 47′4″ east longitude of Koh Thmei Island (Kampuchea) to coordinates 10 degrees 32′4″ north latitude-103 degrees 48′2″ east longitude on the coast of Kampot Province (Kampuchea).

To the north by the coast of Kampot Province stretching from coordinates 10 degrees 32′4″ Lat. N. -103 degrees 48′2″ Long. E. on the terminus of the land border between Vietnam and Kampuchea on the coast.

To the southeast by a line stretching from the terminus of the land border between Vietnam and Kampuchea on the coast to coordinates 10 degrees 04′42″ Lat. N. -104 degrees 02′3″ Long. E. from the An Yet point of Phu Quoc Island (Vietnam) and along the northern coast of this island to the Dat Do point situated at coordinates 10 degrees 02′8″ Lat. N. -103 degrees 59′1″ Long. E. , and from there to coordinates 09 degrees 10′1″ Lat. N. -103 degrees 26′4″ Long. E. of Thu Chu Island (Vietnam) to coordinates 09 degrees 15′0″ Lat. N. -103 degrees 27′0″ Long. E. of Hon Nhan Island in the Tho Chu archipelago (Vietnam).

To the southwest by a straight line stretching from coordinates 09 degrees 55′0″ Lat. N. -102 degrees 53′5″ Long. E. from Puolo Wai Islands (Kampuchea) to coordinates 09 degrees 15′0″ Lat. N. -103 degrees 27′0″ Long. e. of Hon Nhan Island in the Tho Chu archipelago (Vietnam).

Article 2

The two sides will hold at a suitable time negotiations in the spirit of equality, friendship, and respect for each other's independence, sovereignty, territorial integrity, and the legitimate interests of each side in order to delimit the maritime frontier between the two countries in the historical waters mentioned in Article 1.

Article 3

Pending the settlement of the maritime border between the two States in the historical waters mentioned in Article I:

The meeting point O of the two baselines used for measuring the width of the territorial waters of each country situated on the high seas on the straight baseline linking the Tho Chu archipelago and Poulo Wai Islands will be determined by mutual agreement.

The two sides continue to regard the Brévié Line drawn in 1939 as the dividing line for the islands in this zone.

Patrolling and surveillance in these territorial waters will be jointly conducted by the two sides.

The local populations will continue to conduct their fishing operations and the catch of other sea products in this zone according to the habits that have existed so far.

The exploitation of natural resources in this zone will be decided by common agreement.

DONE in Ho Chi Minh City on the 7th of July 1982, in two languages, Vietnamese and Khmer, both being equally valid.

For the Government of the Socialist Republic of Vietnam: Nguyen Co Thach, Minister of Foreign Affairs of the Socialist Republic of Vietnam.

For the Government of the People's Republic of Kampuchea: Hun Sen, Minister of Foreign Affairs of the People's Republic of Kampuchea.

资料来源: K. Kittichaisaree, The Law of the Sea and Maritime Boundary Delimitation in South-East Asia, Oxford: Oxford University Press, 1987。

93

7. Declaration of the Office of the Prime Minister Concerning the Inner Part of the Gulf of Thailand, 22 September 1959 (《1959 年 9 月 22 日泰国总理办公室关于泰国湾内水域的宣告》)

The Council of Ministers has seen fit to issue the following declaration confirming the juridical status of the inner part of the Gulf of Thailand; namely, that the inner part of the Gulf of Thailand situated northward of the baseline which starts from the first point on the Bahn Chong Samsarn Peninsula (latitude 12° 35′45″ north, longitude 100° 57′ 45″ east) and, running westward parallel to the latitude, reaches the second point on the opposite sea coast (latitude 12° 35′ 45″ north, longitude 99° 57′30″ east) is a historic bay and that the waters enclosed within the baselines aforesaid form part of the internal waters of Thailand.

The Kingdom of Thailand has constantly maintained the foregoing position from time immemorial.

资料来源：http：//www. un. org/Depts/los/LEGISLATIONANDTREATIES/ PDFFILES/THA_1959_Declaration. pdf。

8. Proclamation Establishing the Breadth of the Territorial Waters (《(泰国) 关于确立领水宽度的公告》)

Whereas Thailand always maintains that the sovereignty of Thailand extends, beyond its land territory and its internal waters, to a belt of sea adjacent to the coast, described as the territorial sea, including the airspace over the territorial seas as well as its bed and subsoil；

Whereas it is deemed appropriate to establish the breadth of the coastal territorial waters；

It is hereby proclaimed that the breadth of the territorial waters of Thailand is established at twelve nautical miles measured from a baseline used for measuring the breadth of the territorial sea.

资料来源：http://www.un.org/Depts/los/LEGISLATIONANDTREATIES/ PDFFILES/THA_1966_Proclamation.pdf。

9. Announcement of the Office of the Prime Minister Concerning the Straight Baselines and Internal Waters of Thailand(《总理办公室关于泰国直线基线和内水的宣告》)

Whereas the Announcement of the Office of the Prime Minister concerning the Straight Baselines and Internal Waters of Thailand dated 11 June 1970 was made to confirm the status of the straight baselines and internal waters of Thailand；

Whereas there are certain errors in the aforesaid Announcement；

Whereas the name of an island referred to in the aforesaid announcement has now been changed；

The Cabinet, by its decision of 11 August 1992, has amended the aforesaid Announcement as follows：

（1）The geographical names and geographical coordinates of Reference Number 5, Reference Number 12 and Reference Number 22 of Area No. III of the Announcement of the Office of the Prime Minister concerning the Straight Baselines and Internal Waters of Thailand dated 11 June 1970 are hereby repealed and substituted by the following：

（2）The map annexed to the Announcement of the Office of the Prime Minister concerning the Straight Baselines and Internal Waters of Thailand dated 11 June 1970 is hereby repealed and substituted by the map annexed to this present Announcement.

REFERENCE NO.	GEOGRAPHICAL NAME	GEOGRAPHICAL LAT. N.	COORDINATES LONG. E.
5	Ko Kai	07°−44′. 6	98°−37′. 1
12	Ko Bulaobot	07°−04′. 3	99°−23′. 7
22	Ko Khuning	06°−26′. 7	100°−03′. 7

资料来源：http：//www. un. org/Depts/los/LEGISLATIONANDTREATIES/ PDFFILES/THA_1993_Announcement. pdf。

10. Proclamation on Demarcation of the Continental Shelf of Thailand in the Gulf of Thailand，18 May 1973(《1973 年 5 月 18 日泰国关于泰国湾大陆架界限的公告》)

His Majesty the King is graciously pleased to proclaim that

For the purpose of exercising the sovereignty rights of Thailand in exploring and exploiting natural resources of the Gulf of Thailand, the continental shelf shall therefore be demarcated according the map and geographical co-ordinates of each point constituting the continental shelf of Thailand annexed to this Proclamation as the continental shelf of Thailand in the Gulf of Thailand.

The continental shelf has been demarcated on the basis of the right according to the generally accepted principles of international law and the Convocation on the Continental Shelf done at Geneva on 29th April 1958 and ratified by Thailand on 2nd July 1968 has been taken into account.

The map and connecting points determining geographical co-ordinates under this Proclamation are to show the general demarcation lines of the continental shelf. As for the sovereignty rights over the territorial sea adjacent to the territorial sea of the neighbouring countries, which will be taken as starting point of the line dividing the continental shelf, it will be according to future agreement on the basis of the provisions of the Convention on the Territorial Sea and the Contiguous Zone done at Geneva on 29th April 1958.

Given the 18th May B. E. 2516, being the 28th year of the present Reign.

Countersigned by Field Marshall Thanom Kittikachorn Prime Minister.

Geographical coordinates of the connecting points constituting the continental shelf of Thailand in the Gulf of Thailand.

Numerical point	Latitude North	Longitude East
1	11°39′. 0	102°55′. 0
2	09°48′. 5	101°46′. 5
3	09°43′. 0	101°48′. 5
4	09°42′. 0	101°49′. 0
5	09°28′. 5	101°53′. 5
6	09°13′. 0	101°58′. 5
7	09°11′. 0	101°59′. 0
8	08°52′. 0	102°13′. 0
9	08°47′. 0	102°16′. 5
10	08°42′. 0	102°26′. 5
11	08°33′. 0	102°38′. 0
12	08°29′. 0	102°43′. 0
13	07°49′. 5	103°05′. 5
14	07°25′. 0	103°24′. 8
15	06°50′. 0	102°21′. 2
16	06°27′. 8	102°09′. 6
17	06°27′. 5	102°10′. 0
18	06°14′. 5	102°05′. 6

资料来源：Clive Howard Schofield, *Maritime boundary delimitation in the gulf of Thailand*, Durham：Durham University, 1999, pp. 437-438. Available at Durham E-Theses Online：http：//etheses. dur. ac. uk/4351/。

11. Royal Proclamation Establishing the Exclusive Economic Zone of the Kingdom of Thailand, 23 February 1981(《1981 年 2 月 23 日泰王国关于建立专属经济区的皇家公告》)

By Royal Command of His Majesty the King, it is hereby proclaimed that:

For the purpose of exercising the sovereign rights of the kingdom of Thailand with regard to the exploration and conservation of the natural resources, whether living or non-living, of the sea. It is deemed appropriate to establish the exclusive economic zone of the Kingdom of Thailand as follows:

(1) The exclusive economic zone of the Kingdom of Thailand is an area beyond and adjacent to the territorial sea whose breadth extends to two hundred nautical miles measured from the Baselines used for measuring the breadth of the territorial sea.

(2) In the exclusive economic zone, the Kingdom of Thailand has:

(a) sovereign rights for the purpose of exploring and exploiting, conserving and managing the natural resources, whether living or non-linving, of the seabed and subsoil and the superjacent waters, and with regard to other activities for the economic exploration and exploitation of the zone, such as the production of energy from the water, currents and winds.

(b) jurisdiction with regard to :

(i) the establishment and use of artificial islands, installations andstructures;

(ii) marine scientific research;

(iii) the preservation of the marine environment.

(c) other rights as may exist under international law.

(3) In the exclusive economic zone, the freedoms of navigation and

overflight and of the laying of submarine cables and pipelines shall be governed by international law.

（4）In any case where the exclusive economic zone of the Kingdom of Thailand is adjacent or opposite to the exclusive economic zone of another coastal State, the Government of the Kingdom of Thailand is prepared to enter into negotiations with the coastal State concerned with a view to delimiting their respective exclusive economic zones.

Proclaimed on the 23rd day of February, B. E 2524, being the thirty sixth year of the present Reign.

资料来源：http：//www. un. org/Depts/los/LEGISLATIONANDTREATIES/PDFFILES/THA_1981_Proclamation. pdf。

12. Announcement of the Office of the Prime Minister Concerning Straight Baselines and Internal Waters of Thailand Area 4, 17 August 1992(《1992 年 8 月 17 日总理办公室关于泰国区域 4 的直线基线和内水的宣告》)

Whereas the Announcement of the office of the Prime Minister concerning the Straight Baselines and Internal Waters of Thailand dated 11 June 1970 was published in Official Gazette, Special vol. 87, Chapter 52, dated 12 June 1970, （1）to proclaim the straight baselines and internal waters of Thailand in areas.

Whereas the Cabinet has deemed it appropriate to proclaim the straight baselines and internal waters of Thailand in another area, that is Area 4, pursuant to the generally accepted principles of international law, as follows

Whereupon the waters within the aforementioned straight baselines are the internal waters of Thailand.

Area 4

REFERENCE NO.	GEOGRAPHICAL NAME	GEOGRAPHICAL LAT. N.	COORDINATES LONG. E.
1.	KO KONG OK	9°−36′−06″	100°−05′−48″
2.	KO KRA	8°−23′−49″	100°−44′−13″
3.	KO LOSIN	7°−19′−54″	101°−59′−54″
4.	THAI-MALAYSIAN BOUNDARY0	6°−14′−30″	102°−05′−36″

Details of straight baselines and internal waters of Thailand Area 4 in the map annexed to this present Announcement.

Announced on 17 August 1992. （2）

资料来源：http：//www. un. org/Depts/los/LEGISLATIONANDTREATIES/ PDFFILES/THA_1992_Announcement. pdf。

13. Royal Proclamation Establishing the Contiguous Zone of the Kingdom of Thailand，14 August 1995(《1995 年 8 月 14 日泰王国关于建立毗连区的皇家公告》)

By Royal Command of His Majesty the King，it is hereby Proclaimed that：

For the purpose of exercising the rights of the Kingdom of Thailand with regard to the contiguous zone, which are based on generally recognized principles of international law, it is deemed appropriate to establish the contiguous zone of the Kingdom of Thailand as follows：

（1）The contiguous zone of the Kingdom of Thailand is the area beyond and adjacent to the territorial sea of the Kingdom of Thailand, the breadth of which extends to twenty-four nautical miles measured from the baselines used for measuring the breadth of the territorial sea.

（2）In the contiguous zone, the Kingdom of Thailand shall act as necessary to：

（a）Prevent violation of customs, fiscal, immigration or sanitary laws and regulations, which will or may be committed within the Kingdom or its territorial sea；

（b）Punish violation of the laws and regulations defined in（a）, which is committed within the Kingdom or its territorial sea.

Proclaimed on the 14th day of August, B. E. 2538, being the forty-ninth year of the present reign.

资料来源：http：//www. un. org/Depts/los/LEGISLATIONANDTREATIES/ PDFFILES/THA_1995_Proclamation. pdf。

14. Agreement between the Government of the Kingdom of Thailand and the Government of the Socialist Republic of Viet Nam on the Delimitation of the Maritime Boundary between the Two Countries in the Gulf of Thailand, 9 August 1997(《1997 年 8 月 9 日泰王国政府和越南社会主义共和国政府关于两国在泰国湾海域划界的协定》)

The Government of the Kingdom of Thailand and the Government of the Socialist Republic of Viet Nam（hereinafter referred to as "the Contracting Parties"）

Desiring to strengthen the existing bonds of friendship between the two countries,

Desiring to establish the maritime boundary between the two countries in the relevant part of their overlapping continental shelf claims in the Gulf of Thailand,

Have agreed as follows：

Article 1

(1) The maritime boundary between the Kingdom of Thailand and the Socialist Republic of Viet Nam in therelevant part of their overlapping continental shelf claims in the Gulf of Thailand is a straight line drawn from Point C to Point K defined by latitude and longitude as follows:

Point C: Latitude N 07° 48′00″. 0000, Longitude E 103° 02′30″. 0000

Point K: Latitude N 08° 46′54″. 7754, Longitude E 102° 12′11″. 6542

(2) Point C is the northernmost point of the Joint Development Area established by the Memorandum of Understanding between the Kingdom of Thailand and Malaysia on the Establishment of a Joint Authority for the Exploitation of the Resources of the Seabed in a Defined Area of the Continental Shelf of the Two Countries in the Gulf of Thailand, done at Chiangmai on 21 February 1979, and which coincides with Point 43 of Malaysia's continental shelf claim advanced in 1979.

(3) Point K is a point situated on the maritime boundary between the Socialist Republic of Viet Nam and the Kingdom of Cambodia, which is the straight line equidistant from Tho Chu Islands and Poulo Wai drawn from Point O Latitude N09°35′00″. 4159 and Longitude E105°10′15″. 9805.

(4) The coordinates of the points specified in the above paragraphs are geographical coordinates derived from the British Admiralty Chart No. 2414 which is attached as an annex to this Agreement. ① The geodetic and computational bases used are the Ellipsoid Everest-1830-Indian Datum.

(5) The maritime boundary referred to in paragraph 1 above shall constitute the boundary between the continental shelf of the Kingdom of Thailand and the continental shelf of the Socialist Republic of Viet Nam, and shall also constitute the boundary between the exclusive economic zone of the Kingdom of Thailand and the exclusive economic zone of the Socialist Republic of Viet Nam.

---

① For technical reasons, the chart is not reproduced.

（6）The actual location of the above Points C and K at sea and of the straight line connecting them shall, at the request of either Government, be determined by a method to be mutually agreed upon by the hydrographic experts authorized for this purpose by the two Governments.

Article 2

The Contracting Parties shall enter into negotiation with the Government of Malaysia in order to settle the tripartite overlapping continental shelf claim area of the Kingdom of Thailand, the Socialist Republic of Viet Nam and Malaysia which lies within the Thai-Malaysian Joint Development Area established by the Memorandum of Understanding between the Kingdom of Thailand and Malaysia on the Establishment of a Joint Authority for the Exploitation of the Resources of the Seabed in a Defined Area of the Continental Shelf of the Two Countries in the Gulf of Thailand, done at Chiangmai on 21 February 1979.

Article 3

Each Contracting Party shall recognize and acknowledge the jurisdiction and the sovereign rights of the other country over the latter's continental shelf and exclusive economic zone within the maritime boundary established by this Agreement.

Article 4

If any single geological petroleum or natural gas structure or field, or other mineral deposit of whatever character, extends across the boundary line referred to in paragraph 1 of article 1, the Contracting Parties shall communicate to each other all information in this regard and shall seek to reach agreement as to the manner in which the structure, field or deposit will be most effectively exploited and the benefits arising from such exploitation will be equitably shared.

Article 5

Any dispute between the Contracting Parties relating to the interpretation or implementation of this Agreement shall be settled peacefully by consultation or negotiation.

Article 6

This Agreement shall enter into force on the date of the exchange of the instruments of ratification or approval, as required by the constitutional procedures of each country.

IN WITNESS WHEREOF, the undersigned, being duly authorized by their respective Governments, have signed this Agreement.

DONE in duplicate at Bangkok on this 9th day of August, One Thousand Nine Hundred and Ninety-Seven in the Thai, Vietnamese and English languages. In the event of any conflict between the texts, the English text shall prevail.

资料来源：Clive Howard Schofield, *Maritime boundary delimitation in the gulf of Thailand*, (Durham：Durham University, 1999), 469-472. Available at Durham E-Theses Online：http：//etheses. dur. ac. uk/4351/。

15. Treaty between the Kingdom of Thailand and Malaysia Relating to the Delimitation of the Territorial Seas of the Two Countries, 24 October 1979(《1979 年 10 月 24 日泰王国与马来西亚关于两国领海划界的条约》)

THE KINGDOM OF THAILAND AND MALAYSIA,

DESIRING to strengthen the existing historical bonds of friendship between two countries,

NOTING that the coasts of the two countries are adjacent to each other in Northern part of the Straits of Malacca, as well as in the Gulf of

Thailand,

AND DESIRING to establish the common boundaries of the territorial is of the two Countries,

HAVE AGREED AS FOLLOWS:

Article I

(1) The boundary of the Thai and the Malaysian territorial seas in the part of the Straits of Malacca between the islands known as the ' Butang Group ' and Pulau Langkawi where overlapping occurs shall be formed by the straight lines drawn from the point situated in mid-channel between Pulau Terutau and Pulau Langkawi referred to in the Boundary Protocol annexed to the Treaty dated March 10th, 1909 respecting the boundaries of the Kingdom of Thailand and Malaysia, whose co-ordinates are hereby agreed to be Latitude 6° 28′ .5 N Longitude 99° 39′. 2 E, in a north-westerly direction to a point whose co-ordinates are Latitude 6° 30′ .2 N Longitude 99° 33′. 4 E and from there in a south-westerly direction to a point whose co-ordinates are Latitude 6° 28′. 9 N Longitude 99° 30′. 7 E and from there in a south-westerly direction again to the point whose co-ordinates are Latitude 6° 18′. 4 N Longitude 99° 27′. 5 E.

(2) The outer limit of the territorial seas of the islands known as the ' Butang Group ' to the south of the said islands shall be formed by the boundary lines joining the points whose co-ordinates are Latitude 6° 18′. 4 N Longitude 99° 27′. 5 E referred to in paragraph (1) above and from there to the point whose coordinates are Latitude 6° 16′. 3 N Longitude 99° 19′. 3 E and from there to the point whose coordinates are Latitude 6° 18′. 0 Nand Longitude 99°06′. 7E.

(3) The coordinates of the points specified in paragraphs (1) and (2) are geographical coordinates derived from the British Admiralty Charts No. 793 and No. 830 and the boundary lines connecting them are indicated on the charts attached as Annexures ' A(1) ' and ' A(2) ' to this Treaty.

Article II

(1) The boundary of the Thai and the Malaysian territorial seas in the Gulf of Thailand shall be formed by the straight line drawn from a point whose co-ordinates are Latitude 6° 14′. 5 N Longitude 102° 05′ . 6 E to a point whose co-ordinates are Latitude 60° 27′. 5 N Longitude 102″10′. 0 E.

(2) The co-ordinates of the points specified in paragraph (1) are geographical coordinates derived from the British Admiralty Chart No. 3961 and the boundary line onnecting them is indicated on the chart attached as Annexure 'B' to this Treaty.

Article III

(1) The actual location at sea of the points mentioned in Article I and Article II above shall be determined by a method to be mutually agreed upon by the competent authorities of the two Parties.

(2) For the purposes of paragraph (I), 'competent authorities' in relation to the Kingdom of Thailand means the Director of the Hydrographic Department, Thailand, and includes any person authorised by him and in relation to Malaysia, the Director of National Mapping, Malaysia, and includes any person authorised by him.

Article IV

Each Party hereby, undertakes to ensure that all the necessary steps shall be taken at the domestic level to comply with the terms of this Treaty.

Article V

Any dispute between the two Parties arising out of the interpretation or implementation of this Treaty shall be settled peacefully by consultation or negotiation.

Article VI

This Treaty shall be ratified in accordance with the legal requirements of the two Countries.

Article VII

This Treaty shall enter into force on the date of the exchange of the Instruments of Ratification.

DONE IN DUPLICATE AT Kuala Lumpur the Twenty-fourth day of October, Nineteen Hundred and Seventy-nine in the Thai, Malaysian and English Languages. In the event of any conflict' between the texts, the English text shall prevail.

FOR THE KINGDOM OF THAILAND   FOR MALAYSIA
(Signed)   (Signed)
(GENERAL KRIANGSAKCHOMANAN) (DATUK HUSSEINONN)
Prime Minister   Prime Minister

资料来源: Alexander, L. M. and Charney, J. *International Maritime Boundaries*, Vols I and II, Martinus Nijhoff, 1993, pp. 1,096-1,098。

16. Memorandum of Understanding between Malaysia and the Kingdom of Thailand on the Delimitation of the Continental Shelf Boundary between the Two Countries in the Gulf of Thailand, 24 October 1979(《1979 年 10 月 24 日马来西亚和泰王国关于两国在泰国湾划定两国大陆架边界的谅解备忘录》)

MALAYSIA AND THE KINGDOM OF THAILAND,

DESIRING to strengthen the existing historical bonds of friendship between the two Countries,

AND DESIRING to establish the continental shelf boundary of the two countries in the

Gulf of Thailand,

HAVE AGREED AS FOLLOWS:

Article I

(1) The boundary of the continental shelf in the Gulf of Thailand between Malaysia and the Kingdom of Thailand shall consist of straight lines joining in the order specified below the points whose co-ordinates are:

(i) Latitude 6° 27′. 5 N
Longitude 102° 10′. 0 E
(ii) Latitude 6° 27′. 8 N
Longitude 102° 09′. 6 E
(iii) Latitude 6° 50′. 0 N
Longitude 102° 21′. 2 E

(2) The co-ordinates of point (ii) above have been determined by reference to a point whose co-ordinates are Latitude 60 16′. 6 N Longitude 1020 03′. 8, this point being the former position of Kuala Tabar under the Boundary Protocol annexed to the Treaty between Siam and Great Britain signed at Bangkok on the 10th March 1909.

Article II

(1) The co-ordinates of the points specified in Article I above are geographical coordinates derived from the British Admiralty Chart No. 3961 and the boundary lines connecting them are indicated on the chart attached as an Annexure to this Memorandum.

(2) The actual location of these points at sea and of the lines connecting them will be determined by a method to be mutually agreed upon by the competent authorities of the two Countries.

(3) For the purpose of paragraph (2) of this Article, the term "competent authorities" in relation to Malaysia shall mean the Director of National Mapping and include any person authorised by him, and in relation to the Kingdom of Thailand the Director of the Hydrographic Department and include any person authorised by him.

Article III

The Governments of the two Countries shall continue negotiations to complete delimitation of the continental shelf boundary of the two Countries in the Gulf of Thailand.

Article IV

If any single geological petroleum or natural gas structure or field, or any mineral deposit of whatever character, extends across the boundary lines referred to in Article I, the two Governments shall communicate to each other information in this regard and shall seek to reach agreement as to the manner in which the structure, field or deposit will be most effectively exploited; and all expenses incurred and benefits derived therefrom shall be equitably shared.

Article V

Any difference or dispute arising out of the interpretation or implementation the provisions of this Memorandum shall be settled peacefully by consultation or negotiation between the Parties.

Article VI

This Memorandum shall be ratified in accordance with the constitutional requirements of each Country. It shall enter into force on the date of the exchange of the Instruments of Ratification.

DONE IN DUPLICATE at Kuala Lumpur, the Twenty-fourth day of October, One Thousand Nine Hundred and Seventy-nine in the Malaysian, Thai and English languages. In the event of any conflict between the texts, the English shall prevail.

FOR MALAYSIA   FOR THE KINGDOM OF THAILAND

(Datuk Hussein Onn)   (General Tun Kriangsak Chomanan)

Prime Minister   Prime Minister

资料来源：Alexander，L. M. and Charney，J. *International Maritime Boundaries*，Vols I and II，Martinus Nijhoff，1993，pp. 1,105-1,107。

17. Franco-Siamese Boundary Treaty，23 March 1907(《1907 年 3 月 23 日法泰边界条约》)

The President of the French Republic and His Majesty the King of Siam following the delimitation undertaken in execution of the Convention of 13 February 1904, desiring on the one hand to ensure the final settlement of all questions connected with the common boundaries of Indo-China and Siam by a reciprocal and rational system of exchanges, and desiring on the other hand to ease relations between the two countries by the progressive introduction of a uniform legal system and by the extension of the rights of those citizens under French jurisdiction established in Siam, have decided to conclude a new treaty, and have named to this effect their plenipotentiaries as follows：

The President of the French Republic：R. Victor-Emile-Marie-Joseph Collin（de Plancy）Ambassador Extraordinary and Plenipotentiary Minister of the French Republic to Siam, Officer of the Legion of Honour and Public Instruction；

His Majesty the King of Siam：His Royal Highness Prince Devawongse Varoprakar, Knight of the Order of Maha-Chakri, Commanding Officer of the Legion of Honour, etc. , Minister of Foreign Affairs；Who, provided with full authority, which has been found in due and proper form, agreed to the following dispositions：

Article I

The Siamese Government cedes to France the territories of Battambang, Siem-Reap and Sisophon, whose boundaries are defined in

Clause I of the Protocol of Delimitation annexed to this Treaty.

Article II

The French Government cedes to Siam the territories of Dan-Sai and Kratt, whose borders are defined in Clauses I and II of the aforementioned Protocol, also all the islands situated to the south of Cape Lemling as far as and including Koh-Kut.

Article III

The exchange of these territories will take place within twenty days after the date of the ratification of the present Treaty.

Article IV

A Mixed Commission composed of French and Siamese officers and officials, will be named by the two contracting Countries, within four months of the ratification of the present Treaty, and charged with settling the new boundaries. It will commence work as soon as the weather allows and they will follow and conform to the Protocol of Delimitation annexed to the present Treaty.

Article V

Legal arrangements for aliens.

Article VI

Rights of French citizens in Siam.

Article VII

Treaties unaffected by the present Treaty to remain in force.

Article VIII

French version of the Treaty authoritative.

Article IX

Ratification.

Done in Bangkok in duplicate on 23 March 1907.

Annexe 1　Protocol of delimitation

V. Collin (de Plancy)

Devawongse Varoprakar

In order to facilitate the work of the Commission referred to in Article IV of the Treaty dated this day, and to avoid all possibility of difficulty in the delimitation, the Government of the French Republic and His Majesty the King of Siam have agreed as follows:

Clause I

The boundary between French Indo-China and Siam leaves the sea at a point situated opposite the highest point of Koh-Kut island. From this point it follows a northeasterly direction to the crest of Pnom-Krevanh. It is formally agreed that in every case the sides of these mountains which belong to the Klong-Kopo basin remain in French Indo-China.

The boundary follows the crest of the PnomKrevanh in a northerly direction to PnomThom which is found on the main water parting between the rivers which flow into the Gulf of Siam and those which flow towards the Grand Lac. From Pnom-Thorn, the border then follows in a northwesterly direction, then a northerly direction the actual boundary between the Provinces of Battambang on one side and those of Chantaboun and Kratt on the other side, as far as a point where the boundary cuts the river Nam-Sai.

It then follows the course of this river as far as its confluence with the Sisophon river and then the latter to a point situated ten kilometres below the village of Aranh. From this last point it continues in a straight line to a point on the Dang-Reck, halfway between the Chong-Ta-Kob and Chong-Sa-Met passes. It is understood that this line must leave a direct route between Aranh and Chong-Ta-Koh in Siamese territory. From the point mentioned above, situated on the crest of the Dang-Reck, the boundary follows the line of the water-parting between the basin of the Grand Lac and the Mekong on one side and the Nam-Moun on the other side, and reaches the Mekong below Pak Moun, at the mouth of the Huei-Doue, conforming to the line adopted by the previous delimitation Commission of 18 January 1907.

A rough draft of the boundary described above is annexed to the present Protocol.

Clause II

On the side of Luang-Prabang, the boundary leaves the Mekong at the mouth of the Nam-Huong in the south and follows the thalweg of this river as far as its source, which is situated at Phu-Khao-Mieng. From there the boundary follows the water-parting between the Mekong and the Menam, and meets the Mekong at a point cal'led KengPha Dai, conforming to the line adopted by the previous Delimitation Commission of I 6 January 1906.

Clause III

The Delimitation Commission authorised by Article IV of the Treaty of today's date will determine and trace, on the basis of the terrain, that part of the boundary described in Clause I of the present Protocol. If in the course of these operations the French Government desires to obtain a rectification of the boundary with the aim of substituting natural lines for the conventional lines, this rectification must not be made to the detriment of the Siamese Government.

The respective Plenipotentiaries have signed the present protocol and affixed their seals.

Done in duplicate in Bangkok 23 March 1907.

资料来源: J. R. V. Prescott, *Map of Mainland Asia by Treaty*, Melbourne University Press, 1975, pp. 444-446。

18. Continental Shelf Act 1966-Act No. 57 of 28 July 1966, as Amended by Act No. 83 of 1972(《1966 年 (马来西亚) 大陆架法案》-1966 年 7 月 28 日第 57 号法案，于 1972 年通过第 83 号法案修订)

1) (1) This Act may be cited as the Continental Shelf Act, 1966.

(2) (Omitted).

2) In this Act, unless the context otherwise requires-

"continental shelf" means the sea-bed and subsoil of submarine areas adjacent to the coast of Malaysia but beyond the limits of the territorial waters of the States, the surface of which lies at a depth no greater than two hundred metres below the surface of the sea, or, where the depth of the superadjacent waters admits of the exploitation of the natural resources of the said areas, at any greater depth;

"natural resources" means-

(a) the mineral and other natural non-living resources of the sea-bed and subsoil; and

(b) living organisms belonging to sedentary species, that is to say, organisms which, at the harvestable stage, either are immobile on or under the sea-bed or are unable to move except in constant physical contact with the sea-bed or the subsoil;

"petroleum" includes any mineral oil or relative hydrocarbon and natural gas existing in its natural condition in strata, but does not include coal or bituminous shales or other stratified deposits from which oil can be extracted by destructive distillation.

3) All rights with respect to the exploration of the continental shelf and the exploitation of its natural resources are hereby vested in Malaysia

and shall be exercisable by the Federal Government.

4) (1) No person shall explore, prospect or bore for or carry on any operations for the getting of petroleum in the sea-bed or subsoil of the continental shelf except under and in accordance with the Petroleum Mining Act, 1966.

(2) For the purposes of the following subsections, the expression "minerals" shall be construed to mean minerals other than petroleum.

(3) No person shall explore, prospect or bore for or carry on any operations for the getting of minerals in the sea-bed or subsoil of the continental shelf except in pursuance of the licence issued under the following subsections.

(4) The Minister may from time to time, on an application made in that behalf, grant to any person a licence authorising the person to explore, prospect, bore and mine for and to carry on operations for the getting of minerals of any specified kind in any specified area of the continental shelf.

(5) Every application for a licence and every licence granted under subsection (4) shall be in such form and subject to the payment of such fees and other payments as may be prescribed by the Minister and be subject to such conditions as the Minister, when granting the licence, thinks fit to impose in the circumstances of each case, including, but without limiting the generality of the foregoing provisions of this section, conditions requiring the licensee –

(a) to comply with such conditions as to safety as are specified in the licence; and

(b) to pay to the Federal Government in respect of any minerals recovered by the licensee from the continental shelf such royalties as are specified in the licence.

(6) The grant of a licence under subsection (4) shall in every case be in the absolute discretion of the Minister and any number of licences may be granted to the same person; and every licence may be so granted that the rights thereunder are to be enjoyed by the licensee in common

with other licensees to whom licences under subsection (4) may have been granted or may thereafter be granted.

(7) Any person who explores, prospects, bores or mines for, or carries on operations for the recovery of any minerals in the sea-bed or subsoil of the continental shelf otherwise than in pursuance of a licence under subsection (4) and in accordance with the conditions of the licence (not being a condition relating to the payment of royalties to the Federal Government) shall be guilty of an offence, and shall, on conviction, be liable to a fine not exceeding twenty thousand dollars or to imprisonment for a term not exceeding two years or to both; and all machinery, tools, plant, buildings and other property together with any minerals or other products which may be found upon or proved to have been obtained from the area of the continental shelf so unlawfully explored, prospected or mined shall be liable to forfeiture.

5) (1) Subject to this Act, for the purposes of this Act and of every other written law (whether enacted before or after the passing of this Act) for the time being in force in Malaysia-

(a) every act or omission which takes place on or under or above, or in any waters within five hundred metres of, any installation or device (whether temporary or permanent) constructed, erected, placed, or used in, on, or above the continental shelf in connection with the exploration of the continental shelf or the exploitation of its natural resources shall be deemed to take place in Malaysia; and

(b) every installation or device and any waters within five hundred metres of an installation or device as aforesaid shall be deemed to be situated in Malaysia, and for the purposes of jurisdiction shall be deemed to be situated in that part of Malaysia above highwater mark at ordinary spring tides which is nearest to that installation or device; and

(c) every court iin Malaysia which would have jurisdiction (whether civil or criminal) in respect of that act or omission if it had taken place in Malaysia shall have jurisdiction accordingly; and

(d) every power of arrest or of entry or search or seizure or other power that could be exercised under any written law (whether enacted before or after the passing of this Act) in respect of any such act or omission or suspected act or omission if it had taken place or was suspected to have taken place in Malaysia may be exercised on or in respect of any such installation or device or any waters within five hundred metres thereof as if the installation or device or waters were in Malaysia; and

(e) without prejudice to the provisions of the Customs Act, 1967, every installation or device, and any materials or parts used in the construction of an installation or device, which are brought into the waters above the continental shelf from parts beyond the seas shall be deemed to have been imported at the time when the installation or device is constructed, erected, or placed in, on, or above the continental shelf in connection with the exploration of the continental shelf or the exploitation of its natural resources.

(2) The Yang di-Pertuan Agong may from time to time, by order-

(a) modify or exclude any of the provisions of any written law (whether enacted before or after the passing of this Act) to such extent as may be necessary for the purpose of giving full effect to subsection (1);

(b) declare that the provisions of any written law (whether enacted before or after the passing of this Act), with such modifications or exceptions as he thinks fit, shall apply with respect to the continental shelf or any specified part thereof, or to acts or omissions taking place in, on, or above the continental shelf or any specified part thereof, in connection with the exploration of the continental shelf or of that part or the exploitation of its natural resources, and thereupon the provisions of that written law, with those modifications and exceptions, shall apply as if the continental shelf or that part thereof were within Malaysia.

(3) Nothing in this section shall limit the provisions of any written law relating to the liability of persons in respect of acts done or omitted beyond Malaysia or the jurisdiction of any court in Malaysia under any

such written law.

(4) Notwithstanding anything in any other written law, proceedings for the trial and punishment of any person charged with having committed an offence in respect of which the courts in Malaysia have jurisdiction by virtue only of this section shall not be instituted in any court except with the consent of the Public Prosecutor: Provided that a person so charged may be arrested or a warrant for his arrest may be issued and executed, and any such person may be remanded in custody or released on bail, notwithstanding that the consent of the Public Prosecutor to the institution of a prosecution for the offence has not been obtained, but the case shall not be further prosecuted until the consent has been obtained.

(5) In this section the term "device" includes any ship, floating platform, or aircraft that is used in connection with any installation or device.

6) (1) The Yang di-Pertuan Agong may make regulations for-

(a) regulating the construction, erection, or use of installations or devices in, on, or above the continental shelf, or any specified part thereof, in connection with the exploration of the continental shelf or that part thereof or the exploitation of its natural resources;

(b) prohibiting the construction, erection, placing, or use of installations or devices in, on, or above the continental shelf in places where they could cause interference with the use of recognized sea lanes essential to coastwise or international navigation;

(c) establishing safety zones, extending to a distance not exceeding five hundred metres measured from each point of the outer edge of the installation or device, around any such installations or devices in, on, or above the continental shelf;

(d) prescribing such measures as he considers necessary in any such safety zone for the protection of the installation or device with respect to which the safety zone is established;

(e) regulating or prohibiting the entry of ships into any such safety zone;

(f) prescribing measures to be taken in any such safety zone for the protection of the living resources of the sea and the natural resources of the continental shelf from harmful agents;

(g) prescribing the notice to be given of the construction, erection, or placing of installations or devices in, on, or above the continental shelf;

(h) prescribing the permanent means to be installed for the purpose of giving warning to shipping and aircraft of the presence of installations or devices in, on, or above the continental shelf;

(i) providing for the removal of installations or devices constructed, erected, or placed in, on, or above the continental shelf which have been abandoned or become disused;

(j) prohibiting or restricting any exploration of the continental shelf or any specified part thereof or any exploitation of its natural resources which in the opinion of the Yang di-Pertuan Agong could result in any unjustifiable interference with navigation, fishing, or the conservation of the living resources of the sea, or could interfere with national defence or with oceanographic or other scientific research or with submarine cables or pipelines;

(k) providing for such matters as are necessary for giving full effect to this Act and for the due administration thereof; and

(2) prescribing penalties for breaches of the regulations, not exceeding five thousand dollars.

(3) In this section the term "continental shelf" includes the sea-bed and subsoil of the submarine areas within the limits of the territorial waters of the States:

Provided that nothing in this section shall affect the rights and powers of the State Authority under the appropriate land law or any other written law in respect of areas within the limits of the territorial waters of the State.

7) (1) Any prospecting licence, mining lease or agreement issued or made under any written law in force in Sabah and Sarawak immediately

before the 8th November, 1969, for the exploration, prospecting or mining for minerals other than petroleum on the continental shelf shall continue to be in force subject to subsections (2), (3) and(4).

(2) All rights accrued or due to and all liabilities and obligations imposed on or borne by the Governments of Sabah and Sarawak under or by virtue of any prospecting licence, mining lease or agreement referred to in subsection (1) shall accrue and be due to and shall be imposed on and borne by the Federal Government.

(3) The provisions of the prospecting licence, mining lease or agreement referred to in subsection (1) shall be construed subject to this Act.

(4) The Yang di-Pertuan Agong may at any time before the 31st December, 1972, by order make such further transitional or saving provision as he may consider necessary or expedient.

资料来源：http：//www. un. org/Depts/los/LEGISLATIONANDTREATIES/PDFFILES/MYS_1966_Act. pdf。

19. Exclusive Economic Zone Act, 1984, Act No. 311 (《1984 年 (马来西亚) 专属经济区的法案，第 311 号法案》)

An Act pertaining to the exclusive economic zone and certain aspects of the continental shelf of Malaysia and to provide for the regulations of activities in the zone and on the continental shelf and for matters connected therewith.

PART I PRELIMINARY

Short title, application and commencement

1) (1) This Act may be cited as the Exclusive Economic Zone Act

1984 and shall apply to the

exclusive economic zone of Malaysia.

(2) The provisions of this Act pertaining to the continental shelf shall be in addition to, and not in derogation of, the provisions of the Continental Shelf Act 1966.

(3) In the event of any conflict or inconsistency between the provisions of this Act and of any applicable written law, the provisions of this Act shall supersede the conflicting or inconsistent provisions of that applicable written law and the latter shall be construed as so superseded.

(4) The provisions of any applicable written law which are not in conflict or inconsistent with the provisions of this Act shall otherwise continue to apply.

(5) This Act shall come into force on such date as the Yang di-Pertuan Agong may appoint by notification in the Gazette and he may appoint different dates for the coming into force of different provisions of this Act in different areas of the exclusive economic zone and continental shelf.

Interpretation

2) In this Act, unless the context otherwise requires-

"applicable written law" means any written law:

(a) provided to be applicable in respect of the exclusive economic zone, continental shelf or both, as the case may be, by an order made under section 42 or otherwise specifically provided to be so applicable: or

(b) applicable in respect of the continental shelf under the provisions of the Continental Shelf Act 1966, and includes the Continental Shelf Act 1966;

"authorized officer" means any fishery officer as defined in section 2 of the Fisheries Act 1963, any port officer as defined in section 2 of the Merchant Shipping Ordinance 1952, any police officer not below the rank of sergeant as defined in section 2 of the Police Act 1967, any customs officer as defined in section 2 of the Customs Act 1967, any officer of the armed forces as defined in section 2 of the Armed Forces Act 1972, any public officer, irrespective of rank, in command of a vessel belonging to the Government or ay other person or class of persons appointed to be an authorized officer or authorized officers under section 39;

"continental shelf" means the continental shelf of Malaysia as defined in section 2 of the Continental Shelf Act 1966;

"Director-General" means the Director-General of Environmental Quality as defined in section 2 of the Environmental Quality Act 1974;

"dumping" means:

(a) any deliberate disposal of wastes or other matter from vessels, aircraft, platforms or other man-made structures at sea; or

(b) any deliberate disposal of vessels, aircraft or other man-made structures at sea, but "dumping" does not include:

(i) the disposal of wastes or other matter incidental to, or derived from, the normal operations of vessels, aircraft, platforms or other man-made structures at sea and their equipment, other than wastes or other matter transported by or to vessels, aircraft, platforms or other man-made structures at sea, operating for the purpose of disposal of such matter or derived from the treatment of such wastes or other matter on such vessels, aircraft, platforms or structures; or

(ii) placement of matter for a purpose other than the mere disposal thereof, provided that such placement is not contrary to the aims of this Act, any applicable written law or international law;

"exclusive economic zone" or "zone" means the exclusive economic zone of Malaysia determined in accordance with section 3;

"Government" means the Government of Malaysia and includes any Minister charged with responsibility by an order made under the Ministerial Functions Act 1969 for the matter in relation to which the reference to the Government is made under this Act, and any other Minister exercising temporarily the functions of such Minister;

"Malaysian fisheries waters" means all waters comprising the internal waters, the territorial sea and the exclusive economic zone of

Malaysia in which Malaysia exercises sovereign and exclusive rights over fisheries;

"maritime casualty" means a collision of vessels, stranding or other incident of navigation, or other occurrence on board a vessel or external to it resulting in material damage or imminent threat of material damage to a vessel or cargo;

"master", in relation to a vessel, includes every person (except a pilot or port officer as defined in section 2 of the Merchant Shipping Ordinance 1952) having for the time being command or charge of the vessel, or lawfully acting as the master thereof;

"mixture containing oil" means:

(a) a mixture with an oil content of one hundred parts or more in one milllion parts of the mixture; or

(b) a mixture with such oil content as is prescribed by the Minister charged with responsibility for the environment by order in the Gazette to be a mixture containing oil for the purposes of this Act;

"oil" means:

(a) crude oil, diesel oil, fuel oil or lubricating oil; or

(b) any other description of oil which is prescribed by the Minister charged with responsibility for the environment by order in the Gazette to be oil for the purposes of this Act; "owner", in relation to a vessel, means any person or body of persons, whether incorporated or not, by whom the vessel is owned and includes any charterer, sub-charterer, lessee or sub-lessee of the vessel;

"pollutant" means any suibstance which, if introduced into the sea, is liable to create hazards to human health or to harm living resources in the sea or other marine life, or to damage amenities or interfere with other legitimate uses of the sea and, without limiting the generality of the foregoing, includes any substance that is prescribed by the Minister charged with responsibility for the environment by order in the Gazette to be a pollutant for the purposes of this Act;

"State" shall have the meaning assigned to that expression under international law;

"territorial sea" means the territorial waters of Malaysia determined in acccordance with the Emergency (Essential Powers) Ordinance, No. 7/1969;

"this Act" includes regulations and other subsidiary legislation made under this Act and anything done under this Act or under such regulations or other subsidiary legislation;

"vessel" includes every description of ship or floating or submarine craft or structure;

"waste" includes:

(a) any matter, whether liquid, solid, gaseous or radioactive, which is discharged, emitted, deposited or dumped in the marine environment in such volume, composition or manner as to cause an alteration of the environment; or

(b) any matter which is prescribed by the Minister charged with responsibility for the environment by order in the Gazette to be waste for the purposes of this Act.

PART II EXCLUSIVE ECONOMIC ZONE

The exclusive economic zone of Malaysia

3) (1) The exclusive economic zone of Malaysia, as proclaimed by the Yang di-Pertuan Agong vide P. U. (A) 115/80, is an area beyond and adjacent to the territorial sea of Malaysia and. subject to subsections (2) and (4), extends to a distance of two hundred nautical miles from the baselines from which the breadth of the territorial sea is measured.

(2) Where there is an agreement in force on the matter between Malaysia and a State with an opposite or adjacent coast. questions relating to the delimitation of the exclusive economic zone shall be deltermined in accordance with the provisions of that agreement.

（3）The Yang di-Pertuan Agong may cause the limits of the exclusive economic zone to be published in maps or charts from time to time.

（4）Where, having regard to international law, State practice or an agreement referred to in sub-section（2）, the Yang di-Pertuan Agong considers it necessary so to do, he may by order published in the Gazette alter the limits of the exclusive economic zone determined in accordance with subsection（1）.

Sovereign rights in, and jurisdiction over, the exclusive economic zone

4）In the exclusive economic zone Malaysia has

（a）sovereign rights for the purpose of exploring and exploiting, conserving and managing the natural resources, whether living or non-living, of the seabed and subsoil and the superjacent waters, and with regard to other activities for the economic exploitation and exploration of the zone, such as the production of energy from the water, currents and winds;

（b）jurisdiction with regard to

（i）the establishment and use of artificial islands, installations and structures;

（ii）marine scientific research;

（iii）the protection and preservation of the marine environment; and

（c）such other rights and duties as are provided for by international law.

Prohibition of activities in the exclusive economic zone or on the continental shelf except where authorized.

5）Except where authorized in accordance with the provisions of this Act or any applicable written law, no person shall in the exclusive economic zone or on the continental shelf:

（a）explore or exploit any natural resources. whether living or non-living;

（b）carry out any search, excavation or drilling operations;

（c）conduct any marine scientific research; or

(d) construct or authorize and regulate the construction, operation and use of:

(i) any artificial island:

(ii) any installation or structure for any of the purpose provided for in section 4 or for any other economic purpose; or

(iii) any installation or structure which may interfere with the exercise of the rights of Malaysia in the zone or on the continental shelf.

PART III FISHERIES

Seas in the zone to be part of Malaysian fisheries waters

6) The seas comprised in the exclusive economic zone shall be part of Malaysian fisheries waters.

Minister responsible for fisheries in the zone

7) The Minister charged with responsibility for fisheries shall also be responsible for fisheries in the exclusive economic zone.

Written law relating to fisheries to be applicable in the zone and on the continental shelf

8) Except as otherwise provided in this Act, any written law relating to fisheries shall be applicable in the exclusive economic zone and on the continental shelf with such necessary modifications or exceptions as may be provided in an order made under section 42.

PART IV PROTECTION AND PRESERVATION OR THE MARINE ENVIRONMENT

Sovereign right of Malaysia to exploit her natural resources

9) Malaysia has the sovereign right to exploit her natural resources in the exclusive economic zone pursuant to her environmental policies and

in accordance with her duty to protect and preserve the marine environment in the zone.

10) (1) If any oil, mixture containing oil or pollutant is discharged or escapes into the exclusive economic zone from any vessel, land-based source, installation, device or aircraft, from or through the atmosphere or by dumping:

(a) the owner or master of the vessel, if the discharge or escape is from a vessel;

(b) the owner or occupier of the place on land, if the discharge or escape is from land;

(c) the owner or person in charge of the installation or device, if the discharge or escape is from an installation or a device; or

(d) the owner or pilot of the aircraft. if the discharge or escape is from an aircraft, shall each be guilty of an offence and shall be liable to a fine not exceeding one million ringgit.

(2) Where the act or omission of a person other than any of the persons mentioned in subsection (1) caused the discharge or escape mentioned in that subsection, then such other person shall also be guilty of an offence and shall be liable to a fine not exceeding one million ringgit.

(3) Subsection (2) shall not operate to absolve or relieve the persons mentioned in subsection (1) from liability for an offence under subsection (1).

(4) Notwithstanding the provisions of this section, dumping of wastes or other matter may be carried out under a licence issued by the Director-General and subject to such conditions as he may impose.

Defence to a charge under section 10

11) Where a person is charged with an offence under section 10, it shall be a defence to prove that the discharge or escape of the substance mentioned in sub-section (1) of that section was caused for the purpose

of securing the safety of the vessel, the place on land, the installation, device or aircraft concerned, or for the purpose of saving life but a defence under this section shall not operate if the court is satisfied that the discharge or escape was not necessary for the alleged purpose or was not a reasonable step to take in the circumstances.

Requirement for discharge or escape of certain substances to be reported

12) (1) If any oil, mixture containing oil or pollutant is discharged or escapes into the exclusive economic zone from any vessel, land-based source, installation, device or aircraft. the owner or master of the vessel, the owner or occupier of the place on land, the owner or person in charge of the installation or device or the owner or pilot of the aircraft, as the case may be, shall immediately report the occurrence of such discharge or escape to the Director-General.

(2) Any person who fails to comply with this section shall be guilty of an offence and shall be liable to a fine not exceeding ten thousand ringgit.

Measures relating to a maritime casualty

13) (1) The Government may specify measures in relation to the exclusive economic zone which are necessary to protect Malaysia's coastline or any segment or element of the environment or related interests, including fishing, from pollution or threat of pollution following upon a maritime casualty or acts relating to such casualty, which may reasonably be expected to result in major harmful consequences.

(2) The measures referred to in subsection (1) shall be proportionate to the actual or threatened damage to the coastline or segment or element of the environment or related interests, including fishing.

Directions and action to remove, disperse, destroy or mitigate damage

14) (1) Where Malaysia's coastline or any segment or element of the environment or related interests, including fishing in the exclusive economic zone is damaged or threatened to be damaged as a result of any discharge or escape of any substance mentioned in section 10, the Director-General may issue such directions as are, or take such action as is, necessary to remove, disperse, destroy or mitigate the damage or threat of damage.

(2) Any person who fails to comply with any direction given by the Director-General under subsection (1) shall be guilty of an offence and shall be liable to a fine not exceeding ten thousand ringgit.

(3) The owner and the master of the vessel, the owner and the occupier of the place on land, the owner and the person in charge of the installation or device, or the owner and the pilot of the aircraft, as the case may be, from which the substance mentioned in section 10 was discharged or escaped shall be liable jointly and severally for all costs and expenses incurred in carrying out all or any of the work required under subsection (1) to remove, disperse, destroy or mitigate the damage or the damage, and such costs and expenses shall be a first charge on any property or interest held by such person.

(4) Where the Act or omission of a person other than any of the persons mentioned in subsection (3) caused such discharge or escape, then such other person shall also be liable jointly and severally with the persons mentioned in that subsection for all costs and expenses incurred in carrying out all or any of the work required under subsection (1) to remove, disperse, destroy or mitigate the damage or threat of damage, and such costs and expenses shall be a first charge on any property or interest held by such other person.

Power to detain and sell vessel

15) (1) The Director-General may detain any vessel from which the oil, mixture containing oil or pollutant escaped or was discharged in the circumstances mentiioned in subsection (1) of section 14.

(2) The Director-General may release any vessel detained under subsection (1) upon the owner depositing with the Government such sum of money or furnishing such security as, in the opinion of the Director-General, would be adequate to meet all costs and expenses incurred in carrying out the work required to remove, disperse, destroy or mitigate the damage or threat of damage caused by such escape or discharge.

(3) If any vessel which has been detained proceeds to sea without being released under subsection (2), the owner or master of the vessel or any other person who causes the vessel to proceed to sea shall be guilty of an offence and shall be liable to a fine not exceeding one million ringgit.

(4) Where the owner or master of such vessel or any other person found guilty of an offence under this section is unable to pay the fine or the costs and expenses incurred in carrying out the work required under subsection (1) of section 14, the court may, on the application of the Director-General, order the sale of such vessel and the application of the proceeds of the sale towards the payment of the fine and the costs and expenses incurred.

PART V   MARINE SCIENTIFIC RESEARCH

Government consent required for conduct of marine scientific research

16) (1) No marine scientific research may be conducted in the exclusive economic zone or on the continental shelf without the express

consent of and subject to conditions imposed by the Government.

(2) Subject to section 17), the Government shall give its consent where the marine scientific research would be carried out by any State or competent international organization for peaceful purposes and to increase scientific knowledge of the marine environment.

Right to with old consent

17) The Government may withhold its consent to the conduct of a marine scientific research project by any State or competent international organization in the exclusive economic zone or on the continental shelf if it has reason to believe that the project-

(a) is of direct significance to the exploration and exploitation of natural resources, whether living or non-living;

(b) involves drilling into the continental shelf, the use of explosives or the introduction of pollutants into the marine environment;

(c) involves the construction, operation or use of artificial islands, installations or structures;

(d) contains information communicated pursuant to section 18 regarding the nature and objectives of the project which is inaccurate or if the researching State or competent international organization has outstanding obligations to Malaysia from a prior research project; or

(e) would interfere with activities undertaken by Malaysia in the exercise of its sovereign rights and jurisdiction provided for under this Act, any applicable written law or international law.

Duty to provide information.

18) Any State or competent international organization which intends to undertake marine scientific research in the exclusive economic zone or on the continental shelf shall, not less than six months in advance of the expected starting date of the marine scientific research project, provide the Government with a full description of-

(a) the nature and objectives of the project;

(b) the method and means to be used, including name, tonnage, type and class of vessels and a description of scientific equipment;

(c) the precise geographical areas in which the project is to be conducted;

(d) the expected date of first appearance and final departure of the research vessels, or deployment of the equipment and its removal, as appropriate;

(e) the name of the sponsoring institution, its director, and the person in charge of the project; and

(f) the extent to which it is considered that Malaysia should be able to participate or to be represented in the project.

Duty to comply with certain conditions

19) (1) Every State or competent international organization undertaking marine scientific research in the exclusive economic zone or on the continental shelf shall comply with the following conditions;

(a) ensure the right of the Government, if it so desires, to participate or be represented in the marine scientific research project. especially on board research vessels and other craft or scientific research installations, when practicable, without payment of any remuneration to the scientists of Malaysia and without obligation to contribute towards the costs of the project;

(b) provide the Government with preliminary reports, as soon as practicable, and with the final results and conclusions after the completion of the research;

(c) undertake to provide access for the Government, at its request, to all data and samples derived from the project and likewise to furnish it with data which may be copied and samples which may be divided without detriment to their scientific value;

(d) if requested, provide the Government with an assessment of such data, samples and research results or provide assistance in their assessment or interpretation;

(e) ensure, unless otherwise specified by the Government, that the research results are made internationally available through appropriate national or international channels, as soon as practicable;

(f) inform the Government immediately of any major change in the research programme;

(g) unless otherwise agreed. remove the scientific research installations or equipment once the research is completed.

(2) This section is without prejudice to the conditions established by the Government for the exercise of its discretion to give or withhold consent pursuant to section 16) or 17), as the case may be, including requiring prior agreement for making internationally available the research results of a project of direct significance for the exploration and exploitation of natural resources.

Suspension or cessation of marine scientific research activities

20) (1) The Government may order the suspension of any marine scientific research activities in progress within the exclusive economic zone or on the continental shelf if-

(a) the research activities are not being conducted in accordance with the information provided under section 18 upon which the consent of the Government was based; or

(b) the State or competent international organization conducting the research activities fails to comply with the provisions of section 19.

(2) The Government may order the cessation of any marine scientific research activities-

(a) which in deviating from the information provided under section 18 have amounted to a major change in the research project or the research activities; or

(b) if any of the situations contemplated in subsection (1) are not rectified within a reasonable period of time, as determined by the

Government

(3) Following notification by the Government of the order of suspension or cessation, the State or competent international organization shall immediately terminate all or any of the marine scientific research activities that are the subject of such a notification.

(4) An order of suspension under subsection (1) may be lifted by the Government and the marine scientific research activities allowed to continue if the researching State or competent international organization complies with the conditions required under sections 18 and 19 within a reasonable period of time. as determined by the Government.

PART VI ARTIFICIAL ISLANDS, INSTALLATIONS AND STRUCTURES

Prohibition of construction, operation or use of artificial island, etc. except with authorization

21) (1) No person shall construct, operate or use any artificial island, installation or structure in the exclusive economic zone or on the continental shelf except with the authorization of the Government and subject to such conditions as it may impose.

(2) The Government shall have exclusive jurisdiction over artificial islands, installations and structures in the zone and on the continental shelf, including jurisdiction with regard to customs, fiscal, health, safety and immigration laws,

(3) The Government may, where necessary, establish reasonable safety zones around such artificial islands, installations and structures in which it may take appropriate measures to ensure the safety both of navigation and of the artificial islands, installations and structures.

(4) The breadth of the safety zones shall be determined by the

Government, taking into account navigation and of the artificial islands, installations and structures applicable international standards, Due notice shall be given of the extent of the safety zones.

(5) All vessels must respect these safety zones and shall comply with any directions which the Government may give in accordance with generally accepted international standards regarding navigation in the vicinity of artificial islands, installations, structures and safety zones.

PART Ⅶ SUBMARINE CABLES AND PIPELINES

Consent of Government necessary for delineation of course for laying of sub-marine cables and pipelines

22) (1) No person shall lay submarine cables or pipelines in the exclusive economic zone or on the continental shelf without the consent of the Government as to the delineation of the course for the laying of such cables and pipelines

(2) Without prejudice to subsection (1), the Government may impose such conditions as it may consider necessary for the laying or maintenance of such cables and pipelines in the exercise of its right to take reasonable measures for the exploration of the continental shelf. the exploitation of natural resources and the prevention. reduction and control of pollution from such cables or pipelines.

Duty of owner of submarine cable or pipeline

23) The owner of any submarine cable or pipeline which has fallen into disuse or is beyond repair shall forthwith inform the Government thereof and shall, if so directed by the Government, remove such cable or pipeline within such period of time as the Government may direct.

PART Ⅷ   ENFORCEMENT

Powers of authorized officer

24) (1) For the purpose of ensuring compliance with the provisions of this Act or any applicable written law, any authorized officer may, where he has reason to believe that an offence has been committed under this Act or such written law, without a warrant-

(a) stop, board and search any vessel within the exclusive economic zone and inspect any licence, permit, record, certificate or any other document required to be carried on board such vessel under this Act such written law or any generally accepted international rules and standards, and make copies of the same;

(b) make such further enquiries and physical inspection of the vessel, its crew, equipment, gear, furniture, appurtenances stores and cargo as may be necessary to ascertain whether or not a suspected violation of the provisions of this Act or such written law has been committed;

(c) enter and search any place in which he has reason to believe that an offence under this Act or such written law is about to be or has been committed;

(d) arrest any person who he has reason to believe has committed any offence under this Act or such written law;

(e) detain any article which he has reason to believe has been used in the commission of any offence under this Act or such written law;

(f) detain any vessel, including its equipment, gear, furniture, appurtenances, stores and cargo, which he has reason to believe has been used in the commission of any offence or in relation to which any offence has been committed under this Act or such written law.

(2) A written acknowledgement shall be given for any article. vessel

or thing detained under subsection （1）

Hot Pursuit

25）（1）Where any authorized officer has reason to believe that a foreign vessel has contravened any provision of this Act or any applicable written law, he may undertake the hot pursuit of such vessel with a view to stopping and arresting it and bringing it within the exclusive economic zone in accordance with international law.

（2）The powers conferred on an authorized officer under section 24） shall be exercisable pursuant to this section in respect of such vessel beyond the limits of the exclusive economic zone to the extent allowed by international law.

（3）Except as otherwise provided by any regional or bilateral agreement to which Malaysia is a party, the right of hot pursuit shall cease as soon as the vessel pursued enters the territorial sea or exclusive economic zone of its own State or any third State.

How person arrested to be dealt with

26）（1）An authorized officer making an arrest under this Act or any applicable written law shall without unnecessary delay produce the person arrested before a Magistrate.

（2）No authorized officer shall keep in custody a person arrested for a longer period than under all the circumstances of the case is reasonable.

（3）Such period shall not in the absence or after the expiry of a special order of a Magistrate under section 117 of the Criminal Procedure Code exceed twenty-four hours, exclusive of the time necessary for the journey from the place of arrest to the Magistrate's Court. F. M. S. Cap. 6

How detained vessel to be dealt with

27）Any vessel detained under this Part and the crew thereof shall be taken to the nearest or most convenient port and dealt with an accordance with the provisions of this Act or any applicable written law.

Obstruction of authorized officer, etc.

28) Any person who

(a) wilfully obstructs any authorized officer in the exercise of any of the powers conferred on him by this Act or any applicable written law

(b) fails to comply with any lawful order or requirement under this Act or such written law; or

(c) fails to comply with any of the provisions of this Act or such written law for which no punishment is provided for failure to comply therewith shall be guilty of an offence.

PART IX OFFENCES, PENALTIES, LEGAL PROCEEDINGS AND COMPENSATIONS

General penalty

29) Any person who is guilty of an offence under this Act for which no punishment is provided shall be liable to a fine not exceeding one million ringgit.

30) Where any offence under this Act or any applicable written law has been committed by a company, partnership, form or business, every director and every officer of tht company directly connected with the activity resulting in the commission of the offence, every member of that partnership and every person concerned with the management of that firm or business shall each be guilty of that offence and shall be liable to the punishment provided in section 29.

Master liable for offence committed on his vessel

31) Where an offence under this Act or any applicable written law has been committed by any person on board a vessel, the master of such vessel shall also be guilty of that offence and shall be liable to the punishment provided in section 29.

Detention and forfeiture of vessel, etc.

32) (1) Any article, vessel or thing detained under the provisions of

this Act or any applicable written law shal, unless otherwise provided under this Act, be held pending the outcome of any proceedings under this Act or such written law:

Provided, however, that an authorized officer or the court may release the article, vessel or thing so detained upon the furnishing of a bond or other security to the satisfaction of the authorized officer or the court by any person claiming ownership, or acting on behalf of the owner, of the article, vessel or thing to produce the same when required so to do.

(2) Where an article, vessel, or thing is detained under the provisions of this Act or any applicable written law, the authorized officer who detains the article, vessel or thing shall, as soon as may be, cause notice thereof to be given in writing to the owner; and where the owner cannot be found, a notice to that effect shall be published in the Gazette and, if the article, vessel or thing is foreign-owned, the authorized officer shall cause the diplomatic representative in Malaysia of the flag State of the vessel concerned or of the country of which the owner of the article or thing is a national to be informed of such fact through the Ministry responsible for foreign affairs.

(3) If the owner of the article, vessel or thing cannot be found in spite of all courses of action taken under subsection (2) and by reason of the owner not being found proceedings under this Act or any applicable written law cannot be instituted, the article, vessel or thing detained shall be held for a period of one month from the date of the last course of action taken under subsection (2) at the end of which period the article, vessel or thing shall be forfeited to the Government unless a claim is received in respect thereof within the aforesaid period, in which event an enquiry shall be held by a court of competent jurisdiction to determine the validity of the claim and the article, vessel or thing shall be disposed of in such manner as the court may direct.

Power of court to order forfeiture

33) Where any person is found guilty of an offence under this Act or

any applicable written law, the court shall, in addition to any other penalty that may be imposed, order that any article, vessel or thing which was the subject-matter of, or was used in the commission of, the offence be forfeited and that any licence or permit issued or consent given under this Act or such written law be suspended for such period of time as the court may think fit or be cancelled or withdrawn, as the case may be.

Disposal of article, vessel or thing ordered to be forfeited

34) Where it is proved to the satisfaction of a court that any article, vessel or thing detained under the provisions of this Act or any applicable written law was the subject matter of, or was used in the commission of, an offence under this Act or such written law, the court may order the forfeiture of such article, vessel or thing notwithstanding that no person may have been found guilty of such offence.

Sessions Court and Court of Magistrate of First Class to have full jurisdiction and powers under Act or applicable written law

35) (1) Notwithstanding any written law to the contrary, any offence committed under this Act or any applicable written law shall be deemed to have been committed in Malaysia for the purpose of conferring jurisdiction on a court to try that offence, and a Sessions Court or a Court of a Magistrate of the First Class shall each have full jurisdiction and powers for all purposes under this Act or such written law.

(2) Subsection (1) shall not be construed as derogating in any way from the jurisdiction and powers of the High Court to try any offence under any written law.

(3) Any proceedings in respect of an offence under this Act or any applicable written law shall be brough before the Sessions Court or the Court of a Magistrate of the First Class which is nearest the place where the offence was committed, or which is located in the most convenient place for trial in the circumstances of the case as determined by the Public Prosecutor.

（4）This section shall be without prejudice to the provisions of the Criminal Procedure Code relating to the transfer of cases.

36）For the purposes of this Act or any applicable written law, the court shall presume that maps, plans or charts purporting to be made by the authority of:

（a）the Federal Government;

（b）the Government of a State in Malaysia; or

（c）the Government of a State as defined in section 2 and approved by the Federal Government or the Government of any State in Malaysia for use, were so made and are accurate.

Prosecution of offence

37）（1）A prosecution for an offence under this Act or any applicable written law shall not be instituted except by or with the consent of the Public Prosecutor:

Provided that a person who is to be charged with such an offence may be arrested, or a warrant for his arrest may be issued and executed, and any person so arrested may be remanded in custody or released on bail, notwithstanding that the consent of the Public Prosecutor to the institution of a prosecution for the offence has not been obtained, but the case shall not be further prosecuted until tat consent has been obtained.

（2）When a person is brought before a court under this section before the Public Prosecutor has consented to the prosecution, the charge shall be read and explained to him but he shall not be called upon to plead thereto, and the provisions of the Criminal Procedure Code shall be modified accordingly.

Yang di-Pertuan Agong may appoint other persons to be authorized officers

38）Without prejudice to the definition of "authorized officer" in section 2）, the Yang di-Pertuan Agang may, by order in the Gazette, appoint such other person or class of persons as he m ay consider necessary to be an authorized officer or autorized officers for the purposes of this Act or any applicable written law.

(1) Where, by reason of any act or omission in contravention of this Act or any applicable written law, damage is caused to any person or property in or on, or to any segment or element of the environment or related interests within, the exclusive economic zone or continental shelf, the owner and te master of the vessel, the owner and the occupier of the place on land, the owner and the person in charge of the installation ...

(2) Without prejudice to the generality of subsections (1) and (2) such liability shall extend to the payment of compensation for any damage caused to a person, vessel, gear, facility of structure used in any activity, including fishing and related activities, connected with the exercise of the rights of the Government and Malaysian nationals, and of other persons where such rights are exercised with the consent of the Government, in the exclusive economic zone or on the continental shelf, and compensation shall also be paid for policing and surveillance activities and activities for the protection of the environment and shipping necessitated by the damage referred to in subsection (1)

(3) Any claim for compensation under this section may be brought before any High Court, Sessions Court or Court of a Magistrate of the First Class in Malaysia, as the case may be, according to the value or amount of the claim: and where a claim is so brought, the court concerned shall have full jurisdiction and powers to adjudicate thereon.

PART X MISCELLANEOUS

Power to make regulations

39) (1) The Yang di-Pertuan Agong may make regulations for carrying out the provisions of this Act.

(2) Without prejudice to the generality of subsection (1), such

regulations may provide for any of the following matters:

(a) regulating the conduct of marine scientific research within the exclusive economic zone and on the continental shelf;

(b) prescribing measures for the protection and preservation of the marine environment of the exclusive economic zone, including conditions to be complied with by foreign vessels before entering any port or the internal waters of Malaysia or calling at any offshore terminal;

(c) regulating the construction, operation and use of artificial islands and of other installations and structures within the exclusive economic zone or on the continental shelf, including the establishment of safety zones around such islands, installations and structures;

(d) regulating the exploration and exploitation of the exclusive economic zone for the production of energy from the water, currents and winds and for other economic purposes:

(e) providing for such other matters as are necessary or expedient for giving full effect to Malaysia's rights in and jurisdiction over the exclusive economic zone and the continental shelf.

Written laws to be applicable in exclusive economic zone or on continental shelf or both by order

40) (1) The Yang di-Pertuan Agong may, by order in the Gazette, provide for any written law to be applicable in the exclusive economic zone. on the continental shelf or both,

(2) Any order made by the Yang di-Pertuan Agong under this section may provide for such written law to be applicable with such modifications or exceptions thereto as he considers necessary and where he so does. Such written law shall be construed accordingly in its application in the exclusive economic zone, on the continental shelf or both.

(3) The modifications mentioned in subsection (2) may include amendments to such written law which the Yang di-Pertuan Agong may consider necessary-

(a) to make such written law effective in its application in the exclusive economic zone, on the continental shelf or both;

（b）to avoid any conflict or inconsistency between tile provisions of such written law and this Act or 1any other applicable written law; or

（c）to bring the provisions of such written law into accord with the provisions of this Act or any other applicable written law.

（4）Any order made under this section shall be laid before the House of Representatives as soon as may be after it is made and if a motion is moved and carried by that House, within three months of the date on which the order is laid before it, disallowing the order, the order shall thereafter be void but, without prejudice to the validity of anything done under the order or to the making of any new order.

Announcement of the Office of the Prime Minister

资料来源：http：//nghiencuubiendong. vn/en/datbase-on-south-china-sea-study/doc_details/395-malaysias-exclusive-economic-zone-act-1984-act-no-311。

七、1981 年冰岛与挪威扬马延岛共同开发案

1. Agreement between Norway and Iceland on Fishery and Continental Shelf Questions

The Governments of Norway and of Iceland.

Recognizing the need to take effective measures for the conservation, rational exploi-tation and reproduction of the living resources of the sea, and furthermore for the rational exploitation of the natural resources on and in the continental shelf,

Recognizing that under international law it is the two countries, as coastal States, which bear the main responsibility for the effective conservation and rational exploitation of these natural resources,

Recognizing the importance of coordinated, close and friendly cooperation between the two countries in order to secure these aims and recognizing likewise the necessity of coordinated cooperation with other affected countries in order to secure these aims,

Recognizing Iceland's strong economic dependence on the fisheries, cf. Article 71 in the text of the Conference on the Law of the Sea,

Considering that Iceland has established an economic zone of 200 nautical miles and that Norway will in the near future establish a Fishery zone round Jan Mayen,

Recognizing the special circumstances of importance for the drawing up of a dividing line between the two countries in the sea areas concerned for fishery and continental shelf purposes,

Expressing their apprehension with regard to the danger of overfishing which in par-ticular threatens the capelin stock.

Taking account of the work which is being done by the Third United Nations Confer-ence on the Law of the Sea, work which has not yet been completed,

Have agreed as follows:

Article 1

The Parties shall cooperate on practical questions in the fisheries sector, attaching particular importance to measures directed towards conservation, rational exploitation and sound reproduction of the fish stocks which migrate in the sea areas between Iceland and Jan Mayen.

The Parties shall exchange information regarding catch statistics and national fishery measures, coordinate scientific research and pool their experience in respect of developments in the fisheries.

Article 2

A Fisheries Commission shall be established. Each of the two Parties shall appoint one representative and one deputy representative to this Commission. The representatives may be assisted by advisers and experts.

The Commission shall meet at least once each year, alternately in each of the two countries. In addition, the Commission shall meet as often as proves necessary.

In addition to the Commission, a Working Group shall be set up composed of marine research scientists from the two countries. The Group shall assist the Commission with scientific advice in connection with its work.

Article 3

The Commission shall consult on such questions as arise in

connection with the implementation of the regulatory measures for fishing. It shall submit proposals and recommendations to the two Governments concerning the fishing of migrating stocks in the area, including recommendations in respect of the total allowable catch for such stocks and the distribution of this total allowable catch, and shall also discuss and coordinate other conservation measures. Unanimous recommendations from the Commission become binding after two months if neither Party's Government has raised any objection.

The Parties may instruct the Commission to deal with and study other questions which arise.

Article 4

Given the fact that the capelin stock migrates in both Parties' zones, the Parties shall seek to agree on the total allowable catch for capelin. If agreement is not reached, Iceland, as the Party with the greatest interest in the capelin stock, may stipulate the total allowable catch.

If it turns out that the total allowable catch of capelin for the season is altered as compared with the catch volume which formed the basis for the Norwegian quota, Norway's quota shall be adjusted correspondingly during the same or the subsequent fishing season.

Norway may consider herself unbound by the total allowable catch if the stipulation thereof is considered to be clearly unreasonable.

Article 5

Norway's share of the total allowable catch for capelin in the Jan Mayen zone is stipulated for the first four years, including 1980, at 15 per cent.

The distribution of the capelin quota between Norway and Iceland can be reexamined in the Fisheries Commission at the latest at the expiry of the four-year period in the light of the developments which have taken place in fishing and on the basis of research findings with regard to the distribution of the capelin stock between the different zones. If agreement is not reached, the Governments of the two countries shall discuss the situation with a view to arriving at a solution paying due regard to the considerations on which the two Parties have based themselves in drawing up this Agreement.

Article 6

Of that part of the total allowable catch which is due to Iceland pursuant to Article 5, Icelandic fishermen shall be entitled to fish in the Jan Mayen zone a quantity of capelin corresponding to that part of the total allowable catch which is due to Norway pursuant to Article 5.

As regards other migrating stocks, reasonable regard shall be paid to Iceland's dependence on fishing in general and to Iceland's interest in fishing in the Jan Mayen zone. Of that share which is allocated to Iceland in negotiations with Norway and other countries, Iceland may fish a reasonable part in the Jan Mayen zone. Iceland's catch volume in the Jan Mayen zone shall be discussed in the annual consultations in the Fisheries Commission.

Article 7

Each of the Parties may transfer to third countries the right to fish within the quotas they themselves are allocated pursuant to Article 5. Such fishing by third countries may only take place in that Party's own zone.

Article 8

The Parties recognize that effective conservation and rational exploitation of migrating stocks may necessitate consultations and the coordination of fishery measures with other countries, including the stipulation of the total allowable catch and the distribution thereof, in accordance with the principles in Article 63 in the text of the Conference on the Law of the Sea and the provisions of the present Agreement.

Article 9

The question of the dividing line for the shelf in the area between Iceland and Jan Mayen shall be the subject of continued negotiations.

For this purpose the Parties agree to appoint at the earliest opportunity a Conciliation Commission composed of three members, of which each Party appoints one national member. The chairman of the Commission shall be appointed by the Parties jointly.

The Commission shall have as its mandate the submission of recommendations with regard to the dividing line for the shelf area between Iceland and Jan Mayen. In preparing such recommendations, the Commission shall take into account Iceland's strong economic interests in these sea areas, the existing geographical and geological factors and other special circumstances.

The Commission shall adopt its own rules of procedure. The unanimous recommendations of the Commission shall be submitted to the two Governments at the earliest opportunity. The Parties envisage the presentation of the recommendations within five months of the appointment of the Commission.

These recommendations are not binding on the Parties; but during their further negotiations the Parties will pay reasonable regard to them.

Article 10

In the event of activities taking place on the shelf areas between Iceland and Jan Mayen in connection with the exploration for or exploitation of the natural resources on or in the shelf, the Parties undertake to initiate close mutual consultations and close cooperation with regard to the adoption and enforcement of the necessary safety regulations in order to avoid any pollution which might endanger the living resources in these sea areas or otherwise have a harmful effect on the marine environment.

The Parties undertake to submit to each other specific plans for such activities in connection with the exploration for or exploitation of the shelf resources in ample time prior to the commencement of such activities.

Article 11

This Agreement shall not become binding until the Parties, by an exchange of notes, have notified each other that the necessary constitutional steps have been taken.

In witness whereof the respective Plenipotentiaries have signed this Agreement.

Done at Reykjavik the twenty-eighth day of May, nineteen hundred and eighty, in du-plicate in Norwegian and in Icelandic, both texts being equally authoritative.

For the Government of Norway：

[KNUT VOLLEBAEK]

For the Government of Iceland：

[HALLDÓR ÁSGRIMSSON]

资料来源：http：//www. un. org/depts/los/LEGISLATIONANDTREATIES/ PDFFILES/TREATIES/isl-nor1980fcs. pdf。

2.《挪威与冰岛间关于渔业和大陆架问题的协定》

陈思静 译　王阳、梅玉婕 校

挪威政府和冰岛政府，

认识到采取有效措施保护、合理开发和繁殖海中生物资源的需要，以及进一步合理开发大陆架及其附上（水域）的自然资源的需要，认识到依据国际法，这两个海岸相向的国家，需要承担有效保护、合理开发这些自然资源的主要责任，认识到为保障这些目标（的实现），两国之间协调、紧密和友善合作的重要性，以及与其他受影响国家协调合作的必要性，认识到在海洋法会议制定的文本草案第 71 条（的背景下），冰岛对于渔业资源的强烈经济依赖，考虑到冰岛已经建立了一个 200 海里的专属经济区，而在不久的将来，挪威也将在扬马延岛周围建立渔区，表达他们对于过度捕鱼（特别是对毛鳞鱼的过度捕捞）的担忧。借鉴联合国第三次海洋法会议已经完成及尚待完成的工作成果，达成以下协议：

第一条

双方应就渔业部门的实践问题进行合作，（应）特别关注采取直接措施，对在冰岛和扬马延间海域洄游的鱼群进行养护、合理开发和合理培育。

双方应就捕捞的数据、（各自）国内的渔业措施进行信息交换，并协调科学研究、共享渔业发展的经验。

第二条

应当建立一个渔业委员会。双方应各在委员会中派驻一名代表和副代表。代表们应有来自顾问和专家的协助。

委员会应当每年至少会晤一次，会议轮流在两国举行。此外，当确有必要时，委员会应经常召开会议。

除渔业委员会之外，应当建立一个包含两国海洋科学家的工作组。工作组应协助委员会，就与其工作相关的事项，向渔业委员会提供科学建议。

第三条

就与捕鱼的管理措施的执行相关的问题，委员会应展开磋商。它应向两国的政府就两国之间海域中的洄游鱼群的捕捞问题，向两者政府递交意见和建议（包括此类鱼群的总捕捞量和双方的捕捞配额）。同时就其他的养护措施进行讨论和协调。在收到建议的两个月后，若双方政府不提出反对意见，那么委员会的建议就对双方政府具有拘束力。

两国政府可以指示渔业委员会处理或研究（实践中）产生的问题。

第四条

考虑到毛鳞鱼在两国的渔区间洄游的事实，双方应寻求就毛鳞鱼的总捕捞量达成一致意见。如果未能达成一致意见，作为毛鳞鱼最重要的利益相关方，冰岛可以规定总的可捕捞量。

如果证实，某一季节的总捕捞配额，与作为挪威配额基础的捕捞数据相比较，发生了改变，那么挪威本季及其之后的捕捞配额应作出相应的调整。

如果冰岛的规定显然不合理，那么挪威可以考虑，不受总捕捞量规定的约束。

第五条

挪威对于扬马延岛附近海域毛鳞鱼的捕捞配额，自 1980 年开始的第一个四年，皆为总捕捞配额的 15%。

最迟在四年期满后，渔业委员会可以依据与不同捕捞区域中毛鳞鱼的分配相关的调查结果，对挪威和冰岛之间的捕捞配额进行重新审查。如果未能达成一致意见，双方政府应在适当考虑起草本协议时的考量的基础上，就达成一项解决方案进行讨论。

第六条

依据第五条划定的在扬马延岛附近海域的总捕捞配额，除了挪威的捕捞配额，相对应的配额都归冰岛渔民所有。

对其他的溯游种群而言，应当合理关照冰岛对渔业的总体依赖性和冰岛渔民在扬马延岛渔区的捕捞利益。对于挪威和其他国家进行协商以后方能确定的捕捞配额，冰岛可以在扬马延岛渔区中获得一个合理的部分。在每年的渔业委员会会议中，应就冰岛的捕捞配额进行讨论。

第七条

双方都可以将第五条赋予的本国生产捕捞配额转让给第三国。第三国的捕鱼活动只能在其受让的区域进行。

第八条

双方都认识到，依据现阶段的"海洋法公约草案"第 63 条和本协议所规定的原则，使得同其他国家就洄游鱼类的有效养护措施和合理开发措施（包括总捕捞量的规定和分配）进行磋商和合作，很有必要。

第九条

冰岛和扬马延岛之间海域的大陆架划界问题，应是进一步协商的主题。

为此目的，双方同意尽早任命一个由三人组成的调解委员会，其中，两国各指派一个本国国民委员。委员会主席应由两国共同指定。

就冰岛与扬马延岛之间的划界线，调解委员会应当履行提交建议的职责。在准备这样的建议时，调解委员会应当充分考虑冰岛在这些海域中强烈的经济利益、现有的地理、地质因素，以及其他特别情况。

委员会应当制定自身的程序规则。委员会一致通过的建议应尽早递交给两国政府。在调解委员会成员任命完毕后的五个月内，两国应就建议的准备进行审议。

这些建议对两国不具有约束力，但在他们进一步的协商过程中，将对这些建议进行合理的关注。

第十条

若冰岛和扬马延岛之间的大陆架上或大陆架中的活动，与自然资源的勘探、开发有关，为避免对海洋环境造成污染，进而可能危及这些海域中的生物资源，或者对海洋环境产生有害影响，就制定和实施必要的安全规定，双方同意启动密切的共同磋商和密切的合作。

双方同意，在实施与大陆架自然资源的勘探或开发相关的活动前，应提前较长一段时间，相互递交与此类活动(相关的)特别计划。

第十一条

本协定在双方交换照会，互相通知业已完成所需要的宪法程序时生效。

全权代表在此签名，以兹证明。

1980 年 5 月 28 日在雷克雅未克签署，有挪威语和冰岛语两种作准文本，两种文本具有同等效力。

    挪威政府代表：克努特·沃勒贝克

    冰岛政府代表：奥斯格里姆松

3. Additional Protocol to the Agreement of 28 May 1980 between Norway and Iceland concerning Fishery and Continental Shelf Questions and the Agreement derived therefrom of 22 October 1981 on the Continental Shelf between Jan Mayen and Iceland

11 November 1997

The Government of the Kingdom of Norway and the Government of the Republic of Iceland, hereinafter referred to as the Parties,

Having regard to the Agreement of 28 May 1980 between the Parties on Fishery and Continental Shelf Questions and the Agreement derived therefrom of 22 October 1981 on the Continental Shelf between Jan Mayen and Iceland,

Having further regard to consultations between the Kingdom of Norway, the Republic of Iceland and the Kingdom of Denmark concerning the final delimitation of the maritime waters between Jan Mayen, Iceland and Greenland, which led to agreement on the determination of point 1 as described in Article 1 below, where the delimitation lines of the three states intersect,

Have agreed as follows:

Article 1

The delimitation line between the Parties' parts of the continental shelf and between the fishery zones in the area shall include a straight geodetic line between the following points:

Point 1: 69°35′00″N 13°16′00″ W

Point 2: 69°34′42″ N 12°09′24″W

The above-mentioned points are defined by their geographical latitude and longitude in accordance with the World Geodetic System 1984 (WGS 84).

The delimitation line between the above-mentioned points is, for

154

illustrative purposes, drawn on the map appended to this Additional Protocol.

Article 2

This Additional Protocol enters into force when the Parties have notified each other in writing that the procedures necessary thereto have been completed and the Government of the Kingdom of Denmark has notified both Parties in writing that the determination of point 1 as described in Article 1 has been confirmed. The date of entry into force is the date on which these conditions have been fulfilled.

Done at Helsinki on 11 November 1997 in two originals in the Norwegian and Icelandic languages, both texts being equally authentic.

For the Government of the Kingdom of Norway

For the Government of the Republic of Iceland

Map

资料来源：http：//www. un. org/depts/los/LEGISLATIONANDTREATIES/ PDFFILES/TREATIES/NOR-ISL1997FC. PDF。

4.《1980 年 5 月 28 日挪威和冰岛关于渔业与大陆架问题的协定以及 1981 年 10 月 22 日由此衍生的扬马延岛和冰岛间关于大陆架协定之附加议定书》

陈思静 译　王阳、梅玉婕 校

（1997 年 11 月 11 日）挪威王国政府和冰岛共和国政府，后文称双方，考虑到 1980 年 5 月 28 日《关于渔业和大陆架问题的协议》和 1981 年 10 月 22 日《关于冰岛和扬马延岛之间的大陆架协定》，进一步考虑到挪威王国、冰岛共和国以及丹麦王国关于扬马延岛、冰岛和格陵兰岛之间最终海域划界的磋商，已就下文提及的第 1 条中三国划界交界点点 1 的确定达成一致意见，同意以下条款：

第一条

双方此区域中的大陆架部分和渔区的划界线，应当包含以下两点之间的一条测地直线：

点 1：北纬 69 度 35 分 00 秒，西经 13 度 16 分 00 秒

点 2：北纬 69 度 34 分 42 秒，西经 12 度 09 分 24 秒

上述两点的地理经度和纬度，由 1984 年世界测地系统（WGS）加以确定，出于说明的目的，上述两点间的划界线将在本附加议定书的地图附件中标出。

第二条

本附加议定书在双方互相书面通知业已完成的必要法律程序，且丹麦王国政府已书面通知双方已对点 1 加以确认时生效。

1997 年 11 月 11 日在赫尔辛基签署，有挪威语和冰岛语两种语言作准文本，两种文本具有同等效力。

挪威政府代表

冰岛政府代表

地图

5. Agreement between Iceland and Norway concerning Transboundary Hydrocarbon Deposits

The Government of Iceland and the Government of the Kingdom of Norway,

Desiring to maintain and strengthen the good neighbourly relations between Iceland and Norway, and

Referring to the Agreement of 22 October 1981 between Iceland and Norway on the Continental Shelf in the Area between Iceland and Jan Mayen, the Additional Protocol of 11 November 1997 to the Agreement between the Governments of Iceland and Norway on Fisheries and Continental Shelf Issues and the Agreement between the Governments of

Iceland and Norway on the Continental Shelf between Iceland and Jan Mayen, and the Agreement between Iceland and Norway concerning the delimitation of the continental shelf beyond 200 nautical miles to be concluded on the basis of the Agreed Minutes of 20 September 2006 on the Delimitation of the Continental Shelf beyond 200 Nautical Miles between the Faroe Islands, Iceland and Norway in the Southern Part of the Banana Hole of the Northeast Atlantic,

Have agreed as follows:

Article 1

Neither Party can begin exploitation of any hydrocarbon deposit which extends to the continental shelf of the other Party until agreement on the exploitation of the deposit as a unit is reached between the Parties.

Article 2

(1) If the existence of a hydrocarbon deposit in or on the continental shelf of one of the Parties is established and the other Party is of the opinion that the said deposit extends to its continental shelf, the latter Party may notify the former Party accordingly and, at the same time, submit the data on which it bases its opinion.

(2) If such an opinion is submitted, the Parties shall initiate discussions on the extent of the deposit and the possibility for its exploitation. In the course of these discussions, the Party initiating them shall support its opinion with further evidence from geophysical data and/or geological data, including any available drilling data, and both Parties shall make their best efforts to ensure that all relevant information is made available for the purpose of these discussions.

(3) If it is established during these discussions that the deposit extends to the continental shelf of both Parties and that the deposit on the continental shelf of the one Party can be exploited wholly or in part from the continental shelf of the other Party, or that the exploitation of the deposit on the continental shelf of the one Party would affect the

possibility of exploitation of the deposit on the continental shelf of the other Party, agreement on the apportionment of the deposit between the Parties and on the exploitation of it as a unit shall be reached at the request of one of the Parties, including as to the appointment of a unit operator, the manner in which any such deposit shall be most effectively exploited and the manner in which the proceeds relating thereto shall be apportioned. Such agreement shall be reached in the form of a Unitisation Agreement.

Article 3

The Unitisation Agreement to be agreed by the Parties in accordance with Article 2, paragraph 3, concerning the exploitation of a defined transboundary hydrocarbon deposit shall include the provisions set out below:

(1) The transboundary hydrocarbon deposit to be exploited as a unit shall be defined (latitudes and longitudes normally shown in a separate attachment).

(2) The geographical and geological characteristics of the transboundary hydrocarbon deposit and the methodology used for data classification shall be described. The legal persons holding rights to exploit the transboundary hydrocarbon deposit as a unit shall have equal access to any geological data used as a basis for such geological characterisation.

(3) The estimated total amount of the reserves in place in the transboundary hydrocarbon deposit shall be stated. The methodology used for such calculation shall be stated. The apportionment of the reserves between the Parties shall be set out (normally in a separate attachment).

(4) Each Party shall be entitled to copies of all geological data, as well as all other data of relevance for the unitised hydrocarbon deposit, and which are gathered in connection with the exploitation of the

hydrocarbon deposit.

（5） The two Parties shall individually grant all necessary authorisations required by their respective national laws for the development and operation of the transboundary hydrocarbon deposit as a unit in accordance with the Agreement between Iceland and Norway concerning transboundary hydrocarbon deposits.

（6）Each Party shall require the relevant legal persons holding rights to explore for and produce hydrocarbons on its respective side of the delimitation line to enter into a Joint Operating Agreement between them to regulate the exploitation of the transboundary hydrocarbon deposit as a unit in accordance with the Unitisation Agreement.

（7） The following provisions shall apply in relation to the Joint Operating Agreement：

The Joint Operating Agreement shall refer to the Unitisation Agreement to ensure that the provisions contained therein shall prevail.

The Joint Operating Agreement shall be subject to approval by both Parties. Such approval shall be given with no undue delay and shall not be unduly withheld.

A unit operator shall be appointed as the joint agent of the legal persons holding the rights to exploit the defined transboundary hydrocarbon deposit as a unit in accordance with the principles set out in the Unitisation Agreement. The appointment of, and any change of, the unit operator shall be subject to prior approval by the two Parties.

（8）Subject to its national laws, neither Party shall withhold a permit for the drilling of wells by, or on account of, the legal persons holding rights to explore for and produce hydrocarbons on its respective side of the delimitation line for purposes related to the determination and apportionment of the transboundary hydrocarbon deposit.

（9）In due time before the production of hydrocarbons from the transboundary hydrocarbon deposit is about to cease, the two Parties shall agree on the timing of cessation of the production from the transboundary hydrocarbon deposit.

(10) The two Parties shall consult each other with a view to ensuring that health, safety and environmental measures are taken in accordance with the national laws of each Party.

(11) Each Party shall be responsible for inspection of hydrocarbon installations located on its continental shelf and for the hydrocarbon activities carried out thereon in relation to the exploitation of the transboundary hydrocarbon deposit. Each Party shall ensure inspectors of the other Party access to such installations on request, and that they have access to relevant metering systems on the continental shelf or in the territory of either Party. Each Party shall also ensure that relevant information is given to the other Party on a regular basis to enable it to safeguard its fundamental interests including, but not limited to health, safety, environment, hydrocarbon production and metering.

(12) A right to explore for and produce hydrocarbons awarded by one Party, and which applies to a transboundary hydrocarbon deposit that is subject to unitisation in accordance with the Agreement between Iceland and Norway concerning transboundary hydrocarbon deposits, shall not be altered or assigned to new legal persons without prior consultation with the other Party.

Article 4

The Parties shall make every effort to resolve any disagreement as rapidly as possible. If, however, the Parties fail to agree, they shall jointly consider all other relevant options for resolving the impasse.

Article 5

If the Parties fail to agree on exploitation of a transboundary deposit as a unit, the disagreement shall be resolved by negotiation. If any such dispute cannot be resolved in this manner or by any other procedure agreed to by the Parties the dispute shall, at the request of either Party, be submitted to an ad hoc arbitral tribunal composed as follows:

Each Party shall designate one arbitrator, and the two arbitrators so designated shall elect a third arbitrator, who shall be the Chairman. The Chairman shall not be a national of or habitually reside in Iceland or Norway. If either Party fails to designate an arbitrator within three months of a request to do so, either Party may request the President of the International Court of Justice to appoint an arbitrator. The same procedure shall apply if, within one month of the designation or appointment of the second arbitrator, the third arbitrator has not been elected. The tribunal shall determine its own procedure, save that all decisions shall be taken, in the absence of unanimity, by a majority vote of the members of the tribunal. The decisions of the tribunal shall be binding upon the Parties.

Article 6

If the Parties fail to agree on the apportionment of the deposit between themselves, they shall appoint an independent expert to determine the apportionment. The decision of the independent expert shall be binding upon the Parties.

Article 7

Each Party may after commencement of production from the unitised field request discussions to be initiated on review of the apportionment of the deposit. Any request for reapportionment must be based on substantial new geological information. Both Parties shall make their best efforts to ensure that all relevant information is made available for the purpose of these discussions. The Parties may on this basis agree that the deposit shall be reapportioned between themselves according to specified conditions.

Article 8

（1）The provisions of Articles 2-7 of this Agreement shall, where applicable, apply *mutatis mutandis* to any hydrocarbon deposit which may extend across one or more of the lines defined in Article 2 of the Agreement of 22 October 1981 on the Continental Shelf in the Area between Iceland and Jan Mayen, subject to Article 8, paragraph 2, of that Agreement.

（2）Each Party shall ensure that all data necessary to establish whether a hydrocarbon deposit extends beyond one or more of the lines defined in Article 2 of the said Agreement of 22 October 1981 are collected and shall submit all such data to the other Party without undue delay.

Article 9

This Agreement is without prejudice to the respective Parties' views on questions that are not governed by this Agreement, including questions relating to the exercise of sovereign rights or jurisdiction under international law.

Article 10

This Agreement enters into force when the Parties have notified each other in writing that the necessary internal procedures have been completed.

Done at Reykjavik on the 3rd day of November 2008 in the Icelandic, Norwegian and English languages, all texts being equally authentic. In case of any divergence of interpretation, the English text shall prevail.

For Norway

For Iceland

资料来源：https：//treaties. un. org/doc/Publication/UNTS/No%20Volume/50378/Part/I-50378-0800000280321996. pdf。

6.《冰岛与挪威间关于跨界油气矿藏的协定》

陈思静 译　王阳、梅玉婕 校

冰岛政府和挪威王国政府，意欲维持和加强挪威和冰岛之间的睦邻友好关系，并且忆及两国于 1981 年 10 月 22 日签订的《关于冰岛和扬马延岛之间的大陆架协定》，1997 年 11 月 11 日《〈渔业问题和大陆架问题协定〉的附加议定书》，就扬马延岛和冰岛间的大陆架而签订的协定，以及依据 2006 年 9 月 20 日就东北大西洋圈洞南部地区中的，法罗群岛、冰岛和挪威之间的 200 海里外大陆架划界问题而签订的备忘录，进而最终达成的 200 海里外大陆架划界协定，同意以下条款：

第一条

对于延伸到另外一方大陆架上的油气矿藏资源，除非双方达成协议，将该矿藏作为整体进行开发，否则任何一方不能启动开发。

第二条

（1）如果确定一方的大陆架上或大陆架内存有油气矿藏，而另一方则认为该矿藏已延伸至它的大陆架，那么后者可以相应地将这一情况通知前者，并同时附以其作出判断的数据。

（2）在此类意见递交后，双方应就该矿藏的范围及开采的可能性进行讨论。在讨论的过程中，发起讨论的一方应递交进一步的地理和（或）地质数据（包括可以进行钻井的数据）以支持其意见，为讨论的目的，双方应当尽最大的努力，确保所有的相关数据都可以获取。

（3）在讨论的过程中，如果确认，该矿藏在双方的大陆架上均有分布，且一方大陆架上的矿藏可由另一方在其大陆架上部分或整体地加以开采，或者对一方大陆架上矿藏的开采，会影响另外一方开采其本国大陆架上油气资源的可能性，应经由其中一方提议，达成一项协议，将该矿藏作为一个整体进行开采，协议应包括，双方之间的矿藏分配，区块联合经营人的委派，矿藏可以得到最为有效地开采的方式，相应的开采收益分配方式。

这份协议应符合"联合协定"的形式。

第三条

对某一确定的跨界油气矿藏进行开采，应由双方依本协议第2条第3款达成"联合协定"，该协议应包含以下条款：

(1)将待开采的跨界油气矿藏界定为一个整体(通常以另外的附件表明经纬度)。

(2)跨界油气矿藏的地理和地质特征，以及数据分类的方法应予以描述。对视为整体的跨界油气矿藏享有开发权益的法人，应可以平等获取此类地质特征的数据。

(3)应当申明(整体)跨界油气矿藏中的预计储藏总量。应说明这一算方法。应制定双方矿藏的分配方案(通常以单独附件的形式作出)。

(4)双方都应有权获得地质数据的所有复印件、与联合开采的油气矿藏的相关数据的所有复印件、收集得到的与开采矿藏相关的信息的复印件。

(5)双方应依照就跨界油气矿藏签订的协定，根据各自的国内法，对视为整体的跨界油气矿藏的开发活动，单独进行所有必要的授权。

(6)依照"联合协定"，为管制视为整体的跨界矿藏的开采活动，双方应要求，在其各自大陆架上享有开发跨界矿藏、制造油气产品权益的法人，应达成"共同开采协定"。

(7)应适用下列与"共同开采协定"相关的规定：

"共同开采协定"应参照"联合协定"，确保"联合协定"中的条款具有优先地位。

"共同开采协定"应经双方(政府)同意。这一同意应当毫不迟延地作出，且不得不正当地撤回。

依据"联合协定"中规定的原则，对视为整体的某一跨界油气矿藏，应当委派一个联合经营人，作为在其中享有开发权益的法人的共同代理人。联合经营人的任命及任何任命的变更，应当获得双方(政府)的预先同意。

(8)依据双方的国内法，双方不得基于跨界油气矿藏的定性和分配等目的，撤回在其边界一侧享有开发、生产油气产品权益的法人的打井许可。

（9）在跨界油气矿藏将要停止生产前的合理时间段内，双方应就跨界油气矿藏停止开发的时间点达成一致意见。

（10）双方应相互协商，确保依据各自的国内法，采取健康、安全和环境措施符。

（11）双方有责任对位于其大陆架上的油气矿藏开采设备和与跨界油气矿藏开采相关的活动进行监督。一方应确保另一方监督员提出申请后，其可以登临设施，也可以访问对方大陆架上或领土内的相关测量系统。双方也应当确保，定期地相互给予对方一些相关信息，使其可以保障其根本的利益，这些利益包括但不限于健康、安全、环境、油气生产和测量。

（12）经由一方授予的开发和生产油气资源的权利，该权利适用于一块跨界油气矿藏，该矿藏依挪威和冰岛签订的涉及跨界油气矿藏联合开采的协议（划定），在未与对方提前磋商的情况下，不得更改该授权，也不得将授权授予一个新的法人。

第四条

双方应尽一切努力，尽快解决任何分歧。然而，如果双方不能达成一致意见，他们应考虑其他所有可能的方法以化解僵局。

第五条

如果双方对于视为整体的跨界矿藏的开采未能达成一致意见，这项分歧应通过协商解决。如果此类争端不能通过协商解决，也没有通过双方合意的任何其他程序加以解决，应经任何一方的请求，应将（该争端）提交一个特别仲裁庭，该特别仲裁庭依下列方式组成：

双方各委派一名仲裁员，由这两名仲裁员应选举产生第三名仲裁员，第三名仲裁员应是（仲裁庭的）主席。主席不应当是两国国民，其惯常居住地也不得位于冰岛或挪威。若在请求作出之后的三个月内，任何一方未能委派仲裁员，则任何一方可以请求国际法院院长指派一名仲裁员。若在两国分别委派仲裁员后的一个月内，未能选举产生第三名仲裁员，该程序同样适用。仲裁庭应决定其本身的（仲裁）程序，除全票通过的决定应加以执行之外，若未能全票通过，由仲裁庭成员的多数票（作出）决定。仲裁庭的决定应对双方具有拘束力。

第六条

如果双方对于它们之间的矿藏的分配未能达成一致意见，它们应当委派一名独立的专家以决定分配(方案)。独立专家的意见应对双方具有拘束力。

第七条

在联合开发的油田开始生产之后，双方都可以提议讨论，就该矿藏的分配(方案)进行审查。进行重新分配的要求，必须是基于实质的、新的地质信息。双方应尽最大努力确保，为讨论的目的，所有相关信息都可获取。基于此，双方可以同意，在特定条件下，应对它们之间的油气矿藏重新分配。

第八条

(1)在可适用的情况下，1981年《关于冰岛和扬马延岛之间的大陆架协定》第2条所规定的那些跨越一条或多条大陆架边界线的跨界油气矿藏，原本适用1981年协定的第8条第2款，依据情势变更原则，应适用本协定第2-7条的规定。

(2)双方应确保，对确定某一油气矿藏是否属于1981年《关于冰岛和扬马延岛之间的大陆架协定》第2条所规定的那些跨越一条或多条大陆架边界线的跨界油气矿藏的必要信息，应予以收集，并且应毫不迟延地将所有这些信息递交给对方。

第九条

本协定不损害双方对于不受本协定规制的问题的观点，(这些问题)包括依据国际法，与主权性权利或管辖权行使的有关问题。

第十条

本协定在双方业已相互书面通知(对方)，已完成所必要的国内程序时生效。

2008 年 11 月 3 日于雷克雅未克地完成，

有冰岛语、挪威语和英语三种作准本，三种文本具有同等效力。

若对于条约的解释出现了分歧，应以英语文本作准。

冰岛代表   挪威代表

八、1989 年阿拉伯也门共和国与也门 民主人民共和国共同开发案

Aden Summit Agreement between the Yemen Arab Republic and the People's Democratic Republic of Yemen

Aden, 30 November 1989

Entry into force: 30 *November* 1989 *by signature*

Authentic text: *Arabic*

Registration with the Secretariat of the United Nations: *Yemen*, 1 *May* 2007

[TRANSLATION-TRADUCTION]

YEMEN HIGHER COUNCIL

ADEN SUMMIT AGREEMENT

Each side in the two parts of the nation,

Believing in Yemeni unity and the goals of the immortal revolutions of 26 September and 14 October and in fulfilment of the struggle of the Yemeni people and the sacrifices of its martyrs to build a united and independent Yemen,

Responding to the Yemeni will and being desirous of advancing the task of unification between the two parts of the one nation to a higher stage, bringing closer the day of unity, considering that unity is the fate and destiny of our people in both parts of the nation,

Proceeding from the aspirations of our Yemeni masses to achieve unity of the land and people of Yemen and in order to achieve the genuine stability, security, development and growth of the Yemeni nation, particularly given that our achievements in unification have contributed to an enrichment of the climate of unification with additional national and fraternal dimensions, resulting in unification experiences at the popular, governmental, institutional and public organization levels, thereby heightening the anticipation by Yemeni citizens of the transition of their national cause towards the fmalization of the declaration on the establishment of a unified State,

Further to the agreements and declarations signed by the leaderships and officials of both parts of the nation,

Persevering in the creation of the peaceful and democratic climate necessary to implement the unification measures leading to a unified State,

Affirming the commitment to the policy of dialogue and mutual understanding between the two parts of the nation, to the preservation of security and stability and to the maintenance of exchanges and meetings on the unification of the two parts of the nation,

During the visit from 29 to 30 November 1989 by Lieutenant-Colonel Ali Abdullah Saleh, President of the Republic, Commander-in-Chief of the Armed Forces and Secretary-General of the People's General Congress at the head of a large official and popular delegation to join in the celebrations of the Yemeni people on the occasion of the twenty-second anniversary of the independence of the south of the Yemeni nation, the draft permanent constitution of the unified State, completed by the Joint Constitutional Committee on 30 December A. D. 1981 (corresponding to 4 Rabi' I A. H. 1402), was approved and ratified by the leaders of both parts of the nation, represented by Colonel Ali Abdullah Saleh, President of the Republic, Commander-in-Chief of the Armed Forces and Secretary-General of the People's General Congress, and Ali Salim al-Bidh, General Secretary of the Central Committee of the Yemeni Socialist Party, in implementation of paragraph 2 of the Kuwait Agreement, on the understanding that the measures approved in previous agreements, in particular articles 9, 10, 11, 12 and 13 of the Cairo Agreement, would be completed by taking the following steps:

I

(a) The draft constitution shall be referred to the Consultative Council and the People's Council in the two parts of the nation, respectively, for approval in accordance with the constitutional rules of each, within a period of not more than six months,

(b) By mandate from their respective legislative authorities, both Presidents shall arrange for a referendum on the draft constitution and the election of a consolidated legislative body for the new State in accordance with the new constitution.

(c) In implementation of the above, the Presidents of the two parts of the nation shall establish a joint ministerial committee, whose membership shall include both Ministers of the Interior, to supervise this process, within not more than six months from the date of approval of the draft constitution by the legislative bodies in both parts of the nation. This committee shall have all powers necessary to carry out its task.

(d) The Presidents of the two parts of the nation shall invite the League of Arab States to delegate two representatives to participate in the work of the committee.

II

(a) All measures shall be completed in order to implement the Ramadan Agreement (May 1988), including those relating to activation of the work of Yemen Higher Council, the Joint Ministerial Committee and the unification committees between the two parts of the nation and to implementation of the outcome of the first session of 1989 of the Joint

Ministerial Committee (held in Sana'a from 21 to 23 March 1989), and completion of the work of the joint unification committees within a maximum period of two months shall be expedited.

(b) The committee on unified political organization shall be urged to expedite completion, within a maximum period of two months, of the task it began at its first session, in order to ensure preparations for the political activity of the future unified State in the light of its draft constitution, thereby contributing to the promotion of the democratic conduct of political activity

III

The leaderships of both parts of the nation commit themselves to implementing this Agreement within the time frame determined therein.

SIGNED at Aden on 30 November A. D. 1989, corresponding to 1 Jumadah I A. H. 1410.

LIEUTENANT-COLONEL ALI ABDULLAH SALEH

President of the Republic

Commander-in-Chief of the Armed Forces

Secretary-General of the People's General Congress

ALI SALIM AL-BIDH

General Secretary of the Central Committee

of the Yemeni Socialist Party

资料来源: Aden Summit Agreement between the Yemen Arab Republic and the Democratic Republic of Yemen, Aden, 30 November 1989, Yemen Arab Republic—the Democratic Republic of Yemen, U. N. T. S. Vol. 2429. pp. 131-141, https: //treaties. un. org/doc/Publication/UNTS/Volume% 202429/ v2429. pdf。

九、1995 年英国与阿根廷共同开发案

1. Joint Statement of 15 February 1990 Re-establishing Diplomatic Relations between Britain and Argentina

(1) Delegations of the British and Argentine Governments, as agreed at their meeting in Madrid in October 1989, met again in Madrid on 14 and 15 February 1990. The British delegation was led by Sir Crispin Tickell, United Kingdom Permanent Representative to the United Nations, and the Argentine delegation by Ambassador Lucio Garcia del Solar, Special Representative of the Government of Argentina.

(2) Both delegations reaffirmed that the formula on sovereignty over the Falkland Islands (Islas Malvinas), South Georgia and the South Sandwich Islands and the surrounding maritime areas, recorded in paragraph 2 of the Joint Statement of 19 October 1989, applied to this meeting and its consequences.

(3) Both Governments, wishing to develop further friendship and co-operation between their two peoples, agreed to re-establish diplomatic relations following notification of the Protecting Powers. Embassies will be re-opened shortly and Ambassadors appointed in accordance with international practice.

(4) The British delegation announced the decision of the British Government to lift the Protection Zone established around the Falkland Islands (Islas Malvinas).

(5) Both Governments approved with satisfaction the final report of

the "British-Argentine Working Group about measures to build confidence and avoid incidents in the military sphere" and decided, under the terms of the formula on sovereignty referred to in paragraph 2 of this Joint Statement, the following:

(a) To establish an "Interim reciprocal information and consultation system" for movements of units of their armed forces in areas of the South West Atlantic. The aims of this system are to increase confidence between the United Kingdom and Argentina and to contribute to achieving a more normal situation in the region without unnecessary delay. (The text of this agreement is included as Annex I to this Joint Statement.)

(b) To establish a direct communication link between the Falkland Islands (Islas Malvinas) and the mainland in order to reduce the possibility of incidents, to limit their consequences in the case of occurrence, and to increase common knowledge of military activities in the South West Atlantic. (See Annex I.)

(c) To agree on a set of rules of reciprocal behavior for naval and air units of their armed forces when operating in proximity. (See Annex II.)

(d) To agree on a mechanism for emergencies aimed at facilitating air and maritime search and rescue operations in the South-West Atlantic. (See Annex III.)

(e) To establish a system of exchange of information on the safety and control of air and maritime navigation. (See Annex IV.)

(f) To continue bilateral consideration of these matters and to review the measures agreed upon within one year from their coming into force.

(6) The agreements described in paragraph 5 will enter into force on the 31st of March 1990. On the same day the decision mentioned in paragraph 4 will be implemented.

(7) Both delegations expressed the satisfaction of their Governments with the report of the Working Group on fisheries which met in Paris on 18 and 19 December 1989. It was agreed that both Governments should proceed-through their respective Foreign Ministries-to exchange available

information on the operations of the fishing fleets, appropriate catch and effort statistics and analyses of the status of the stocks of the most significant off-shore species in the maritime area of the Atlantic Ocean between latitude 45 degrees S altitude 60 degrees S. They also agreed to assess jointly such information, and to explore bilaterally the possibilities for co-operation and conservation.

(8) Both Governments decided to set up a Working Group on South Atlantic Affairs with the mandate to continue consideration of the issues entrusted to the two working groups mentioned in paragraphs 5 and 7 of this Joint Statement. The Working Group will meet as frequently as the parties consider necessary; its first meeting will be held within one year of the date of this Joint Statement.

(9) Both delegations considered the situation regarding contacts between the Falkland Islands (Islas Malvinas) and the mainland and agreed to continue considering this matter. The British Delegation Recognized the Argentine readiness to facilitate communications and trading opportunities between the Islands and the mainland.

(10) Both delegations expressed their agreement to a visit to the cemetery on the Falkland Islands (Islas Malvinas) by close relatives of Argentine nationals buried there. The visit-based on humanitarian considerations-will take place under the auspices of the International Committee of the Red Cross (ICRC). Both Governments will seek the good offices of the ICRC and agree, through diplomatic channels, on the arrangements for and timing of the visit.

(11) Both delegations agreed that the feasibility and desirability of a general co-operation agreement should be examined through diplomatic channels.

(12) Both Governments, recognizing that the promotion and reciprocal protection of investments should encourage private initiative and increase prosperity in both states, agreed to begin, through diplomatic channels, the negotiation of an Investment Promotion and Protection Agreement.

（13）Both delegations agreed that it would be appropriate to abolish the requirement for visas for nationals of each country wishing to visit the other. This measure would become effective once negotiations had been concluded through diplomatic channels.

（14）Both Governments, conscious of the need to increase efforts to protect the environment, will work to ensure bilateral consultation and co-operation, including within the international institutions.

（15）Both Governments, recognising the threat which illicit drugs and drug abuse have created for all countries, agreed to explore ways of collaborating in this field, including exchanges of information, control of trafficking and an agreement to trace, freeze and confiscate the proceeds of drug trafficking. The Argentine delegation announced that its Government would be represented at the world conference on "Demand Reduction and the Cocaine Threat" to be held in London in April 1990.

（16）Both delegations, noting the importance of current international trends towards greater political and economic interdependence and integration, agreed to consult through diplomatic channels on these trends, particularly those concerning the European Community and Latin America.

（17）It was agreed that both Governments would jointly send the text of the present statement and its annexes to the Secretary General of the United Nations for distribution as an official document of the General Assembly, under Item 35 of the Agenda of the 44th regular session, and of the Security Council. The United Kingdom will transmit this Joint Statement to the Presidency and Commission of the European Community, and the Government of Argentina will do likewise to the Organization of American States.

（18）In conclusion, both delegations expressed their thanks to the Spanish Government for its generous hospitality and support.

资料来源：福克兰群岛协会网站，http：//www. fiassociation. com/shopimages/ pdfs/5. %201990% 20Joint% 20British-Argentine %20Statement%20on% 20the% 20Reestablishment% 20of% 20Diplomatic% 20Relations. pdf。

2.《1990 年 2 月 15 日英国和阿根廷恢复外交关系的共同声明》

王阳 译　陈思静、梅玉婕 校

（1）基于 1989 年 10 月英国政府和阿根廷政府在马德里会议上达成的共识，两国政府代表于 1990 年 2 月 14 日至 15 日再次在马德里会晤。英国代表（团）由英国常驻联合国代表克里斯宾·迪克尔爵士率领，阿根廷政府的特别代表是卢西奥·加西亚大使。

（2）两国代表重申，两国政府于 1989 年 10 月在马德里达成的共同声明第 2 段中所载之有关福克兰群岛（马尔维纳斯群岛）、南乔治亚和南桑威奇群岛及其周边海域的主权方案，适用于此次会议及其结果。

（3）为进一步提升英阿两国人民之间的友好关系，在接到保证国的通知之后，英国和阿根廷同意恢复两国外交关系，两国使馆将尽速重新开放，外交大使也将根据国际实践任命。

（4）英国代表宣布，英国政府决定废除在福克兰群岛（马尔维纳斯群岛）周边海域设置的保护区之规定。

（5）两国政府对于"提升英阿政治互信和避免军事摩擦工作组"的最终报告表示满意，决定予以批准，并依据本共同声明第 2 段所达成的主权方案，作出下列决定：

a）为指导两国武装力量在西南大西洋的活动，建立"临时互相通报和磋商机制"。该机制旨在增进两国互信，并毫不迟延地促成更加正常的地区局势的实现。（此协定的文本包含在声明附件一中）

b）为降低发生对立事件的可能性，并在冲突一旦爆发时限制其后果，在福克兰群岛（马尔维纳斯群岛）和大陆之间建立直接通信联系，并增进两国在西南大西洋军事活动的共识。（参见附件一）

c）同意达成两国海空军单位接近的一系列对等行为规则。（参见附件二）

d）同意达成一项机制，在紧急情况下，为西南大西洋海空搜救提供便利。（参见附件三）

e)建立海空航行管制信息交换系统。(参见附件四)

f)继续推进对于上述事项的双边磋商,并在上述措施生效之日起一年内重新审查。

(6)本声明第5段所指的协定将于1990年3月31日生效。声明第4段提到的决定也将于同日执行。

(7)两国政府对双方渔业工作组于1989年12月18日至19日在巴黎会晤后形成的报告表示满意。两国政府同意,由两国外交部长牵头,在南纬45°至南纬60°区域内,继续交换与渔船运营、适度捕捞数据、珍稀近海物种储量现状分析有关的信息,并同意对上述信息进行共同评估,探索双边合作和保护的可能性。

(8)两国政府决定建立"南大西洋事务工作组",授权其继续考虑本联合声明第5段和第7段委托的两个工作组所考虑的事项,该工作组将在两国政府认为必要时会晤,工作组第一次会晤将在本联合声明达成之日起一年内举行。

(9)双方代表业已考虑有关福克兰群岛(马尔维纳斯群岛)和大陆之间联系的现状并同意继续关注此事项。英国代表承认,阿根廷对便利大陆和群岛之间的贸易往来和商业交流作出了迅速的反应。

(10)双方代表对于便利阿根廷国民吊谒安葬于福克兰群岛(马尔维纳斯群岛)的亲属达成一致意见。基于人道主义考虑,该吊谒行为将由国际红十字委员会监督。两国政府将寻求国际红十字委员会的调停,并通过外交渠道就吊谒时间及相应安排达成一致。

(11)两国代表同意,对于两国总体合作的可行性及意愿,应当通过外交途径进行审查。

(12)两国政府,意识到促进和保护投资能够激发私人的创造力并且可以推动两国经济繁荣,同意通过外交途径启动两国《促进和保护投资协定》的谈判。

(13)两国代表同意废除两国国民往来的签证要求。一旦两国之间通过外交途径达成相关成果,该项措施将生效。

(14)两国政府,意识到采取行动保护环境的重要性,将会采取措施,确保开展双边磋商与合作,包括在相关国际组织内的双边磋商与合作。

(15)两国政府,意识到毒品贩运和毒品滥用对于国际社会的威胁,同意探索在这一领域开展合作的方式，包括信息交换、非法交易行为的管制、资产追踪和冻结协定的达成以及毒品交易的获利的没收。阿根廷代表宣布阿根廷政府将会出席1990年4月在伦敦举办的"抑制可卡因需求与威胁"大会。

(16)两国代表，注意到目前国际政治和经济形势相互依存和一体化的重大发展趋势，同意通过外交途径，就这一趋势特别是涉及欧洲共同体和拉丁美洲的事项开展磋商。

(17)两国政府同意共同将这一声明的文本及附件提交联合国秘书长，作为第44届联合国大会第35项的议题，(使之成为)联合国大会和安理会的官方文件进行传播，英国政府会将本联合声明提交欧共体主席与欧共体委员会，相应地，阿根廷政府会将本联合声明提交美洲国家组织。

(18)最后，两国代表对西班牙政府的慷慨款待和支持表示感谢。

3. UK-Argentina Joint Statement on the Conservation of Fisheries

1) The Government of the Argentine Republic and the Government of the United Kingdom of Great Britain and Northern Ireland agreed that the following formula on sovereignty, contained in the Joint Statement issued at Madrid on 19 October 1989, applies to this Statement and its results:

(1) Nothing in the conduct or content of the present meeting or of any similar subsequent meetings shall be interpreted as:

(a) a change in the position of the United Kingdom with regard to sovereignty or territorial and maritime jurisdiction over the Falkland Islands, South Georgia and the South Sandwich Islands and the surrounding maritime areas;

(b) a change in the position of the Argentine Republic with regard to sovereignty or territorial and maritime jurisdiction over the Falkland Islands, South Georgia and the South Sandwich Islands and the surrounding maritime areas;

(c) recognition of or support for the position of the United Kingdom or the Argentine Republic with regard to sovereignty or territorial and maritime jurisdiction over the Falkland Islands, South Georgia and the South Sandwich Islands and the surrounding maritime areas.

(2) No act or activity carried out by the United Kingdom, the Argentine Republic or third parties as a consequence and in implementation of anything agreed to in the present meeting or in any similar subsequent meetings shall constitute a basis for affirming, supporting, or denying the position of the United Kingdom or Argentine Republic regarding the sovereignty or territorial and maritime jurisdiction over the Falkland Island, South Georgia and the South Sandwich Islands and the surrounding maritime areas.

2) In order to contribute to the conservation of fish stocks, the two Governments agreed to open the way for cooperation in this field on an ad-hoc basis; this will be done:

(a) by means of the establishment of the "South Atlantic Fisheries Commission", composed of delegations from both states, to assess the state of fish stocks in the South Atlantic in accordance with paragraph 7 of the Joint Statement issued at Madrid on 15 February 1990;

(b) by means of the temporary total prohibition of commercial fishing by vessels of any flag in the maritime area defined in the Annex to this Joint Statement, for conservation purposes.

The two Governments further agreed to review this Joint Statement annually, in particular the duration of the total prohibition.

3) The Commission will be composed of a delegation from each of the two states, and will meet at least twice a year, alternately in Buenos Aires and London. Recommendations shall be reached by mutual agreement. In accordance with paragraph 7 of the Madrid Joint Statement of 15 February 1990, the maritime area which the Commission will consider in relation to the conservation of the most significant off-shore species will be waters between latitude 45S and latitude 60S.

4) The Commission will have the following functions:

(a) In accordance with paragraph 7 of the Joint Statement issued at Madrid on 15 February 1990, to receive from both States the available information on the operations of the fishing fleets, appropriate catch and effort statistics and analyses of the status of the stocks of the most significant off-shore species. Both governments will provide such information in the form recommended by the Commission.

(b) To assess the information received and to submit to both Governments recommendations for the conservation of the most significant off-shore species in the area.

(c) To propose to both Governments joint scientific research work on the most significant off-shore species.

(d) In accordance with international law, to recommend to both Governments possible actions for the conservation in international waters of migratory and straddling stocks and species related to them.

(e) To monitor the implementation of the prohibition and make recommendations in this regard to both Governments.

5) The prohibition in paragraph 2(b) will take effect on 26 December 1990; both Governments agreed to cooperate in order to implement it.

6) Each Government will take the appropriately related administrative measures in accordance with this Joint Statement.

资料来源：David Freestone, UK/Argentina Co-operation on Fisheries Conservation, International Journal of Estuarine and Coastal Law, Vol. 145, No. 6, 1991, pp. 146-148。

ANNEX

The area referred to in paragraph 2 (b) is the one encompassed by the lines of the type specified in the second column, joining points in the first column defined to the nearest minute of arc on WGS 72 Datum by coordinates of Latitude and Longitude in the order given.

Column 1	Column 2
Coordinates of Latitude and Longitude	Line Type
1. 47° 42′S, 60° 41′W	1-2 rhumb line along meridian.
2. 49° 00′S, 60° 41′W	2-3 parallel of latitude.
3. 49° 00′S, 60° 55′W	3-4 rhumb line along meridian.
4. 49° 20′S, 60° 55′W	4-5 arc of the circle which has a radius of 150 nautical miles and its center at Latitude 51° 40′ S, Longitude 59° 30′W, moving clockwise.
5. 54° 02′S, 58° 13′W	5-6 rhumb line
6. 54° 38′S, 58° 02′W	6-7 meridian
7. 55° 30′S, 58° 02′W	7-8 rhumb line
8. 56° 14′S, 58° 31′W	8-9 a line draw anti-clockwise along the maximum limit of jurisdiction over fisheries in accordance with international law.
9. 47° 42′S, 60° 41′W	

The area mentioned above is described for the sole purpose of the total prohibition in paragraph 2（b）of this Joint Statement and, in particular, the formula on sovereignty in paragraph 1 of this Joint Statement applies to it.

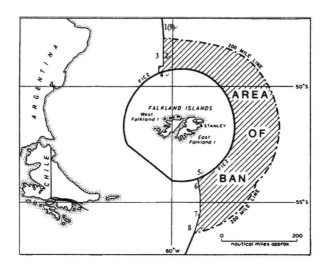

资料来源：David Freestone, UK/Argentina Co-operation on Fisheries Conservation, *International Journal of Estuarine and Coastal Law*, Vol. 145, No. 6, 1991, p. 150。

4.《联合王国和阿根廷关于渔业保护的共同声明》

王阳 译　陈思静、梅玉婕 校

1) 阿根廷共和国政府与大不列颠及北爱尔兰联合王国政府同意，基于两国在 1989 年 10 月发布的"马德里共同声明"中所包含的下述主权方案，适用于本声明及其结果：

(1)此会议和任何后续类似会议之行为和内容不应当解释为：

(a)改变联合王国对于福克兰群岛、南乔治亚和南桑威奇群岛及周边海域所享有的主权或者领土以及海域管辖权的立场。

(b)改变阿根廷共和国对于福克兰群岛、南乔治亚和南桑威奇群岛及周边海域所享有的主权或者领土以及海域管辖权的立场。

(c)承认或者支持联合王国或者阿根廷共和国对于福克兰群岛、南乔治亚和南桑威奇群岛及周边海域所享有的主权或者领土以及海域管辖权的立场。

(2)联合王国、阿根廷共和国或者第三方在执行本会议或者后续类似会议的任何协定，或者作为本会议及后续类似会议结果的行为或者活动，均不应当构成对于联合王国或者阿根廷共和国就福克兰群岛、南乔治亚和南桑威奇群岛及周边海域所享有的主权或者领土以及海域管辖权立场的确认、支持或者反对。

2) 在临时安排的基础上，为使保护渔业资源有所裨益，两国政府同意在这一领域首开先河，合作将会以下列方式展开：

(a)依据 1990 年 2 月 15 日两国在马德里达成的共同声明第 7 段，通过建立由两国代表组成的"南大西洋渔业委员会"的方式，在南大西洋评估渔业储量状况；

(b)在本共同声明附件中，通过划定禁渔区的方式，禁止悬挂任何国家国旗的渔船在该区域进行商业性捕鱼，从而保护渔业资源。

两国政府同意在未来对该声明进行年度审查，特别是禁渔的期限。

3）委员会由两国代表组成，每年至少会晤两次，会晤在布宜诺斯艾利斯和伦敦轮流举行。委员会的建议由双方共同协议确定。根据 1990 年 2 月 15 日"马德里共同声明"第 7 段，为保护珍稀近海种群，委员会将会制定保护措施，该措施的适用范围是南纬 45°至南纬 60°的区域。

4）委员会的职能有：

（a）依据两国在 1990 年 2 月 15 日达成的"马德里共同声明"第 7 段，接收可用信息，（这些信息）包括两国渔船运营、适度捕捞的数据、珍稀近海物种储量现状分析的信息。两国会以建议的方式通过委员会提供上述信息。

（b）评估收集的信息，为保护区域内珍稀近海物种，向两国政府提出建议。

（c）向两国政府提议，对珍稀近海物种进行联合科学研究。

（d）根据国际法，在国际水域内，为保护迁徙和回溯鱼类种群以及与该种群相关的物种，就可能采取的行动向两国政府提出建议。

（e）监督禁令的执行，并就此向两国政府提出建议。

5）本声明第 2 段 b 项所规定之禁令将在 1990 年 12 月 26 日生效，为执行该禁令，两国政府同意开展合作。

6）依据本声明，两国政府将采取相关适当的行政措施。

附　　件

共同声明第 2 段 b 项规定之区域，是由第 2 列的线按照第 1 列的点，依照附件中提供的点的经纬度顺序，由 WGS72 坐标系上最近的弧线连接而成。

第 1 列 点的经纬度坐标	第 2 列 线的种类
1. 南纬 47 度 42 分　西经 60 度 41 分	1-2 沿着经度的恒向线
2. 南纬 49 度　　西经 60 度 41 分	2-3 纬线
3. 南纬 49 度　　西经 60 度 55 分	3-4 沿着经度的恒向线
4. 南纬 49 度 20 分　西经 60 度 55 分	4-5 以南纬 51 度 40 分 西经 59 度 30 分为圆心，以 150 海里为半径顺时针所画出的半圆

续表

第 1 列	第 2 列
点的经纬度坐标	线的种类
5. 南纬 54 度 02 分　西经 53 度 18 分	5-6 恒向线
6. 南纬 54 度 38 分　西经 58 度 02 分	6-7 经线
7. 南纬 55 度 30 分　西经 58 度 02 分	7-8 恒向线
8. 南纬 56 度 14 分　西经 58 度 31 分	8-9 根据国际法以逆时针方式画出的渔业
9. 南纬 47 度 42 分　西经 60 度 41 分	管辖的最大范围

划定上述区域的唯一目标是落实共同声明第 2 段 b 项之禁渔规定，特别需要明确的是，共同声明第 1 段规定的主权方案适用于这一区域。

5. Joint Declaration of 27 September 1995 Cooperation Over Offshore Activities in the South West Atlantic

1）The Government of the United Kingdom of Great Britain and Northern Ireland and the Government of the Argentine Republic agreed that the following formula on sovereignty, based on that contained in the Joint Statement issued at Madrid on 19 October 1989, applies to this Joint Declaration and to its results:

（1）Nothing in the content of the present Joint Declaration or of any similar subsequent Joint Statements and meetings shall be interpreted as:

（a）a change in the position of the United Kingdom with regard to sovereignty or territorial and maritime jurisdiction over the Falkland Islands, South Georgia and the South Sandwich Islands and the surrounding maritime areas.

（b）a change in the position of the Argentine Republic with regard to sovereignty or territorial and maritime jurisdiction over the Falkland Islands, South Georgia and the South Sandwich Islands and the surrounding maritime areas.

（c）recognition of or support for the position of the United Kingdom or the Argentine Republic with regard to sovereignty or territorial and maritime jurisdiction over the Falkland Islands, South Georgia and the South Sandwich Islands and the surrounding maritime areas.

(2) No act or activity carried out by the United Kingdom, the Argentine Republic or third parties as a consequence and in implementation of anything agreed to in the present Joint Declaration or in any similar subsequent Joint Statements and meetings shall constitute a basis for affirming, supporting, or denying the position of the United Kingdom or the Argentine Republic regarding the sovereignty or territorial and maritime jurisdiction over the Falkland Islands, South Georgia and the South Sandwich Islands and the surrounding maritime areas. The areas subject to the controversy on sovereignty and jurisdiction will not be extended in any way as a consequence of this Joint Declaration or its implementation.

This Joint Declaration does not apply to the maritime areas surrounding South Georgia and the South Sandwich Islands.

2) The two Governments agreed to cooperate in order to encourage offshore activities in the South West Atlantic in accordance with the provisions contained herein. Exploration for and exploitation of hydrocarbons by the offshore oil and gas industry will be carried out in accordance with sound commercial principles and good oil field practice, drawing on the Governments' experience both in the South West Atlantic and in the North Sea. Cooperation will be furthered:

(a) by means of the establishment of a Joint Commission, composed of delegations from both sides;

(b) by means of coordinated activities in up to 6 tranches, each of 3,500 square kilometers, the first ones to be situated within the sedimentary structure as identified in the Annex.

3) The Commission will be composed of a delegation from each of the two states, and will meet at least twice a year. Recommendations shall be reached by mutual agreement.

4) The Commission will have the following functions:

(a) to submit to both Government recommendations and proposed standards for the protection of the marine environment of the South West Atlantic, taking into account relevant international conventions and recommendations of competent international organizations.

(b) to coordinate activities in the tranches referred to in paragraph 2(b) above, as areas for special cooperation. This will be done by the establishment of a subcommittee which shall meet regularly, subordinate to the Commission, charged with:

(i) encouraging commercial activities in each tranche by means such as joint ventures and consortia from the two sides;

(ii) seeking nominations from companies for each tranche, to be offered upon terms appropriate for a challenging environment;

(iii) making recommendations on proposals made to the two Governments by companies for development projects in each tranche, including the limits of the tranches;

(iv) seeking close coordination in regard to all aspects of future operations, including the overall level of fees, royalties, charges and taxes, the harmonization of timing, commercial terms and conditions, and compliance with the recommended standards;

(v) recommending on the basis of geological data known to both sides, additional tranches either within the sedimentary structure referred to in the Annex or in a further area to be agreed by the Governments on the recommendation of the Commission;

(c) to promote the exploration for and exploitation of hydrocarbons in maritime areas of the South West Atlantic subject to a controversy on sovereignty and jurisdiction, and to this end:

(i) to promote cooperation between industry on both sides, including the formation of joint ventures and the elaboration of joint projects for exploration, production and use of infrastructure;

(ii) to receive from both sides and from operating companies the available information on scientific research, development of activities and commercial operations relating to the seabed, whilst respecting commercial confidentiality;

(iii) to propose to both Governments coordinated research work by commercial undertakings;

(iv) to submit to both Governments recommendations for standards for offshore activities in safety, health and monitoring;

Both Governments will take the appropriate measures in order to ensure that the companies will keep the Commission informed on the development of their activities;

(d) on the basis of geological data known to both sides, to propose to the two Governments at the appropriate time further areas of special cooperation, on terms similar to those contained in paragraph 4 (b) above;

(e) to consider and submit recommendations to the two Governments on any related matter which may arise in the future, including the possible need to agree on the unitization of any discoveries in accordance with good oil field practice, on pipeline operations and on the efficient use of infrastructure.

5) The arrangements regarding search and rescue set out in the Joint Statements of 25 September 1991 and 12 July 1993 or any future arrangements between the Parties on the same subject will apply to offshore activities. Civilian helicopter traffic will be the subject of future discussion.

6) Each Government will take the appropriately related administrative measures in accordance with this Joint Declaration for the exploration for and exploitation of hydrocarbons in the areas referred to in paragraph 4 above. They agreed that such measures regulating the activities of the companies would be subject to the formula on sovereignty in paragraph 1 above. The Parties will create the conditions for substantial participation in the activities by companies from the two sides. The Parties will communicate to each other relevant information relating to the conduct of exploration and exploitation activities in the areas. Both Parties agreed to abstain from taking action or imposing

conditions designed or tending to inhibit or frustrate the possibility of carrying out hydrocarbons development in the areas.

7) In order to implement the different arrangements in this Joint Declaration, which form an interdependent whole, the two Governments agreed to cooperate throughout the different stages of offshore activities undertaken by commercial operators, including the regime for the eventual abandonment of installations.

For the United Kingdom For the Argentine Republic

New York, 27 September 1995

(Signed by The Right Horourable Malcolm Rifkind MP for Britain and His. Excellency Dr. Guido Di Tella for the Argentine Republic)

资料来源：福克兰群岛协会网站，http：//www. fiassociation. com/shopimages/ pdfs/7. %201995% 20Joint% 20Declaration% 20on% 20Cooperation% 20Over% 20Offshore%20Activities%20in%20the%20South%20West%20Atlantic. pdf。

ANNEX TO JOINT DECLARATION DATED 27 SEPTEMBER 1995

Special Area

The Area is bounded by line of the type described in Column 2 joining the points defined to the nearest minute of arc by coordinates of latitude and longitude on WGS 72 Datum specified in Column 1.

Column 1	Column 2
Coordinates of Latitude and Longitude	Line Type
1. 52° 00′S, 63° 36′W	1-2 meridian
2. 53° 10′S, 63° 36′W	2-3 parallel of latitude
3. 53° 10′S, 62° 48′W	3-4 meridian
4. 53° 25′S, 62° 48′W	4-5 parallel of latitude
5. 53° 25′S, 61° 48′W	5-6 meridian
6. 53° 40′S, 61° 48′W	6-7 parallel of latitude
7. 53° 40′S, 61° 00′W	7-8 meridian
8. 53° 00′S, 61° 00′W	8-9 parallel of latitude

Column 1 Coordinates of Latitude and Longitude	Column 2 Line Type
9. 53° 00′S, 62° 00′W	9-10 meridian
10. 52° 30′S, 62° 00′W	10-11 parallel of latitude
11. 52° 30′S, 62° 36′W	11-12 meridian
12. 52° 00′S, 62° 36′W	12-13 parallel
13. 52° 00′S, 63° 36′W	

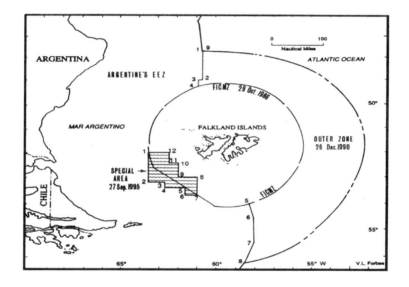

资料来源：Patrick Armstrong, Vivian Forbes, The Falkland Islands and their Adjacent Maritime Areas, *IBRU Maritime Briefing*, Vol. 2, No. 3, 1997, p. 15。

6.《1995 年 9 月 27 日关于西南大西洋近海活动合作的共同宣言》

王阳 译　陈思静、梅玉婕 校

1）阿根廷共和国政府与大不列颠及北爱尔兰联合王国政府同意，基于两国在 1989 年 10 月达成的"马德里共同声明"中所包含之下述主权方案，适用于本共同宣言及其结果。

(1)此会议及任何后续类似会议之行为与内容不应当解释为：

(a)改变联合王国对于福克兰群岛、南乔治亚和南桑威奇群岛及周边海域所享有的主权或者领土以及海域管辖权的立场。

(b)改变阿根廷共和国对于福克兰群岛、南乔治亚和南桑威奇群岛及周边海域所享有的主权或者领土以及海域管辖权的立场。

(c)承认或者支持联合王国或者阿根廷共和国对于福克兰群岛、南乔治亚和南桑威奇群岛及周边海域所享有的主权或者领土以及海域管辖权的立场。

(2)联合王国、阿根廷共和国或者第三方，在执行本共同宣言的过程中，共同宣言的任何规定，或者后续共同声明和会议，或者作为本共同宣言，以及后续共同声明和会议结果的行为或者活动，均不应当构成对于联合王国或者阿根廷共和国，就福克兰群岛、南乔治亚和南桑威奇群岛以及周边海域所享有的主权或者领土以及海域管辖权立场的确认、支持或者反对。本宣言及其执行结果所确立的主权和管辖权争议区域，不应以任何形式扩展。

本宣言对于南乔治亚和南桑威奇群岛及周边海域不予适用。

2)依据本宣言之规定，为鼓励西南大西洋近海活动，两国政府同意开展合作。对油气资源的勘探和开发将会依据合理的商业原则和良好采油实践，并在吸收英阿两国政府分别在北海和西南大西洋开发经验的基础上进行。双方合作将依据下列方式进一步深化：

(a)建立联合委员会，该委员会由两国代表组成；

(b)通过协调双方在六个区块活动的方式，每个区块面积约3500平方千米，第一个区块位于附件中所标识区域的沉积构造中。

3)委员会由双方代表组成，每年至少会晤两次。委员会所作的建议应当由双方协议达成。

4)委员会拥有以下职能：

(a)为保护西南大西洋海洋环境，在考虑相关国际条约和国际组织建议的基础上，向两国政府提出保护意见并提议相关标准。

(b)在本宣言2段b项所规定之特别合作区域内协调双方行动。这项工作将由隶属于联合委员会的次级委员会执行。该委员会应当定期会晤，其职能是：

（ⅰ）在每个区块内通过设立合营公司的方式鼓励双方的商业性活动；

（ⅱ）为选定每一区块内的合营公司，寻求在候选公司中提名，所提名的公司为适当保护环境提供相应条件；

（ⅲ）为每一区块内合营公司项目的运营，包括区块范围，对两国政府提出的方案提供建议；

（ⅳ）在未来运营的所有方面中寻求紧密合作，包括总体费用、特许使用费、运费、税款、以及时间的协调，商业性条款及条件，推荐标准的使用；

（ⅴ）基于双方已知的地理数据，在附件中规定沉积构造的区域范围内，或者未来两国政府根据联合委员会的建议所达成的相关区域，就(区块的选择)作出推荐。

（c）为促进西南大西洋主权和管辖权争议海域内油气资源的勘探和开发，两国的目标是：

（ⅰ）促进双方产业合作，包括合营公司的组成，以及为开发、生产和基础设施的使用为目的，进行的合营项目的运营；

（ⅱ）从两国政府和合营公司获取有用信息，包括与海床有关的科学研究、活动开展和商业运营的信息，并遵守商业秘密；

（ⅲ）建议两国政府通过商业企业开展研究工作；

（ⅳ）为保证海洋活动安全、健康、有序进行，向双方政府提出建议。

为确保运营公司就开发活动向委员会尽速通知，两国政府将会采取适当措施。

（d）在双方已知的地理数据的基础上，建议两国政府，根据类似本声明第 4 段 b 项之内容，在适当时间促进未来特别区域内的合作；

（e）考虑未来可能出现的任何问题，向两国政府提出建议，（这些建议)包括根据良好采油实践、管道运营和基础设施有效利用所达成的，就所有探明油气资源进行统一运营的可能需求。

5）两国在 1991 年 9 月 25 日和 1993 年 7 月 12 日共同声明中所达成的搜救安排，或者双方在未来就相同事项达成的安排，将适用于近海活动。民用直升机活动将是未来两国讨论的主题。

6）为勘探和开发油气资源，两国政府将在本宣第 4 段规定的区域内，采取相关适当的管理措施。双方同意，这种规制公司活动的措施，将会服从本宣言第 1 段所达成的主权方案。双方将对来自两国实际参与开发活动的公司创造条件。对于在特别区域内勘探和开发活动有关的信息，双方将会互相交流。双方同意，避免采取扰乱或影响未来在特别区域内油气活动的开展行动，或者施加（此类）先决条件，或者避免（此类）趋势的出现。

7）为了执行本共同宣言中的不同安排，这些安排构成了相互依赖的整体，两国政府同意通过商业运营者承担不同阶段的开发活动，进行合作。这一合作（的内容）包括最终拆除设施的制度。

联合王国和阿根同共和国

1995 年 9 月 27 日于纽约

由马尔科姆·里夫金德议员代表联合王国签署

由迪特利亚博士阁下代表阿根廷共和国签署

《1995 年 9 月 27 日共同宣言的附件》

特别区域

特别区域由第 2 列中的经线和纬线，按照第 1 列中的坐标依次连接构成，第 1 列中各点的位置由 WGS84 坐标系确定。

第 1 列 点的经纬度坐标	第 2 列 线的种类
1. 南纬 52 度，西经 63 度 36 分	1-2　经线
2. 南纬 53 度 10 分，西经 63 度 36 分	2-3　纬线
3. 南纬 53 度 10 分，西经 62 度 48 分	3-4　经线
4. 南纬 53 度 25 分，西经 62 度 48 分	4-5　纬线
5. 南纬 53 度 25 分，西经 61 度 48 分	5-6　经线
6. 南纬 53 度 40 分，西经 61 度 48 分	6-7　纬线
7. 南纬 53 度 40 分，西经 61 度	7-8　经线
8. 南纬 53 度，西经 61 度	8-9　纬线
9. 南纬 53 度，西经 62 度	9-10　经线
10. 南纬 52 度 30 分，西经 62 度	10-11　纬线
11. 南纬 52 度 30 分，西经 63 度 36 分	11-12　经线
12. 南纬 52 度，西经 62 度 36 分	12-13　纬线
13. 南纬 52 度，西经 63 度 36 分	

7. Declaration of the British Government with regard to the Joint Declaration signed by the British and Argentine Foreign Ministers on Cooperation over Offshore Activities in the South West Atlantic

The British Government welcomes the understanding reached with Argentina on cooperation over offshore activities in the South West Atlantic.

The understanding will facilitate mutually beneficial cooperation, promoting the development of hydrocarbons. It will further improve relations with Argentina since the Madrid Joint Statement of February 1990 [which reestablished diplomatic relations]. At the same time, it will offer commercial opportunities to British companies, as well as to the Falkland Islands which will launch a licensing round in October.

The Joint Declaration safeguards British sovereignty and jurisdiction over the Falkland Islands and the surrounding maritime areas. HMG have no doubts about the sovereignty and jurisdiction of the UK.

HMG are aware that Argentina proposed to enact legislation purporting to impose charges on companies working in maritime areas surrounding the Falkland Islands. HMG do not accept any Argentine claim to impose such charges on companies by reason only of their activities on the continental shelf around the Falkland Islands under Falklands license. HMG will be working with the Falkland Islands Government in development of the forthcoming licensing round. We welcome the understanding as a beneficial factor which will reassure the oil industry and improve the climate for exploration for and exploitation of hydrocarbons in a frontier area.

Appropriate legislation will be introduced in order to take account of the Joint Declaration, including a new Ordinance in the Falkland Islands.

资料来源：福克兰群岛协会网站，http：//www.fiassociation.com/shopimages/pdfs/7.％201995％ 20Joint％ 20Declaration％ 20on％ 20Cooperation％ 20Over％ 20Offshore％ 20Activities％ 20in％ 20the％ 20South％ 20West％ 20Atlantic..pdf。

8.《英国政府关于〈英国与阿根廷外交部长签订有关在西南大西洋近海活动合作的共同宣言〉之宣言》

王阳 译　陈思静、梅玉婕 校

英国政府对于与阿根廷政府达成的，在西南大西洋进行近海活动合作的谅解表示欢迎。

此谅解将便利两国互利合作，促进油气资源开发。自 1990 年 2 月"马德里声明"（该声明恢复两国外交关系）签署以来，它将进一步促进两国关系的提升。同时，该谅解将向英国公司和福克兰群岛提供商业机遇，与油气资源开发相关的招标许可程序将于（1995 年）十月份启动。

共同宣言保障了英国对于福克兰群岛及其周边海域的主权和管辖权。女王陛下政府对联合王国拥有这一主权和管辖权确信无疑。

女王陛下政府注意到阿根廷政府拟颁布法令，向在福克兰群岛附近海域作业的英国公司收取费用。阿根廷政府认为这些公司在福克兰群岛大陆架上的活动仅得到了福克兰群岛政府的许可，女王陛下政府不接受阿根廷的这一主张。女王陛下政府将会在即将到来的招标许可阶段，与福克兰群岛政府进行合作。该谅解作为有利因素，有利于消除石油产业（经营者）的疑虑，并改善勘探和开发油气资源的氛围，女王陛下政府对之表示欢迎。

女王陛下政府拟根据该宣言颁布相关法律，包括在福克兰群岛（颁布）一项新的法律。

9. Statement by the Argentine Government with regard to the Joint Declaration signed by the Foreign Ministers of Argentina and the United Kingdom on Exploration and Exploitation of Hydrocarbons

The Argentine Government welcomes the achievement of an understanding with the United Kingdom on matters concerning cooperation over exploration and exploitation of hydrocarbons in the maritime areas subject to a dispute of sovereignty in the South West Atlantic.

That understanding will preserve the cordial relations existing between the two countries at the current high level. At the same time, it will offer commercial opportunities to Argentine companies, and it will contribute to the economic prosperity of the country, particularly in the Patagonian region.

The understanding safeguards the imprescriptible rights of the Argentine Republic over the Malvina Islands, South Georgia and South Sandwich Islands and their surrounding maritime areas, as it emerges from the text of the declaration, and as it shall be reflected by the implementation of its dispositions. As both parties have convened, it shall not be interpreted in any way as recognition or support of the position of the United Kingdom in respect of sovereignty over the referred Islands or the surrounding maritime areas.

On the basis of this understanding, the Argentine Republic shall benefit, without prejudice to its legitimate rights, of the activities to be carried out in the areas subject to the dispute of sovereignty, through a provisional *modus vivendi* until both parties resolve that dispute by the peaceful means established by international law. The benefits to be perceived shall be related to the exploration areas or the volumes of hydrocarbons produced. In accordance with paragraph 6 of the Joint

Declaration, the Executive Power shall introduce in the Honorable National Congress nondiscriminatory legislation which will impose charges on national and foreign companies operating in the area to the benefit of the nation. The understanding and its implementation do not imply and shall not be interpreted in any way as an acceptance of a claimed right to call a licensing round for the development of hydrocarbons in the maritime areas surrounding the Malvinas Islands.

The Executive Power considers that the assistance of the Honorable National Congress is absolutely necessary in order to make the present Declaration operative. To this end it will introduce the pertinent bills for their legislative consideration.

资料来源：福克兰群岛协会网站，http：//www. fiassociation. com/shopimages/ pdfs/7. %201995% 20Joint% 20Declaration% 20on% 20Cooperation% 20Over% 20Offshore% 20Activities% 20in% 20the% 20South% 20West% 20Atlantic. . pdf。

10.《阿根廷政府关于〈阿根廷外交部长与英国签订有关油气勘探与开发共同宣言〉之声明》

王阳 译　陈思静、梅玉婕 校

阿根廷政府对于与英国政府达成的，关于在西南大西洋主权争议区域进行油气资源勘探和开发合作的谅解表示欢迎。

此谅解将在更高层面上，维持两国的友好关系。同时，它将向阿根廷公司提供商业机遇，并且能够促进阿根廷特别是巴塔哥尼亚地区的经济繁荣。

此谅解，正如宣言文本中体现，以及宣言执行中将会反映（的那样），保障了阿根廷共和国对于马尔维纳斯群岛、南乔治亚和南桑威奇群岛及其周边海域所享有的不可剥夺的权利。双方约定，该宣言将不会解释为以任何方式承认或支持英国对于上述岛屿及其附近海域的主权。

　　基于此谅解，在不损害阿根廷政府合法权益的基础上，依据国际法最终和平解决两国争端之前，通过两国达成的临时办法，阿根廷共和国将会受益于主权争议区域内活动的执行。预期利益将与开发区或油气资源的产量相关。根据共同宣言第 6 段，行政机关将会采用国民议会非歧视的立法，为国家利益计，该立法将(规定)，对在开发区域内作业的本国和外国公司收取费用。该谅解以及其未来的执行，将不会暗含及解释为，以任何方式接受(联合王国政府)为开发马尔维纳斯群岛附近海域的油气资源进行许招标的权利主张。

　　行政机关认为，为执行本宣言，接受国民议会的协助相当必要。为此目的，行政机关将会向立法机关提出相关立法建议。

十、1995 年丹麦与挪威共同开发案

Agreement between the Kingdom of Denmark and the Kingdom of Norway Concerning the Delimitation of the Continental Shelf in the Area Between Jan Mayen and Greenland and Concerning the Boundary Between the Fishery Zones in the Area. 18 December 1995

The Government of the Kingdom of Norway and the Government of the Kingdom of Denmark,

Referring to the Judgment of the International Court of Justice of 14 June 1993 in the case concerning maritime delimitation in the area between Greenland and Jan Mayen,

Having agreed to draw the delimitation line between the fishery zones and to delimit the continental shelf in accordance with that judgment,

Having in this connection completed a geodetic calculation of the delimitation criteria laid down by the Court,

Desiring to continue cooperation on reciprocal fisheries and on the flexible exploitation of the living marine resources in the area,

Having also agreed that a final determination of the further course of the delimitation line south of point No. 4 as specified in the Agreement must be effected in consultation with Iceland,

Have agreed as follows:

Article 1

The delimitation line between the Parties' parts of the continental shelf in the area between Greenland and Jan Mayen is established as straight lines between the following points, in the order indicated below:

Point No. 1: 74° 21' 46. 9″N   05° 00' 27. 7″ W

Point No. 2: 72° 49' 22. 2″N   11° 28' 28. 7″ W

Point No. 3: 71° 52' 50. 8″N   12° 46' 01. 3″ W

Point No. 4: 69° 54' 34. 4″N   13° 37' 46. 4″ W

All straight lines are geodetic lines.

The points listed above are defined by geographic latitude and longitude in accordance with the World Geodetic System 1984 (WGS84).

By way of illustration, the delimitation line and the points listed above have been drawn on the sketch-map annexed to this Agreement.

Article 2

If natural resources are discovered in or on the continental shelf of one of the Parties and the other Party is of the opinion that the said resources extend onto its continental shelf, the latter Party may by presenting the evidence on which the opinion is based, e. g. geological or geophysical data, submit this opinion to the first-mentioned Party.

If such an opinion is put forward, the Parties shall institute deliberations, at which the information available to both of the Parties is submitted, on the extent of the resources and the possibility of exploitation. If it is established in the course of these deliberations that the resources extend across both Parties' parts of the continental shelf and that the resources in one of the Parties' areas are exploitable, wholly or in part, from that of the other Party or that the exploitation of the resources in one of the Parties' areas would affect the possibility of exploiting the resources in that of the other Party, an agreement shall be made, at the request of either of the Parties, concerning exploitation of the said resources.

Article 3

The boundary between the fishery zone around Jan Mayen and the fishery zone around Greenland coincides with the delimitation line specified in article 1.

Article 4

This Agreement shall be signed and enters into force upon signature.

IN WITNESS WHEREOF the undersigned, being duly authorized by their respective Governments for that purpose, have signed the present Agreement.

DONE in duplicate at Oslo on 18 December 1995 in the Norwegian and Danish languages, both texts being equally authoritative.

资料来源：http：//www. un. org/depts/los/LEGISLATIONANDTREATIES/
PDFFILES/TREATIES/DNK-NOR 1995CS. PDF。

十一、1997 年丹麦与冰岛共同开发案

Agreement between the Government of the Kingdom of Denmark along with the Local Government of Greenland on the one hand, and the Government of the Republic of Iceland on the other hand on the Delimitation of the Continental Shelf and the Fishery Zone in the Area between Greenland and Iceland, 11 November 1997

The Government of the Kingdom of Denmark along with the Local Government of Greenland on the one hand and the Government of the Republic of Iceland on the other hand,

Wishing to maintain and strengthen the good-neighbourly relations between Denmark/Greenland and Iceland,

Have agreed as follows:

Article 1

The boundary line between the Parties' parts of the continental shelf and the fishery zone in the area between Greenland and Iceland is based on the median line between the relevant coastlines of Greenland and Iceland together with the negotiating results of 28 June 1997 and is fixed as straight lines between the following points in the order which is indicated below:

    A. 69°35′. 0″N   13°16′. 0″W

    B. 69°21′. 4″N   13°33′. 6″W

    C. 69°05′. 1″N   15°21′. 3″W

D. 69°03′.0″N   15°45′.1″W

E. 68°45′.8″N   17°20′.2″W

F. 68°24′.5″N   20°00′.0″W

G. 68°08′.2″N   21°45′.0″W

H. 67°49′.5″N   23°21′.6″W

I. 67°37′.8″N   24°26′.5″W

J. 67°22′.9″N   25°36′.0″W

K. 67°03′.9″N   26°33′.4″W

L. 66°57′.3″N   26°59′.7″W

M. 66°38′.4″N   27°45′.9″W

N. 66°12′.7″N   28°58′.7″W

O. 65°13′.0″N   29°51′.4″W

P. 63°55′.4″N   30°34′.9″W

Q. 63°18′.8″N   30°51′.8″W

All straight lines are geodesic lines. The agreed-upon line is defined by geographic latitude and longitude in accordance with the World Geodesic System 1984 (WGS84). The line shall be subject to a technical revision before 1 January 1999.

By way of illustration, the boundary line and the above-mentioned points have been drawn on the sketch map annexed to this Agreement.

(1)The boundary point A has been established in cooperation with the Kingdom of Norway and shall be confirmed through bilateral agreements with the Government of the Kingdom of Norway

Article 2

If natural resources are found in or on the continental shelf of one of the Parties and the other Party is of the opinion that the resources extend onto its continental shelf, the latter Party may, by presenting the evidence upon which the opinion is based, e. g. , geological or geophysical data, submit this to the first-mentioned Party.

If such an opinion is submitted, the Parties shall initiate discussions on the extent of the resources and the possibility for exploitation, with a presentation of each of the Parties' information hereon. If it is established during these discussions that the resources extend across both Parties' parts of the continental shelf and also that the resources in the area of one Party can be exploited wholly or in part from the area of the other Party or that the exploitation of the resources in the area of one Party would affect the possibility of exploitation of the resources in the area of the other Party, an agreement concerning the exploitation of the resources shall be made at the request of one of the Parties.

Article 3

This Agreement is without prejudice to other delimitation questions between the Kingdom of Denmark and the Republic of Iceland.

Article 4

This Agreement shall enter into force when the Parties have informed each other in writing that the necessary procedures have been concluded. However, the provision on the coordinates of boundary point A shall only enter into force when the Government of the Kingdom of Norway has informed the Parties in writing that the determination of that point has been confirmed.

DONE at Helsinki on 11 November 1997 in duplicate in the Danish and Icelandic languages, both texts being equally authentic.

For the Government   For the Local Government   For the Government of the

of the Kingdom of Denmark   of Greenland   Republic of Iceland

资料来源：http：//www. un. org/depts/los/LEGISLATIONANDTREATIES/PDFFILES/TREATIES/DNK-ISL1997CS. PDF。

十二、2000 年尼日利亚与赤道几内亚共同开发案

Treaty between the Federal Republic of Nigeria and the Republic of Equatorial Guinea concerning Their Maritime Boundary, 23 September 2000

The Governments of the Federal Republic of Nigeria and the Republic of Equatorial Guinea,

CONSIDERING that they are moved by the desire to strengthen the strong and brotherly relations between them as neighboring countries and to preserve peace in their relations and on the African continent,

DESIRING to establish the boundary between their respective exclusive economic zones to the south and west of Point (i) described in Article 2 below,

INTENDING subsequently to establish the further sector of the maritime boundary to the north and east of the said Point (i),

THE TWO PRESIDENTS declare their will to conclude this maritime boundary delimitation Treaty that safeguards the sovereign rights and economic interests of each country in accordance with the international law of the sea, and to that end

HAVE AGREED as follows:

Article 1

The purpose of this Treaty is to establish the partial maritime boundary between the Federal Republic of Nigeria and the Republic of Equatorial Guinea described in Article 2, and provide for the remainder of the maritime boundary in accordance with Article 3.

Article 2

Southwards and westwards from Point (i) identified below, the maritime boundary between the Federal Republic of Nigeria and the Republic of Equatorial Guinea shall be constituted by successive straight lines connecting the following points:

(i) Latitude 4° 01'37. 0"N, Longitude 8° 16'33. 0"E

(ii) Latitude 3° 53'01. 8"N, Longitude 8° 04'10. 7"E

(iii) Latitude 3° 51'54. 8"N, Longitude 8° 04'58. 9"E

(iv) Latitude 3° 51'20. 2"N, Longitude 8° 04'04. 0"E

(v) Latitude 3° 52'25. 8"N, Longitude 8° 03'18. 5"E

(vi) Latitude 3° 42'37. 0"N, Longitude 7° 49'10. 0"E

(vii) Latitude 3° 38'42. 4"N, Longitude 7° 49'10. 3"E

(viii) Latitude 3° 26'46. 5"N, Longitude 7° 35'40. 7"E

(ix) Latitude 3° 15'12. 0"N, Longitude 7° 22'. 35. 8"E

(x) Latitude 2° 52'10. 9"N, Longitude 7° 22'. 37. 8"E

Article 3

Northwards and eastwards from Point (i) identified in Article 2 the maritime boundary shall be established by the Contracting Parties, and recorded in a Protocol to this *Treaty*, following completion of the maritime aspects of the case before the International Court of Justice between the Federal Republic of Nigeria and the Republic of Cameroon, concerning the land and maritime frontier between them.

Article 4

North and west of the maritime boundary established by this Treaty, the Republic of Equatorial Guinea shall not claim or exercise sovereign rights or jurisdiction over the waters or seabed and subsoil. South and east of the maritime boundary established by this Treaty, the Federal Republic of Nigeria shall not claim or exercise sovereign rights or jurisdiction over the waters or seabed and subsoil.

Article 5

The geographic positions set forth in Article 2 are referenced to the *World Geodetic System 1984* (WGS-84). All lines referred to in Article 2 are geodetic lines.

Article 6

1. Should the maritime boundary established by this *Treaty* run through any field of hydrocarbon deposits so that part of the field lies on the Nigerian side of the boundary and part lies on the Equatorial Guinea side, the Contracting Parties shall seek to reach appropriate unitisation arrangements for each such field.

2. In implementing paragraph 1 of this Article within the area formed by straight lines connecting points (ii), (iii), (iv) and (v) set forth in Article 2, the Contracting Parties shall authorise the relevant government entities in association with the relevant concession holders to establish appropriate unitisation and other arrangements to enable this area to be developed in a commercially feasible manner. Such arrangements shall not be effective until the entry into force of this Treaty.

Article 7

1. This *Treaty* shall be subject to ratification.

2. This *Treaty* shall enter into force upon the exchange of the instruments of ratification.

3. Without prejudice to paragraph 2 of this Article, and subject to review if no arrangements have been agreed within a reasonable time in accordance with Article 6.2, this *Treaty* shall be provisionally applied as from today's date.

Article 8

As soon as possible after this Treaty has entered into force, it shall be registered with the Secretary General of the United Nations in accordance with Article 102 of the Charter of the United Nations.

Done at Malabo, the 23rd of September 2000, in two originals in each of the English and Spanish languages, both language texts being equally authoritative.

H. E. OLUSEGUN OBASANJO   H. E. OBIANG NGUEMA MBASOGO

President Federal Republic Nigeria   President Republic of Equatorial Guinea

资料来源: Treaty between the Federal Republic of Nigeria and the Republic of Equatorial Guinea concerning their maritime boundary, 23 September 2000, Federal Republic of Nigeria-the Republic of Equatorial Guinea, U. N. T. S. Vol. 2205, p. 325, https://treaties. un. org/doc/Publication/UNTS/Volume%202205/v2205. pdf。

十三、2010 年挪威与俄罗斯共同开发案

1. Joint Statement on Maritime Delimitation and Cooperation in the Barents Sea and the Arctic Ocean

Recognising our mutual determination to strengthen our good neighbourly relations, secure stability and enhance cooperation in the Barents Sea and the Arctic Ocean, we are pleased to announce that our negotiating delegations have reached preliminary agreement on the bilateral maritime delimitation between our two countries in these areas, which has been the object of extensive negotiations over the years.

As stated in the Ilulissat Declaration of the coastal States around the Arctic Ocean of 28 May 2008, both Norway and the Russian Federation are committed to the extensive legal framework applicable to the Arctic Ocean, as well as to the orderly settlement of any possible overlapping claims.

The negotiations have covered all the relevant issues concerning the maritime delimitation. The two delegations recommend, in addition to a maritime delimitation line, the adoption of treaty provisions that would maintain and enhance cooperation with regard to fisheries and management of hydrocarbon resources. A comprehensive Treaty concerning maritime delimitation and cooperation in the Barents Sea and the Arctic Ocean is thus envisaged. Such a Treaty shall not prejudice rights and obligations under other international treaties to which both the the Kingdom of Norway and the Russian Federation are parties.

The two delegations recommend a delimitation line on the basis of international law in order to achieve an equitable solution. In addition to the relevant factors identified in this regard in international law, including the effect of major disparities in respective coastal lengths, they have taken into account the progress achieved in the course of long-standing negotiations between the parties in order to reach agreement. They recommend a line that divides the overall disputed area in two parts of approximately the same size.

Bearing in mind the developments in the Arctic Ocean and the role of our two States in this region, they highlight the bilateral cooperation with regard to the determination of the outer limits of the continental shelf, in accordance with the United Nations Convention on the Law of the Sea.

In the field of fisheries, the two delegations underline the special economic importance of the living resources of the Barents Sea to Norway and the Russian Federation and to their coastal communities. The need to avoid any economic dislocation of coastal regions whose inhabitants have habitually fished in the area is stressed. Moreover, the traditional Norwegian and Russian fisheries in the Barents Sea are highlighted. They recall the primary interest and responsibility of Norway and the Russian Federation, as coastal States, for the conservation and rational management of the living resources of the Barents Sea and the Arctic Ocean, in accordance with international law. The conclusion of a Treaty on maritime delimitation and cooperation in the Barents Sea and the Arctic Ocean shall therefore not adversely affect the fishing opportunities of either State. To this end, provisions to the effect of continued close cooperation of the two States in the sphere of fisheries and preservation of relative stability of their fishing activities are recommended. The same applies to provisions concerning continued cooperation in the Norwegian-Russian Joint Fisheries Commission, as well as necessary transitional arrangements.

In the field of hydrocarbon cooperation, the two delegations recommend the adoption of detailed rules and procedures ensuring efficient and responsible management of their hydrocarbon resources in cases where any single oil or gas deposit should extend across the delimitation line.

Recalling our common desire to complete the maritime delimitation, we express our firm intention to take, in accordance with the requirements of the legislation of each State, all necessary measures to conclude a Treaty on Maritime Delimitation and Cooperation in the Barents Sea and the Arctic Ocean at the earliest possible date.

Oslo, 27 April 2010

Jonas Gahr Støre	Sergey Lavrov
Foreign Minister	Foreign Minister
of the Kingdom of Norway	of the Russian Federation

资料来源：挪威政府网站，https：//www. regjeringen. no/globalassets/ upload/ud/vedlegg/folkerett/030427_english_4. pdf。

2.《关于在巴伦支海和北冰洋海域划界与合作的联合声明》

陈思静 译　王阳、梅玉婕 校

认识到我们两国在巴伦支海和北冰洋增进睦邻友好关系、确保稳定和加强合作方面的共同决心，我们双方的代表很高兴地宣布，我们已经就巴伦支海的划界事宜——我们双方过去多年来广泛谈判的目标，达成了初步协定。

正如 2008 年 5 月 28 日环北冰洋沿岸国家在《伊卢利萨特宣言》中所声明的那样，挪威和俄罗斯联邦承诺，遵守适用于北冰洋的广泛法律框架，也将致力于可能的重叠(海域)主张的有序处理。

磋商涉及海域划界的所有相关问题。双方代表建议，除划界外，将会草拟相关条款，维持和提升双方在渔业和油气资源方面的合作。如此，将会缔结一个涉及巴伦支海和北冰洋海域划界与合作的综合性条约。对于挪威王国和俄罗斯联邦作为当事国的其他条约，这一条约，并不损害挪威王国和俄罗斯联邦依其他条约而享有的权利、承担的义务。

为达成一项公平的解决方案,双方的代表依照国际法提出了一项划界线的建议。除国际法已经承认的划界线因素(包括双方海岸线长度的不成比例)外,双方还考虑到在长期谈判过程中,为达成协议而采取的立场。他们提出的划界线建议,将所有的争议区域划为面积大致相等的两部分。

考虑到北冰洋的发展以及两国在北冰洋的角色,他们特别强调,依照《联合国海洋法公约》,进行外大陆架划界的双边合作。

在渔业领域,双方代表强调巴伦支海的生物资源对于两国及其沿岸的居民具有特殊的经济重要性。(双方也)强调,需要避免巴伦支海两岸长期捕鱼的渔民的经济利益出现任何失衡。此外,还应对俄罗斯与挪威的传统渔业予以重视。两国忆及,作为沿岸国,依据国际法,他们有养护、合理利用巴伦支海和北冰洋生物资源的重要利益和责任。因此,划界条约的缔结、北冰洋和巴伦支海的合作,将不会损害双方的捕鱼机会。为此目的,两国建议加入在渔业领域持续紧密合作、保证他们渔业活动相对稳定的规定。这些规定,对两国在挪威——俄罗斯渔业委员会中的持续合作也适用,对必要的过渡协议也同样适用。

在油气资源合作领域,两国代表提议,制定详细的规则和程序,确保在单一地质矿藏跨越两国大陆架划界线时,可以进行有效的、负责任的管理。

忆及我们完成海域划界的共同愿望,我们表达我们的坚定意向,依据两国国内法的要求,采取所有必要的措施,尽早订立一项在巴伦支海和北冰洋海域划界与合作的协定。

奥斯陆,2010 年 5 月 27 日

约纳斯·加尔·斯特勒　　　　谢尔盖·拉夫罗夫

挪威外交部长　　　　　　　　俄罗斯联邦外交部长

十四、2001 年东帝汶与澳大利亚共同开发案

1. Timor Sea Designated Authority for the Joint Petroleum Development Area "Guidelines for Applications for Production Sharing Contracts and Criteria for Assessment of Applications"

Introduction

This guideline is issued under Article 5 of the Petroleum Mining Code for the purpose of assisting companies in lodging applications for Production Sharing Contract Areas in the Joint Petroleum Development Area ('JPDA'). The terms used in this guideline have the same meaning as those used in the Petroleum Mining Code.

Guideline 1   Applications for Production Sharing Contracts

1) Application Details

Applications lodged under Article 5 of the *Petroleum Mining Code* must:

(a) be made in writing in triplicate on size A4 paper;

(b) be delivered in a sealed envelope marked strictly confidential;

(c) be made within the period specified in the official advertisement;

(d) include a fixed non-refundable processing fee of US $10, 000, payable to "The Timor Sea Designated Authority" at a bank nominated by the Designated Authority, for each Production Sharing Contract Area included in the application;

(e) be for one Contract Area , and all documents concerning the application shall be clearly identified as pertaining to an application for a certain Contract Area, and a company (or any company that controls it) cannot be, directly or indirectly, part of more than one bid for a certain Contract Area;

(f) include a summary of their application in the form of a table; and

(g) be submitted via secure delivery to the Darwin Office of the Timor Sea Designated Authority ('TSDA'), located at Level 8, 22 Mitchell Street, Darwin, NT, 0801 or the Dili Office of the TSDA located at No. 5 Avenida de Portugal, Farol, Dili, Timor-Leste.

2) Application Content

Applications must contain the following information:

(1) Technical Assessment

(a) the applicant's assessment of the petroleum potential of the Contract Area, including a geological and geophysical review and technical assessment of the Contract Area, and the concepts underlying the proposed exploration work program and expenditure commitments;

(b) the applicant's proposed exploration Work Programme and Budget commitments for the first three (3) contract years covering data evaluation, seismic surveys and exploration wells to be drilled, on the basis that none of the items of the work program are conditional on the discovery of hydrocarbons. The first three (3) years of the proposal should only include work and expenditure expected to involve a substantial exploration component;

(c) the applicant's proposal (in terms of operational activity or estimated expenditure) for data evaluation, seismic surveys and exploration wells to be drilled, for each of the remaining four (4) years of the contract term.

(2) Particulars of the Applicant

(a) Documents and other relevant information concerning the legal details of the applicant (s) (including a certificate of incorporation or registration in the country of origin);

(b) the technical capability of the applicant including information on the relevant experience and expertise of the applicants relating to development work, research, safety, and work in difficult operating conditions, including (if applicable to the Contract Area) deepwater, high temperature or pressure operation and environmentally sensitive areas, and how this expertise and experience may contribute to the efficient exploration of, and the production of petroleum from, the Contract Area in question.

(c) the technical knowledge and ability of the corporation proposed as contract Operator and of its employees;

(d) the financial capability of the applicant, including evidence of the applicant's ability to fund the proposed work program and expenditure commitments, information on their short and long term financial commitments, and a copy of the last three (3) annual reports for each applicant company;

(e) where relevant, the viability of the consortium lodging the application, including evidence that a satisfactory agreement has been, or can be, reached on the joint operating agreement (a copy of a heads of agreement document will generally suffice), and the viability of the corporation appointed and authorised to be the contract Operator;

(f) details of the applicant corporation (s), the percentage participating interest of each corporation, the nominated contract Operator, and the contract Operator's address;

(g) any relationship that a director of an applicant company had with any company that had defaulted over the previous five (5) years;

(h) any permit, licence or contract cancellations, defaults on work program conditions or adverse criminal findings under relevant legislative schemes of any of the applicant companies (or any company in control of one of the applicant companies) over the previous five (5) years, and why the applicant believes the prior failure is irrelevant to the current application.

(3) Timor-Leste's Economic Development

(a) proposals for training, and giving preference in employment, to nationals and permanent residents of Timor-Leste;

(b) proposals for the acquisition of goods and services from persons based in Timor-Leste;

(c) proposals for the improvement of the technical capabilities of Timor-Leste through research to be undertaken in Timor-Leste;

(d) proposals for the transfer of technology and skills to Timor-Leste nationals and permanent residents;

(4) Health Safety and the Environment

(a) proposals for securing the health, safety and welfare of persons involved in petroleum activities;

(b) proposals for protecting the natural and marine environment, and for preventing, minimising and remedying pollution and other environmental harm;

(5) Other

(a) a statement that:

(i) the applicant acknowledges that acceptance of the model Production Sharing Contract terms and conditions is a prerequisite for making an application to bid;

(ii) the applicant accepts that the application is a formal offer that may be accepted by the Designated Authority to form a final Production Sharing Contract without any further negotiation with the applicant;

(b) proposals for insurance; and

(c) such other information as the applicant wishes to be taken into account in consideration of the application.

Guideline 2   Criteria for Assessment of Applications for Production Sharing Contracts

1) General

Companies will be expected to have taken into account all relevant information and any special conditions, such as those related to environment protection, applying in Contract Areas. All relevant information and details of special conditions will be made known to potential applicants by the Designated Authority when blocks forming Contract Areas are advertised.

2) Assessment Criteria

(a) The Designated Authority's key objective will be to identify the exploration work program bid which will best and expeditiously evaluate the petroleum potential of the Contract Area. The primary criteria for assessment of applications are therefore:

(i) acceptance of the Production Sharing Contract;

(ii) the substance and quality of exploration work in each of the first three contract years; and

(iii) the extent to which the first three (3) years' work program and expenditure commitments, including the drilling program, data evaluation and geophysical surveying activities, reflects the available technical information on exploration prospects in the Contract Area, seeks to follow up existing leads, and seeks to identify and evaluate new exploration prospects in previously unexplored parts of the Contract Area. The work program commitments and associated expenditure will be assessed by the Designated Authority on the basis of a detailed review of the objectives of the individual items of work proposed.

The Designated Authority will not negotiate changes to the work program bids in assessing those bids.

(b) The capacity of the applicant to undertake the proposed work program commitments will also be considered, particularly:

(i) the adequacy of financial capability and technical knowledge and ability available to each applicant:

(aa) the evaluation of financial capacity will be based on the company's annual reports or if they are providing a parent guarantee then an assessment of the parent company's annual report and any other publicly available information on the finances of those companies;

(bb) technical knowledge and ability will be assessed on the basis of company's performance in offshore operations or as appropriate on the company's financial capacity to acquire the necessary technological resources to work offshore; and

(ii) the future viability of any group of corporations lodging an application, including evidence that a joint operating agreement can be, or has been, reached between those corporations for cooperation in relation to petroleum activities in the Contract Area.

(c) The following additional criteria shall also be used to choose between the applications:

(i) the application which maxmises participation of Timor-Leste nationals involvement in petroleum exploration and associated and subsequent activities;

(ii) the extent to which the applicant undertakes to source goods and services in Timor-Leste,

and to transfer technology and skills to Timor-Leste nationals and permanent residents;

(iii) any undertaking by consortia members to research exploration techniques and technology

in Timor-Leste; and

(iv) the amount and quality of work proposed for contract years' four (4) to seven (7).

3) Process for Assessing Applications

(a) Applications will be assessed against the selection criteria by a panel of officials representing the Designated Authority. The panel will prepare a report for the Designated Authority containing recommendations as to the winning bid.

(b) Applications will be assessed on the basis of the information contained in the written applications together with any additional information requested by the Designated Authority, which should also be submitted in writing. Applicants may be invited to attend an interview with the assessment panel and information provided during that interview will also be taken into account.

(c) It should be noted that the composition and timing of the work program proposed in the original application as part of the competitive bidding process cannot be amended by the provision of additional information or through the interview process.

(d) In the event that a winning applicant cannot be chosen on the basis of the information contained in the written application and provided during interview, the two (2) or more parties that the Designated Authority considers as equally deserving of the grant of the Production Sharing Contract, will be invited to submit supplementary written bids as a basis for the selection of a successful applicant.

4) Refusal to Grant a Permit

Applicants should note that the Designated Authority is not obliged to award an Applicant a Production Sharing Contract and the re-release of acreage will be at the discretion of the Designated Authority in consultation with the Joint Commission.

2. Timor Sea Designated Authority for the Joint Petroleum Development Area "Interim Directions Issued under Article 37 of the Interim Petroleum Mining Code Specific Requirements as to Petroleum Exploration and Exploitation in the Joint Petroleum Development Area"

Part I Introductionry

Clause 101 Application of Directions

(1) These Directions are issued for the purpose of elaborating various parts of the Treaty and its Annexes, and the Interim Petroleum Mining Code.

(2) Where there is any inconsistency, the Treaty and its Annexes, and the Interim Petroleum Minig Code prevail.

Clause 102　Definitions

In these Directions unless inconsistent with the context or subject matter:

"approval" or "approved" means the approval of or approved by the Managing Director.

"Managing Director" is the person appointed by the Executive Director of the Designated Authority from time-to-time to be the Managing Director of the Technical Directorate responsible for petroleum activities in the JPDA

Part Ⅱ　Production Entitlements Including the Recovery of Investment Credits and Operating Costs

Division 1　General Requirements and Principles

Clause 201　Production Sharing Entitlements

(1) References to Sections, sub-sections and sub-paragraphs in this Part II, unless otherwise stated, are references to Sections, sub-sections and sub-paragraphs in the Production Sharing Contract.

(2) The contractor will be entitled to a share of petroleum production as provided in Section 7.

(3) Claims for recoverable investment credits and operating costs will be provided by the contract operator to the Designated Authority for the purpose of calculating the contractor's production entitlement from actual expenditures incurred, as follows:

(a) if the costs were incurred in any other currency than United States dollars, expenditure will be converted to United States dollars at the opening mid-rate quoted by the United States Federal Reserve Bank on the day on which the expenditure was paid.

（b）estimates of investment credits and operating costs may be applied on a monthly basis, pending the aggregation of actual quarterly or annual expenditure provided in sub-clause（c）below. Such estimates will be based on or be consistent with:

（i）approved exploration and work program and agreed budget of operating costs;

（ii）exploration, capital and non-capital cost estimates included in breakdowns to be provided by "company authority for expenditure"（CAFE）or company equivalent internal expenditure approval as advised to the Designated Authority by the contract operator;

（iii）anticipated disbursements predicted for the month.

（c）each quarter the contract operator will revise estimates of expenditure, referred to in sub-clause 3（b）above, to actual expenditure on the basis of actual expenditures disbursed and these expenditures will be reported in expenditure reports as provided in Clause 227.

（d）the contract operator will include only such expenditure as has been disbursed, rather than be accrued, in the books of account within a claim for a particular quarter or calendar year for the purpose of its inclusion in the calculation of the contractor's production entitlements for that quarter or calendar year as provided in Clause 227.

（e）expenditure may be claimed where this is incurred on, or directly related to, petroleum activities in the contract area but will exclude ineligible costs provided in sub-section 6.9.

（f）when expenditure is other than a cost incurred directly in the conduct of petroleum activities in the contract area, but includes allocations of overhead, general and administration costs which can be demonstrated to have been incurred in relation to petroleum activities in the contract area, the Designated Authority will approve the eligibility of such expenditure only after it has made or has otherwise independently obtained a detailed study, to determine how such expenditure may be identified, controlled and reported.

（g）labour costs of the contract operator which are included in capital costs will only include labour which is employed in the physical construction and installation of facilities referred to in sub-section 6. 7 subparagraphs (a), (b), (c) and (f).

(h) where natural gas, as defined in sub-section 7. 5, is marketed separately from crude oil, budgets and reports of expenditure will separately identify investment credits and operating costs associated with natural gas production.

Division 2   Reporting and Data Submission

Clause 220   Petroleum Production Forecasts

As part of the annual work program and budget of operating costs referred to in Clause 225 below, the contract operator will provide details of petroleum production forecasts for the year.

Clause 221   Valuation of Petroleum Production

(1) The general principles are defined in Section 8.

(2) Petroleum sold to third parties shall be valued f. o. b. the contract area provided in sub-section 8. 1. Accordingly petroleum sales contracts should be negotiated on an f. o. b. basis. However, if an f. o. b. sales contract becomes impracticable, and a sales contract provides a c. i. f. price at the port of destination, a price f. o. b. the contract area will be calculated, as provided in sub-section 8. 1 (c), by allowing the following deductions:

(i) freight (including bunkers);

(ii) insurance;

(iii) demurrage at the port of destination;

(iv) wharfage at the port of destination;

(v) heating costs in the case of crude oil when required of the oil;

(vi) cargo surveys;

(vii) in the case of crude oil, a volumetric loss of up to 0. 05% of the volume loaded in the contract area.

(3) Contracts for the sale of petroleum will be written in United States dollars.

(4) Nominations of tanker arrivals and loadings will be provided to the Managing Director-Technical of the Designated Authority. Consistent with the requirements of sub-section 8. 7, tanker arrivals and loading nominations will also be advised to the Managing Director-Finance of the Designated Authority, together with the customer, the port of destination and the contract volumes and price and other relevant terms for c. i. f. contracts.

Clause 222　Estimated Expenditure

The contract operator will provide a series of estimates and planning documents to the Designated Authority, which may use these estimates and planning documents to review month to month claims for investment credits and operating costs, where these are based on estimates. The following estimates and planning documents, referred to in Clauses 222 to 225, may also be required for other purposes.

Clause 223　Exploration and Appraisal Strategy

The contract operator will prepare 2 months prior to the beginning of each contract year, an exploration and appraisal strategy for the contract area to be presented at a meeting between the contract operator and the Designated Authority.

Clause 224　Annual Work Program and Budget of Operating Costs (Exploration Phase)

(1) An annual work program and budget of operating costs will be submitted by the contract operator for the approval of the Designated Authority one (1) month before the start of the calendar year.

(2) The budgetary aspect of the annual work program and budget of operating costs will include estimates of the costs of each activity for the contract year-that is, the estimated aggregate cost of each data

evaluation, seismic survey and well drilling will be stated. The contract operator will separately identify any budgeted exploration costs not covered by Section 6.5.

（3）Where petroleum activities include the separate marketing of natural gas, or the prospective marketing of natural gas, as defined in sub-section 7.5, estimates provided under sub-clause 2 above will separately identify estimates relating specifically to natural gas.

（4）Budgeted expenditure will be supported by detailed account line codes using typical oil industry codes.

Clause 225   Annual Work Program and Budget of Operating Costs (Development and Production Stage)

（1）The annual work program and budget of operating costs shall be submitted by the contract operator for the approval of the Designated Authority one (1) month before the start of the calendar year.

（2）In addition to the information required to be provided in the program and budget in relation to exploration, the contract operator will submit information on the technical aspects of the annual program for development work, maintenance and production (estimated monthly production). The budgetary aspects shall include aggregate estimates of capital costs separately identifying these items covered by sub-section 6.7 subparagraphs (b), (c) and (d) from those included under sub-section 6.7 subparagraphs (a), (e) and (f), non-capital costs, miscellaneous receipts, and ineligible expenditures for the calendar year. The program and budget will also include the organisation structure and the relevant personnel budget.

Budgeted expenditure will be supported by detailed account line codes using typical oil industry codes.

Clause 226   Company Authority for Expenditure

For the information of the Designated Authority, the contract operator shall provide a copy of its internal "company authority for expenditure" (CAFE) or other authority for expenditure. It is expected that the CAFE would provide a full breakdown of the cost estimates for each proposed activity for the calendar year, identifying various capital and non-capital costs. The CAFE will be compared with tenders at the time the tenders are submitted for approval. No Designated Authority approvals are required.

Clause 227　Reporting of Operating Costs, Miscellaneous Receipts and Investment Credits

(1) In those contract areas where there has been no declaration of a discovery area defined under Article 16 of the Interim Petroleum Mining Code, the contract operator will provide the Designated Authority with detailed annual and semi-annual returns of operating costs, miscellaneous receipts and investment credits, in the format provided in the attached Forms A and B "Return of Operating Costs, Miscellaneous Receipts and Investment Credits Under Sections 6 and 7 of the Production Sharing Contract" for each 12 month period ending 31 December. Form A will be returned to the Designated Authority by 28 February, and Form A, with a completed auditor's report, will be returned by 30 April in each year. The attached Form B, "Return of Operating Costs, Miscellaneous Receipts and Investment Credits Under Sections 6 and 7 of the Production Sharing Contract" for each 6 month period ending 30 June, will be returned to the Designated Authority by 31 August in each year.

(2) In those contract areas where there has been a declaration of a discovery area defined under Article 16 of the Interim Petroleum Mining Code, the contract operator will provide the Designated Authority with detailed annual and quarterly returns of expenditure and miscellaneous receipts, for the purposes of the calculation of production entitlements under Clauses 228 and 229. The annual return of expenditure and miscellaneous receipts is to be analysed in the format provided in the attached Form C "Return of Operating Costs, Miscellaneous Receipts and Investment Credits Under Sections 6 and 7 of the Production Sharing

Contract" for each 12 month period ending 31 December, with effect from 31 December, following the first declaration of a discovery area in the contract area. Form C will be returned to the Designated Authority by 31 January, and Form C, with a completed auditors report, will be returned by 30 April in each year. The attached Form D, which is a quarterly return is to be completed for the first, second and third quarters of each year, is to be returned to the Designated Authority reporting the cumulative operating costs for the one, two or three quarters ending 31 March, 30 June, and 30 September by 10 April, 10 July and 10 October in each year. (The dates set for the completion of the annual return is consistent with the requirements of sub-section 8. 5, while the date set for the completion of the quarterly return is consistent with the 10 day payment cycle provided under sub-section 9. 3.)

(3) Depreciation will be calculated, as provided in sub-paragraph 6. 10 (a), on the basis of the capitalised actual expenditure incurred, beginning in the year that the asset is placed into service. "Placed into service" will be when the asset is used in petroleum activities but not, for example, when the asset is installed ready for use, but is not yet in operation.

(4) Where petroleum activities include the separate marketing of natural gas, or the prospective marketing of natural gas, as defined by sub-section 7. 5, reports of expenditure and miscellaneous receipts as required under sub-paragraph 6. 10 (d), will separately identify expenditures specific to the production of natural gas.

(5) For the purposes of the calculation of production entitlements under Clauses 228 and 229, the contract operator will calculate, based on the amounts of quarterly operating costs as returned under sub-clause 227. 2 above, the amounts of operating costs which are recoverable and any excess operating costs carried forward from previous years, as provided under sub-sections 6. 3 and 7. 2, together with investment credits recoverable under sub-section 7. 10.

(6) Expenditure reports provided under paragraph 1 and 2 above will

include account line codes details using typical oil industry account codes.

(7) Where there is a significant difference of more than 25% between the budget estimates referred to in Clauses 224 and 225 and the actual expenditure reported under paragraphs 1 and 2 above, the contract operator will provide an explanation to the Designated Authority, including detailed comparisons between budget and actual expenditure by account line numbers.

Clause 228　Calculation of Production Entitlements (Crude Oil)

(1) Without prejudice to the principle of production sharing, production entitlements as provided in Section 7 will be calculated by the contract operator as at the end of each month and to be provided to the Designated Authority within ten days of the end of each month, based on:

(a) year to date production volumes being the aggregate volume of petroleum cargoes loaded from a contract area into tankers (Symbol V);

(b) the cumulative number of days from 1 January up to and including the last day of the month for which production entitlements are being calculated;

(c) the aggregate value of all cargoes, detailed on a cargo by cargo basis, loaded in the calendar year (Symbol C);

(d) the Contractors Claim of Unrecovered Investment Credits and Operating Costs provided in sub-clause 227.3 above (Symbol U).

(2) The calculation of the value of production entitlements of first tranche petroleum receivable by both the Designated Authority and the Contractor in accordance with sub-section 7.9 (Symbol F) will be based on the aggregate values of all cargoes provided in sub-paragraph 1(c) above-(Symbol C).

(3) The calculation of the Designated Authority's revenue from its production entitlements in accordance with sub-section 7.3 and 7.4, or 'share oil', will be based on a calculation of the residual margin (Symbol R) expressed in United States dollars per barrel being revenue,

excluding first tranche petroleum, net of investment credits and operating costs, calculated according to the following formula:

During First Five Years of Production   Thereafter

$$R = \frac{(C-F)-U}{0.9V}$$ 　　　　$$R = \frac{(C-F)-U}{0.8V}$$

The value of R will be applied against the year to date actual production volumes in each tranche, net of first tranche petroleum, and prorated between the Designated Authority and the contractor according to the production sharing formula applicable to each tranche. Where U exceeds (C-F) no such calculation is necessary as all production, excluding first tranche petroleum, will be applied in the recovery of investment credits and operating costs.

(4) The revenue attributable to the Designated Authority's share of petroleum production at the end of each month will be calculated by taking the cumulative value of its share of first tranche petroleum for the calendar year to the end of that month, net of aggregate first tranche petroleum proceeds paid to the Designated Authority in respect of prior months of the calendar year. Similarly the Designated Authority's cumulative share of share oil (as described in sub-clause 3 above) will be calculated for the calendar year to date. The Designated Authority will then be entitled to receive that amount net of any amounts paid to the Designated Authority in respect of share oil in prior months of the calendar year.

(5) The contract operator will calculate the apportionment of revenue between the Designated Authority and the contractor using a sufficient number of decimal places such that the sum of the proceeds of first tranche petroleum, the recovery of investment credits and operating costs and the value of share oil (as described in sub-clause 3 above) equals the aggregate value of all cargoes loaded in the calendar year.

(6) The contract operator will pay the Designated Authority the proceeds of the Designated Authority's share of production, as calculated

under sub-clause 4 above, in United States dollars on, or before the tenth (10th) day of the month following the end of the month in which the obligation to make such payment is incurred, excepting that the payment to be made in January of each year in respect of the then completed calendar year will be made thirty (30) days after the end of the calendar year as provided in sub-section 8.5.

(7) The contract operator, if directed by the Designated Authority, will hold the Designated Authority's share of receipts from petroleum sales, received but not yet paid to the Designated Authority, in an interest bearing trust account at a bank nominated by the Designated Authority.

Clause 229   Calculation of Production Entitlements (Natural Gas)

(1) For the purposes of this clause, natural gas is as defined in sub-section 7.5.

(2) Entitlements to natural gas production will be calculated as at the end of each month and provided to the Designated Authority within ten days of the end of each month, based on:

(a) year to date production volumes, being the aggregate volume of gas delivered from a contract area (Symbol GV);

(b) the cumulative number of days from 1 January up to and including the last day of the month for which production entitlements are being calculated;

(c) the aggregate value of all natural gas deliveries in the calendar year (Symbol GC); and

(d) the Contractor's Claim of Unrecovered investment credits and operating costs associated with natural gas operations (Symbol GU).

(3) The value of first tranche petroleum entitlements from natural gas production receivable by the Designated Authority and the Contractor (Symbol GF), based on the aggregate value of all natural gas deliveries as reported in accordance with sub-clause 2 above (Symbol GC), will be split in equal shares as provided in sub-section 7.5.

（4）The Designated Authority's revenue from its natural gas production entitlement will be based on a calculation of the entitlement remaining after first tranche petroleum, and the recovery of investment credits and operating costs. This residual entitlement, or 'share gas', (Symbol GR), will be calculated according to the following formula:

$$GR = (GC - GF) - GU$$

The value of share gas (GR) will be split fifty (50) percent to the Designated Authority and fifty (50) percent to the Contractor.

（5）The Designated Authority's share of natural gas production at the end of each month will be the cumulative calendar year to date share of revenue from first tranche natural gas production (GF) plus the Designated Authority's cumulative calendar year to date share gas entitlement (GR) less any amounts paid to the Designated Authority in respect of natural gas production in prior months of the calendar year.

（6）The provisions of sub-clauses 228. 5, 228. 6 and 228. 7 will also apply to the calculation of apportionments, payment of sale proceeds and the holding of Designated Authority sales receipts.

Clause 231 Independent Audit of Returns of Operating Costs, Miscellaneous Receipts and Investment Credits

（1）An independent audit of the Annual Returns of Operating Costs, Miscellaneous Receipts, and Investment Credits is required to be completed as part of the submission of such Returns as provided by Clause 227. 1 and 227. 2 above for every calendar year during which a production sharing contract is in force. A pro forma audit report for completion by the independent auditor is to be provided with the Annual Return.

（2）Once the Designated Authority has declared, under Article 16 of the Interim Petroleum Mining Code, the initial discovery area in a contract area, the Financial Managing Director of the Designated Authority will review the scope and findings of the independent audit (or audits) of the annual Returns of Operating Costs, Miscellaneous

Receipts, and Investment Credits of the preceding calendar year; and prior calendar years. Thereafter, such review will be annual and directed principally at the annual Return of Operating Costs, Miscellaneous Receipts, and Investment Credits of the preceding calendar year. The object of the review will be to assess the overall strength and integrity of internal check and control over operations; and to provide accurate and consistent reporting in the Returns of Operating Costs, Miscellaneous Receipts and Investment Credits. The contract operator will be represented during such review. This review will include at least the following 5 review components:

（a） relevant internal control procedures, accounting policies including: procedures and controls to ensure that the costs as reported in US $ fairly represent actual costs incurred; the controls on the measurement, transfer and sale of petroleum as prescribed by Clause 622 of the Regulations, together with effective control and custody of documentation showing measurement of, and transfer of title to, petroleum sold; the procedure and controls for the implementation of the calculation of petroleum production entitlements as provided under Clauses 228 and 229 of the Directions; the system for the control of inventory movements as provided by Clause 622 of the Directions; the system for charging overheads; account code classifications for operating costs; delegated authorities; service agreements with both third parties and affiliated/parent companies; organisation charts (see also Clause 301 of these Directions) including those employees for whom a part of their time is charged to the contract operator; and details of other related control and organisational structures;

（b） the scope of the audit carried out by the independent corporate auditor (and the internal auditor if applicable) of the contract operator and assess in particular the adequacy of specific consideration given to the provisions of the Production Sharing Contract in the context of the Designated Authority's responsibilities to the Contracting States;

（c） review any internal control memoranda sent by the corporate external auditor (or internal auditor) to the contract operator and follow-up actions taken;

(d) the supplementary information to the returns of Operating Costs, Miscellaneous Receipts and Investment Credits to be provided annually following the declaration of a discovery area under Clause 233 below; and

(e) the findings under the specific audit checks and procedures to be undertaken by the independent auditor of a contract operator under Clause 234.

(3) In relation to the initial audit review following the declaration of a discovery areas provided in Clause 231. 2 above, the Designated Authority will consider the scope of the audits as completed for prior calendar years, particularly the extent of supplementary information available as provided for under Clause 233 and the audit checks and procedures specified under Clause 234, and the adequacy of information under Clause 233 and the adequacy of the scope of audit checks in relation to Clause 234. The Designated Authority will then advise the contract operator in writing of any additional information required, or audit checks to be completed.

(4) The independent audit referred to under sub-clauses 1 and 2 above of this Clause, consistent with the provisions of sub-section 14. 2 of the PSC, and Article 41 of the Interim Petroleum Mining Code, shall not prejudice the rights of the Designated Authority to inspect and audit the contractor's books and accounts.

Clause 232　Audit by the Designated Authority

The Designated Authority reserves the right to inspect and audit the books and records of the contract operator. An audit conducted by the Designated Authority may include the review of the additional information for prior contract years as provided in Clause 231. 3 above, or at the discretion of the Designated Authority, may be extended to other matters.

Clause 233 Supplementary Information to the Returns of Operating Costs, Miscellaneous Receipts and Investment Credits to be Provided Annually following the Declaration of a Discovery Area

Additional information will be provided of general and administrative charges, and any costs charged by an affiliated corporation, or affiliate (as defined in Section 1 of the PSC). This information will provide the basis of the review, as provided by Section 6.10 (b) of the PSC, of the determination of a method whereby such charges may be allocated consistent with the overriding requirement that such costs are demonstrated as being directly related to current year petroleum activities in the contract area. All costs charged to the contract operator, other than costs charged by a third party non-affiliated corporation or entity, will be set out on a schedule, or schedules. The schedule, or schedules, will include the following details:

(a) corporate cost centres from which charges have been made to the contract operator, the basis on which charges are made from such costs centres, and the extent to which within these costs centres that over or under recoveries of costs have been made;

(b) details of any reviews made of the cost recoveries made by corporate cost centres;

(c) details of any service agreements, or other agreements, under which such costs are charged;

(d) the amount of such costs charged;

(e) the nexus between the charge and its relationship to current calendar year's petroleum activities in the contract area;

(f) the affiliated corporation, or affiliate, making such charges; and

(g) any other charges made, or costs incurred, not charged by a third party, including goods, materials and supplies.

The schedule, or schedules, containing these details will be reviewed by the independent auditor, who will report whether the details provided are a "true and fair statement of the details of the costs charged to the contract operator, other than costs charged by a third party non-affiliated corporation or affiliate".

Clause 234　Specific Audit Checks and Procedures to be Undertaken by the Independent Auditor of a Contract Operator following the Declaration of a Discovery Area.

（1）The contract operator will instruct the independent auditor, in addition to the audit review process with the Designated Authority as provided in Clause 231.2, to include in the audit review to be undertaken those enquiries and checks as set out in paragraphs 2, 3, 4 and 5 below. The audit review program as set out below is framed to review the amounts included in the Returns of Operating Costs, Miscellaneous Receipts and Investment Credits and compliance with certain Treaty obligations. The independent auditor will report to the Designated Authority their specific findings on the specific issues addressed in the audit review program. (It is not intended that the audit review, as provided below, should result in the exclusion of other areas audit otherwise required from a corporate management/control perspective.)

（2）Review of contract administration and purchase orders:

（a）Obtain a summary of payments made under contracts. Compare these payments under these contracts against the CAFEs (or AFEs) issued in accordance with Clause 226 of the Directions. Document exceptions where payments are made outside approvals provided by the CAFEs.

（b）Ascertain the extent to which contracts were tendered, and all findings are to be documented.

（c）Obtain the "annual work program and budget of operating costs" for the year as approved by the Designated Authority. Compare this against actual operating costs as reported, and obtain explanations for major differences, ascertaining the extent of Designated Authority approvals to such variations.

(d) Carry out in-depth test checks on the management of selected contracts (including principal contracts under exploration expenditures and capital costs under development program). Obtain summaries of contract conditions, if available, and if not establish how contract information is disseminated to maintain effective contract controls. Review such summaries/ information against the contract as appropriate, particularly for progress payment provisions; review the internal controls on progress payments; contract variations; and final payments made on completion of contracts. At each stage consider the extent of information available to decision makers, particularly those responsible for approving progress payments. Document the extent to which overall system of internal control is satisfactory.

(e) Ascertain the extent to which third party goods and services have been provided outside the tender provisions of Section 10 of the PSC. Review the operation of internal controls on such purchases, particularly purchase orders. Conduct in-depth test checks to ascertain: why any contract was not tendered; the authority for issuing a purchase order; alternative purchasing processes followed outside of contract or purchase order procedures; the extent of quotes obtained and the documentation of those quotes; the extent to which the scope/coverage of purchase orders was subsequently extended to cover additional items or numbers of items. All findings are to be documented.

(f) Review the process and control of cost collections for consolidation in the Return of Operating Costs, Miscellaneous Receipts and Investment Credits. (Schedules are to have been provided with these returns which will provide documentation, though generally expressed in US $). Extend the in-depth test of cost items tested in Clause 234.2 a). to e). above, and Clause 234.3 a). to d). below to their inclusion on the Return. Assess in each case whether the basis on which these specific costs items is returned is consistent with the criterion that the costs relate directly to the current calendar year's operations in the contract area. All findings are to be documented.

(g) Schedules 1 (a), 4 (a), and 4 (c) of the Return of Operating Costs, Miscellaneous Receipts and Investment Credits refer to materials used. Identify the extent of inventories of unused materials on a schedule, and compare this against the inventories shown in the Financial Statements of the contract operator. Ascertain whether such costs have been included in Return of Operating Costs, Miscellaneous Receipts and Investment Credits. All findings are to be documented.

(3) Review cost collections of internal allocations and non-third party supplies of goods and services:

(a) Ascertain which supplies of goods are sourced from internal corporate/affiliate supply or inventory sources. By enquiry and test checks establish whether such items were charged at the original cost price to the affiliate purchasing the goods from a third party, and if not the extent to which the price to the contract operator exceeded, or was less than, the cost price. Document the basis on which cost has been determined (eg LIFO (last in first out), FIFO (first in first out) or average costs) and record the evidence obtained of costs of purchases. In particular test check the supply arrangements for tubulars used in drilling wells and related drilling equipment supplied to the contract operator from affiliated corporations. Ascertain the pricing procedure adopted and test from stock records and/or other substantive records on what basis such inventory items were supplied to the contract operator. Ascertain whether or not these arrangements were specifically approved by the Designated Authority. Assess whether the transfer price was reasonable as compared to the initial purchase cost of the items to the affiliated corporation, or affiliate. If possible obtain prices for supplies ex third party suppliers. Document whether or not prescribed supply and pricing practices are followed, and where alternative practices are provided for, and the criteria on which alternative practices were selected.

(b) Give careful consideration to whether general administrative overheads have been included under Schedules 1 and 4, which do not "directly relate to the current calendar year's operations in the contract area", and identify and report any exceptions. For example accounting staff employed directly on the accounting of current calendar year's operations in the contract area are allowable, while a corporate accounting overhead is not allowable. Where specific accounting/finance functions such as payroll, purchasing and treasury are charged, a specific basis will need to have been established. (See sub-section 6.9 (h) of the PSC). All findings are to be documented.

(c) Check by sampling whether the direct labor costs returned under Schedules 1 (a) iv), 1 (b) iv) and 6 exclude oncosts or overheads such as office rentals, and document the extent of any such overheads or charges are included. Assess whether the time writing records provide reasonable assurance that the activity was related to "the current calendar years exploration operation in the contract area". All findings are to be documented.

(d) Direct costs of survey support services for data processing, dark room and drawing office services, which are charged out based on time costs directly to exploration operations in the contract area, may be included as an exploration cost under sub-section 6.5 (b) item iii). Similarly direct costs of design support services for data processing, dark room and drawing office services, which are charged directly to an item of capital cost, directly related to petroleum activities in the contract area, such expenditure may be included as a cost of that item under sub-section 6.7. When these services are not charged out on a time cost basis, but as an overhead, these costs will be considered as being technical and related services, which may be claimed under sub-section 6.6 (b) item i). Test check how charges for such services have been made and whether their treatment complies with item c) of the "Directions for the Completion of this Return". All findings are to be documented.

(e) Costs of office, services and general administration directly related to the petroleum activities carried in the contract area including technical and related services, office supplies, office rentals, other rentals of services and property, and personnel expenses will constitute neither "exploration costs" (sub-section 6.5) nor "capital costs" (sub-section 6.7); but may be returned only under sub-section 6.6 (b), providing the test of directness within the meaning of that sub-section is met. Establish and document the overall extent and scope of charges, and how such charges have been returned.

(f) Rentals claimed under sub section 6.6 (b), as office rentals, other rentals of services and property, may include charges for:

(i) rental charges for office space at commercial rates, including property taxes if applicable, for space occupied by persons directly engaged in petroleum activities in the contract area; and

(ii) rental charges for other assets used in relation to petroleum activities in the contract area, based on the cost of the asset and its useful life, where no other charge for such asset usage is included under charges for services or other operating costs.

Review the basis on which office rentals, other rentals for services and property have been set, and whether they conform with item j) of the "Directions for the Completion of this Return".

(g) Obtain and review the extent to which service contracts have been entered into, and that the charging of costs under such is consistent with the necessary direct relationship " to current calendar year's operations in the contract area". Identify and report any exceptions.

(4) Review costs of labor, materials and services incurred as part of exploration costs, non-capital costs and capital costs.

(a) Establish through test checks the extent and effectiveness of controls for the enforcement of contract conditions for contracted staff and specialist staff employed under sub-contracts consistent with Treaty Article 11. All findings are to be documented.

(b) Establish whether or not the obligation to provide terms and conditions, that are no less favourable than those which would apply from time to time to comparable categories of employment in Australia and

Timor-Leste. Document how these arrangements have been effected.

(c) Review the overall procedures for the control of numbers of employees, and the steps taken to ensure that employment levels are consistent with minimum staffing levels from operational and safety standards. All findings are to be documented.

(d) Test check salaries paid against contracts, time records, and income tax records. Include in the test nationals/permanent residents of Australia, Timor-Leste and third countries. Taxation of the salaries of Australian and Timor-Leste residents is payable to the respective Australian and Timor-Leste taxation authorities, while taxation on the salaries of nationals of third countries is taxable, subject to a rebate entitlement against the tax payable in each Contracting State of the reduction percentage of the gross tax payable in the Contracting State. All findings are to be documented.

(e) Review the "direct labor cost" as returned on Schedules 1 (a) iv), 1 (b) iv), 4 (a) i), 4 (b) i) and ii) and ensure by comprehensive test checks that direct labor costs are consistent with Direction d) of the "Directions for the Completion of this Return" and exclude allocations additional to direct salary costs. All findings are to be documented.

(f) The contract operator must be able to substantiate the allocation of direct labor costs by reference to time sheets or employment records, which demonstrate that such labor costs were directly related to petroleum activities in the contract area in relation to "exploration costs" (sub-section 6. 5), "non-capital costs" (sub-section 6. 6) and "capital costs" (sub-section 6. 7). Test check direct labor costs against the above criterion. All findings are to be documented.

(g) Eligible costs will in the normal course of events be incurred in the first instance by the contract operator and accounted for in the first instance in the books of account of the contract operator. Alternatively where the costs are charged onto the contract operator by an affiliated corporation, eligible costs will be supported by one of the following:

(i) actual time based charges for such eligible costs incurred;

(ⅱ) allocations of eligible costs incurred, based on a system which is demonstrated as being fairly formulated, and is subject to frequent and regular review;

(ⅲ) a service agreement which provides for a reasonable recovery of eligible costs.

Test allocations from affiliated corporations against the above criterion. All findings are to be documented.

(h) Review by test checks the adequacy and effectiveness of controls over ordering, purchasing, inventory, payment, budget and costing records for purchases of goods and materials. Establish by tests and enquiry at what point in time goods and materials are charged as an operating cost under sub-section 6. 6 a), in particular are such purchases of goods and materials expensed at time of purchase, and if so assess the extent of prospective inventory levels in quantitative and monetary terms. All findings are to be documented.

(5) Review specific issues requiring particular treatment, or consideration, under the Production Sharing Contract.

(a) Ascertain from the contract operators corporate accounts, cash books receipt summaries and other available sources the extent to which Miscellaneous Receipts as provided in Section 6. 8 of the PSC may have been received during the calendar year. All findings are to be documented.

(b) Ascertain whether any Ineligible Costs as provided under sub-section 6. 9 have been excluded in the Return. From audit enquiries, and a general overview, including a review of charges against particular account codes where ineligible costs may have been charged, ascertain whether Ineligible Costs have been identified, and excluded from the amounts returned. Document Ineligible Costs as excluded and any costs which may be considered to be Ineligible Costs, which have not been excluded from the Return.

(c) Unless otherwise approved by the Designated Authority, costs incurred by the contractors other than the contract operator, will be ineligible costs (sub-paragraph 6.9 (k)). During the exploration phase of petroleum activities, individual contractors may, subject to Designated Authority approval, insure their individual interests in exploration activity under world wide, or separate policies, rather than a policy effected for the contract as a whole by the contract operator. Two criterion have to be met:

(i) the basis of the allocation of such insurance premiums paid has to be consistent between all contractors for that contract area; and

(ii) the basis of allocation is to reflect the relationship of exploration activity in the contract area to the overall exploration activity of the contractor.

Confirm that such criterion have been met. All findings are to be documented.

(d) With the declaration of a discovery areas provided under Article 16 of the Interim Petroleum Mining Code, the Designated Authority will consider proposals from the contract operator, and if appropriate will agree the procedure for the conversion of a non-US $ currency transactions to US $ for the purpose of returning Operating Costs, Miscellaneous Receipts and Investment Credits. Test check major items of expenditure to ensure that the rate of exchange as applied was the rate applicable on the date the payment was made. All findings are to be documented.

(e) Consider the overall integrity of the system of internal controls and internal check, where an integrated set of books of account are not maintained in US $, to ensure that amounts returned in the Returns of Operating Costs, Miscellaneous Receipts and Investment Credits, can be reconciled back to total expenditures as recorded in the books of account in non-US $ currencies. All findings are to be documented.

(f) Review and document the extent of accrued liabilities provided by the contract operator and the extent to which these are included in the Return of Operating Costs, Miscellaneous Receipts and Investment Credits. In principle the recovery of operating costs through entitlements to shares of petroleum production arises on costs incurred on a cash basis. All findings are to be documented.

(g) The review of expenditures on capital costs is to have been reviewed under Clause 234. 2 & 234. 3, in relation to payments made under contracts, and allocations for labour and overheads. Review the related progress reports tenders and quotes on the construction/ supply of these items, and inspection, test or delivery reports together with any other documentation recording progress on the fabrication, construction and delivery of these items. Establish whether those items claimed to have been "placed into service", meet the criterion for placed into service as provided in Clause 227. 3 of the Directions. Check the calculation of depreciation on capital costs on a 20% straight line basis.

(h) Review the extent to which the audit has covered the amounts included in the Return of Operating Costs, Miscellaneous Receipts and Investment Credits, and set out on a schedule those cost items not reviewed.

Part Ⅲ   Reporting on Organization Structure

Clause 301   Organization Structure and Personnel Establishment

The contract operator will provide the Designated Authority annually with:

(1) A chart of its Organization Structure which will be submitted together with the documents under Clause 224 and 225.

(2) A report of the Personnel Establishment filling positions in the above Organization Structure (as referred to in Clause 225. 2), including the names and job-titles of the officers, and the anticipated percentage of time-allocation in case of part-time assignees.

(3) Its program by which it will meet its obligations under Section

5. 2 (i) of the contract.

Part IV　Service Contracts

Clause 401　Reporting on Service Contracts

The contract operator will report to the Designated Authority monthly in brief, on service contracts entered into, as required under Section 10. 5 of the Contract, by listing particulars, including:

(1) The name of the persons/individuals contracted, their nationality, effective date, term, kind of service provided, contract-sum, and terms of payments; and

(2) Progress of service completion and details of payments made during the month and cumulative; expenditures on each service contract.

Clause 402　Service Preference Program

The contract operator will provide the Designated Authority annually with its program to meet its obligations under section 5. 2 (h) of the contract.

Clause 403　Subcontracting for Services

(1) Pursuant to subsection 5. 2 of the Production Sharing Contract, the Contract Operator shall ensure that any of its subcontracts contain a stipulation that the parties thereto shall comply with the requirements of the Treaty, including the Interim Petroleum Mining Code and the regulations and directions issued thereunder, the Production Sharing Contract, and the Taxation Code.

(2) The Designated Authority requires the Contract Operator to take appropriate measures that in any subcontract within the JPDA preference is given to employment of Timor-Leste nationals and permanent residents, with due regard to efficient operations and to good oilfield practice （based on Article 11 of the Treaty）.

（3）To ensure due compliance with this requirement, the measures should be taken from an early stage of the process of subcontracting.

Part Ⅴ　Preparation and Presentation of a Development Plan and Commencement of Development

Clause 501　Development Plan

（1）As provided by Section 2.4 of the contract and Article 16.1 of the Interim Petroleum Mining Code, the Designated Authority shall declare a discovery area and the contract operator shall commence development, provided that the Designated Authority and the contract operator can agree that a discovered petroleum pool can be produced commercially.

（2）To facilitate the means for considering commerciality referred to in the above paragraph, the subsequent declaration of a discovery area, and for commencing work on the development of a petroleum discovery pursuant to Section 4.9 of the contract, the contract operator shall prepare and submit to the Designated Authority, a Development Plan.

（3）The Development Plan, which will be based on all pertinent operating and financial data, shall set out details such as:

（a）The proposed petroleum reservoir development and recovery management program;

（b）the reservoir-drainage pattern adopted, and projection of the production profile for the expected life of the project;

（c）production facilities, including the layout, field production processing system, petroleum storage and loading facilities, and the supply and logistics system of personnel and goods;

（d）feasibility of fabrication, hauling, installation and project commissioning stages of the facilities, the project implementation schedule, and estimates of the capital and non-capital expenditures of the plan; together with the estimated percentage of the total to be expended in Australia and Timor-Leste;

(e) projection of costs of operation/production; together with the relevant percentages of the total to be spent on Australian and Timor-Leste services and personnel;

(f) calculation of the economics to show commerciality of the Development Plan.

Clause 502　Commencement of Development

(1) Upon the Designated Authority and the contract operator agreeing that a discovered petroleum pool can be produced commercially in accordance with section 2.4 of the contract, then as to that particular block or blocks of the contract area and Designated Authority shall declare a discovery area and the contract operator shall commence development.

(2) Subject to paragraph 1. above, all necessary steps shall be taken to enable the commencement of exploitation of the petroleum resource, consistent with the Development Plan, as soon as possible. Specifically in the case of the natural gas development project however, the Designated Authority may allow the contract operator the time necessary for making gas marketing arrangements and conclusion of a gas sales contract.

Part Ⅵ　Equipment Entering or Leaving JPDA

Division 1　Principles and Responsibilities
Clause 601　Movements of Equipment

(1) The Treaty requires that the Designated Authority controls all movements into, within and out of the JPDA including the movements of equipment which includes vessels, aircraft, structures and equipment

employed in exploration for and exploitation of petroleum resources.

(2) The contract operator will ensure that equipment and goods do not enter structures in the JPDA without first entering Timor-Leste or Australia, where they are subject to customs control in accordance with the laws of the Contracting State through which entry into the JPDA is to be made.

(3) The Designated Authority's responsibility to control such movements of equipment including materials and goods is also related to the need to correlate operating costs recoveries against equipment and goods entering or leaving the JPDA, as:

(a) items purchased for inventory shall be recoverable as operating costs at such time as the items are landed in the JPDA;

(b) depreciation of capital costs begin in the calendar year the asset is placed into service which takes place in the contract area in the JPDA; and

(c) the value of property, the cost of which is an operating cost, when the property ceases to be used in petroleum activities in the contract area would constitute a miscellaneous receipt.

Division 2　Control on Movements of Equipment
Clause 620　Equipment Owned by Service Companies

Designated Authority control on movements into, within and out of the JPDA of equipment owned by service companies, including their aircraft, seismic, drill, supply and service vessels engaged in petroleum activities, with their onboard equipment and inventory, is provided under Clause 216, 401 and 501 of these Regulations; it is not subject to Clause 621 subsequent hereto.

Clause 621　Equipment Acquired by Contract Operators

(1) A contract operator shall maintain and lodge with the Managing Director, a master list of all equipment shipped into JPDA and shall include materials and goods acquired and owned by the contract operator

for use or installation in its contract area. The "master list" shall list the items according to their cost category, ie. exploration cost, non-capital cost or capital cost.

(2) The master list should also indicate:

(a) the name(s) or identification of the item(s) or lots of items listed, the manufacturer/fabricator and country of origin;

(b) the United States dollar value of the items(s) or lots of items listed;

(c) for capital cost item(s) or lots of capital cost items, the segment of production system to which the item(s) belong eg. oil/gas wells, platform structure, production processing, pipeline/flowlines segment, crude oil storage etc. ;

(d) for lots of non-capital cost items (eg. for inventory, consumables, spare-parts), the reference number (s) of detail documents of such lots of items (eg. packing lists, confirmed purchase orders) in lieu of listing the items themselves;

(e) name and address of carrier, and reference number of the Bill of Lading;

(f) the place of final destination in the contract area;

(g) the signature of the contract operator's authorised officer responsible for correctness of the master list's contents;

(h) the date of lodgement; and

(i) the signature and stamp of the Timor-Leste or Australian customs evidencing that the equipment and goods listed have been duly cleared pursuant to Section 5.2 (k).

(3) For equipment including materials and goods leaving the contract area, the contract operator shall also lodge with the Managing Director a similar master list, except that it should also indicate:

(a) the place in the contract area the items have been taken away from;

(b) the destination;

(c) the reason for taking away from the contract area; and

（d）the date of lodgement.

（4）Any equipment including materials and goods acquired and owned by a contract operator entering or leaving its contract area not covered by such master list(s), represents a default on the part of the contract operator.

（5）When the contract operator considers it helpful for the purpose of obtaining clearance through either the Timor-Leste or Australian customs, the contract operator may request the Managing Director to sign and stamp the master list（s）in order to provide evidence of the Designated Authority's authorisation for the items listed to enter or leave the JPDA, whichever is the case.

Clause 622   Reporting of Inventory Movements

（1）After commencement of production, a contract operator shall quarterly report movements during the quarter, of materials and equipment inventory in the contract area used/to be used in petroleum activities in accordance with subsection 6.10（e）of the Production Sharing Contract, expressed in United States dollars as follows：

（a）total value of items purchased and added or returned to such inventory；

（b）total value of items taken out from inventory for use in petroleum activities；

（c）value of non-moving inventory items, subdivided into values of items which have not moved for：

（i）less than 1 year；

（ii）1 to 2 years；and

（iii）more than 2 years.

（d）value of items used outside the contract area, soled or otherwise removed from the contract area；and

（e）total value of inventory level at end of quarter.

（2）Contract operator will also include in the report：

（a）the locations where the inventory items are stored；and

(b) a bar chart depicting the above quarterly inventory movements.

Part Ⅶ Insurance

Division 1 General Principles
Clause 701 Strict Liability of Contractor

Insurance is required to be taken out and maintained by the Contractor on a strict liability basis under Article 25 of the Interim Petroleum Mining Code. The Contractor is accordingly liable for any damage or injury arising in connection with the carrying out of petroleum activities and other activities associated with those operations, whether or not it exercised reasonable care; such liability being non-delegable.

Clause 702 Independent Contractor

The Contract Operator, having the exclusive right and responsibility to undertake petroleum activities in a contract area, is and shall act as an independent contractor, and all personnel assigned to the petroleum activities by the Contract Operator shall in no sense be nor be deemed to be agents or employees of the Designated Authority.

Clause 703 Damage or Expenses incurred from Pollution

The Contractor shall be liable for damage or expenses incurred as a result of pollution of the marine environment arising out of petroleum activities and other activities associated with those operations.

Clause 704 Insurance Cover and Limits

Insurance cover and limits specified in policies, cannot be construed in any way as limiting the Contractor's liability or as constituting acceptance by the Designated Authority of responsibility for any financial or other liabilities of the Contractor.

Clause 705　Claims

The word "Claims" includes any and all claims, liens, judgements, awards, remedies, debts, damages, injuries, costs, losses, expenses or causes of action of whatever nature, including, without limitation, punitive or exemplary damages and those made or enjoyed by dependents, heirs, claimants, executors, administrators, successors, survivors or assigns.

Division 2　Insurance Requirements
Clause 730　Additional Insured

The Contract Operator shall ensure that the Designated Authority is named as additional insured on all policies (other than Employer's liability and Worker's Compensation Insurance) which Contractor is required to effect arising out of or with respect to its petroleum activities and other activities associated with those operations.

Clause 731　Waiver of Rights of Subrogation

Each Contractor shall provide the Designated Authority with written confirmation that the Contractor's insurers have agreed to waive all rights of subrogation against the Designated Authority with respect to the Contractor's petroleum activities and other activities associated with those operations.

Clause 732　Subcontractors' Insurance

The Contract Operator must ensure that each sub-contractor engaged by it in the conduct of petroleum activities under the Contract takes out and maintains for the duration of the Contract, employer's liability, worker's compensation and other insurances required by law, together with such other insurance as Contract Operator may consider necessary. Any deficiencies in the cover or policy limits of sub-contractors' insurances shall be the sole responsibility of Contract Operator. Contract

Operator shall also procure that its sub-contractors and their respective insurers waive all express or implied rights of subrogation against the Designated Authority; and that in their sub-contractors' insurances the Designated Authority is named as an additional insured.

Clause 733 Indemnity

Contract Operator shall procure that, notwithstanding:

(a) any negligence of the sub-contractor, its employees, servants and agents;

(b) defects in or unfitness of any equipment, building or structure;

(c) the place where any loss, damages, destruction or injury occurs; or

(d) the negligence of the Contract Operator and the Designated Authority or either of them,

each sub-contract provides for the sub-contractor to protect, defend, indemnify and hold harmless the Designated Authority from and against any and all claims, demands, liabilities and damages arising out of:

(a) illness or injury to, or death of, the employees, servants and agents of such sub-contractor and/or its sub-contractors or their employees, servants or agents, and/or

(b) loss of, or destruction of property, owned or hired, or equipment, materials and supplies of such sub-contractor, its sub-contractors, and its or their respective employees, servants or agents, where such loss or injury is occasioned by, incidental to, or arises out of or in conjunction with the sub-contract.

Clause 734 Deductibles

Any deductibles applicable to the insurances shall be for the account of Contract Operator, or its sub-contractors as may be expressly provided in their contracts.

Clause 735 Evidence of Insurances Effected

(1) Before or on the commencement of petroleum activities, the

Contract Operator shall provide to the Designated Authority certified copies of the Contractor's insurance policies. Renewal policies shall be obtained by Contract Operator as and when necessary and certified copies thereof shall be forwarded promptly to the Designated Authority.

(2) Should an individual corporation, being one of the contracting corporations to a Production Sharing Contract, wish to effect insurance for the exploration phase, through individual policies pursuant to Clause 761 of these Directions, rather than through a single policy effected for that Contract as a whole, it shall be deemed to have satisfied the requirement under paragraph (1) of this Clause by promptly providing the Designated Authority with an original copy of a "Declaration of Insurances" in accordance with the format in Annex A to Part Ⅶ of these Directions; and renewals thereof shall also be promptly forwarded to the Designated Authority.

(3) Where the Contract Operator has effected insurances for the exploration phase through a policy, or policies, for the Production Sharing Contract as a whole, the Contract Operator may satisfy the requirements under paragraph (1) of this Clause by promptly providing the Designated Authority with an original copy of a "Declaration of Insurances" in accordance with the format in Annex A to Part Ⅶ of these Directions; and renewals thereof shall also be promptly forwarded to the Designated Authority. The Designated Authority reserves the right, however, to be provided with certified copies of the Contract Operator's insurance policies as provided by paragraph (1) of this Clause.

(4) The Contract Operator shall also furnish the Designated Authority with copies of the certificates of sub-contractors' insurances stating: (a) kinds and amounts of insurance; (b) insurance company (ies) carrying the coverages; (c) effective and expiration dates of policies; (d) that an endorsement of waiver of subrogation has been attached to all policies; and (e) that the other requirements of Clauses 732 and 733 have been met.

(5) Any material change in or cancellation of the documents required

to be submitted to the Designated Authority under this Clause, shall be notified by the Contractor at least 30 days prior to such change or cancellation, and the Designated Authority shall be provided with the replacement copy as applicable.

(6) If the Designated Authority is not satisfied with the arrangements for insurances that have been made as evidenced by the documents required to be submitted to the Designated Authority under this Clause, including inadequacy of the quality of cover and security of the insurer, it will so notify the Contractor for due rectification thereof.

Clause 736   Acquisition of Insurances

Subject to Article 25 of the Interim Petroleum Mining Code, Contract Operator shall take out and maintain insurance in accordance with subsection 5.2 of the Contract.

Division 3   Types of Insurances
Clause 760   Insurances to be effected

Pursuant to Article 25 of the Interim Petroleum Mining Code, and without prejudice to the liabilities and responsibilities of the Contractor and Contract Operator set forth above, Contract Operator shall take out and maintain with respect to and for the duration of petroleum activities under the Contract, insurances which shall include:

(1) Workers Compensation and Employers' Liability Insurance, to limits in compliance with applicable laws.

(2) Insurance to cover damage to Contract Operator's properties, including equipment, installations, machinery and all other equipment of any description to be furnished by Contract Operator to conduct petroleum activities under the Contract.

(3) General Third Party Liability Insurance against any property damage and/or loss and/or personal injury or death arising out of or in any way connected with petroleum activities.

(4) Insurance to cover expenses and liabilities associated with clean-

up, remedy and control of the seepage and the escape of petroleum from within the contract area (including costs to regain control of a well), polluting the environment.

(5) Insurance to cover for costs of or incidental to, the actual or attempted raising, removal or destruction of the wreckage or debris (howsoever caused) of property of the Contract Operator and of other contracted parties in connection with petroleum activities not otherwise insured.

Any such coverage to be provided hereunder, shall not stop the collection of claims that may become apparent after the end of the operations by virtue of having "claims made" policies or the like.

Clause 761 Insurance Effected by the Individual Corporations, being one of the Contracting Corporations to a Production Sharing Contract

Insurance may be effected by individual corporations, which are one of the contracting corporations to a Production Sharing Contract (PSC), only during the exploration phase of petroleum activities. The requirement to be met should such corporations wish to effect insurance through individual policies held by them, rather than through a single policy effected for the PSC as a whole, are:

(1) the requirements of Article 25 of the Interim Petroleum Mining Code, together with the Directions under this Part Ⅶ, are to be met under the policies effected by such corporations;

(2) the requirements of Section 10 of the PSC are met in such a way that the contract operator can demonstrate that the aggregate cost of insurance effected by the individual corporations, is competitive against the cost of independent tenders/quotes, based on the same terms of reference, for the insurance of the risk when insured for the block as a whole; and

(3) that the contract operator sets out for consideration of the Designated Authority the system/method on which the cost of corporate package insurance policies may be allocated to the PSC by the respective parent (or affiliated) of such corporations, with the sum of the insurance premiums charged as an operating cost of the PSC.

Once a discovery area has been declared as provided in Article 16 of the Interim Petroleum Mining Code, insurance as required under Article 25 of the Interim Petroleum Mining Code, relating to the development and production phases of petroleum activities in, or from the discovery area will be effected by the contract operator in respect of all interests under the PSC.

This Direction is restricted to the exploration phase of petroleum activities.

3. Timor Sea Designated Authority for the Joint Petroleum Development Area "Interim Administrative Guidelines for the Joint Petroleum Development Area"

Introduction

These guidelines are issued for the purpose of assisting companies by elaborating various parts of the Treaty and its Annexes, and the Interim Petroleum Mining Code. Where there is any inconsistency the Treaty and its Annexes, and the Interim Petroleum Minig Code prevail.

These guidelines are not comprehensive as there are a number of other matters in the Treaty, the Interim Petroleum Mining Code and the Production Sharing Contracts which could be elaborated for the benefit of the Designated Authority and companies.

Guideline 1 Applications under the work program bidding system for Production Sharing Contracts in the Joint Petroleum Development Area

Applications to Enter into Contracts

Applications lodged under Article 10 of the Interim Petroleum Mining Code will be made in duplicate and should be accompanied by:

（a）（i）the applicant's assessment of the petroleum potential of the contract area, including a geological and geophysical review and technical assessment of the contract area, and the concepts underlying the proposed exploration work program and expenditure commitments;

（ii）the applicant's proposed exploration work program and expenditure commitments for the first three contract years covering data evaluation, seismic surveys and exploration wells to be drilled, on the basis that none of the items of the work program are conditional on the discovery of hydrocarbons. The first three years of the proposal should only include work and expenditure expected to involve a substantial exploration component-appraisal work should not be included;

（iii）the applicant's proposal（in terms of operational activity or estimated minimum expenditure）for data evaluation, seismic surveys and exploration wells to be drilled, for each of the remaining three years of the contract term. This proposal for exploration work and expenditure covering contract years four to six, may be renegotiated. It should only include work and expenditure expected to involve a substantial exploration component-appraisal work should not be included.

（iv）a statement of the applicant's acceptance of the terms of the Production Sharing Contract.

（v）the production sharing contract（PSC）with details of the applicant company（ies）（PSC preamble）the nominated contract operator（PSC subsection 1.1）, the proposed work program and expenditure（PSC subsection 4.2）, the proposed amount of insurance cover（PSC paragraph 5.2（j））, the proposed place and language of arbitration（PSC subsection 12.6）, the contract operator's address（PSC subsection 15.2）, and the proposed law to apply to the contract（PSC subsection 15.6）.

（b）Particulars of:

（i）the technical knowledge and ability of the company to be appointed contract operator and of its employees;

（ii）the technical advice available to the contract operator;

(iii) the financial capability of the applicant, including evidence of the applicant's ability to fund the proposed work program and expenditure commitments and a copy of the latest annual report for each applicant company;

(iii) where relevant, the viability of the consortium lodging the application, including evidence that an agreement can be reached between the corporations for cooperation in petroleum activities in the contract area (a copy of a Principles of Agreement document will generally suffice), and the corporation appointed and authorised to be the Contract Operator responsible on behalf of the group of corporations for petroleum activities and all dealings with the Designated Authority under the contract;

(v) plans to be implemented to meet the obligations specified under paragraph 5.2(i) of the contract concerning employment of Timor-Leste nationals and permanent residents; and

(vi) the percentage participating interest of each limited liability corporation specifically established for the sole purpose of the contract.

(c) Such other information as the applicant wishes to be taken into account in consideration of the application including:

(i) past performance in offshore exploration;

(ii) intentions as to the sourcing of goods and services in Australia and the Timor-Leste to be used in operations;

(iii) proposals to improve technical capabilities through research to be undertaken in Australia and Timor-Leste; and

(iv) proposals to transfer technology and skills to Timor-Leste nationals and permanent residents.

(d) A fee, payable to a bank to be designated by the Designated Authority and to be in United Stated dollars, will be paid for each contract area for which an application is lodged (the amount is set out in Article 44 of the Interim Petroleum Mining Code).

Assessment of Applications

Applications will be assessed principally on the acceptance of the

Production Sharing Contract, and the amount and quality of the exploration work and expenditure commitment bid, subject to applicants having sufficient financial capability and technical knowledge and ability to carry out the proposed work program and expenditure commitments. Details of the assessment criteria are provided in Administrative Guideline No. 2.

Guideline 2   Criteria for assessment of applications under the work program bidding system for production sharing contracts the Joint Petroleum Development Area

（1）Pursuant to Article 11 of the Interim Petroleum Mining Code, this document sets out the criteria to be followed by the Designated Authority in assessing applications lodged for production sharing contracts.

（2）Companies will be expected to have taken into account all relevant information and any special conditions, such as environment protection, applying in contract areas. All relevant information and details of special conditions will be made known to potential applicants by the Designated Authority when blocks forming contract areas are advertised.

（3）Applications will be assessed on the basis of the information contained in the written applications, which may be elaborated on during any interview to discuss the application with officials of the Designated Authority.

Assessment Criteria

（4）The Designated Authority's key objective will be to identify the exploration work program and expenditure commitment bid which will

257

best and expeditiously evaluate the petroleum potential of the contract area. The successful applicant is likely to be the one who is willing to undertake the greatest exploration effort which results in the most comprehensive assessment of the exploration/geological play concepts relevant to the whole contract area. The primary criteria for assessment of applications are therefore:

(a) acceptance of the Production Sharing Contract;

(b) the number of wells to be drilled in each of the first three contract years; and

(c) the extent to which the first three years' work program and expenditure commitments, including the drilling program, data evaluation and geophysical surveying activities, reflects the available technical information on exploration prospects in the contract area, seeks to follow up existing leads, and seeks to identify and evaluate new exploration prospects in previously unexplored parts of the contract area. The work program and expenditure commitments will be assessed by the Designated Authority on the basis of a detailed review of the objectives of the individual items of work proposed.

The Designated Authority will not negotiate changes to the work program and expenditure bids in assessing those bids.

(5) The capacity of the applicant to undertake the proposed work program and expenditure commitments will also be considered, particularly:

(a) the adequacy of financial capability and technical knowledge and ability available to each applicant

(i) the evaluation of financial capacity will be based on assessment of parent/related company annual reports and any other publicly available information on the finances of the company;

(ii) technical knowledge and ability will be assessed on the basis of company's performance in offshore operations or as appropriate on the company's financial capacity to acquire the necessary technological resources to work offshore; and

(b) the future viability of any group of corporations lodging an application, including evidence that an agreement can be reached between those corporations for cooperation in petroleum activities in the contract area or can be reached and the corporation appointed and authorised to be the Contract Operator responsible on behalf of the group of corporations for petroleum activities and all dealings with the Designated Authority under the contract.

(6) In the event that the assessment of applications against the above criteria does not identify one applicant as superior to other applicants for a particular contract area, some of the following additional criteria can be used (but not in any priority order) to choose between the competing applications:

(a) consistent with the Designated Authority's wish to see a continuing and significant level of Timor-Leste involvement in petroleum exploration, preference may be given to consortia with Timor-Leste participation;

(b) consideration may be given to the intent of consortia members to source goods and services in Timor-Leste, and to transfer technology and skills to Timor-Leste nationals and permanent residents; and

(c) consideration may be given to the intent of consortia members to undertake research into exploration techniques and technology in Timor-Leste.

Where preference is given in paragraphs (a), (b) and (c) to Timor-Leste, preference should then be given to Australia followed by other countries.

(7) In the event that the best applicant cannot be chosen on the basis of these criteria, consideration will be given to the amount and quality of work or the amount of expenditure proposed for contract years four to six.

Guideline 3 Guidelines for handling work program and expenditure commitment variations, and contract terminations.

(1) This document summarises some of the conditions applying to a contract entered into under Article 12 of the Interim Petroleum Mining Code, the procedures to be followed in monitoring the status of contracts and guidelines for handling work program and expenditure commitment variations, and contract terminations.

The guideline deals with matters addressed in Articles 28 and 48 of the Interim Petroleum Mining Code, and Sections 4, 13 and 15 of the Production Sharing Contract.

Monitoring of Contract Commitments

(2) The prime responsibility for ensuring that all contract commitments are met rests with the contract operator. The Designated Authority, will ensure that petroleum activities executed by the contract operator are consistent with the contract, the Interim Petroleum Mining Code and its Regulations and Directions.

(3) At least two months prior to the beginning of each contract year (except the first contract year), the contract operator is expected to prepare and submit to the Designated Authority:

(a) a summary of current year exploration and development activity in the contract area;

(b) plans to undertake any remaining work program and expenditure commitments due in the current contract year; and

(c) an exploration and appraisal strategy for the following contract year which briefly describes the exploration and geologic play concepts, the extent to which leads and prospects are identified, and a brief description of the data reviews, seismic surveys and wells planned for the

260

year.

(4) This procedure is aimed at ensuring that, at an early stage, any problems or difficulties being experienced by the contract operator are brought to the attention of the Designated Authority as soon as practicable. Failure to meet contractual requirements may result in termination of the contract.

(5) If more than the required amount of exploration work or expenditure is completed in any contract year, the excess will be counted toward meeting the obligations of the succeeding contract year. The Designated Authority cannot require the operator to undertake more exploration work or expenditure than the minimum amount specified for the contract year.

(6) At least one month before the beginning of each calendar year, the contract operator will prepare and submit to the Designated Authority an annual work program and budget of operating costs. The annual work program and budget of operating costs will be based on the approved exploration and appraisal strategy, and will cover the work planned for the contract area for the year, including the minimum amount of data review, seismic surveying and wells specified in the contract, and any additional discretionary work.

(7) The budgetary aspect of the work program and budget of operating costs will include estimates of the costs of each activity for the calendar year, that is, the estimated aggregate cost of each data evaluation, seismic survey, well, development activity and maintenance work will be stated. The budget will be useful in providing to the Designated Authority an early estimate of aggregate capital, non-capital and exploration costs for the calendar year.

(8) At the exploration stage, the Designated Authority's assessment of cost estimates will be limited to the identification and query of aggregate costs outside the "normal" range for the type of work proposed, and fulfilment of exploration work and expenditure commitments. At this stage, the Designated Authority would arrange with

the relevant Timor-Leste and Australian authorities, contract operator requirements for establishing onshore facilities.

(9) At the development stage, information provided in the work program and budget of operating costs will included the technical aspects of the annual program for development work, maintenance and production (estimated monthly production). An organisation structure and a staffing budget will also be provided.

Work Program Conditions for Contract Years One to Three

(10) A contract operator will undertake each component of the first three years' work program commitments in the designated year or earlier and, unless conditions of 'force majeure' apply, failure to do so will result in the Designated Authority recommending to the Joint Commission that the contract be terminated. The first three years' work program commitments will not be reduced once the contract has been entered into.

(11) The contract operator may apply at any time, consistent with Section 15 of the Production Sharing Contract, for a variation of work program commitments under Section 4 of the Production Sharing Contract on the grounds of "force majeure".

Work Program Conditions for Contract Years Four to Ten

(12) In any of contract years four to six, the contract may be terminated if the amount of exploration work or expenditure required is not completed. However, if the contract is not terminated, the work or expenditure will be completed in the following contract year.

(13) Sixty days before the end of the sixth contract year, the contract operator may request the Designated Authority to extend the contract term to ten years. The Designated Authority and the contract operator will agree to an exploration work program and expenditures for years seven to ten.

(14) The contract operator and Designated Authority may negotiate changes to the work program or expenditure commitment covering

contract years four to ten. The changes will be made at least three months prior to the beginning of the contract year affected by the changes. Any changes to the work program or expenditure commitment should not substantially change the general objective, quantity and quality of the work program.

Other Contract Conditions

(15) Any work undertaken to appraise a discovery which is made during the contract term will not be eligible for credit against the work program or expenditure commitments unless, on application by the contract operator, the Designated Authority is satisfied the work contains a major exploration component.

(16) The Contractor will comply with the provisions of the Interim Petroleum Mining Code, and with the terms and conditions of the contract, including any special conditions imposed by the contract (e. g. special environmental requirements).

Contract Termination

(17) Contracts will not be terminated during the first three contract years unless termination procedures are instituted under Article 48 of the Interim Petroleum Mining Code for breach of contract conditions.

(18) Contracts may be terminated at any time after the third contract year by mutual agreement of the contractor and the Designated Authority. When the contractor notifies the Designated Authority that they wish to terminate the contract, the Designated Authority will consider the application in the context of these guidelines.

(19) The Designated Authority will only agree to terminate the contract if the agreed work or expenditure commitments for the year have been completed. The Designated Authority's agreement to terminate the contract will be conditional on the termination taking effect in the contract year in which the agreement is made. If not, additional work program or expenditure commitments will be incurred.

(20) In considering whether the contractor has complied with the conditions of the contract and the provisions of the Interim Petroleum Mining Code, the Designated Authority will take into account all relevant requirements, particularly:

(a) whether all fees and monies due to the Designated Authority have been paid and whether all work program or expenditure commitments have been completed;

(b) the reporting requirements as set out in the Regulations and Directions issued by the Designated Authority to the contract operator under the Interim Petroleum Mining Code and whether all reports and data have been lodged (e. g. reports on specified activities, quarterly reports, annual reports);

(c) the action taken by the contract operator to ensure that the contract area is clear of all debris resulting from operations and that all wells have been plugged or closed; and

(d) whether on completion of production of petroleum, the contract operator has removed all platforms, structures, pipelines, and associated structures and equipment as provided for in Articles 27 and 48(3) of the Interim Petroleum Mining Code and subsection 5(2)(e) of the Production Sharing Contract in accordance with any generally accepted international standard established in this regard by the competent international organisation.

(21) Where the Designated Authority notifies a contractor of its intention to recommend to the Joint Commission that the contract be terminated because of failure to meet contract conditions, the contractor can provide the Designated Authority with reasons why the contract should not be terminated. These will be provided within 30 days of receipt of notice of the intention to terminate, and the Designated Authority will give full consideration to these reasons.

(22) If the contract is terminated, the contractor remains liable for its obligations for the period prior to the termination. In particular, the contractor will take all necessary action to clean-up the contract area and

remove all property brought into that area, as well as paying any outstanding debts to the Designated Authority.

Guideline 4   Prospecting approvals and access approvals in the Joint Petroleum Development Area

(1) This document sets out the circumstances in which prospecting approvals and access approvals may be issued by the Designated Authority under Articles 32 and 33 of the Interim Petroleum Mining Code. Issue of these approvals will not require publication in the Australian or Timor-Leste Government Gazettes.

Prospecting Approvals

(2) A prospecting approval may be issued by the Designated Authority to corporations wishing to undertake approved petroleum exploration activities (excluding the drilling of petroleum exploration wells) in blocks not in contract areas, prior to the advertisement of those blocks for production sharing contracts. The maximum term of a prospecting approval will normally be six months.

(3) The conditions applicable to a prospecting approval will include:

(a) the area over which petroleum exploration activities will be conducted;

(b) the period for which the prospecting approval will be in force;

(c) compliance with the Interim Petroleum Mining Code and any Regulations and Directions issued by the Designated Authority, or as otherwise approved by the Joint Commission;

(d) reporting requirements; and

(e) public release at any time by the Designated Authority of the data collected from the exploration activities.

(4) The Designated Authority may issue a number of prospecting

approvals over the same blocks. Where this is the case, the Designated Authority will notify each holder of a prospecting approval of the activities to be undertaken by, and conditions applicable to, the holders of every other prospecting approval.

(5) Applications for a prospecting approval will normally include information similar to that outlined in Attachment A.

Access Approvals

(6) An access approval may be issued by the Designated Authority to a holder of a prospecting approval, a person under-taking marine scientific research or a contract operator to enter a contract area, not being its contract area, to undertake petroleum exploration activities (not including the drilling of exploration wells). The Designated Authority will consult with the contract operator of the contract area into which access is sought before giving the access approval.

(7) Applications for access approvals will include:

(a) particulars of activities to be undertaken;

(b) the location of the exploration activity;

(c) reasons access is required; and

(d) the expected time period over which access is required.

(8) Conditions applicable to all access approvals issued will include:

(a) compliance with the Interim Petroleum Mining Code and any Regulations and Directions issued by the Designated Authority;

(b) reporting requirements;

(c) the date that data from the exploration activity will become publicly available;

(d) supplying data to the affected contract operator, if feasible; and

(e) any other conditions.

(9) Access approvals may also be issued to a contract operator to lay and fix petroleum production facilities on the seabed in a contract area not being its contract area, provided that such activities do not interfere with petroleum activities.

Attachment A   Details to accompany applications for a prospecting approval to undertake a Marine Geophysical Survey

The application will be submitted in duplicate and accompanied by the following details of the geophysical survey:

(1) Name of Survey   ....

(2) Name and Address of Sub-Contractor   ....

(3) Name of Survey Vessel   ....

(4) Port from which Vessel Will Operate   ....

(5) Geophysical Technique Proposed   ....

(6) Energy Source Proposed   ....

(7) Proposed Commencement Date   ....

(8) Estimated Duration   ....

(9) Navigational System   ....

(10) Estimated Length of Survey(Time, Kms)   ....

(11) Estimated Cost of Survey ($ US)   ....

(12) Object of Survey (attach statement if insufficient space)

....

(13) All enquiries concerning the application should be directed

.........of.............

(Tel·····················)

Attachments Required:

(1) Two copies of a map showing the proposed lines and blocks.

(2) Technical details of the vessel (if not previously supplied).

(3) A statement of any other matters that the applicant wishes the Designated Authority to consider.

Guideline 5   Guideline for the preparation of Environmental Impact Assessments of petroleum activities

（1）The Designated Authority is responsible for approving all petroleum activities in the Joint Petroleum Development Area, including those which could have a significant effect on the environment, but will consult with the relevant environment authorities in each Contracting State on proposals to construct and install petroleum production structures. The types of petroleum activities likely to be undertaken in the JPDA are seismic surveys, drilling operations, construction and installation of petroleum production structures, and production of petroleum.

（2）The Designated Authority does not require environmental assessments for seismic operations, but does require assessments for all other operations pursuant to clauses 305 and 501 of the Regulations issued under Article 37(1) of the Interim Petroleum Mining Code.

（3）Environmental assessments are required by the Designated Authority when a contract operator applies for approval to drill, and to construct and install petroleum production structures. The contract operator will provide the Designated Authority with information describing the environmental impact of the petroleum activities. For petroleum production projects, the Designated Authority requires contract operators to submit an environmental management plan pursuant to Section 5.2 paragraph（d）of the Production Sharing Contract, including an environmental monitoring program.

（4）This guideline sets out the procedures to be followed by contract operators when providing environmental impact information to the Designated Authority pursuant to clauses 305 and 501 of the Regulations and Section 5.2 paragraph（d）of the Production Sharing Contract.

Drilling

(5) In accordance with clause 501, Part V, of the Regulations issued under Article 37 of the Interim Petroleum Mining Code, an application to drill a well will include a statement which assesses any impact the drilling of the well will have on the environment.

(6) This statement will:

(a) describe the environment in the vicinity of the well site;

(b) assess the potential impact of the drilling on the environment;

(c) describe and assess the effectiveness of any safeguards or standards intended to be adopted for the protection of the environment, including the emergency response manual required under clause 202, Part II, of the Regulations and the identification of blow out prevention equipment and procedures consistent with Part V of the Regulations; and

(d) where the proposal relates to production drilling, describe any proposed changes to the environmental management plan, including the monitoring program (see below).

Construction and Installation of Petroleum Production Structures

(7) In accordance with clause 305, Part III, of the Regulations issued under Article 37 of the Interim Petroleum Mining Code, a preliminary environmental report will be included with an application for approval to construct and install petroleum production structures. The following information will be supplied in this report:

(a) a description of the environment in the vicinity of the proposed structure, including baseline data;

(b) a statement of the potential impact of the structure on the environment, including information on the primary, secondary, short term, long term, adverse and beneficial effects of the proposed structure;

(c) a description of safeguards or standards which will be adopted to protect the environment, including the emergency response manual requirements outlined in clause 202, Part II of the Regulations; and

(d) the proposed environmental management plan, including the environmental monitoring program.

(8) A more detailed description of the requirements for items 7(a) and 7(b) is at Attachment A.

(9) The preliminary environmental report will be assessed by the Designated Authority, or by independent experts engaged by the Designated Authority. The Designated Authority will also refer the report to relevant Timor-Leste and Australian authorities for comment. In determining if further environmental information, and hence an environmental impact statement (EIS) is required, the Designated Authority will take into account to what extent the petroleum development will result in:

(a) a substantial impact on the eco-systems of an area including a significant diminution of the scientific value or other environmental qualities of an area;

(b) the endangering, or further endangering, of any species of fauna or flora;

(c) important long term effects on the environment;

(d) the degradation of the quality of the environment;

(e) the pollution of the environment; and

(f) environmental problems associated with the disposal of waste.

(10) If, according to the above criteria, the Designated Authority determines an EIS is not required, it still may direct that changes be made to the development proposal and the environmental management plan including the monitoring program. Reasons for the Designated Authority's decision not to require an EIS will be made available to the relevant Timor-Leste and Australian authorities

(11) However, if the Designated Authority decides an EIS is necessary, the contract operator will submit a draft EIS which will be referred by the Designated Authority to relevant Timor-Leste and Australian authorities for comment. Each authority will assess the draft EIS according to its own procedures.

（12）An EIS will:

（a）state the objectives of the petroleum development;

（b）contain a description of the petroleum development;

（c）include information and technical data adequate to permit a careful assessment of the impact on the environment of the petroleum development;

（d）examine any feasible and prudent alternative to the development plans;

（e）describe the environment in the vicinity of the proposed structures, including baseline data;

（f）assess the potential impact on the environment of the petroleum development, including the primary, secondary, short-term, long-term, adverse and beneficial effects on the environment of the petroleum development;

（g）describe, and assess the effectiveness of, any safeguards or standards for the protection of the environment intended to be adopted or applied in respect of the petroleum development. The means of implementing and monitoring arrangements to be adopted in respect to safeguards or standards will be described;

（h）cite any sources of information relied upon during the preparation of the EIS; and

（i）include any other relevant information.

（13）Procedures for comment on the draft EIS are at Attachment B. The Designated Authority may require the Contract Operator to alter the EIS. The Designated Authority will give approval for the petroleum development to go ahead in accordance with the final EIS. Approval may include special conditions relating to the development.

Environmental Management Plan

（14）The environmental management plan will set out the procedures and equipment proposed to be used by the contract operator to reduce or prevent the possible harmful effects which could be caused during various stages of the project, including construction, installation, and commissioning of structures, and production.

(15) The plan will include information on:

(a) the types of environmental emergencies for which contingency plans will be in place;

(b) pursuant to clause 202 of the Regulations, details of the contingency plans including the general emergency response organization, chain of command and key areas of responsibility;

(c) the capabilities and limitations of countermeasure equipment and techniques;

(d) the plans for the disposal of recovered pollutants, waste, and debris;

(e) the contract operator's program for gathering data about the physical environment during the life of the project (environmental monitoring program); and

(f) procedures to be undertaken if physical environment monitoring suggests a significant degradation of the environment.

Environmental Monitoring Program

(16) As indicated in paragraph 15(e), the contract operator will provide the Designated Authority with an environmental monitoring program which will include:

(a) information needed to provide a suitable baseline for subsequent monitoring;

(b) the types of project effects that are likely to need monitoring;

(c) the ecosystem parameters to be monitored;

(d) policies for evaluating and amending the monitoring program; and

(e) the predicted effects on the environment after mitigative measures have been followed. This will include a prediction of the expected effects from a clean-up operation after an oil spill.

(17) The Designated Authority may direct that changes be made to

the environmental management plan, including the monitoring program before approving an application to construct and install petroleum production structures.

Attachment A   Information to be included in the Preliminary Environmental Report

(1) Description of the environment required in paragraph 7(a) of the guideline will include baseline data (i. e. data collected on the following factors prior to construction and installation of structures) on:

(a) location;

(b) geology;

(c) climate, including rainfall, cyclone probability, ambient air temperature, relative humidity and winds;

(d) oceanography, including sea water temperature, wave data, water depth and information on currents; and

(e) marine life of the area affected by the petroleum development.

(2) Discussion of the potential environmental impact as required in paragraph 7(b) of the guideline will include:

(a) the effects of the structures on the marine life of the area, with information on events which may cause major ecological disruptions, including oil spill trajectory studies;

(b) any cumulative effect of the petroleum development;

(c) requirements for further monitoring, research or data collection;

(d) the effects related to oil discharges from all sources on marine life;

(e) the quantities and composition of liquid wastes and their disposal;

(f) the quantities and composition of atmospheric emissions; and

(g) sea bed disturbances and solid wastes discharges.

Attachment B   Procedures for comment on draft Environmental Impact Statements

(1) The contract operator will provide the Designated Authority with three copies of the draft Environmental Impact Statement (EIS), including commercial-in-confidence information.

(2) The Designated Authority will request comment on the draft EIS from the relevant Timor-Leste and Australian environmental authorities. These authorities may seek comment from interested parties. The Australian environmental authorities may request the Designated Authority to require the Contract Operator to meet the cost of advertising the draft EIS for public comment in Australia. The Designated Authority will allow at least 60 days for comment.

(3) The Designated Authority may direct the contract operator to revise the draft EIS where necessary.

(4) The contract operator will then provide three copies of the final EIS to the Designated Authority. The Designated Authority may, at any time, review and assess any of the environmental aspects of the petroleum development.

Guideline 6   Guideline for the Graticulation of the JPDA, the Identification and Application of Blocks

(1) Pursuant to Article 2 of the Interim Petroleum Mining Code, the Designated Authority shall be responsible for the division of the JPDA into 5×5 minutes Graticular Sections, and their further subdivision ultimately into smaller Blocks.

(2) This guideline distinguishes the term "Block", being the result of the ultimate subdivision of each Graticular Section provided under

paragraph 2 of Article 2 of the Interim Petroleum Mining Code, from the term "Graticular Section" of 5 x 5 minutes.

(3) This guideline sets out the procedure to be followed for processing the graticulation of the JPDA into Blocks and their identification system, and the follow-up required from each Contract Operator in processing the proper definition and identification of such Blocks in their respective Contract Areas.

(4) Having distinguished the term Block from Graticular Section, another purpose of this guideline is to point out the application of such Blocks under certain provisions of the Interim Petroleum Mining Code and the Production Sharing Contract.

Graticular Sections

(5) The surface of JPDA is divided by the Designated Authority into Graticular Sections defined by meridians of five (5) minutes longitude (reference the meridian of Greenwich) and by parallels five (5) minutes latitude (reference the equator).

(6) Contract Areas of the Joint Petroleum Development Area are identified by the prefix letters "JPDA", and are further identified by:

(a) the year of release, e. g. 03, 04, 05, etc. ;

(b) the allocated Contract Area number, e. g. 01, 02, 03, etc.

The Contract Areas are each composed of whole Graticular Sections and parts of Graticular Sections, which are squares or truncated squares. These Graticular Sections are assigned a sequential numbering system.

Subdivision of Graticular Sections

(7) Each Graticular Section of 5×5 minutes shall ultimately be subdivided by meridians of 1 (one) minute longitude and by parallels of 1 (one) minute latitude, thereby forming a Block.

(8) Each Block as defined under paragraph 7 above, shall be allocated a discreet identifying number as per following examples.

Examples:

(a) Graticular Section 351 (square)

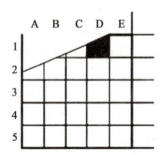

The shaded Block in column C on line 3 is identified as "Block 351-C3".

Heavy 5×5 minutes lines

Light 1×1 minute lines

(b) Graticular Section 132 (truncated square)

The shaded Block in column D on line 1 is identified as "Block 132-D1"

(9) Contract Areas within JPDA shall be described in terms of the component Blocks. Each Contract Operator shall therefore prepare for their respective Contract Areas:

(a) the subdivision of Graticular Sections in the Contract Area into Blocks;

(b) determine the accurate coordinates of the points where the side-lines of such Blocks cross; and

(c) assign the proper identifying number to each such Block; consistent with the guidelines described above.

This graticulation shall be submitted to the Designated Authority for approval.

Application of Blocks

(10) For the operation of the following provisions of:

(a) the Interim Petroleum Mining Code

- Article 16　Declaration of Discovery Area;

- Article 22　Block Relinquishment;

- Article 23　Surrender of Blocks; and

(b) the Production Sharing Contract

- Section 2　Term of this Contract;

- Section 3　Relinquishment of Blocks;

the term Block referred in such provisions, are the component Blocks as meant under paragraph 9 of this Guideline.

Guideline 7　Administrative guideline on tendering and reporting on drilling operations in the Joint Petroleum Development Area

A. Tendering for Petroleum Activities

(1) The Contract Operator shall draw invitations to tender for subcontracts to the attention of Timor-Leste subcontractors (Subsections 10.1, 5.2.(h), and 5.2.(i) of the PSC for guidance in inviting Tenders).

(2) The Designated Authority requires the Contract Operator to take appropriate measures that in subcontracting operations for JPDA preference is given to employment of Timor-Leste nationals and permanent residents, having due regard to safe and efficient operations and good oilfield practice (Subsection 5.2.(i) of the PSC and Article 11 of the Treaty).

(3) The Designated Authority shall be notified by the Contract Operator, as follows:

(a) Notification of Intention to Tender for Subcontract, one (1) week prior to tender invitation;

(b) A tender period of at least 30 days should apply for subcontracts estimated up to US $ 2 million and 60 days should be allowed for subcontracts likely to exceed US $ 2 million;

(c) Notification of Subcontract Award, as soon as practicable after evaluation of the tender,

(d) The full financial details of the sub-contract, irrespective of the amount of the expenditure involved (Subsection 10.5 of the PSC), to be attached to the Notification of Subcontract Award.

(4) Tenders shall be subject to the approval of the Designated Authority, Subsection 10.2 of the PSC, except as provided for in Subsection 10.4 of the PSC.

B. Drilling

(1) Prior to drilling commencing, the Contract Operator will provide the Designated Authority with an environmental assessment in accordance with Administrative Guideline No 5 (Guideline for the preparation of Environmental Impact Assessment of Petroleum activities and Clause 501 of the Regulations)

(2) The Contract Operator is required to obtain approval for drilling a well in the JPDA. The attached Application for Approval to Drill a Well in the JPDA is to be submitted in duplicate to the Designated Authority at least one month before the commencement of drilling of each well (Clause 501 of the Regulations).

(3) The Contract Operator is required to obtain approval for materials and equipment to be used in the drilling operations which do not satisfy Clause 502 of the Regulations.

(4) The Contract Operator is required to obtain approval for Drill Vessels, Workboats (Anchor handling and Supply Vessels), and Aircraft both fixed and rotary wing, to enter the JPDA (paragraph g Annex C of the Treaty) and all personnel (including employees of Contract Operator) who are employed in petroleum activities in the JPDA (Clause 208 of the Regulations).

C. During Drilling Operations

(1) Designated Authority approval is required for:

(a) Moving of a Mobile Offshore Drilling Unit (MODU) within JPDA (Clause 302 of the Regulations);

(b) Production or Drill Stem Testing of a well, not being a producing well (Clause 513 of the Regulations);

(c) Abandoning or suspending of a well (Clause 514 of the Regulations); and

(d) Completion of a well (Clause 608 of the Regulations).

(2) The Designated Authority must be notified by the Contract Operator for the following:

(a) Any significant variations to the prescribed setting depth of casing (Clause 504 of the Regulations);

(b) Any reason to suspect a faulty cementing operation (Clause 505 of the Regulations);

(c) Removing blow out prevention equipment for repairs (Clause 506 of the Regulations);

(d) Results of analyses of cuttings and cores as soon as practicable after the completion of the analyses (Clause 456 of the Regulations);

(e) Logging and the results of logging analyses of the objective formations as soon as practicable after the completion of the analyses;

(f) Production or Drill Stem Testing with not less than 24 hours notice of the date and time of that test (Clause 513 of the Regulations); and

(g) When an emergency occurs, a report to be made within 48 hours of the occurrence (Clause 286 of the Regulations).

D. Reports

(1) The following reports are required:

(a) Daily reports for the previous 24 hours, with a copy sent to the Designated Authority's Head Office in Darwin (Clause 551 of the

Regulations）;

（b）Weekly reports（two copies）including a summary of daily reports, daily driller's logs and weekly rig inspection report（Clause 552 of the Regulations）;

（c）Record of personnel entering and leaving JPDA（Clause 208 of the Regulations）;

（d）Notifications to the appropriate authorities（Custom Service）of proposed movements of vessels or aircraft（Clause 216 of the Regulations）;

（e）Report on Modification, Abandonment or Suspension of a well（Clause 553 of the Regulations）; and

（f）Final Reports on Wells（three copies）shall be made available as soon as practicable but within 6 months after such completion（Clause 454 of the Regulations）.

（2）Unless otherwise advised, all reports and correspondence relating to drilling activities should be addressed to the Managing Director-Technical.

E. Inspection by the Designated Authority

The following will be subject to inspection by the Designated Authority:

（a）MODU's will be inspected before its first entry into the JPDA unless it has been inspected in either Australia or Timor-Leste within the preceding nine（9）months（Clause 503 of the Regulations）; and

（b）Supporting Vessels and Aircraft both fixed and rotary wing will be inspected by an Inspector designated by the Managing Director before their entry into the JPDA（paragraph g Annex C of the Treaty）.

Attachments

（1）Notification of Intention to Tender for Subcontract.

（2）Notification of Subcontract Award.

（3）Application For Approval to drill a well in the JPDA.

Attachment 1　Notification of Intention to Tender for Subcontract(To be submitted on Contract Operator Corporate letterhead)

To be submitted prior to tendering for services. The Contract Operator shall notify their intention to tender for petroleum activities by providing the following information and supporting documents.

To: Managing Director-Technical

From:

Contract Area : JPDA ...

Contract Operator Contact:　　　　　　Phone No :

　　　　　　　　　　　　　　　　　　Facsimile :

B. Brief Scope of Work to be tendered:

C. Estimate of Contract Value: US $

D. Estimated Contract Duration:

E. Proposed Date of Invitation to Tender:

F. Total Number of Tenderers Invited:　　Timor-Leste : (　　)

Others : 　(　　)

(*A list of Invited Tenderers is required to be attached, giving company name, full address and contact name*)

(*Refer to Subsections* 5. 2. (*h*) *and* 5. 2. (*i*) *of the PSC and Article* 11 *of the Treaty as guidance for selecting Invited Tenderers*)

G. Proposed Date for Contract Award:

H. Specific Details of Tender Process:

The following, which outlines the tender evaluation process, is required by the Designated Authority.

* Justification to go to tender,

* Selection criteria for invitations to tender,

* Selection criteria for tenderers,

* Tender receipt procedure covering confidentiality and communication

with tenderers,

    * Criteria for evaluation and award.

    * Other relevant information.

Attachment 2　Notification of Subcontract Award
(*To be submitted on Contract Operator Corporate letterhead*)

To: Managing Director-Technical

From:

Contract Area:　　　　　　JPDA ...

A. Contract Value: US $

B. Contract Duration:

C. Date of Subcontract Award:

D. Total Number of Tenders Received: Timor-Leste: 　(　)

Others: 　(　)

E. Summary of Tenders Received:

Give details of all tenders and methods used to evaluate along with the justification for award to a particular tender. List all tenders in order of evaluation result and preference.

(*Refer to Subsections* 5. 2. (*h*) *and* 5. 2. (*i*) *of the PSC and Article* 11 *of the Treaty as guidance for selecting preferred Subcontractor*)

F. Subcontractor details:

Provide details of the selected Subcontractor name, organisation (Indicate the employment of Timor-Leste nationals and permanent residents in the organisation), past performance and place of subcontractor/company registration.

G. Notifications and Approvals:

(*Refer to Subsections* 10. 2 *and* 10. 4 *of the PSC for details where approval is to be sought and given*)

Is Designated Authority Approval Required Prior to Award:

                                                                YES / NO

Approval requested by: ······································ (Applicant)

·· (Title)

Approval is hereby granted by: ······························ (Title)

Attachment 3   Application for Approval to Drill a Well in the JPDA
(*To be submitted on Contract Operator Corporate letterhead*)

This application is required to be submitted to the Managing Director-Technical not later than one month prior to the commencement of drilling of each well.

(1) Contract Operator:

Name:

Address:

(2) Contract Area: JPDA ...

(3) Prime Contact:

Name:

Phone & Facsimile (B/H): Phone & Facsimile (A/H):

(4) Drilling Subcontractor:

Name:

Address:

(5) Name and Address of all other Subcontractors involved:

(to be listed on Attachment A)

(6) Name and Type of MODU:

(7) Well Name, Number and Well Code:

(8) Drilling Objectives:

Primary:

Secondary:

(9) Well Location:

SP: Seismic Line No.:

Lat: Long:

Location in accordance with TSDA's grid system:

(10) Water Depth (m):

(11) Proposed Total Depth (m):

(12) Estimated Spud Date:

(13) Estimated Drilling Time (days):

(14) Estimated Total Cost in US. $:

(*to be itemized on Attachment B*)

(15) Name or Registration Number of attendant craft including Aircraft which will provide services:

(*list on Attachment C*)

(16) Other Information to be attached:

* Map showing well location (A4-size)

* Details of MODU and Blow-out Prevention Equipment (*Including diagram, description, and method of operation*)

* Geological Prognosis (*including Predicted Section and Targets*)

* Drilling Prognosis (*including Time vs. Depth Prediction Graph*)

* Drilling Procedural Manual

* Pollution Control Measures and Oil Spill Contingency

* Statement on any significant impact on Environmental Policies

* Drilling Safety Manual and Emergency Response Manual

* Safety and Accident Record of the drilling subcontractor for the past 3 year period

* Current valid certifications for MODU, vessels, aircraft and any other equipment used in the operation:

MODU: Summary Report of Class Surveys, Certificate of Inspection, International Load Line Certificate, Crane Certificate, and the latest Inspection Report & Safety Audit.

Vessel: Certificate of Classification/Seaworthiness, Safety Equipment Certificate, Safety Radio Certificate, Safety Construction Certificate, International Load Line Certificate, International Tonnage Certificate, Hull & Machinery Certificate, and International Oil Pollution Prevention Certificate, and the latest Inspection Report & Safety Audit.

Aircraft: Airworthiness Certificate, Air Operator's Certificate, and the latest Inspection Report & Safety Audit.

∗ Details of all personnel required to enter the JPDA including Name, Position, Nationality and copies of their Passports. For non-Australian and non-Timor-Leste nationals or permanent residents copies of visas are to be included.

∗ Details of insurance as required of under PART VII of the Directions.

∗ Copy of Subcontractors' acceptance to work in accordance with the PSC.

∗ Attach copies of Drilling and Geological and any other Report Forms (daily, weekly, etc) to be used.

Guideline 8 Administrative guideline for the payment of the proceeds to the Designated Authority of its share of First Tranche Petroleum (FTP)

Applicable Treaty documents provisions and underlying Regulations and Directions:

(1) Consistent with the Designated Authority's powers and functions under the Treaty, the management functions shall include: collecting and, with approval of the Joint Commission, distributing between the two Contracting States the proceeds of the Designated Authority's share of petroleum production from contracts.

(2) The Production Sharing Contract provides at sub-section 7.9 that:

"in the initial five (5) calendar years of production from the contract area, the Parties shall be entitled to take and receive a quantity of petroleum equal to ten (10) per cent of the petroleum production in those years, called "first tranche petroleum" before any recovery of investment credits and operating costs. In each subsequent calendar year, the first tranche petroleum shall be equal to twenty (20) per cent of the petroleum produced in those years. The quantity of first tranche petroleum from crude oil production for each calendar year shall be shared between the Designated Authority and the contractor in accordance with the sharing percentages as provided under subsection 3 of this Section, …:"

(3) Subsection 7.3 of the PSC provides the following sharing of production, applicable to FTP, as provided in sub-section 7.9:

"(a) the Designated Authority fifty (50) per cent and the contractor fifty (50) per cent for the tranche of 0 to 50, 000 barrels daily average of all crude oil production from the contract area for the calendar year;

(b) the Designated Authority sixty (60) per cent and the contractor forty (40) per cent for the tranche of 50, 001 to 150, 000 barrels daily average of all crude oil production from the contract area for the calendar year; or

(c) the Designated Authority seventy (70) per cent and the contractor thirty (30) per cent for the tranche of more than 150, 000 barrels daily average of all crude oil production from the contract area for the calendar year. "

(4) Article 4.3 of the Interim Petroleum Mining Code provides inter alia;

"Except as provided in paragraph 5 of this Article, the Designated Authority shall authorise the marketing of its share of petroleum production by the contractor who shall market all the petroleum in the contract area.. "

Article 4.5   of the Interim Petroleum Mining Code provides inter alia;

" The Designated Authority, with the approval of the Joint Commission, may market any or all petroleum production. " The paragraph continues to set out the basis for the valuation of petroleum, and other marketing arrangements for sales of petroleum production by the Designated Authority. These arrangements are outside the scope of this Administrative Guideline.

(5) Sub-section 7. 1 of the PSC provides:

"The contractor is authorised by the Designated Authority and obliged to market all petroleum produced and saved from the contract area subject to the following provisions."

The provisions of Section 7 of the PSC provide the production sharing arrangements, including those set out in 2 and 3 above. The contractor refers collectively to the party, or parties, contracted under the PSC to the Designated Authority. (Note, however, that sub-section 7. 11 of the Production Sharing Contract reserves the right for the Designated Authority to market any or all of the petroleum, when the Designated Authority secures a net realized price f. o. b. the contract area, greater than the price which can be realized by the contractor.

(6) The individual contracting parties to a PSC, under PSC sub-section 5. 3 (d), may exercise their right to market their respective, shares of petroleum production, consistent with Section 8 of the PSC. Section 8 of the PSC provides for a net realized price f. o. b. the contract area, or the determination of a fair and reasonable f. o. b. price/value.

(7) The Contract Operator is required to by the 10th day of each month to meet the reporting requirements on shipments of petroleum as set out in Clause 656 of Designated Authority Regulations.

Administrative Guideline Provisions

(1) Where the individual contracting parties to a PSC exercise their right to market their respective shares of petroleum production, the cargo contract, pricing and notification procedures as between these individual contracting parties (lifting parties) and the Designated Authority must be agreed between the lifting parties and the Designated Authority. Subject to such agreement, the Designated Authority will be a party to each contract for the sale of petroleum to the extent of its share of FTP production during that period when the investment credits and operating costs, recoverable by the individual contracting parties, exceed the value of the quantity of petroleum produced from the contract area, excluding

FTP.

（2）The negotiated terms and contractual conditions for the sale of a cargo, or cargoes, of petroleum production will be set out in an initial Cargo Transaction Report. The initial Cargo Transaction Report, together with the contract for the sale of the petroleum, will be provided to the Designated Authority as soon as the contract conditions are settled.

（3）The Designated Authority's revenue from its share of FTP will be the applicable proceeds, net of its share of agreed expenses, as set out in a preliminary Cargo Transaction Report. This revenue will be lodged into the Designated Authority's interest bearing account（denominated in US $）with the Chase Manhattan Bank, New York, on the same day as the gross proceeds are received by the lifting party.

（4）The Designated Authority will receive a final Cargo Transaction Report from the lifting party. The Designated Authority will have five（5）working days within which to approve, or otherwise call for explanation of expenditures claimed against petroleum revenues. This report will form the basis of:

（a）an additional payment to be lodged into the Designated Authority's account with Chase Manhattan on receipt of the Designated Authority's acceptance of the final Cargo Transaction Report; or

（b）if the initial payment, based on the preliminary Cargo Transaction Report, exceeds the amount payable to the Designated Authority on the basis of the final Cargo Transaction Report, the Designated Authority will repay the overpayment within five（5）working days of the receipt of final Cargo Transaction Report.

If the Designated Authority calls for an explanation and has received a reply, it may accept the explanation, or seek further review. Where the lifting party has paid additional costs to a third party, the Designated Authority will pay its share of outstanding costs to the lifting party, subject to reserving a right of recompense. Similarly the Designated Authority may reserve a right of recompense against a cost included on the preliminary Cargo Transaction Report which is carried forward to the final Cargo Transaction Report. The Designated Authority reserves the right to audit the receipt of sales revenues and the disbursement of costs made against those revenues as provided under subsection 14.2 of the PSC.

（5）The Designated Authority will maintain a minimum balance of US $10, 000 in its Chase Manhattan account. This minimum balance will be available to cover repayments as provided in 4 (b) above. The balance in the Designated Authority's Chase Manhattan Bank account in excess of US $10, 000 on the 15th day of each month, or next banking day, will be transferred in equal shares to bank accounts nominated by the Contracting States. Transfer costs will be for the account of the Contracting States.

4. Timor Sea Treaty Designated Authority（Privileges and Immunities）Regulations 2003

Statutory Rules 2003 No. 451
Dated 7 April 2003

1）Name of Regulations
These Regulations are the Timor Sea Treaty Designated Authority (Privileges and Immunities) Regulations 2003.

2）Commencement
These Regulations are taken to have commenced on the commencement of section 5B of the International Organisations (Privileges and Immunities) Act 1963.

3）Australia-Indonesia Zone of Cooperation（Privileges and Immunities) Regulations — repeal
The following Statutory Rules are repealed：
· 1990 No. 228
· 1991 No. 444.
4）Definitions

In these Regulations:

Act means the International Organisations (Privileges and Immunities) Act 1963.

Treaty has the same meaning as in the Petroleum (Timor Sea Treaty) Act 2003.

Note For the meaning of Designated Authority, see section 5B of the Act.

5) Designated Authority to have juridical personality and legal capacities

The Designated Authority:

(a) is a body corporate; and

(b) is capable, in its corporate name:

(i) of entering into contracts; and

(ii) of acquiring, holding and disposing of real and personal property; and

(iii) of suing and being sued.

6) Privileges and immunities of the Designated Authority

The Designated Authority has the privileges and immunities specified in paragraph 7 of the First Schedule to the Act in relation to:

(a) income tax within the meaning of the Income Tax Assessment Act 1936; and

(b) income tax within the meaning of the Income Tax Assessment Act 1997; and

(c) fringe benefits tax within the meaning of the Fringe Benefits Tax Assessment Act 1986.

7) Privileges of officers of the Designated Authority

(1) Subject to subregulation (2), a person who holds an office in the Designated Authority and is not:

(a) a resident of Australia within the meaning of the Income Tax Assessment Act 1936; or

(b) an Australian resident within the meaning of the Income Tax Assessment Act 1997;

has the privileges and immunities specified in paragraphs 2 and 7 of Part I of the Fourth Schedule to the Act.

(2) In relation to the importation of furniture and effects, the privileges and immunities specified in paragraph 7 of Part I of the Fourth Schedule to the Act apply for a period of 6 months, or such further time as in exceptional circumstances is allowed by the Minister, from a person's first entry into Australia for the purpose of taking up a post with the Designated Authority.

(3) However, the privileges and immunities specified in paragraph 7 of Part I of the Fourth Schedule to the Act cease to apply to imported goods that are sold, donated or otherwise disposed of in Australia:

(a) within 2 years after the goods were imported; and

(b) otherwise than in accordance with an agreement between the officer of the Designated Authority and the Commonwealth.

Note

Notified in the Commonwealth of Australia Gazette on 7 April 2003.

5. Petroleum Mining Code for the Joint Petroleum Development Area

Part I   Definitions

Article 1   Definitions

(1) For the purposes of this Petroleum Mining Code:

(a) "block" means a block constituted in accordance with Article 2 of this Petroleum Mining Code;

(b) "calendar year" means a period of twelve (12) months commencing on 1 January and ending on the following 31 December, according to the Gregorian Calendar;

(c) "contract operator" means the contractor appointed and authorized by the contractors to be responsible for petroleum operations and all dealings with the Designated Authority under the contract on behalf of the contractors;

(d) "contract year" has the meaning specified in each production sharing contract;

(e) "discovery area" means the blocks declared by the Designated Authority under Article 16 of this Petroleum Mining Code to contain petroleum;

(f) "operating costs" means those costs defined in a production sharing contract which are incurred and are recoverable by the contract operator in the course of undertaking petroleum operations;

(g) "petroleum pool" means a discrete accumulation of petroleum under a single pressure system;

(h) "pipeline" means a pipe or system of pipes and associated equipment necessary for conveying petroleum;

(i) "work program and budget of operating costs" means the details of petroleum operations to be carried out in or related to the contract area and the aggregate cost estimates for those operations;

(j) "Treaty" means the Timor Sea Treaty signed on 20 May 2002.

(2) The terms used in this Petroleum Mining Code shall, unless otherwise specified, have the same meaning as those in the Treaty.

Part II   Joint Petroleum Development Area

Article 2   Graticulation of the Joint Petroleum Development Area

(1) The surface of the Joint Petroleum Development Area shall be divided by the Designated Authority into graticular sections defined by meridians of five (5) minutes of longitude (reference the meridian of Greenwich) and by parallels of latitude of five (5) minutes (reference the

Equator). A block shall constitute a graticular section as described above and shall include part graticular sections. Each block in the Joint Petroleum Development Area shall be allocated a discrete identifying number.

(2) The Designated Authority may subdivide each block into graticular sections. Where this is done, the graticular sections shall be defined by meridians of longitude and by parallels of latitude, and each section shall form a block. Each block so defined shall be allocated a discrete identifying number.

(3) Contract areas within the Joint Petroleum Development Area shall be described in terms of the component blocks.

Article 3   Geodetic datum

Whenever it is necessary to determine the position of a line in the Joint Petroleum Development Area that position shall be determined by reference to a spheroid having its centre at the centre of the earth and a major (equatorial) radius of 6378160 metres and a flattening of 100/29825 and by reference to the position of the Johnston Geodetic Station in the Northern Territory of Australia. That station shall be taken to be situated at 133 degrees, 12 minutes and 30. 0771 seconds of East Longitude and at 25 degrees, 56 minutes and 54. 5515 seconds of South Latitude and to have a ground level of 571. 2 metres above the spheroid referred to above.

Part Ⅲ   The Contract

Article 4   Rights conferred by contract

(1) A production sharing contract entered into by the Designated Authority, with the approval of the Joint Commission, shall give to the contractor the exclusive right and the responsibility to undertake petroleum operations in a contract area, subject to the provisions of the

Treaty, relevant regulations and directions issued by the Designated Authority, and the terms and conditions of the contract.

(2) During each calendar year, any petroleum production shall be shared between the Designated Authority and the contractor.

(3) The contract shall not confer on the contractor ownership of petroleum in the ground but shall provide for the contractor to take a share of petroleum production as payment from the Designated Authority for the petroleum operations undertaken by the contract operator pursuant to the contract. Ownership of the Designated Authority's share of petroleum production shall remain with the Designated Authority. Except as provided in paragraph 5 of this Article, the Designated Authority shall authorize the marketing of its share of petroleum production by the contractor who shall market all petroleum produced from the contract area.

(4) Title to the contractor's share of petroleum production:

(a) In the case of petroleum exported by tanker: shall pass to the contractor at the point of tanker loading. Petroleum production shall be measured at the point of tanker loading. For the purposes of a production sharing contract, all such measured production shall be deemed to have been produced on the day of the commencement of tanker loading.

(b) In the case of petroleum exported by pipeline: shall pass to the contractor at the input flange of the export pipeline. Petroleum production shall be measured at the input flange of the export pipeline. For the purposes of a production sharing contract, all such measured production shall be deemed to have been produced on the day on which the petroleum enters the input flange of the export pipeline.

(c) In the case of any means other than those specified in subparagraphs (a) and (b) of this paragraph: shall pass at the point as heretofore or hereafter agreed between Australia and Timor-Leste. Such agreement shall include a provision on the point at which petroleum is measured and the day on which production is deemed to have been produced.

Subject to paragraph 5 of this Article the contractor shall have the right to lift, dispose of and export its share of petroleum, and retain abroad the proceeds obtained therefrom. Except where the Designated Authority markets petroleum as provided in paragraph 5 of this Article, the contract shall require the contractor to pay to the Designated Authority, at regular periods during each calendar year, an amount of money estimated to be equal to the value of the Designated Authority's share of petroleum production lifted for those periods. The contract shall specify the length of each period, monthly if workable, the means by which the value of the Designated Authority's share of petroleum production is estimated for each period, and when each payment shall be made. The estimated value of the Designated Authority's share of petroleum production for each period shall be based on the work program and budget of operating costs and revisions to it, and the expected value of quantities of petroleum to be produced. The estimated value shall be revised during the calendar year having regard to the actual operating costs and value of sales of petroleum.

(5) The Designated Authority, with the approval of the Joint Commission, may market any or all petroleum production subject to such conditions as may be specified in the production sharing contract. Where it is the Designated Authority's share of petroleum production which is to be marketed by the Designated Authority, the method of determining the estimated value of the Designated Authority's share shall be based on that method described in paragraph 4 of this Article. Where petroleum production marketed by the Designated Authority includes the contractor's share, the contract shall require the Designated Authority to pay to the contractor, at regular periods during each calendar year, an amount of money estimated to be equal to the value of the contractor's share of petroleum production so lifted for those periods. The method of determining the estimated value of the Designated Authority's and the contractor's shares shall be based on that method described in paragraph 4 of this Article. The contract operator shall be obliged to coordinate the

efficient lifting of the petroleum production, including tanker nomination and scheduling.

(6) The contract shall also specify that within thirty (30) days after the end of each calendar year, adjustments and cash settlements between the contractor and the Designated Authority shall be made on the basis of the actual quantities, amounts and prices involved, in order to ensure that the Designated Authority receives the correct share of petroleum production for each calendar year.

(7) In the case of a contract entered into with a group of corporations, each corporation shall be jointly and severally liable for meeting the conditions of the contract, and for complying with the requirements of this Petroleum Mining Code and the regulations and directions issued by the Designated Authority. Each corporation shall be a signatory to the contract with the Designated Authority.

Article 5   The contract

Without limiting the matters to be dealt with, the contract shall be concluded on the basis of the Model Production Sharing Contract and shall include:

(a) the definition of the responsibilities and rights of the contractor, the contract operator and the Designated Authority;

(b) the term of the contract and block relinquishment provisions;

(c) the work program and expenditure commitments;

(d) the definition of operating costs and the method of recovery of those costs by the contract operator;

(e) the petroleum production share to be allocated to the contractor;

(f) provisions for the termination of the contract;

(g) provisions for exemption from and variation of contract conditions;

(h) provisions for the resolution of disputes between the contractor and the Designated Authority; and

(i) any other provisions that are consistent with the Treaty.

Article 6   Contract operator

（1）Where a number of corporations enters into a contract with the Designated Authority, the corporations shall appoint and authorize one of their number to be the contract operator responsible, on behalf of the group of corporations, for petroleum operations and all dealings with the Designated Authority under the contract.

（2）The contract operator shall undertake petroleum operations in an efficient manner which minimizes costs and in a manner in accordance with the provisions of the production sharing contract. Costs incurred by the contract operator in undertaking petroleum operations shall not include any component of profit which accrues to the contract operator solely by virtue of its role as contract operator.

（3）All communications on matters related to the contract shall be effected between the contract operator and the Designated Authority. The contract operator shall establish an office in either Timor-Leste or Australia.

Article 7   Term of contract

（1）Subject to the provisions of this Article, and Articles 22 and 48 of this Petroleum Mining Code,:

（a）Production Sharing Contract 03-12 shall expire on 6 February 2022;

（b）Production Sharing Contract 03-13 shall expire on 17 December 2021;

（c）Production Sharing Contract 03-19 shall expire on 3 October 2026; and

（d）Production Sharing Contract 03-20 shall expire on 15 November 2026.

（2）In addition, the provisions of the production sharing contract shall include

（a）an obligation on the Designated Authority to give sympathetic consideration to an extension of the term of the contract beyond the expiration date if petroleum production has not ceased by that year; and

(b) automatic extension of the term of the contract to allow continuation of petroleum production to meet natural gas sales contracts the terms of which extend beyond the expiration date of the production sharing contract.

(3) The production sharing contract may also include a specified term after which the contract may be terminated if a discovery is not made.

(4) Production sharing contracts 03-01, 03-16 and 03-21 shall expire six months from the later of:

(a) the date on which the Joint Commission approves the Petroleum Mining Code provided for in Article 7(a) of the Treaty; and

(b) the date on which the Joint Commission approves the model production sharing contract.

Part Ⅳ   Petroleum Exploration and Exploitation

Article 8   Advertisement of blocks

(1) The Designated Authority shall invite applications to enter into a contract over specific blocks. The invitation for applications shall specify:

(a) the blocks over which the rights shall be granted;

(b) the bidding system to apply;

(c) the basis on which bids shall be assessed;

(d) details of the contract to be entered into including the rights and responsibilities of the parties to the contract; and

(e) the period within which applications may be made.

(2) Details of the invitation for applications shall be published in official Australian and Timor-Leste Government Gazettes and in such

other ways as the Designated Authority decides.

Article 9　Bidding system

(1) The Designated Authority shall invite applications to enter into a contract over parts of the Joint Petroleum Development Area using a work program bidding system which identifies annual exploration work program and expenditure commitments to be undertaken in the contract area.

(2) The Designated Authority shall make available full details of the bidding system to be used at the time applications are invited.

Article 10　Application for contracts

(1) The Designated Authority shall set out in formal guidelines the form in which applications shall be prepared and lodged. As a minimum requirement a draft contract based on the Model Production Sharing Contract shall be completed and lodged, and applications shall set out details of the work program and expenditure commitments, and the financial capability and technical knowledge and ability available to the applicant.

(2) Where an application is lodged by a group comprising several corporations, the application shall be accompanied by evidence that an agreement can be reached between those corporations for cooperation in petroleum operations in the contract area.

(3) The application shall be accompanied by the fee specified in Article 44 of this Petroleum Mining Code.

Article 11　Consideration of application

(1) The Designated Authority shall set out in formal guidelines the basis on which applications will be considered and the relevant criteria which applicants will be expected to meet. Contracts shall be offered in accordance with the published criteria for that bidding round. The principal criteria shall be the amount and quality of the exploration work bid.

(2) The Designated Authority shall be satisfied that an applicant has the necessary financial capability and technical knowledge and ability to carry out petroleum operations in a manner consistent with the terms and conditions of the contract and this Petroleum Mining Code, including the necessary environmental and safety requirements.

Article 12   Grant or refusal of contracts

(1) The Designated Authority shall seek prior approval from the Joint Commission to enter into a contract with the preferred applicant or group of applicants.

(2) Subject to that approval, the Designated Authority shall notify in writing the successful applicant that it has Joint Commission approval to enter into a contract with the applicant covering petroleum operations in a specified contract area on terms and conditions set out in the contract. The applicant shall have thirty (30) days within which to accept or refuse the offer in writing. On the applicant accepting the offer, paying the contract service fee, and providing evidence that it has fulfilled any prerequisite conditions such as insurance cover, the Designated Authority shall enter into the contract with the applicant.

(3) Unsuccessful applicants shall be advised accordingly.

Article 13   Publication of contracts

The Designated Authority shall publish in official Australian and Timor-Leste Government Gazettes summary details of:

(a) contracts entered into; and

(b) termination of contracts.

Article 14   Commencement of work

The contract operator shall commence petroleum operations within six (6) months from the date the contract is entered into, except for reasons of force majeure.

Article 15   Discovery of petroleum

(1) The contract operator shall notify the Designated Authority in writing within twenty four hours (24) whenever any petroleum is discovered and on request by the Designated Authority shall provide details in writing of the:

(a) chemical composition and physical properties of the petroleum; and

(b) the nature of the sub-soil in which the petroleum occurs.

(2) The contract operator shall provide the Designated Authority with any other information concerning the discovery on request by the Designated Authority.

(3) The contract operator shall also do such things as the Designated Authority requests to determine the chemical composition and physical properties of any petroleum discovered, and to determine the geographical extent of any petroleum pool and the quantity of petroleum in that pool.

Article 16   Declaration of discovery area

(1) The Designated Authority shall declare the blocks within the contract area covering a petroleum pool as a discovery area, provided that the Designated Authority and contract operator agree that the petroleum pool can be produced commercially. These blocks shall form a single contiguous area.

(2) At any time after a discovery area has been declared, the Designated Authority may, of its own volition or on request from the contract operator, agree that certain blocks be included in or excluded from the discovery area. Blocks included in the discovery area in this way shall be from within the contractor's contract area.

Article 17   Approval to produce petroleum

The contract operator shall not construct any production structures without the approval of the Designated Authority. The Designated Authority shall not unreasonably withhold approvals.

Article 18　Approval to construct pipeline

（1）The contract operator shall not construct a pipeline for the purpose of conveying petroleum within or from the Joint Petroleum Development Area without the approval of the Joint Commission, nor shall the contract operator operate or remove that pipeline without the approval of the Joint Commission.

（2）The Joint Commission may direct a contract operator owning a pipeline to enter into a commercial agreement with another contract operator to enable the second mentioned operator to transport petroleum.

Article 19　Petroleum production work

Unless otherwise agreed between the contract operator and the Designated Authority, work on a permanent structure to produce petroleum shall commence within six（6）months of approval to construct the structure.

Article 20　Rates of production

The Designated Authority may direct and make regulations about the commencement of petroleum production and the specific rates of petroleum production. In giving such directions and making such regulations the Designated Authority shall take account of good oilfield practice.

Article 21　Unitization

Where a petroleum pool is partly within a contract area and partly within another contract area, but wholly within the Joint Petroleum Development Area, the Designated Authority shall require the contractors to enter into a unitization agreement with each other within a reasonable time, as determined by the Designated Authority, for the purpose of securing the more effective and optimized production of petroleum from the pool. If no agreement has been reached within such reasonable time, the Designated Authority shall decide on the unitization agreement. Without limiting the matters to be dealt with, the unitization agreement shall define or contain the approach to define the amount of petroleum in each contract area, the method of producing the petroleum, and shall appoint the contract operator responsible for production of the petroleum covered by the unitization agreement. The Designated Authority shall approve the unitization agreement before approvals under Article 17 of this Petroleum Mining Code are given. Any changes to the unitization agreement shall be subject to approval by the Designated Authority.

Article 22   Block relinquishment

（1）The contract shall contain provisions for the progressive relinquishment of blocks from the contract area.

（2）In calculating the relinquishment requirements, the blocks in a discovery area shall not be counted as part of the original number of blocks in the contract area.

（3）In the event that no discovery area has been declared in the contract area before the end of an initial period specified in the contract, the contract operator shall either relinquish all remaining blocks in the contract area and the contract shall be terminated, or the contract operator shall exercise the option provided in the contract to extend the term of the contract.

Article 23   Surrender of blocks

（1）The contractor may surrender some or all of the blocks in a contract area provided the conditions of the contract have been met to the satisfaction of the Designated Authority. Blocks surrendered in this way shall be credited towards the block relinquishment requirement in Article 22 of this Petroleum Mining Code.

（2）Before agreeing to an application to surrender some or all of the blocks in a contract area, the Designated Authority may direct the contract operator to clean up the contract area or remove structures, equipment and other property from the contract area and the contract operator shall comply with that direction.

Part V   General Arrangements

Article 24   Work practices

It shall be the responsibility of the contract operator to ensure that petroleum operations are carried out in a proper and workmanlike manner and in accordance with good oilfield practice. The contract operator shall take the necessary action to:

(a) protect the environment in and about the contract area; and

(b) secure the safety, health and welfare of persons engaged in petroleum operations in or about the contract area.

Article 25   Insurance

(1) The Designated Authority shall require the contractor to maintain to the satisfaction of the Designated Authority, insurance on a strict liability basis and for an amount determined by the Designated Authority in consultation with applicants for contracts. It shall also agree with the contractor on a mechanism whereby compensation claims can be determined. The insurance shall cover expenses or liabilities or any other specified things arising in connection with the carrying out of petroleum operations and other activities associated with those operations in the contract area, including expenses associated with the prevention and clean-up of the escape of petroleum.

(2) The contract operator shall ensure that transportation of petroleum in bulk as cargo from the Joint Petroleum Development Area only takes place in tankers with appropriate insurance commensurate with

relevant international agreements.

Article 26   Maintenance of property

The contract operator shall be responsible for maintaining in safe and good condition and repair all structures, equipment and other property in the contract area.

Article 27   Removal of property

(1) As directed by the Designated Authority, the contract operator shall remove all property brought into the contract area and comply with regulations and directions concerning the containment and clean-up of pollution.

(2) In the event that the contract operator does not remove property or pollution to the satisfaction of the Designated Authority or take such other action as is necessary for the conservation and protection of the marine environment in that contract area, the Designated Authority may direct the contract operator to take such remedial action as the Designated Authority deems necessary. If the contract operator does not comply with that direction, the contractor shall be liable for any costs incurred by the Designated Authority in rectifying the matter.

Article 28   Exemption from or variation of conditions

(1) Subject to paragraph 2 of Article 28, the Designated Authority may agree to exempt the contractor from complying with the conditions of the contract. The Designated Authority may also agree to vary those conditions.

(2) The Designated Authority shall not exempt the contractor from or vary the following conditions of a contract without prior approval of the Joint Commission:

(a) the Designated Authority's or the contractor's production shares;

(b) the operating cost recovery provisions;

(c) the term of the contract;

(d) the block relinquishment provisions;

(e) the annual contract service fee;

(f) obligations aimed at protecting the environment and preventing and cleaning up pollution as provided under the Treaty including the Petroleum Mining Code and the contract; and

(g) the exploration work program required to be performed by a contractor in the first three (3) years of a contract.

Article 29   Provision of information

(1) The Designated Authority may direct the contractor to provide the Designated Authority with data, documents or information relating to petroleum operations including but not limited to routine production and financial reports, technical reports and studies relating to petroleum operations.

(2) The Designated Authority may require the contractor to provide that information in writing within a specified period. The Designated Authority shall have title to all data obtained from the petroleum operations.

(3) A contractor shall not be excused from furnishing information on the grounds that the information might tend to incriminate the contractor but the information shall not be admissible in evidence against the contractor in criminal proceedings.

Article 30   Safety zones

(1) The Designated Authority may declare a safety zone around any specified structure in the Joint Petroleum Development Area, and may require the contract operator to install, maintain or provide thereon, navigation, fog and illumination lighting, acoustic and other devices and equipment necessary for the safety of the petroleum operations. A safety zone may extend up to five hundred (500) metres from the extremities of the structure. Unauthorized vessels shall be prohibited from entering the safety zone.

(2) Additionally, a restricted zone of one thousand two hundred and fifty (1250) metres may be declared around the extremities safety zones and pipelines in which area unauthorized vessels employed in exploration for and exploitation of petroleum resources are prohibited from laying anchor or manoeuvring.

Article 31　Records to be kept

The Designated Authority shall require the contractor to keep accounts, records or other documents, including financial records, in connection with petroleum operations and to furnish to the Designated Authority in a specified manner data, reports, returns or other documents in connection with those activities. These arrangements shall also apply to cores, cuttings and samples taken in connection with petroleum operations in the contract area.

Article 32　Prospecting approval

The Designated Authority may issue a prospecting approval to any person to carry out petroleum exploration activities in blocks not in contract areas. The prospecting approval shall specify those conditions to which the person shall be subject. The conditions of a prospecting approval shall not include any preference for or rights to enter into a contract over those blocks. All data reports resulting from such activities shall be submitted to the Designated Authority for its own free use.

Article 33　Access approval

(1) In order to promote the optimum exploration for and exploitation of petroleum resources in the Joint Petroleum Development Area, the Designated Authority may give approval to a contract operator, and persons holding prospecting approvals or undertaking marine scientific research, to enter a contract area, not being its contract area, to carry out activities in accordance with that approval. The Designated Authority shall consult with the contract operator of the contract area into which

access is sought before giving approval. The terms and conditions of approval shall include an obligation to furnish to the Designated Authority in a specified manner data, reports, returns or other documents in connection with activities carried out under the access approval and a prohibition on the drilling of exploration wells.

(2) The Designated Authority may also give approval to a contract operator to lay and fix petroleum production facilities on the seabed in a contract area not being its contract area, provided that such activities do not interfere with the petroleum operations in the first contract area.

Article 34   Inspectors

(1) The Designated Authority may appoint a person to be an inspector for the purposes of this Petroleum Mining Code, the regulations and directions issued under Article 37 of this Petroleum Mining Code, and contract terms and conditions applying to petroleum operations in the Joint Petroleum Development Area. A person so appointed shall, at all reasonable times and on production of a certificate of appointment：

(a) have the right to enter any structure, vessel or aircraft in the Joint Petroleum Development Area being used for petroleum operations;

(b) have the right to inspect and test any equipment being used or proposed to be used for petroleum operations; and

(c) have the right to enter any structure, vessel, aircraft or building in which it is thought there are any documents relating to petroleum operations in the Joint Petroleum Development Area and may inspect, take extracts from and make copies of any of those documents.

(2) The contractor shall provide an inspector with all reasonable facilities and assistance that the inspector requests for the effective exercise of the inspector's powers.

Article 35   Service of notices

(1) A document to be served on a person other than the Designated Authority or a corporation shall be served：

(a) by delivering the document to that person;

(b) by posting the document as a letter addressed to that person;

(c) by delivering the document to that address and leaving the document with a person apparently in the service of that person;

(d) by sending the document in the form of a telex or facsimile to that person's telex or facsimile number, as appropriate; or

(e) by sending the document as a telegram addressed to that person.

(2) A document to be served on a corporation shall be served by complying with sub-paragraphs (b), (c), (d) or (e) of paragraph 1 of this Article.

(3) A document to be served on the Designated Authority shall be served by leaving it with a person apparently employed in connection with the Designated Authority, at a place of business of the Designated Authority specified in the contract or by posting the document as a letter or telegram addressed to the Designated Authority at that place of business or by sending the document as a telex or facsimile to the Designated Authority's telex or facsimile number.

(4) Where a document is posted as a letter, service shall be deemed to have been effected within seven (7) days of the letter having been posted, unless the contrary is proved.

Article 36　Release of information and data

(1) The Designated Authority may make such use as it wishes of information and data contained in a report, return or other document furnished to the Designated Authority, provided that information and data is not made publicly known before the periods of confidentiality identified below have expired.

(2) Basic information and data about petroleum operations in a contract area may be released two (2) years after it was lodged with the Designated Authority or when the blocks to which that information and data relates cease to be part of the contract area, if earlier. However, conclusions drawn or opinions based in whole or in part on that

information and data shall not be released until five (5) years after that information and data was lodged with the Designated Authority.

(3) Information and data relating to a seismic or other geochemical or geophysical survey shall be deemed to have been lodged no later than six (6) months after the survey was essentially completed. Information and data on wells shall be deemed to have been lodged no later than three (3) months after the well was essentially completed.

(4) Notwithstanding paragraph 2 of this Article, the contract operator shall have the right to have access to and use all information held by the Designated Authority relating to the blocks in the Joint Petroleum Development Area adjacent to its contract area. Where information and data has been released by the person or some party acting on the person's behalf, the Designated Authority shall not be obliged to maintain the confidentiality of that information and data.

(5) The Designated Authority shall be free to use any information and data relating to relinquished, surrendered and other blocks outside the contract area, including releasing it to any party.

(6) Contractors shall not use such information and data outside Australia or Timor-Leste without the approval of the Designated Authority.

(7) Officials of the Australian and Timor-Leste Governments may have access to information and data provided to the Designated Authority under this Petroleum Mining Code, provided such officials comply with the provisions of this Article.

Article 37   Regulations and directions

(1) The Designated Authority shall issue regulations and directions to apply to persons, consistent with the Treaty including this Petroleum Mining Code, in order to carry out its functions. In particular, the regulations and directions shall deal with, but are not limited to, the following matters:

(a) the exploration for petroleum and the carrying on of operations, and the execution of works, for that purpose;

(b) the production of petroleum and the carrying on of operations, and the execution of works, for that purpose;

(c) the measurement and the sale or disposal of the Designated Authority's and the contractor's petroleum production, and the carrying on of operations for that purpose, including procedures for transfer of title to petroleum and measurement and verification of petroleum so transferred;

(d) the conservation, and prevention of the waste of, the natural resources, whether petroleum or otherwise;

(e) the construction, erection, maintenance, operation, use, inspection and certification and re-certification of structures, pipelines or equipment;

(f) the control of the flow or discharge, and the prevention of the escape, of petroleum, water or drilling fluid, or a mixture of water or drilling fluid with petroleum or any other matter;

(g) the clean-up or other remedying of the effects of the escape of petroleum;

(h) the prevention of damage to petroleum-bearing strata;

(i) the prevention of the waste or escape of petroleum;

(j) the removal from a contract area of structures, equipment and other property brought into the contract area for or in connection with petroleum operations;

(k) the carrying on of petroleum operations in a safe and environmentally sound manner;

(l) the preparation of assessments of the impact of petroleum operations on the environment;

(m) the authorization by the Designated Authority of entry into the Joint Petroleum Development Area by the employees of contractors and the employees of their sub-contractors; and

(n) the control of movement into, within and out of the Joint Petroleum Development Area of vessels, aircraft, structures and equipment employed in petroleum operations.

(2) The Designated Authority may, by instrument in writing served

on a person or class of persons, make a regulation or direction on a matter consistent with the above to apply specifically to that person or class of persons.

Article 38   Register of contractors

The Designated Authority shall maintain a register setting out summary details of:

(a) areas over which contracts are in force;

(b) the contract operator and the contractor for each contract area;

(c) work and expenditure commitments relating to the contract area;

(d) changes to contract conditions, the contract operator and the undivided participating interest of the contractor in a contract area;

(e) blocks relinquished or surrendered from contract areas;

(f) changes in names and addresses of the contract operator and the contractor; and

(g) unitization agreements.

Article 39   Approval of contractors

Corporations wishing to hold an undivided participating interest which would result in changes to the contractor or the contract operator in a contract area shall be required to obtain the Designated Authority's approval of those changes. The Designated Authority shall note such approval in the register. Until such approval is given by the Designated Authority, with the prior consent of the Joint Commission, the new participating interest holders' agreement shall not be recognized by the Designated Authority, and the contractor's and contract operator's liabilities under a contract shall remain unchanged.

Article 40   Inspection of register

The Designated Authority shall ensure the register is available for inspection by any person at all convenient times.

Article 41   Auditing of contractor's books and accounts

The contractor's books and accounts shall be subject to audit by the Designated Authority, which shall be conducted annually. The Designated Authority may issue regulations and directions with respect to the auditing of books and accounts.

Article 42   Security of structures

(1) Operators of vessels, drilling rigs and structures in the Joint Petroleum Development Area shall be responsible for controlling access to their facilities; providing adequate surveillance of safety zones and their approaches; and establishing communications with, and arranging action by, the appropriate authorities in the event of an accident or incident involving threat to life or security.

(2) To assist operators in meeting these responsibilities, the Designated Authority shall appoint persons, to be stationed at the office of the Technical Directorate of the Designated Authority, responsible for liaising with appropriate Australian and Timor-Leste authorities.

Article 43   Amendment of Petroleum Mining Code

Except in the case of amendments to Part VI of this Petroleum Mining Code, where the provisions of this Petroleum Mining Code are amended, to the extent that the amendments are not consistent with the provisions of contracts in force prior to the amendments, those amendments may only apply to such contracts by agreement between the contract operator and the Designated Authority.

Part VI   Fees

Article 44   Application fees

(1) The fee to be lodged with applications for production sharing

contracts is US $ ten thousand (10, 000).

(2) The fee to be lodged with applications for a prospecting approval is US $ six thousand (6000).

(3) Application fees shall not be refunded to unsuccessful applicants.

Article 45   Contract service fee

(1) At the beginning of each contract year, the contract operator shall pay to the Designated Authority a contract service fee of US $ one hundred and sixty thousand (160,000). Upon termination of a contract during the first six (6) contract years of the term of the contract, the contractor must immediately pay the Designated Authority the sum of US $ nine hundred and sixty thousand (960,000) less any contract service fee previously paid by the contractor, to compensate the Designated Authority for any expense or loss incurred or suffered by the Designated Authority as a result of the termination of the contract.

(2) In addition, if one or more discovery areas have been declared in the contract area, the contract operator shall pay to the Designated Authority at the beginning of the contract year a service fee of:

(a) US $ fifty thousand (50, 000) for the first discovery area; and

(b) US $ twenty-five thousand (25, 000) for each additional discovery area within the contract area.

(c) US $ ten thousand (10, 000) for each full or partial 5' by 5' block in a discovery area to commence when a development plan is lodged with the Designated Authority and to cease when production ceases.

Article 46   Registration fees

For the approval and registration of agreements between corporations which result in changes to the undivided participating interests of the contractor in a contract area, a fee of US $ two thousand five hundred (2, 500) shall be payable.

Article 47　Amendment of fees

With the approval of the Joint Commission, the Designated Authority may change the fees specified in this Part to reflect any changes in the costs of administration. Those changes in fees shall not be made more frequently than once a year and shall not be applied retrospectively.

Part Ⅶ　Penal Provisions

Article 48　Termination of contracts

(1) Where the contractor has not complied with the provisions of this Petroleum Mining Code, the regulations and directions issued by the Designated Authority, or the terms of the contract the Designated Authority may recommend to the Joint Commission that the contract be terminated. The Designated Authority shall give thirty (30) days written notice to the contractor of the Designated Authority's intention to recommend termination of the contract.

(2) The Joint Commission shall not agree to the termination of the contract until the contractor has had an opportunity to provide the Designated Authority with reasons why the contract should not be terminated, and the Designated Authority has given full consideration to those reasons. The contractor must provide reasons for non-termination within thirty (30) days of receipt of notice of the Designated Authority's intention to terminate.

(3) Notwithstanding the termination of a contract, the contractor shall remain liable to take such action as is necessary to clean-up the contract area and remove all property brought into that area. The contractor shall remain liable to the Designated Authority to pay any outstanding debts due to the Authority.

6. Taxation of Bayu-Undan Contractors Act

República Democrática de Timor-Leste, National Parliament, Law No. 3/ 2003 of 1 July

The Timor Sea Treaty signed by Timor-Leste and Australia on 20 May 2002 and ratified by the National Parliament on 17 December 2002 permits development of petroleum resources to proceed in the area of the Timor Sea called the JPDA.

The Timor Sea Treaty permits, with certain limitations, each of the two governments to apply its tax regime to the petroleum activities in the JPDA. Under the Treaty, Timor-Leste may apply its tax regime to 90 percent of the petroleum activities; Australia may apply its tax regime to 10 percent.

The Bayu-Undan field is the largest discovery in the JPDA so far. The production and tax revenues from this field will represent a very significant portion of Timor-Leste's national budget and GDP from mid-2004, when the field is scheduled to go into production.

This Law establishes a tax regime for the development of the Bayu-Undan field.

The purpose of this Law is to encourage the Bayu-Undan contractors to proceed with the gas phase of the project, in addition to the liquids phase. Development of the gas phase of the project will permit Timor-Leste to maximize its total revenues from the Bayu-Undan field.

This Law enters into force when the Joint Commission has approved Production Sharing Contracts JPDA 03-12 and JPDA 03-13 (including annexes thereto providing for the valuation of natural gas), the Development Authority has approved the amendment to the Development Plan relating to the export of gas, and contracts for the transportation and sale of natural gas by the contractors have become binding and effective with conditions precedent satisfied.

The National Parliament decrees, in accordance with article 92, part b) of paragraph 2 of article 95, and paragraphs 1 and 2 of article 139 of the Constitution of the Republic, with the weight of the law, the following:

Part 1　Preliminary

Article 1　Short Title

This Act may be cited as the Taxation of Bayu-Undan Contractors Act, 2003.

Article 2　Definitions

(1) In this Act:

"Bayu-Undan" means the Bayu-Undan discovery area as defined in Production Sharing Contracts JPDA 03-12 and JPDA 03-13;

" Commissioner " means the Commissioner of the East Timor Revenue Service;

"contractor" means a Tax Subject that:

(a) has entered into Production Sharing Contract JPDA 03-12 or JPDA 03-13 or a successor Production Sharing Contract pursuant to Annex F to the Timor Sea Treaty; or

(b) is a successor or assignee of a Tax Subject referred to in paragraph (a) as permitted under Production Sharing Contract JPDA 03-12 or JPDA 03-13, as the case may be,

and is registered as a contractor under the *Petroleum Mining Code*;

"Designated Authority" means the Designated Authority established under Article 6 of the *Timor Sea Treaty*;

"Elang Kakatua Kakatua North" means the Elang Kakatua Kakatua North discovery area as defined in Production Sharing Contract JPDA 03-

12；

"export pipeline" means an export pipeline as defined in Production Sharing Contracts JPDA 03-12 and JPDA 03-13；

"Joint Commission" means the Joint Commission established under Article 6 of the Timor Sea Treaty；

"Law on General Tax Provisions and Procedures" means the Law on General Tax Provisions and Procedures applicable in *Timor-Leste* under UNTAET Regulation No. 1999/1；

"Law on Income Tax" means the Law on Income Tax applicable in Timor-Leste under UNTAET Regulation No. 1999/1；

"Law on Value Added Tax on Goods and Services and Sales Tax on Luxury Goods" means the Law on Value Added Tax on Goods and Services and Sales Tax on Luxury Goods applicable in *Timor-Leste* under UNTAET Regulation No. 1999/1；

"petroleum" means：

（a）Any naturally occurring hydrocarbon, whether in a gaseous, liquid, or solid state；

（b）Any naturally occurring mixture of hydrocarbons, whether in a gaseous, liquid, or solid state；

（c）Any naturally occurring mixture of one or more hydrocarbons, whether in a gaseous, liquid, or solid state, as well as other substances produced in association with such hydrocarbons,

and includes any petroleum as defined in paragraphs（a）,（b）, and（c）that has been returned to a natural reservoir；

"petroleum activities" means all activities undertaken to produce *petroleum*, authorized or contemplated under a contract, permit, or licence, and includes exploration, development, initial processing, production, transportation, and marketing, as well as the planning and preparation for such activities；

"Petroleum Mining Code" means the Code referred to in Article 7 of the *Timor Sea Treaty*；

"petroleum project" means *petroleum activities* undertaken in relation to Bayu-Undan and does not include *petroleum activities* undertaken in relation to *Elang Kakatua Kakatua North*;

"subcontractor" means any Tax Subject supplying goods or services directly or indirectly to a *contractor* in respect of the petroleum project;

"Timor-Leste", when referring to a geographic area, means the territory of República Democrática de Timor-Leste as defined in Section 4 of the Constitution of the República Democrática de Timor-Leste and the East Timor Maritime Zones Act; and

"Timor Sea Treaty" means the Timor Sea Treaty dated 20 May 2002 between the Government of Timor-Leste and the Government of Australia.

(2) Unless the context indicates otherwise, terms used in this Act and not defined in sub-article 1 have the same meaning as in the *Law on Income Tax*, *Law on Value Added Tax on Goods and Services and Sales Tax on Luxury Goods*, and *Law on General Tax Provisions and Procedures* (*as these laws apply in Timor-Leste*), UNTAET Regulation No. 2000/18 (as amended), and the *Timor Sea Treaty*, as the case may be.

(3) In the event of a conflict between this Act and the *Law on Income Tax*, *Law on Value Added Tax on Goods and Services and Sales Tax on Luxury Goods*, *Law on General Tax Provisions and Procedures* (as these laws apply in *Timor-Leste*) or UNTAET Regulation No. 2000/18 (as amended), this Act prevails.

Part 2   Taxation Regime for Contractors
Undertaking the Petroleum Project

Article 3   Taxation of a Contractor Undertaking
the Petroleum Project

(1) A *contractor* undertaking the petroleum project is subject to tax in accordance with the *Law on Income Tax*, *Law on Value Added Tax on*

319

Goods and Services and Sales Tax on Luxury Goods, *and the Law on General Tax Provisions and Procedures*, as modified by UNTAET Regulation No. 2000/18 (as amended), and subject to the modifications in this Part.

(2) The application of the *Law on Income Tax*, *Law on Value Added Tax on Goods and Services and Sales Tax on Luxury Goods*, and the *Law on General Tax Provisions and Procedures to contractors* undertaking the petroleum project is in accordance with UNTAET Regulation No. 1999/1.

(3) The rate of corporate tax applicable to a contractor for a fiscal year is 30%.

(4) Notwithstanding sub-article 1, Tax Subjects are exempt from *Timor-Leste* taxes, including taxes applicable pursuant to the *Law on Income Tax*, *Law on Value Added Tax on Goods and Services and Sales Tax on Luxury Goods*, and the *Law on General Tax provisions and Procedures*, as modified by UNTAET Regulation No. 2000/18 (as amended) with respect to income and activities relating to the construction, installation and operation of an export pipeline.

Article 4   Decommissioning Costs Reserve

(1) For the purposes of calculating the taxable income of a *contractor* for a fiscal year and notwithstanding Article 9(1) (c) of the *Law on Income Tax*, the *contractor* is allowed a deduction for the year for the amount carried to the decommissioning costs reserve for the year in respect of the *petroleum project*.

(2) A deduction is not allowed for any decommissioning expenditure incurred by a *contractor* in a fiscal year (referred to as the "current fiscal year") except to the extent that the total amount of decommissioning expenditure incurred by the *contractor* in the current fiscal year and previous fiscal years exceeds the amount calculated according to the following formula:

$$(A+B)-C$$

Where:

A is the total amount allowed to the *contractor* as a deduction under sub-article 1 in the current fiscal year and previous fiscal years;

B is the total amount allowed to the *contractor* as a deduction under this sub-article in previous fiscal years; and

C is the total amount included in the *contractor's* taxable income in the current fiscal year and previous fiscal years pursuant to sub-article 5.

(3) The decommissioning costs reserve is calculated by reference to the Total Approved Decommissioning Costs. The amount carried to the reserve for a fiscal year is the amount allowed to the *contractor* for that year under the Production Sharing Contract between the *Designated Authority* and the *contractor* governing the project.

(4) No deduction is allowed under sub-article 1 for any fiscal year prior to 1 January 2008.

(5) Where, at any time, the total amount allowed as a deduction under this article exceeds the Total Approved Decommissioning Costs, the amount of the excess is included in the gross income of the *contractor* for the fiscal year in which such excess occurs.

(6) In this Article:

"Decommissioning Plan", in relation to the *petroleum project*, means the Decommissioning Plan approved by the *Designated Authority* under the Production Sharing Contract between the *Designated Authority* and the *contractor* governing the project;

"Development Plan", in relation to the *petroleum project*, means the Development Plan approved by the *Designated Authority* under the Production Sharing Contract between *Designated Authority* and the *contractor* governing the project; and

"Total Approved Decommissioning Costs", means the total decommissioning costs approved by the *Designated Authority* in accordance with the *Decommissioning Plan* for the *petroleum project*, as revised from time to time.

Article 5　Depreciation and Amortization

(1) The following modifications apply to Article 11 of the *Law on Income Tax* as it applies to a *contractor* undertaking the *petroleum project*：

(a) The depreciation of tangible property used in *petroleum activities* in respect of the project is calculated individually on a straight-line basis only；

(b) The straight-line depreciation rates applicable to tangible property used in *petroleum activities* in respect of the project are as follows：

Useful life of the property	Depreciation rate
1-4 years	25%
more than 4 years	20%

(c) The depreciation of tangible property referred to in paragraph (a) acquired or constructed before first production commences from the date of first production；and

(d) Subject to sub-articles 4 and 5, the amount of depreciation allowed as a deduction for a fiscal year in respect of an item of tangible property is calculated according to the following formula：

$$A \times B$$

where：

A is the cost of the property；and

B is the depreciation rate determined under paragraph (b).

(2) The following modifications apply to Article 11A of the *Law on Income Tax* as it applies to a *contractor* in respect of the *petroleum project*：

(a) The amortization of intangible property and other expenditure of an intangible nature (hereafter referred to as an "intangible") relating to *petroleum activities* in respect of the project is calculated individually on a straight-line basis only；

(b) The straight-line amortization rates applicable to an intangible used in *petroleum activities* in respect of the project are as follows:

Useful life of the intangible	Amortization rate
1-4 years	25%
more than 4 years	20%

(c) The amortization of an intangible acquired, developed, or incurred before first production commences from the date of first production; and

(d) Subject to sub-article 4 and 5, the amount of amortization allowed as a deduction for a fiscal year in respect of an intangible is calculated according to the following formula:

$$A \times B$$

where:

A is the cost of the intangible; and

B is the amortization rate determined under paragraph (b).

(3) The following provisions apply where *petroleum activities* in *Elang Kakatua Kakatua North* have ceased, the *contractor* has made a loss for income tax purposes in respect of the activities, and the *contractor* has undertaken the *petroleum project*:

(a) The amount of the loss that has not been deducted under Article 6(2) of the *Law on Income Tax* is treated as expenditure incurred by the *contractor* in respect of the project;

(b) The expenditure is treated as having been incurred at the later of:

(i) The date on which the *Elang Kakatua Kakatua North* activities ceased; or

(ii) The date of first production for the *petroleum project*;

(c) The expenditure is treated as having a useful life of five years; and

(d) The expenditure is amortized under Article 11A of the *Law on Income Tax*, as modified by Article 5(2) of this Act, on a straight-line basis.

(4) In the fiscal year in which first production occurs, the amount

323

allowed as a deduction under sub-article 1(d) and 2(d) is computed according to the following formula:

$$A \times B/C$$

where:

A is the amount computed under sub-article 1(d) or 2(d), as the case may be;

B is the number of days from the date of first production to the end of the fiscal year in which first production occurs; and

C is the number of days in the fiscal year.

(5) In the last fiscal year of depreciation or amortization, the amount allowed as a deduction under sub-article (1)(d) and 2(d), as the case may be, for any tangible property or intangible to which sub-article 4 applied is calculated according to the following formula:

$$A - B$$

A is the amount computed under sub-article 1(d) or 2(d), as the case may be, for the fiscal year of first production without regard to sub-article 4; and

B is the amount allowed as a deduction for the fiscal year of first production under sub-article 1(d) or 2(d), as modified by sub-article 4.

(6) For the purposes of this Article-

(a) First production occurs where there has been a minimum of thirty days commercial production and the commencement of first production is on the first day of the thirty day period; and

(b) The last fiscal year of depreciation or amortization –

(i) in the case of any tangible property or intangible with a useful life of 1 – 4 years, is the fourth fiscal year after the fiscal year of first production; or

(ii) in the case of any tangible property or intangible with a useful life of more than 4 years, is the fifth fiscal year after the fiscal year of first production.

Article 6 Special Calculation Norm

(1) For the purposes of Article 15 of the *Law on Income Tax*, the

net income of a permanent establishment engaged in oil and gas drilling activities for the *petroleum project* is six percent (6%) of gross income. This is the basis for calculating the tax installment payments of the permanent establishment under Article 25 of the *Law on Income Tax*.

(2) For the purposes of Article 15 of the *Law on Income Tax*, the net income of a permanent establishment engaged in shipping or air service activities for the *petroleum project* is two point four percent (2.4%) of gross income. This is the basis for calculating the tax installment payments of the permanent establishment under Article 25 of the *Law on Income Tax*.

Article 7   Estimated Net Income

The estimated net income determined under Article 23(2) of the *Law on Income Tax* for the purposes of Article 23(1) (c) (2) of the *Law on Income Tax* applicable to –

(a) Compensation paid by a *contractor* or *subcontractor* for oil and gas drilling support services acquired for the *petroleum project* is twelve percent (12%) of gross compensation;

(b) Compensation paid by a *contractor* or *subcontractor* for technical, management, accounting and bookkeeping, legal consulting, and tax consulting services acquired for the *petroleum project* is sixteen percent (16%) of gross compensation; and

(c) Compensation paid by a *contractor* or *subcontractor* for rent or other income pertaining to the use of property for the *petroleum project* is sixteen percent (16%) of gross compensation.

Article 8   Withholding Tax

(1) The withholding tax rate for the purposes of Article 23(1) (a) (3) of the *Law on Income Tax* shall be six percent (6%) of the gross amount paid by a *contractor* or *subcontractor* with respect to the *petroleum project*.

(2) The withholding tax rates determined under Article 4(2) of the

Law on Income Tax applicable to compensation paid for services acquired for the *petroleum project* shall be as follows:

(a) Zero point eight percent (0.8%) with respect to construction services; and

(b) One point six percent (1.6%) with respect to consulting services.

(3) The withholding tax rate for the purposes of Article 26(1) (c) and (d) of the Law on Income Tax applicable to compensation paid by a contractor or *subcontractor* for services acquired for the *petroleum project* is eight percent (8%) of the gross amount of the compensation.

(4) Notwithstanding sub-article 3, the withholding tax rate for the purposes of Article 26(1) (d) of the Law on Income Tax applicable to compensation paid by a contractor or *subcontractor* to employees for services acquired for the *petroleum project* is twenty percent (20%) of the gross amount of the compensation.

Article 9   Branch Profits Tax

Article 26 (4) of the *Law on Income Tax* does not apply to a *contractor* or *subcontractor* in respect of income derived from the *petroleum project*, including income from the disposal of an interest in the project.

Article 10   Value of Gas

(1) For the purposes of calculating the taxable income of a *contractor* undertaking the *petroleum project*:

(a) The valuation of natural gas produced and saved, and not used in field operations, is made in accordance with the Production Sharing Contract between the *Designated Authority* and the *contractor* governing the project; and

(b) No deduction is allowed for any export cost charge incurred by a *contractor* in a fiscal year except to the extent that the export cost charge has not been taken into account in the determining the valuation of natural gas produced and saved pursuant to paragraph (a).

(2) In this Article:

"export cost charge", in relation to a *contractor* in respect of the *petroleum project*, has the meaning in the Production Sharing Contract between the *Designated Authority* and the *contractor* governing the project; and

"natural gas" means all gaseous hydrocarbons, including wet mineral gas, dry mineral gas, casinghead gas and residue gas remaining after the extraction of liquid hydrocarbons from wet gas.

Part 3   Additional Profits Tax

Article 11   Imposition of Additional Profits Tax

(1) A *contractor* undertaking the petroleum project that has a positive amount of accumulated net receipts for the project for a fiscal year is liable to pay additional profits tax.

(2) The additional profits tax payable by a *contractor* for a fiscal year is calculated according to the following formula:

$$A \times 22.5\% / (1-r)$$

where:

A is the accumulated net receipts of the contractor for the year; and r is the corporate rate of tax as specified in sub-article 3 of Article 3.

(3) Additional profits tax imposed under this Article is in addition to the income tax imposed on the taxable income of the *contractor* for the fiscal year.

(4) Additional profits tax paid by a *contractor* is allowed as a deduction in calculating the taxable income of the *contractor* in the fiscal year in which the tax was paid.

Article 12   Accumulated Net Receipts

(1) The accumulated net receipts of a *contractor* for a fiscal year for

the *petroleum project* is calculated according to the following formula:

$$((A \times 116.5\%) - (1 \times (1-r))) + B$$

where:

A is the *contractor*'s accumulated net receipts for the project at the end of the previous fiscal year;

B is the *contractor*'s net receipts for the project for the current fiscal year;

I is the interest expense and other financial charges paid by the *contractor* in respect of the project in the current fiscal year (and is entered in the formula as a negative number); and

r is the corporate rate of tax as specified in sub-article 3 of Article 3.

(2) Where additional profits tax is payable by a *contractor* for a fiscal year, the amount of the accumulated net receipts of the *contractor* at the end of that year is zero for the purposes of calculating the accumulated net receipts of the *contractor* for the next year.

(3) Where component ($A \times 116.5\%$) of the formula in sub-article 1 is negative for a fiscal year, the subtraction of component ($1 \times (1-r)$) for that year shall not reduce the amount of ($(A \times 116.5\%) - (1 \times (1-r))$) to an amount that is less than A. The amount of any excess is not carried forward or carried back to any fiscal year.

(4) The following provisions apply to a *contractor* to which Production Sharing Contracts JPDA 03-12 and JPDA 03-13 apply:

(a) The formula in sub-article 1 is to be applied to the *contractor* for the period 25 October-31 December 1999 on the basis that the initial total accumulated net receipts of all *contractors* as at 25 October, 1999 was negative $233 million;

(b) The formula in sub-article 1 is to be applied to the *contractor* for the period 1 January-31 December 2000 on the basis that the amount calculated under paragraph (a) is the accumulated net receipts of the *contractor* as at 31 December, 1999;

(c) The formula in sub-article 1 is to be applied to the *contractor* for the period 1 January-31 December 2001 on the basis that the amount calculated under paragraph （b） is the accumulated net receipts of the *contractor as at* 31 December, 2001; and

（d） The amount calculated under paragraph （c） is the accumulated net receipts of the *contractor* as at 31 December, 2001 for the purposes of applying the formula in sub-article 1 to the *contractor* for the fiscal year commencing on 1 January, 2002.

Article 13   Net Receipts

The net receipts of a *contractor* for the *petroleum project* for a fiscal year is the gross receipts of the *contractor* for the project for the year less the total deductible expenditure of the *contractor* for the project for the year. The net receipts of a *contractor* for a fiscal year may be a negative amount.

Article 14   Gross Receipts

The gross receipts of a *contractor* for a fiscal year for the *petroleum project* is the sum of the following amounts:

（a） The gross income for income tax purposes accrued by the *contractor* in the year from the project, including amounts received from the hiring or leasing out of, or the granting of rights to use property, but not including interest income;

（b） The consideration received by the *contractor* in the year for the disposal, destruction, or loss of any property （including materials, equipment, plant, facilities, and intellectual property or rights） used in the project where the expenditure incurred in acquiring the property was deducted in computing the net receipts of the *contractor* for any fiscal year;

（c） Any amount received by the *contractor* in the year from the provision of information or data obtained from any survey, appraisal, or study relating to the project where the expenditure incurred in undertaking the survey, appraisal, or study was previously deducted in computing the net receipts of the *contractor* for any fiscal year;

(d) Any other amount received by the contractor in the year that is a reimbursement, refund, or other recoupment of an amount previously deducted in computing the net receipts of the contractor for the project for any fiscal year; and

(e) Where property has been destroyed or lost by a *contractor*, any compensation, indemnity, or damages received by the *contractor* in respect of the property under an insurance policy, indemnity agreement, settlement, or judicial decision.

(2) Notwithstanding sub-article 1, and subject to Article 16, the gross receipts of a contractor does not include any amount received or accrued as consideration for the transfer of an interest in the petroleum project.

(3) Where an amount referred to in sub-article 1 is attributable to the *petroleum project* and some other activity of the *contractor*, only that portion that relates to the *petroleum project* is included in the gross receipts of the *contractor* in calculating the net receipts of that project.

Article 15   Deductible Expenditure

(1) The total deductible expenditure of a *contractor* for a fiscal year for the *petroleum project* is the sum of the following amounts:

(a) Any expenditure incurred by the *contractor* in the year in respect of the project and allowed as a deduction (other than as a depreciation or amortization deduction) in computing taxable income, including interest and financing charges;

(b) Any capital expenditure incurred by the *contractor* in the year in acquiring or constructing a tangible or intangible asset for use in the project;

(c) Any exploration expenditure incurred by the *contractor* in the year in respect of the project; and

(d) An amount of *Timor-Leste* corporate income tax of the *contractor* for the year calculated by applying the corporate rate of tax as specified in sub-article 3 of Article 3 to the taxable income of the *contractor for the year before deduction of additional profits tax.*

（2）Notwithstanding sub-article 1, and subject to Article 16, the deductible expenditure of a contractor does not include any amount incurred as consideration for the acquisition of an interest in the petroleum project.

（3）Where an amount referred to in sub-article 1 is attributable to the *petroleum project* and to some other activity of the *contractor*, only that portion that relates to the *petroleum project* is allowed as deductible expenditure of the *contractor* in computing the net receipts of that project.

Article 16　Transfer of Interest in the Petroleum Project

（1）Where the whole of a *contractor's* interest in the *petroleum project* is transferred to another *contractor*, the transferee *contractor* is treated as having the same gross receipts and deductible expenditures in respect of the interest as the transferor had immediately before the transfer. For the purposes of calculating the transferee *contractor's* accumulated net receipts for the fiscal year in which the transfer occurred, the transferor *contractor's* accumulated net receipts at the end of the previous fiscal year is treated as the transferee contractor's accumulated net receipts for that previous year.

（2）Where part of a *contractor's* interest in the *petroleum project* is transferred to another *contractor*:

（a）The transferee *contractor* is treated as having the gross receipts and deductible expenditures in respect of that partial interest as the transferor *contractor* had in relation to the whole interest immediately before the transfer multiplied by the transferred percentage factor; and

（b）For the purposes of calculating the transferee *contractor's* accumulated net receipts for the fiscal year in which the transfer occurred, the transferor *contractor's* accumulated net receipts at the end of the previous fiscal year multiplied by the transferred percentage factor is treated as the transferee *contractor's* accumulated net receipts for that previous fiscal year.

(3) In this Article, "transferred percentage factor" means the transferor *contractor's* percentage ownership in the *petroleum project* that is transferred divided by the transferor *contractor's* total percentage ownership in the *petroleum project* prior to the transfer.

Article 17   Procedure Relating to Additional Profits Tax

(1) A *contractor* undertaking the *petroleum project* in a fiscal year shall deliver to the *Commissioner* an additional profits tax return for the year.

(2) The additional profits tax return for a fiscal year shall be delivered in the same manner and by the same due date as the annual income tax return of the *contractor* for that year.

(3) Additional profits tax for a fiscal year is due and payable by a *contractor* on the same date as the income tax of the *contractor* for that year is due and payable.

(4) Subject to Article 18, the *Law on General Tax Provisions and Procedures*, as modified by UNTAET Regulation No. 2000/18 (as amended) applies, with any necessary changes made:

(a) To the assessment and collection of additional profits tax and additional tax imposed in respect of an additional profits tax liability, including the keeping of records and investigations;

(b) To appeals relating to a liability for additional profits tax or to additional tax imposed in respect of an additional profits tax liability; and

(c) To the application or refund of additional profits tax overpaid.

(5) Chapter XI of UNTAET Regulation No. 2000/18 (as amended) applies to the additional profits tax on the basis that:

(a) The reference to "tax" in that Chapter includes the additional profits tax imposed under this Regulation; and （b）The reference to "tax form" in that Chapter includes the additional profits tax return required to be delivered under sub-article 1.

Article 18　Instalments of Tax

（1）A contractor shall pay monthly instalments of additional profits tax for each fiscal year. Instalments of additional profits tax are payable by the 15th day after the end of the month to which they relate. Where the due date for payment of an instalment of additional profits tax does not fall on a business day, the due date is the next business day.

（2）The amount of each instalment is one-twelfth of the amount of additional profits tax estimated by the *contractor* to be due for the fiscal year. Every *contractor* shall deliver to the Commissioner an estimate of additional profits tax for a fiscal year by the due date for payment of the first instalment for the year.

（3）An estimate delivered under sub-article 2 remains in force for the whole of the fiscal year unless the *contractor* delivers a revised estimate to the *Commissioner*. A revised estimate applies to the calculation of instalments of additional profits tax due both before and after the date the revised estimate was delivered. The amount of any underpayment of instalments made prior to the revised estimate shall be paid by the *contractor* together with the first instalment due after the revised estimate is delivered. The amount of any overpaid instalments shall be refunded to the *contractor* within 30 days of the revised estimate being delivered.

（4）Where a *contractor* fails to deliver an estimate of additional profits tax as required under sub-article 2, the estimated additional profits tax of the *contractor* for the year is such amount as estimated by the *Commissioner*. The *Commissioner*'s estimate remains in force for the whole of the fiscal year unless revised by the *contractor* in accordance with sub-article 3.

（5）Where a *contractor*'s estimate (including any revised estimate) of additional profits tax for a fiscal year is less than ninety percent of the contractor's assessed additional profits tax liability for that year, the contractor is liable for additional tax –

(a) if the under-estimate is due to fraud or wilful neglect, fifty percent (50%) of the amount by which the actual additional profits tax liability exceeded the estimated liability for the year; or

(b) in any other case, ten (10%) percent of the amount by which the actual additional profits tax liability exceeded the estimated liability for the year.

Part 4 Final Provisions

Article 19 Regulations

The Minister responsible for finance may make regulations for the effective carrying out of the provisions of this Act.

Article 20 Entry into Force and Application

(1) This Act enters into force on the date when all of the following are satisfied-

(a) the Timor Sea Treaty has entered into force;

(b) the Joint Commission has approved Production Sharing Contracts JPDA 03-12 and JPDA 03-13, including annexes thereto providing for the valuation of natural gas;

(c) the Designated Authority has approved the amendment to the Development Plan for *Bayu-Undan* (providing for export of gas through the *export pipeline* and relevant contracts for the transportation and sale of natural gas by the contractors); and

(d) the contracts for the transportation and sale of natural gas referred to in paragraph (c) have become binding and effective with conditions precedent satisfied.

（2）This Act applies from 1 January 2002.

（3）The additional profits tax imposed under Article 11 applies for the fiscal year commencing 1 January 2002 and subsequent fiscal years.

Approved on 3 June 2003

The President of the National Parliament

Francisco Guterres "Lu-Olo"

Taxation of Bayu-Undan Contractors Act
Explanatory Memorandum
República Democrática de Timor-Leste

Introduction

This memorandum provides an explanation of the Taxation of Bayu-Undan Contractors Act (referred to as the " the Act") , which provides for the taxation of contractors undertaking petroleum projects in Bayu-Undan. The basic effect of the Act is to preserve the existing income tax treatment of such contractors subject to the modifications provided for in the Act, including the imposition of additional profits tax.

（1）Short Title

This article provides that the Act may be cited as the Taxation of Bayu-Undan Contractors Act, 2003.

（2）Definitions

This article provides for the interpretation of words and terms used in the Act.

Sub-article 1 provides definitions of commonly used terms in the Act. The definitions of "petroleum" and "petroleum activities" are the same as in the Timor Sea Treaty. " Petroleum project" is defined to mean petroleum activities taking place in Bayu-Undan. It is expressly provided that petroleum activities taking place in Elang Kakutua Kakutua North do not constitute a petroleum project for the purposes of the Act. This is particularly relevant for article 5 of the Act.

A "contractor" is defined to mean a Tax Subject that has entered into Production Sharing Contract JPDA 03-12 or 03-13, or a successor contract. The definition also includes any successor or assignee of such a Tax Subject. For a Tax Subject to be a contractor, it must be registered as a contractor under the Petroleum Mining Code.

Sub-article 2 provides that terms not defined in sub-article 1 have their ordinary meaning under the *Law on Income Tax*, *Law on Value Added Tax on Goods and Services and Sales Tax on Luxury Goods*, *Law on General Tax Provisions and Procedures*, *UNTAET Regulation No.* 2000/18 (as amended) and the *Timor Sea Treaty*, as the case may be. As regards the *Law on Income Tax*, *Law on Value Added Tax on Goods and Services and Sales Tax on Luxury Goods*, and the *Law on General Tax Provisions and Procedures*, terms have the meaning in those laws to the extent that those laws are applicable in East Timor as determined under *UNTAET Regulation No.* 1999/1.

Sub-article 3 provides a priority rule in the event of a conflict between the Act and *Law on Income Tax*, *Law on Value Added Tax on Goods and Services and Sales Tax on Luxury Goods*, *Law on General Tax Provisions and Procedures* (as these laws apply in Timor-Leste) or UNTAET Regulation No. 2000/18 (as amended). In the event of such conflict, the Act prevails.

(3) Taxation of a Contractor Undertaking a Petroleum Project

This article states the general principle of taxation of contractors undertaking the petroleum project.

Sub-article 1 provides that a contractor is subject to tax in accordance with the Law on Income Tax, Law on Value Added Tax on Goods and Services and Sales Tax on Luxury Goods, and Law on General Tax Provisions and Procedures. This is subject to several qualifications. First, sub-article 2 makes it clear that it is only to the extent that those Laws apply in East Timor. This is determined in accordance with *UNTAET Regulation* 1999/1. Secondly, the application of the Laws is subject to the modifications in *UNTAET Regulation* 2000/18 (as amended). See, in particular, Chapters VII (wages income tax), X (taxation procedure) and XI (additional tax, offences and penalties). Thirdly, the application of those Laws is also subject to the modifications in Part 2 of the Act explained in these notes.

Sub-article 3 provides that the rate of corporate tax applicable to a contractor is 30%.

Sub-article 4 exempts Tax Subjects from tax with respect to income and activities relating to the construction, installation and operation of an export pipeline (as defined in article 2).

(4) Decommissioning Costs Reserve

This article allows a contractor to claim a deduction for the amount carried to the decommissioning costs reserve for a fiscal year in respect of a petroleum project.

Sub-article 1 states the principle of deductibility. It is expressly provided that sub-article 1 overrides Article 9 (1) (c) of the *Law on Income Tax*, which provides that no deduction shall be allowed for the establishment or accumulation of a reserve fund. The amount allowed as a deduction for a fiscal year is the amount carried to the decommissioning costs reserve for the year. Decommissioning costs actually incurred during a fiscal year are either deductible under Article ·6 of the *Law on Income Tax* or amortized under Article 11A of the *Law on Income Tax*, depending on the useful life of the costs incurred.

Sub-articles 3 and 4 provide for two important limitations on the deduction. First, sub-article 3 provides that the establishment and carrying of amounts to the decommissioning costs reserve must be based on the total decommissioning costs approved by the Designated Authority in accordance with the contractor's Decommissioning Plan. This includes any revision of the total decommissioning costs estimated to be incurred, provided the Designated Authority approves the revised amount. The amount carried to the reserve is determined under the relevant Production Sharing Contract.

Secondly, sub-article 4 provides that no deduction is to be allowed for amounts carried to the decommissioning costs reserve for any fiscal year prior to 1 January 2008.

The deduction allowed under sub-article 1 is for amounts carried to the decommissioning costs reserve. Sub-article 2 ensures that there is no double deduction when decommissioning costs are actually incurred. In broad terms, there is no deduction for actual costs incurred unless they exceed the amount carried to the reserve.

Sub-article 5 applies if, at any time, the total amount allowed as a deduction under this article exceeds the total approved decommissioning costs. In this case, the amount of the excess is included in the contractor's gross income for the fiscal year in which the excess occurs.

(5) Depreciation and Amortization

This article provides for the depreciation of tangible property, and the amortization of intangible property and other expenditure in respect of the petroleum project.

Sub-article 1 applies to the depreciation of tangible property. The effect of the sub-article is that the depreciation rules in Article 11 of the *Law on Income Tax* apply to tangible property acquired by a contractor for use in exploration in respect of a petroleum project subject to the modifications in paragraphs (a)-(d).

Under Article 11 of the *Law on Income Tax*, a taxpayer may use either the diminishing value or straight-line methods of depreciation for tangible property. The depreciation is to be based on the useful life of the asset and is calculated on the basis of pooling of assets. Paragraphs (a)-(d) set out four modifications in the calculation of the amount of depreciation in relation to tangible property-

① Paragraph (a) limits contractors to straight-line depreciation calculated on a single asset basis.

② Paragraph (b) sets out the depreciation rate schedule.

③ Paragraph (c) provides that the depreciation of any property acquired before first commercial production commences from the date of first commercial production. This is determined under sub-article 6(a).

④ Paragraph (d) provides for the calculation of the amount of depreciation. As stated above, this is straight-line depreciation on a single asset basis.

Sub-article 2 makes equivalent modifications to Article 11A of the *Law on Income Tax* in its application to intangible property used, and other expenditures incurred by a contractor in relation to the petroleum project.

Sub-article 3 provides for the treatment of a terminal loss incurred by a contractor in respect of petroleum activities in Elang Kakutua Kakutua North. If the contractor has undertaken a petroleum project, the undeducted amount of the loss is treated as an amount of notional expenditure incurred by the contractor in respect of the project. The expenditure is treated as having been incurred at the later of the date the Elang Kakutua Kakutua North activities ceased or the date of first commercial production for the Bayu-Undan project. This means that the loss cannot be amortized before the date of first commercial production for the Bayu-Undan project. The expenditure is treated as having a useful life of five years and is amortized under Article 11A of the *Law on income Tax* in calculating the contractor's taxable income for the Bayu-Undan project.

Sub-article 4 provides for apportionment of the amount allowed as a deduction under sub-article 1 (d) or 2 (d) in the fiscal year of first production. Sub-article 5 provides for an adjustment in the last fiscal year of depreciation or amortization (as defined in sub-article 6(b)) to ensure that relevant asset or expenditure is fully depreciated or amortized.

(6) Special Calculation Norm

This article specifies a Special Calculation Norm for the purposes of calculating the taxable income of a permanent establishment of a contractor in certain circumstances.

Article 15 of the *Law on Income Tax* provides that Special Calculation Norms may be specified for the purposes of calculating the net income of certain taxpayers. The Special Calculation Norms apply in priority to the normal rules for the calculation of taxable income under Article 16 of the *Law on Income Tax*.

Sub-article 1 provides that the net income of a permanent establishment of a contractor engaged in oil and gas drilling activities for the petroleum project is 6% of the gross income. Sub-article 2 provides that the net income of a permanent establishment of a contractor engaged in shipping and air service activities for the petroleum project is 2. 4% of the gross income. "Gross income" and "permanent establishment" have their meanings in the *Law of Income Tax*. It is expressly provided that the Special Calculation Norm applies for the purposes of calculating the tax instalment payments of the permanent establishment under Article 25 of the *Law on Income Tax*.

(7) Estimated Net Income

This Article provides for the calculation of the estimated net income applicable to compensation paid by a contractor for certain services relating to petroleum projects for the purposes of Article 23(1) (c) (2) of the *Law on Income Tax*.

Paragraph (a) applies to compensation paid by a contractor or subcontractor for oil and gas drilling support services, acquired for the petroleum project. It reduces the estimated net income from 30% to 12% of the gross compensation. Tax under Article 23 of the *Law on Income Tax* is withheld at the rate of 15%. This means that the amount to be withheld from such compensation is 1. 8% of the gross compensation.

Paragraph (b) applies to compensation paid by a contractor or subcontractor for technical, management, accounting and book-keeping, legal consulting and tax consulting services acquired for the petroleum project. It reduces the estimated net income from 40% to 16% of the gross compensation. Tax under Article 23 of the *Law on Income Tax* is withheld at the rate of 15%. This means that the amount to be withheld from such compensation is 2. 4% of the gross compensation.

Paragraph (c) applies to compensation paid by a contractor or subcontractor for rent or other income relating to the use of property for the petroleum project. The estimated net income is reduced to 16%. Tax under Article 23 of the Law on Income Tax is withheld at the rate of 15%. This means that the amount to be withheld from such compensation is 2.4% of the gross compensation.

(8) Withholding Tax

This article modifies the withholding tax rates applicable to certain items of income.

Sub-article 1 reduces the withholding tax rate applicable under Article 23(1) (c) (3) of the *Law on Income Tax* on royalties paid by a contractor or subcontractor from 15% to 6% of the gross amount of the royalty paid.

Sub-article 2 provides that the withholding tax rates determined under Article 4(2) of the *Law on Income Tax* applicable to compensation for construction services acquired for the project is 0.8% and consulting services is 1.6%.

Sub-article 3 applies to compensation paid by a contractor or subcontractor for services acquired in respect of the petroleum project. It reduces the withholding tax rate under Article 26(1) (c) and (d) of the *Law on Income Tax* for such services from 20% to 8% of the gross amount of compensation. This is subject to sub-article 4, which provides that the withholding tax rate under Article 26 (1) (d) applicable to compensation paid to employees is 20%.

(9) Branch Profits Tax

This article provides that the branch profits tax in Article 26(4) of the Law on Income Tax does not apply to a contractor or subcontractor in respect of income derived from a petroleum project.

(10) Value of Gas

This article provides for the valuation of natural gas (as defined in sub-article 2) for the purposes of calculating the taxable income of a contractor in respect of the petroleum project. Paragraph (a) of sub-article 1 provides that the valuation of natural gas produced and saved, and not used in field operations, is to be made in accordance with the Production Sharing Contract governing the project. Paragraph (b) makes it clear that no deduction is allowed for any export cost charge except to the extent that the charge has not been taken into account in determining the valuation of natural gas produced and saved pursuant to paragraph (a).

(11) Imposition of Additional Profits Tax

This article provides for the imposition of additional profits tax ("APT") on a contractor undertaking the petroleum project.

Sub-article 1 imposes APT on a contractor who has a positive amount of accumulated net receipts for the project for a fiscal year. The accumulated net receipts of a contractor for a fiscal year is calculated according to the formula in article 12. By virtue of article 20, APT is imposed for the fiscal year commencing 1 January, 2002 and subsequent fiscal years.

Sub-article 2 provides for the calculation of the APT payable by a contractor a fiscal year. In broad terms, the APT payable is the accumulated net receipts of the contractor for the year multiplied by 22.5%, with the resulting amount grossed-up by the income tax rate specified in Article 3(3) (i. e. , 30%).

Sub-article 3 makes it clear that any APT payable by a contractor for a fiscal year is in addition to the contractor's ordinary income tax liability for the year.

Sub-article 4 provides that any APT paid by a contractor is a deduction in the calculation of the taxable income of the contractor for the fiscal year in which the APT is paid.

(12) Accumulated Net Receipts

This Article provides for the calculation of the accumulated net receipts of a contractor for the petroleum project.

Sub-article 1 provides that the contractor's accumulated net receipts for a fiscal year is calculated according to the specified formula. Component A is the contractor's accumulated net receipts at the end of the previous fiscal year. Sub-article 2 provides that the amount of component A for a fiscal year is zero if the contractor paid APT for the previous fiscal year. This means that component A will always be either zero or a negative amount. Sub-article 4 provides a transitional measure for a contractor under Production Sharing Contracts JPDA 03-12 and 03-13. Component A of the formula for the fiscal year commencing on 1 January, 2002 (i. e. , the first fiscal year of the APT) is to be calculated on the basis that the accumulated net receipts of the contractor as at 25 October, 1999 was negative $233 million. The contractor is to notionally apply the formula in sub-article 1 for the period 25 October, 1999-31 December, 2001. The resulting amount is treated as component A of the formula for the fiscal year commencing 1 January, 2002,

Component B is the contractor's net receipts for the current fiscal year. This is calculated in accordance with Article 13.

Component I is the total of any interest or other financial charges paid by the contractor for the current fiscal year. It is entered as a negative amount. Sub-article 3 provides that where component (A x 116.5%) is negative for a fiscal year, the subtraction of component I(1-r) for that year is not to reduce the amount of ((A x 116.5%)-I(1-r)) to an amount that is less than component A. For example, if A is-$200m for a fiscal year, then the amount entered in the formula for the year as I (1-r) is not to exceed $33m. The amount of any excess is not carried forward or carried back to any fiscal year.

Component r is the corporate tax rate specified in Article 3(3).

(13) Net Receipts

This article provides for the calculation of the net receipts of a contractor for a petroleum project for a fiscal year. The net receipts are the gross receipts of the contractor for the year less the total deductible expenditure of the contractor for the year. The gross receipts of the contractor are calculated in accordance with Article 14 and the total deductible expenditure is calculated in accordance with Article 15. It is expressly provided that the net receipts of a contractor for a fiscal year may be negative.

The net receipts of a contractor for a fiscal year is component B of the formula in article 12 for that year.

(14) Gross Receipts

This article provides for the calculation of the gross receipts of a contractor for a fiscal year for the petroleum project. It is relevant to the calculation of the contractor's net receipts for the project for the year under Article 13.

Sub-article 1 provides that the gross receipts of a contractor for a fiscal year for the project is the sum of the following amounts –

① Paragraph (a) includes the gross income of the contractor received in the fiscal year for the project. The reference to "gross income" is a reference to the concept of gross income that forms the basis for the computation of taxable income under Article 6 of the *Law on Income Tax*. This is basically the sum of the amounts specified in Article 4 of the *Law on Income Tax*. It is expressly provided that the contractor's gross income includes any amounts received from the hiring or leasing out of, or the granting of rights to use property. It is also expressly provided that gross income for the purposes of calculating gross receipts does not include the contractor's interest income.

② Paragraph (b) includes the consideration received by the contractor in the year for the disposal, destruction or loss of any property used in the project where the expenditure incurred in acquiring the property was deducted under article 15 in calculating the net receipts of the contractor for any fiscal year. "Property" is to be interpreted broadly. It expressly includes any materials, equipment, plant facilities and intellectual property or rights.

③ Paragraph (c) includes the consideration received by the contractor in the year from the provision of information or data obtained from any survey, appraisal or study relating to the project where the expenditure incurred in undertaking the survey, appraisal or study was deducted under article 16 in calculating the net receipts of the contractor for any fiscal year.

④ Paragraph (d) includes the total of any other amounts received by the contractor in the year that is a reimbursement, refund or other recoupment of an amount previously deducted in computing the net receipts of the contractor for any fiscal year.

⑤ Paragraph (e) includes the consideration received in respect of property includes any compensation, indemnity or damages received by the contractor for the loss or destruction of the property.

Sub-article 2 provides that the gross receipts of a contractor does not include any amount received as consideration for the transfer of an interest in the petroleum project. This is subject to Article 16.

Sub-article 3 provides for apportionment of any amount derived or received that is only partly attributable to a petroleum project.

(15) Deductible Expenditure

This Article provides for the calculation of the total deductible expenditure of a contractor for a fiscal year for the petroleum project. It is relevant to the calculation of the contractor's net receipts for the project for the year under Article 14.

Sub-article 1 provides that the total deductible expenditure of a contractor for a fiscal year for the project is the sum of the following amounts –

① Paragraph (a) includes the total of amounts incurred in the year by the contractor in respect of the project and allowed as a deduction under Article 6 of the *Law on Income Tax* in calculating the taxable income of the contractor. It is expressly provided that this includes interest expense and financing charges. Paragraph (a) does not include depreciation and amortization deductions as the full amount of the expenditure is deductible under paragraph (b).

② Paragraph (b) includes the total capital expenditure incurred by the contractor in the year in acquiring assets (tangible and intangible) for use in the project.

③ Paragraph (c) includes the total exploration expenditure incurred

345

by the contractor in the year in respect of the project.

④ Paragraph (d) includes the East Timor income tax of the contractor for the year calculated by applying the corporate specified in Article 3(3) (i. e. , 30%) to the taxable income of the contractor for the year computed before allowance of the deduction of APT.

Sub-article 2 provides that the deductible expenditure of a contractor does not include any amount incurred as consideration for the transfer of an interest in the petroleum project. This is subject to Article 16.

Sub-article 3 provides for apportionment of any amount paid that is only partly attributable to a petroleum project.

(16) Transfer of Interest in a Petroleum Project

This Article applies where a contractor disposes of its interest in a petroleum project. In this case, the transferee contractor takes over the transferor's gross receipts and deductible expenditure for the fiscal year in which the transfer takes place calculated as at the date of the transfer. The transferee contractor also takes over the transferor's component A of the formula in article 13 for the fiscal year in which the transfer takes place.

(17) Procedure Relating to Additional Profits Tax

This article provides for procedural matters relating to the imposition of APT.

Sub-articles 1 and 2 oblige a contractor to lodge an APT return for a fiscal year. The return must be lodged by the same date as the contractor's annual income tax return for the year. According to Article 3 of the *Law on General Tax Provisions and Procedures*, this is three months after the end of the fiscal year.

Sub-article 3 provides that a contractor's APT for a fiscal year is due and payable on the same date as the contractor's income tax is due and payable for that year. APT is collected in instalments as determined under Article 18.

Sub-article 4 provides that the procedural rules in the *Law on General tax Provisions and Procedures* (as amended by *UNTAET*

Regulation No. 2000/18) apply for the purposes of the assessment and collection of APT and any additional tax imposed in relation to an APT liability, and for appeals against a contractor's assessed liability for APT or additional tax.

Sub-article 5 provides that Chapter XI of *UNTAET* Regulation No. 2000/18 applies for the purposes of APT. The combined operation of sub-article 5 and Chapter XI of UNTAET Regulation No. 2000/18 results in the imposition of additional tax in the following cases –

① A failure to lodge an APT return by the due date.

② A failure to pay APT or an instalment of APT by the due date.

③ An understatement of the amount of APT declared in an APT return.

④ A failure to create and retain records for the purposes of APT.

The combined operation of sub-article 5 and Chapter XI of *UNTAET* Regulation *No.* 2000/18 also results in the following offences –

① A failure to create and retain records for the purposes of APT.

② Obstructing or hindering the Commissioner in enforcing APT.

③ A failure to provide information or the provision of false information concerning APT.

④ Evasion of APT.

(18) Instalments of Tax

This article provides for the payment of APT by instalments.

Sub-article 1 provides for monthly instalments of APT. Each instalment is due on the 15th day after the end of the month. The first instalment for the fiscal year is for the month of January and is due on 15 February. If that date is not a business day, then the APT is due on the next business day. This treatment mirrors that applicable to the payment of the ordinary income tax.

Sub-article 2 obliges a contractor to deliver to the Commissioner an estimate of contractor's additional profits tax liability for a fiscal year by the payment date of the first instalment for that year (i. e. , 15 February). The amount of each instalment is one-twelfth of the estimate.

Sub-article 3 provides that the estimate remains in force for the whole of the fiscal year unless the contractor delivers a revised estimate to the Commissioner. A revised estimate applies to instalments due both before and after the revised estimate was delivered to the Commissioner. The sub-article also provides for the treatment of underpaid and overpaid tax as a result of a revised estimate.

Sub-article 4 provides that the Commissioner is to estimate the APT payable by a contractor for a fiscal year where the contractor fails to deliver an estimate as required under sub-article 2. The Commissioner's estimate remains in force for the whole of the year unless the contractor revises the Commissioner's estimate in accordance with sub-article 3.

Sub-article 5 provides for the imposition of additional tax where the contractor's APT estimate for a year is less than 90% of the actual APT payable by the contractor for the year.

(19) Regulations

This article provides that the Minister responsible for finance has the power to make regulations for the effective carrying out of the provisions of the act.

(20) Entry into Force and Application

This article provides that the Act enters into force upon satisfaction of the conditions specified in sub-article 1. APT applies for the fiscal year commencing on 1 January, 2002 and subsequent fiscal years.

7. Greater Sunrise Unitisation Agreement Implementation Act 2004, No. 47, 2004

[Assented to 21 April 2004]

The Parliament of Australia enacts:

1) Short title

This Act may be cited as the Greater Sunrise Unitisation Agreement

Implementation Act 2004.

2）Commencement

（1）Each provision of this Act specified in column 1 of the table commences, or is taken to have commenced, in accordance with column 2 of the table. Any other statement in column 2 has effect according to its terms.

Commencement information		
Column 1	Column 2	Column 3
Provision(s)	Commencement	Date/Details
1. Sections 1 to 3 and anything in this Act not elsewhere covered by this table	The day on which this Act receives the Royal Assent.	21 April 2004
2. Section 4	At the same time as the provision(s) covered by table item 3.	7 February 2007
3. Schedule 1, items 1 to 86	A single day to be fixed	7 February 2007 by Proclamation (*See* F2007L0025)
4. Schedule 1, items 87 and 88	The later of: (a) immediately after the commencement of section 4 of this Act; and (b) immediately after the commencement of item 1 of Schedule 3 to the *Petroleum (Submerged Lands) Amendment Act 2003.*	7 *February* 2007 (*paragraph (a) applies*)
5. Schedule 1, items 89 to 110	At the same time as the provision(s) covered by table item 3	7 February 2007
6. Schedule 1, Part 2	Immediately after the Commencement of item 47 of Schedule 1 to the Petroleum (Submerged Lands) Legislation Amendment *Act* (*No.*1) 2000	7 March 2000

Commencement information		
Column 1	Column 2	Column 3
Provision(s)	Commencement	Date/Details
7. Schedule 2	At the same time as the provision(s) covered by table item 3.	7 February 2007

Note: This table relates only to the provisions of this Act as originally passed by the Parliament and assented to. It will not be expanded to deal with provisions inserted in this Act after assent.

(2)Column 3 of the table contains additional information that is not part of this Act. Information in this column may be added to or edited in any published version of this Act.

3) Schedule(s)

Each Act that is specified in a Schedule to this Act is amended or repealed as set out in the applicable items in the Schedule concerned, and any other item in a Schedule to this Act has effect according to its terms.

4) Regulations

(1) The Governor-General may make regulations in relation to transitional matters arising out of the amendments made by this Act.

(2) The Governor-General may make regulations making provision (including provision by way of modification or adaptation of any Act) for or in relation to matters consequential on amendments made by this Act.

(3) The Governor-General may make regulations that:

(a) in the Minister's opinion, are necessary or convenient for giving effect to any provision of the Greater Sunrise unitisation agreement; and

(b) are not inconsistent with any amendment made by this Act.

(4)In this section:

Greater Sunrise unitisation agreement means the Agreement between the Government of Australia and the Government of the Democratic Republic of Timor-Leste relating to the Unitisation of the Sunrise and Troubadour Fields done at Dili on 6 March 2003.

Note: In 2004, the text of the agreement was available in the Australian Treaties Database of the Department of Foreign Affairs and Trade, accessible on the Internet through that Department's world-wide web site.

Schedule 1   Petroleum (Submerged Lands) Act 1967

Part 1   Amendments implementing the Greater Sunrise unitisation agreement

1) Subsection 5(1)

Insert:

Eastern Greater Sunrise area means the part of the adjacent area in respect of the Northern Territory that is described in Schedule 8 under the heading that refers to the Eastern Greater Sunrise area.

2) Subsection 5(1)

Insert:

Greater Sunrise unit area means the area described in Schedule 8 under the heading that refers to the Greater Sunrise unit area.

3) Subsection 5(1)

Insert:

Greater Sunrise unitisation agreement means the Agreement between the Government of Australia and the Government of the Democratic Republic of Timor-Leste relating to the Unitisation of the Sunrise and Troubadour Fields done at Dili on 6 March 2003.

Note: In 2004, the text of the agreement was available in the Australian Treaties Database of the Department of Foreign Affairs and Trade, accessible on the Internet through that Department's world-wide web site.

4) Subsection 5(1)

Insert:

Greater Sunrise unit reservoir licence means a licence in respect of one or more blocks within the Eastern Greater Sunrise area that would allow the licensee to recover petroleum from either or both of the Greater Sunrise unit reservoirs.

5) Subsection 5(1)

Insert：

Greater Sunrise unit reservoirs means the Unit Reservoirs within the meaning of the Greater Sunrise unitisation agreement.

6) Subsection 5(1)

Insert：

Greater Sunrise visiting inspector means an inspector who is specified in the certificate given to that inspector under subsection 125(2) as being a Greater Sunrise visiting inspector.

7) Subsection 5(1)

Insert：

Principal Northern Territory PSL area means the part of the adjacent area in respect of the Northern Territory that is comprised of all of that adjacent area apart from the Eastern Greater Sunrise area.

8) Subsection 5(1) (definition of *Register*)

After "adjacent area", insert ", or a part of an adjacent area".

9) Subsection 5(1) (at the end of subparagraph (a) (iii) of the definition of the *Designated Authority*)

Add ", or a part of an adjacent area".

10) Subsection 5(1) (at the end of paragraph (b) of the definition of *the Designated Authority*)

Add ", or a part of an adjacent area".

11) Subsection 5(1) (at the end of the definition of *the Designated Authority*)

Add ", or that part of an adjacent area".

12) Subsection 5(1) (at the end of subparagraph (a)(iii) of the definition of *the Joint Authority*)

Add ", or a part of an adjacent area".

13) Subsection 5(1) (at the end of paragraph (b) of the definition of *the Joint Authority*)

Add ", or a part of an adjacent area".

14) Subsection 5 (1) (at the end of the definition of *the Joint Authority*)

Add ", or that part of an adjacent area".

15) Subsection 5(1)

Insert:

Timor Sea Treaty means the Timor Sea Treaty between Australia and East Timor done on 20 May 2002 as amended from time to time.

Note: The text of the Treaty is set out in the Australian Treaty Series at [2003] ATS 13. In 2004 this was available in the Australian Treaties Database of the Department of Foreign Affairs and Trade, accessible on the Internet through that Department's world-wide web site.

16) Subsection 5(1)

Insert:

Timor Sea Treaty Designated Authority means the Designated Authority within the meaning of the *Petroleum (Timor Sea Treaty) Act* 2003.

17) Subsection 5(1)

Insert:

Western Greater Sunrise area means the area described in Schedule 8 under the heading that refers to the Western Greater Sunrise area.

Note: Activities occurring in the Western Greater Sunrise area in relation to the exploration, development and exploitation of the Greater Sunrise unit reservoirs are dealt with under the *Petroleum (Timor Sea Treaty) Act* 2003.

18) Subsection 8A (3)

Repeal the subsection, substitute:

(3) For the purposes of this Act, the Joint Authority:

(a) in respect of the adjacent area in respect of the Northern Territory; and

(b) consisting of the Commonwealth Minister and the Territory Minister; and

(c) known as the Commonwealth-Northern Territory Off-shore Petroleum Joint Authority; and

(d) that was established by this section before the commencement of Part 1 of Schedule 1 to the *Greater Sunrise Unitisation Agreement Implementation Act* 2004;

is continued in existence under that name as the Joint Authority in respect of the Principal Northern Territory PSL area.

(4) For the purposes of this Act, there is established in respect of the Eastern Greater Sunrise area a Joint Authority consisting of the Commonwealth Minister, and that Joint Authority is to be known as the Greater Sunrise Off-shore Petroleum Joint Authority.

19) Section 8C

After "adjacent area", insert ", or the part of an adjacent area,".

20) Subsection 8D (1)

After "a Joint Authority", insert "consisting of 2 members".

21) Subsection 8D (2)

Omit "If the members of a Joint Authority", substitute "If a Joint Authority consists of 2 members and they".

22) Subsection 8D (3)

Omit "A", substitute "If a Joint Authority consists of 2 members, a".

23) Before subsection 8H(1)

Insert:

(1A) This section only applies in respect of a Joint Authority consisting of 2 members.

Note: The heading to section 8H is altered by adding at the end "— other than Greater Sunrise Off-shore Petroleum Joint Authority".

24) Subsection 8H(1)

Omit "two persons together.", substitute:

two persons together, each of whom is one of the following:

（a）an APS employee who is an SES employee or acting SES employee;

（b）an employee of a State, or of the Northern Territory.

Note 1: The expressions *APS employee*, *SES employee and acting SES employee* are defined in section 17AA of the Acts Interpretation Act 1901.

Note 2: See also sections 34AA and 34AB of the Acts Interpretation Act 1901.

25）Subsection 8H(2A)

Omit "Without", substitute "Subject to subsection (1), and without".

26）At the end of Part IA

Add:

8J Greater Sunrise Off-shore Petroleum Joint Authority—consultations

The Greater Sunrise Off-shore Petroleum Joint Authority may consult with the Timor Sea Treaty Designated Authority before exercising any power, or performing any function, that is conferred on it under this Act, under an Act that incorporates this Act or under the regulations.

8K Delegation by Greater Sunrise Off-shore Petroleum Joint Authority

（1）The Greater Sunrise Off-shore Petroleum Joint Authority may, by written instrument, delegate to:

（a）an APS employee who is an SES employee or acting SES employee; or

（b）an employee of the Northern Territory;

any or all of the powers or functions of the Joint Authority under this Act, under an Act that incorporates this Act or under the regulations.

Note 1: The expressions *APS employee*, *SES employee* and *acting SES employee* are defined in section 17AA of the *Acts Interpretation Act* 1901.

Note 2: See also sections 34AA and 34AB of the *Acts Interpretation Act* 1901.

(2) If the Greater Sunrise Off-shore Petroleum Joint Authority delegates a power or function under this section, the delegation continues in force despite:

(a) a vacancy in the office of Joint Authority; or

(b) a change in the identity of the holder of the office of Joint Authority.

(3) Despite subsection (2), a delegation under this section may be revoked by the Greater Sunrise Off-shore Petroleum Joint Authority in accordance with subsection 33(3) of the *Acts Interpretation Act* 1901.

(4) A copy of each instrument making, varying or revoking a delegation under this section must be published in the *Gazette*.

27) Subsection 14(1)

After "adjacent area", insert "(other than the adjacent area in respect of the Northern Territory)".

Note: The heading to section 14 is altered by adding at the end "—adjacent areas other than the Northern Territory adjacent area".

28) Subsections 14(5) and (6)

Repeal the subsections.

29) After section 14

Insert:

14A Designated Authorities—Northern Territory adjacent area

Principal Northern Territory PSL area

(1) For the purposes of this Act, the Designated Authority:

(a) in respect of the adjacent area in respect of the Northern Territory; and

(b) consisting of the Northern Territory Minister; and

(c) that was established by subsection 14(1) of this Act before the commencement of Part 1 of Schedule 1 to the *Greater Sunrise Unitisation Agreement Implementation Act* 2004;

is continued in existence as the Designated Authority in respect of the Principal Northern Territory PSL area.

(2) The functions and powers of the Northern Territory Minister as

356

the Designated Authority in respect of the Principal Northern Territory PSL area may be performed and exercised by another Northern Territory Minister acting for and on behalf of that Minister.

Eastern Greater Sunrise area

（3）For the purposes of this Act, there is to be a Designated Authority in respect of the Eastern Greater Sunrise area.

（4）The Designated Authority in respect of the Eastern Greater Sunrise area is the Commonwealth Minister.

14B Eastern Greater Sunrise Designated Authority—consultations

The Designated Authority in respect of the Eastern Greater Sunrise area may consult with the Timor Sea Treaty Designated Authority before exercising any power, or performing any function, that is conferred on it under this Act, under an Act that incorporates this Act or under the regulations.

30) Subsection 15(1)

Repeal the subsection, substitute：

（1）A Designated Authority may, by written instrument, delegate to：

（a）an APS employee who is an SES employee or acting SES employee; or

（b）an employee of a State, or of the Northern Territory；

any or all of the powers or functions of the Designated Authority under this Act, under an Act that incorporates this Act or under the regulations.

Note 1：The expressions APS employee, SES employee and acting SES employee are defined in section 17AA of the Acts Interpretation Act 1901.

Note 2：See also sections 34AA and 34AB of the Acts Interpretation Act 1901.

31) After subsection 41(1)

Insert：

（1A）An application under section 39A or 40A for the grant of a Greater Sunrise unit reservoir licence must also：

(a) nominate a person to be the unit operator, as defined in the Greater Sunrise unitisation agreement; and

(b) be accompanied by each Joint Venturers' Agreement, as defined in the Greater Sunrise unitisation agreement; and

(c) be accompanied by a copy of the proposed Development Plan, as defined in the Greater Sunrise unitisation agreement.

32) Subsection 43(1A)

After "must,", insert "subject to subsection (1B),".

33) After subsection 43(1A)

Insert:

(1B) The Greater Sunrise Off-shore Petroleum Joint Authority must not tell an applicant for the grant of a Greater Sunrise unit reservoir licence that the Joint Authority is prepared to grant to the applicant such a licence unless:

(a) the Joint Authority has given to the Timor Sea Treaty Designated Authority a written notice that:

(i) states that the Joint Authority is considering granting the licence to the applicant and naming the person who the applicant has nominated to be the unit operator; and

(ii) is accompanied by a copy of each Joint Venturers' Agreement that accompanied the application; and

(iii) is accompanied by a copy of the proposed Development Plan that accompanied the application; and

(b) the Joint Authority has approved:

(i) a unit operator in respect of the development of the Greater Sunrise unit reservoirs in the blocks to which the licence relates; and

(ii) each Joint Venturers' Agreement in respect of that development; and

(iii) the Development Plan in respect of that development; and is satisfied that the Timor Sea Treaty Designated Authority has approved the same unit operator, Joint Venturers' Agreements and Development Plan in respect of that development; and （c）the Joint Authority has determined the conditions subject to which the licence is to be granted.

34）After paragraph 43（3）（b）

Insert：

or（c）in the case of an application for the grant of a Greater Sunrise unit reservoir licence—the Joint Authority is not satisfied that the Timor Sea Treaty Designated Authority has given the approvals mentioned in paragraph（1B）（b）；

35）Paragraph 59（1）（a）

After "petroleum pool", insert "（other than either of the Greater Sunrise unit reservoirs）".

36）Subsection 59B（1）

After "Designated Authority", insert "in respect of an adjacent area or a part of an adjacent area".

37）Subsection 59B（1）

After "Joint Authority", insert "in respect of the adjacent area or the part of an adjacent area".

38）Paragraph 59B（2）（b）

After "adjacent area,", insert "or a part of an adjacent area".

39）Subsection 60(1)

Omit "the adjacent area", substitute "an adjacent area, or a part of an adjacent area".

40）Subsection 60(4)

Omit "the adjacent area", substitute "an adjacent area, or a part of an adjacent area".

41）Subsection 60(5)

Omit "the adjacent area", substitute "an adjacent area, or a part of an adjacent area".

42）Subsection 60(6)

Omit "The", substitute "A".

43）Subsection 62(1)

After "Designated Authority", insert "in respect of an adjacent area, or a part of an adjacent area,".

44) At the end of paragraph 62(1)(d)

Add ", or the part of an adjacent area".

45) Section 63

After "Designated Authority", insert "in respect of an adjacent area, or a part of an adjacent area,".

46) Section 63

Omit "in an adjacent area", substitute "in the adjacent area, or the part of an adjacent area,".

47) Subsection 65(1)

After "an adjacent area", insert ", or a part of an adjacent area,".

48) Subsection 65(1)

After ", adjacent area", insert ", or a part of an adjacent area".

49) Subsection 65(2)

After "an adjacent area", insert ", or a part of an adjacent area,".

50) Subsection 65(2A)

After "an adjacent area", insert ", or a part of an adjacent area,".

51) Subsection 65(3)

After "an adjacent area", insert ", or a part of an adjacent area,".

52) Paragraph 66(a)

Omit "an adjacent area", substitute "the adjacent area, or the part of an adjacent area, specified in the pipeline licence".

53) Subparagraph 66(a) (i)

After "that adjacent area", insert ", or that part of an adjacent area,".

54) Paragraph 66(c)

After "adjacent area", insert ", or that part of an adjacent area,".

55) At the end of subsection 76(1)

Add ", or the part of the adjacent area, in respect of which the Designated Authority is the Designated Authority".

56) Section 92

After "adjacent area", insert ", or a part of the adjacent area,".

57）Subsection 101(1)

Omit " The Designated Authority ", substitute " A Designated Authority in respect of an adjacent area, or a part of an adjacent area".

58）Paragraph 101(2)（b）

After " the adjacent area" (wherever occurring), insert ", or the part of the adjacent area,".

59）Subsection 101(2)

After "person who is in the adjacent area", insert ", or the part of the adjacent area,".

60）Subsection 101(2C)

After "Designated Authority", insert "in respect of an adjacent area, or a part of an adjacent area,".

61）Subsection 101(2C)

Omit "in an adjacent area", substitute "in the adjacent area, or the part of an adjacent area".

62）Subsection 102(1A)

Omit " by the Joint Authority ", substitute " by a Joint Authority comprised of 2 members".

63）At the end of section 103A

Add:

(6) For the purposes of subsection (5):

(a) the Commonwealth-Northern Territory Off-shore Petroleum Joint Authority; and

(b) the Greater Sunrise Off-shore Petroleum Joint Authority;

are taken to have been established in relation to the Northern Territory.

64）Subsection 107(2)

After "The Designated Authority", insert ", in respect of an adjacent area, or a part of an adjacent area,".

65）Subsection 107(2)

Omit " is a permittee, lessee, licensee, infrastructure licensee or pipeline licensee ", substitute " holds a permit, lease, licence, infrastructure licence, or pipeline licence, in respect of one or more blocks in that adjacent area, or that part of an adjacent area".

66) Paragraph 107(2)(a)

Omit "part of", substitute "area in".

67) Paragraph 107(2)(a)

Omit "or part by", substitute "by".

68) Paragraph 107(2)(b)

Omit "or part".

69) Paragraph 107(2)(c)

Omit "or part".

70) Paragraph 107(2)(d)

Omit "or part".

71) Subsection 112(1)

After "Designated Authority", insert "in respect of the adjacent area, or the part of the adjacent area, in which the blocks that the permit, lease or licence relates to are located,".

72) Subsection 112(1)

Omit "being part of the adjacent area", substitute "being part of that adjacent area, or that part of an adjacent area,".

73) Subsection 112(1C)

After "within an adjacent area", insert ", or a part of an adjacent area,".

74) Subsection 112(1C)

After "that adjacent area", insert ", or that part of an adjacent area,".

75) Subsection 112(1C)

After "in an adjacent area", insert ", or a part of an adjacent area,".

76) Subsection 112(1C)

After "first-mentioned adjacent area", insert ", or part of an adjacent area".

77) Subsection 112(4)

After "the Designated Authority", insert ", in respect of an adjacent area, or a part of an adjacent area,".

78) Subsection 112(4)

After "block" (wherever occurring), insert "in that adjacent area, or that part of an adjacent area,".

79) Subsection 112(4A)

After "adjacent area", insert ", or the part of an adjacent area,".

80) Subsection 112(4B)

After "adjacent area", insert ", or the part of an adjacent area,".

81) Subsection 115(1)

After "an adjacent area", insert ", or a part of an adjacent area,".

82) Subsection 115(1)

After "recovery of petroleum", insert "(including the measurement of the amount of petroleum recovered)".

83) Subsection 115(1)

After "that adjacent area,", insert "or that part of an adjacent area,".

84) Subsection 119(1)

After "an adjacent area", insert ", or a part of an adjacent area".

85) Subsection 122(1)

After "Designated Authority", insert " in respect of an adjacent area, or a part of an adjacent area,".

86) Subsection 122(1)

Omit "in an adjacent area", substitute "in the adjacent area, or the part of an adjacent area,".

87) Paragraph 122A (1)(a)

After "adjacent area", insert ", or a part of an adjacent area,".

88) Paragraph 122A (2)(a)

After "adjacent area", insert ", or a part of an adjacent area,".

89) Subsection 123(1)

Omit "The Designated Authority", substitute "A Designated Authority in respect of an adjacent area, or a part of an adjacent area,".

90) Subsection 123(1)

Omit "in an adjacent area", substitute "in the adjacent area, or the part of an adjacent area,".

91) Subsection 123(3)

After "the adjacent area", insert ", or the part of the adjacent area,".

92) Subsection 125(1)

After "adjacent area" (first occurring), insert ", or a part of an adjacent area,".

93) At the end of subsection 125(1)

Add ", or that part of an adjacent area".

94) After subsection 125(2)

Insert:

(2A) The Designated Authority in respect of the Eastern Greater Sunrise area may specify in a certificate given to an inspector under subsection (2) that the inspector is a Greater Sunrise visiting inspector.

95) Subsection 126(1)

After "an inspector", insert "(other than a Greater Sunrise visiting inspector)".

96) Paragraph 126(1) (a)

After "the adjacent area", insert "or the part of an adjacent area,".

97) Paragraph 126(1) (a)

After "that area" (wherever occurring), insert "or part".

98) Paragraph 126(1) (b)

After "that area", insert "or part".

99) Paragraph 126(1) (c)

After "in that area", insert "or part".

100) After subsection 126(1)

Insert:

(1A) For the purposes of paragraph (1) (c), the Eastern Greater Sunrise area is taken to be specified in Schedule 2 as being an adjacent area in respect of the Northern Territory.

(1B) For the purposes of this Act and the regulations, a Greater Sunrise visiting inspector who produces, at a reasonable time, a certificate given to him or her under section 125:

(a) is to be given access to the regions in:

(i) the Eastern Greater Sunrise area; or

(ii) the Principal Northern Territory PSL area; specified in the certificate; and

(b) is to be given access to any structure, ship, aircraft or building in that region that, in his or her opinion, contains any equipment used to measure amounts of petroleum recovered from one or more of the Greater Sunrise unit reservoirs; and

(c) may inspect and test any equipment that, in his or her opinion, is being used in that region to measure amounts of petroleum recovered from one or more of the Greater Sunrise unit reservoirs.

101) Subsection 126(2)

After "subsection (1)", insert "or (1B)".

102) Section 127

After "if petroleum", insert ", other than petroleum from the Greater Sunrise unit reservoirs,".

103) At the end of section 127

Add:

(2) Subject to this Act, if an amount of petroleum is recovered at a particular time from one of the Greater Sunrise unit reservoirs by a permittee, lessee or licensee in the permit area, lease area or licence area:

(a) the current apportionment percentage of the amount of the petroleum becomes the property of the permittee, lessee or licensee; and

(b) property in the remainder of the amount of petroleum is determined under the Timor Sea Treaty; and

(c) the amount of petroleum is not subject to any rights of other persons (other than any person to whom the person whose property the petroleum becomes, under paragraph (a) or (b), assigns or otherwise disposes of the petroleum or an interest in the petroleum).

(3) In this section:

current apportionment percentage, in relation to an amount of petroleum recovered at a particular time, means 79.9% unless, before that time, the Apportionment Ratio set out in article 7 of the Greater Sunrise unitisation agreement has changed, at least once, because it has been:

(a) redetermined due to a technical redetermination undertaken in accordance with paragraph 8(1) of the agreement; or

(b) altered due to an agreement in accordance with paragraph 8(2) of the Greater Sunrise unitisation agreement;

in which case it means the percentage of the production of petroleum from the Greater Sunrise unit reservoirs that is apportioned to Australia under the Greater Sunrise unitisation agreement immediately after the most recent change to the Apportionment Ratio.

104) Subsection 137(1)

After "adjacent area", insert ", or a part of an adjacent area,".

105) At the end of subsection 137(1)

Add ", or that part of an adjacent area".

106) Subsection 157(3)

After " rights ", insert ", and compliance with Australia's obligations,".

107) At the end of subsection 157(3)

Add "(whether in an adjacent area or not)".

108) Subclause 29(1) of Schedule 7

After "an inspector", insert "(other than a Greater Sunrise visiting inspector)".

109) Subclause 29(1) of Schedule 7

After "adjacent area", insert ", or a part of an adjacent area,".

110) At the end of the Act

Add:

Schedule 8   Greater Sunrise areas

Note 1: See subsection 5 (1) (definitions of Greater Sunrise unit area, Western Greater Sunrise area and Eastern Greater Sunrise area).

Note 2: For datum, see section 150M.

Greater Sunrise unit area

The Greater Sunrise unit area is the area the boundary of which commences at the point of Latitude 9° 50′ 00″ South, Longitude 127° 55′ 00″ East and runs:

(a) thence easterly along the rhumb line to the point of Latitude 9° 50′ 00″ South, Longitude 128° 20′ 00″ East;

(b) thence northerly along the rhumb line to the point of Latitude 9° 40′ 00″ South, Longitude 128° 20′ 00″ East;

(c) thence easterly along the rhumb line to the point of Latitude 9° 40′ 00″ South, Longitude 128° 25′ 00″ East;

(d) thence northerly along the rhumb line to the point of Latitude 9° 30′ 00″ South, Longitude 128° 25′ 00″ East;

(e) thence westerly along the rhumb line to the point of Latitude 9° 30′ 00″ South, Longitude 128° 20′ 00″ East;

(f) thence northerly along the rhumb line to the point of Latitude 9° 25′ 00″ South, Longitude 128° 20′ 00″ East;

(g) thence westerly along the rhumb line to the point of Latitude 9° 25′ 00″ South, Longitude 128° 00′ 00″ East;

(h) thence south-westerly along the rhumb line to the point of Latitude 9° 30′ 00″ South, Longitude 127° 53′ 20″ East;

(i) thence westerly along the rhumb line to the point of Latitude 9° 30′ 00″ South, Longitude 127° 52′ 30″ East;

(j) thence southerly along the rhumb line to the point of Latitude 9°

367

35′ 00″ South, Longitude 127° 52′ 30″ East;

(k) thence westerly along the rhumb line to the point of Latitude 9° 35′ 00″ South, Longitude 127° 50′ 00″ East;

(l) thence southerly along the rhumb line to the point of Latitude 9° 37′ 30″ South, Longitude 127° 50′ 00″ East;

(m) thence westerly along the rhumb line to the point of Latitude 9° 37′ 30″ South, Longitude 127° 45′ 00″ East;

(n) thence southerly along the rhumb line to the point of Latitude 9° 45′ 00″ South, Longitude 127° 45′ 00″ East;

(o) thence easterly along the rhumb line to the point of Latitude 9° 45′ 00″ South, Longitude 127° 50′ 00″ East;

(p) thence southerly along the rhumb line to the point of Latitude 9° 47′ 30″ South, Longitude 127° 50′ 00″ East;

(q) thence easterly along the rhumb line to the point of Latitude 9° 47′ 30″ South, Longitude 127° 55′ 00″ East;

(r) thence southerly along the rhumb line to the point of commencement.

Eastern Greater Sunrise area

The Eastern Greater Sunrise area is the area the boundary of which commences at the point of Latitude 9° 50′ 00″ South, Longitude 128° 03′ 22. 51″ East and runs:

(a) thence easterly along the rhumb line to the point of Latitude 9° 50′ 00″ South, Longitude 128° 20′ 00″ East;

(b) thence northerly along the rhumb line to the point of Latitude 9° 40′ 00″ South, Longitude 128° 20′ 00″ East;

(c) thence easterly along the rhumb line to the point of Latitude 9° 40′ 00″ South, Longitude 128° 25′ 00″ East;

(d) thence northerly along the rhumb line to the point of Latitude 9° 30′ 00″ South, Longitude 128° 25′ 00″ East;

(e) thence westerly along the rhumb line to the point of Latitude 9°

30′ 00″ South, Longitude 128° 20′ 00″ East;

（f）thence northerly along the rhumb line to the point of Latitude 9° 25′ 00″ South, Longitude 128° 20′ 00″ East;

（g）thence westerly along the rhumb line to the point of Latitude 9° 25′ 00″ South, Longitude 128° 00′ 00″ East;

（h）thence south-westerly along the rhumb line to the point of Latitude 9° 28′ 00″ South, Longitude 127° 56′ 00″ East;

（i）thence south-easterly along the geodesic to the point of Latitude 9° 29′ 57″ South, Longitude 127° 58′ 47″ East;

（j）thence south-easterly along the geodesic to the point of commencement.

Western Greater Sunrise area

The Western Greater Sunrise area is the area the boundary of which commences at the point of Latitude 9° 28′ 00″ South, Longitude 127° 56′ 00″ East and runs:

（a）thence south-westerly along the rhumb line to the point of Latitude 9° 30′ 00″ South, Longitude 127° 53′ 20″ East;

（b）thence westerly along the rhumb line to the point of Latitude 9° 30′ 00″ South, Longitude 127° 52′ 30″ East;

（c）thence southerly along the rhumb line to the point of Latitude 9° 35′ 00″ South, Longitude 127° 52′ 30″ East;

（d）thence westerly along the rhumb line to the point of Latitude 9° 35′ 00″ South, Longitude 127° 50′ 00″ East;

（e）thence southerly along the rhumb line to the point of Latitude 9° 37′ 30″ South, Longitude 127° 50′ 00″ East;

（f）thence westerly along the rhumb line to the point of Latitude 9° 37′ 30″ South, Longitude 127° 45′ 00″ East;

（g）thence southerly along the rhumb line to the point of Latitude 9° 45′ 00″ South, Longitude 127° 45′ 00″ East;

（h）thence easterly along the rhumb line to the point of Latitude 9°

45′ 00″ South, Longitude 127° 50′ 00″ East;

(i) thence southerly along the rhumb line to the point of Latitude 9° 47′ 30″ South, Longitude 127° 50′ 00″ East;

(j) thence easterly along the rhumb line to the point of Latitude 9° 47′ 30″ South, Longitude 127° 55′ 00″ East;

(k) thence southerly along the rhumb line to the point of Latitude 9° 50′ 00″ South, Longitude 127° 55′ 00″ East;

(l) thence easterly along the rhumb line to the point of Latitude 9° 50′ 00″ South, Longitude 128° 03′ 22. 51″ East;

(m) thence north-westerly along the geodesic to the point of Latitude 9° 29′ 57″ South, Longitude 127° 58′ 47″ East;

(n) thence north-westerly along the geodesic to the point of commencement.

Part 2   Technical corrections

111) Subsection 44(1)

Omit "an instrument under subsection 43(1)", substitute "a notice under subsection 43(1A)".

112) Subsection 44(1)

Omit "instrument on", substitute "notice on".

113) Subsection 44(1)

Omit "first-mentioned instrument", substitute "notice".

114) Subsection 44(2)

Omit "an instrument under subsection 43(1)", substitute "a notice under subsection 43(1A)".

115) Subsection 44(4)

Omit "an instrument under subsection 43(1)", substitute "a notice under subsection 43(1A)".

116) Paragraph 44A(b)

Omit "subsection 43(1)", substitute "subsection 43(1A)".

Schedule 2　Amendment of other Acts
Petroleum Resource Rent Tax Assessment Act 1987

1) Section 2

Insert：

apportionment percentage figure has the meaning given by subsection 2C(2).

2) Section 2

Insert：

current apportionment percentage has the meaning given by subsection 2C(1).

3) Section 2

Insert：

Greater Sunrise project means a petroleum project for the recovery of petroleum from one or more of the Greater Sunrise unit reservoirs.

4) Section 2

Insert：

Greater Sunrise unit area has the same meaning as in the *Petroleum (Submerged Lands) Act* 1967.

5) Section 2

Insert：

Greater Sunrise unit reservoirs has the same meaning as in the *Petroleum (Submerged Lands) Act* 1967.

6) Section 2 (definition of *production licence*)

Repeal the definition, substitute：

production licence means：

(a) a production licence for petroleum under Part III of the *Petroleum (Submerged Lands) Act* 1967; or

(b) a lawful authority or right (however described) to undertake activities in the Western Greater Sunrise area for the recovery of petroleum from one or more of the Greater Sunrise unit reservoirs.

7) Section 2 (definition of *production licence area*)

Repeal the definition, substitute:

production licence area means a licence area within the meaning of the *Petroleum (Submerged Lands) Act* 1967 and, in relation to a Greater Sunrise project, includes the Western Greater Sunrise area.

8) Section 2 (note at the end of the definition of *transferable exploration expenditure*)

Omit "Note", substitute "Note 1".

9) Section 2 (at the end of the definition of *transferable exploration expenditure*)

Add:

Note 2: Special rules apply in relation to the transfer of Greater Sunrise exploration expenditure: see Part 1A of the Schedule.

10) Section 2

Insert:

Western Greater Sunrise area has the same meaning as in the *Petroleum (Submerged Lands) Act* 1967.

11) After section 2B

Insert:

2C Greater Sunrise apportionments

(1) For the purposes of this Act, *current apportionment percentage* means the percentage applying from time to time under the definition of *current apportionment percentage* in subsection 127(3) of the *Petroleum (Submerged Lands) Act* 1967.

(2) For the purposes of this Act, *apportionment percentage figure*, in relation to a year of tax, means:

(a) if the current apportionment percentage did not change during the year of tax—the numerator of the fraction with a denominator of 100 that represents the current apportionment percentage that applied during that year; or

(b) if the current apportionment percentage changed during the year of tax—means the amount worked out using the following formula:

$$\frac{\{\text{Second \% figure} \quad \text{Subsequent days}\} + \{\text{First\% figure} \quad \text{Prior days}\}}{\text{Days in tax year}}$$

where:

days in tax year means the number of days in the year of tax. *first % figure*, in relation to a year of tax in which the current apportionment percentage changed, means the numerator of the fraction with a denominator of 100 that represents the current apportionment percentage applying before the change.

prior days, in relation to a year of tax in which the current apportionment percentage changed, means the number of days in that year before the current apportionment percentage changed.

second % figure, in relation to a year of tax in which the current apportionment percentage changed, means the numerator of the fraction with a denominator of 100 that represents the current apportionment percentage applying after the change.

subsequent days, in relation to a year of tax in which the current apportionment percentage changed, means the number of days in that year from and including the day on which the current apportionment percentage changed.

12) At the end of section 22 (after the note)

Add:

Allowing for Greater Sunrise apportionments

(2) However, if the petroleum project is a Greater Sunrise project, the person is taken for the purposes of this Act to have a taxable profit

in relation to the project and the year of tax of an amount worked out using the following formula:

$$\frac{\text{Initial taxable profit . Apportionment percentage figure}}{100}$$

where:

apportionment percentage figure has the meaning given by subsection 2C(2).

initial taxable profit means the amount of taxable profit worked out under subsection (1) ignoring this subsection.

13) Subsection 23(1)

Omit "subsection (2)", substitute "subsections (2) and (3)".

14) At the end of section 23

Add:

(3) For the purposes of this Act, assessable receipts, in relation to a Greater Sunrise project, are to be calculated as if each amount of the petroleum recovered from a Greater Sunrise unit reservoir became the property of the person who recovered that amount as soon as it was recovered.

(4) Subsection (3) has effect despite subsection 127(2) of the *Petroleum (Submerged Lands) Act* 1967.

15) At the end of section 46

Add:

Greater Sunrise closing-down credits

(2) However, for the purposes of the operation of paragraph (1)(a) in relation to a Greater Sunrise project, the amount that is so much of the excess as does not exceed the amount of the closing-down expenditure is taken to be the amount worked out using the following formula:

$$\frac{\text{Initial excess. Apportionment percentage figure}}{100}$$

where:

apportionment percentage figure has the meaning given by subsection 2C(2).

initial excess means the amount that is so much of the excess as does not exceed the amount of the closing-down expenditure under paragraph (1)(a) ignoring this subsection.

16) After Part 1 of the Schedule

Insert:

Part 1A   Special rules relating to the transfer
of Greater Sunrise expenditure

4A   Certain Greater Sunrise expenditure is not transferable

Despite paragraphs 7(b), 8(5)(c), 11(b), 12(4)(c) and 18(3)
(e) of this Schedule and subclauses 18(1) and 18(2) of this Schedule,
amounts of exploration expenditure incurred in relation to the Western
Greater Sunrise area before 6 March 2003 are not transferable under
section 45A, 45B or 45C.

4B   Greater Sunrise transferable exploration expenditure must be adjusted

Transfers from a Greater Sunrise project

(1) If, in relation to a year of tax, transferable exploration
expenditure is transferred from a Greater Sunrise project to a petroleum
project other than a Greater Sunrise project, the amount of that
expenditure for the purposes of the other petroleum project is taken to be
the amount worked out using the following formula:

$$\frac{\text{Amount transferred. Apportionment percentage figure}}{100}$$

where:

amount transferred means the amount transferred, in relation to the
year of tax, from the Greater Sunrise project before that amount is
reduced by the operation of this subclause.

apportionment percentage figure has the meaning given by
subsection 2C(2).

Transfers to a Greater Sunrise project

(2) If, in relation to a year of tax, transferable exploration
expenditure is transferred to a Greater Sunrise project from a petroleum
project other than a Greater Sunrise project, the amount of that

expenditure for the purposes of the Greater Sunrise project is taken to be the amount worked out using the following formula:

$$\frac{\text{Amount transferred} \cdot 100}{\text{Apportionment percentage figure}}$$

where:

amount transferred means the amount transferred, in relation to the year of tax, from the project other than the Greater Sunrise project before that amount is increased by the operation of this subclause.

apportionment percentage figure has the meaning given by subsection 2C(2).

17) At the end of clause 20 of the Schedule

Add:

Note: Special rules apply in relation to the transfer of Greater Sunrise exploration expenditure: see Part 1A of this Schedule.

18) At the end of clause 29 of the Schedule

Add:

Note: Special rules apply in relation to the transfer of Greater Sunrise exploration expenditure: see Part 1A of this Schedule.

Radiocommunications Act 1992

19) At the end of paragraph 16(1)(d)

Add "or 17A".

20) After section 17

Insert:

17A Western Greater Sunrise area

(1) Subject to subsection (2), this Act applies in relation to the Western Greater Sunrise area as if references in this Act to Australia, when used in a geographical sense, included references to the Western Greater Sunrise area.

(2) The extended application given to this Act by subsection (1)

extends only in relation to:

(a) acts, matters and things directly or indirectly connected with exploration of, or exploitation of the resources of, either or both of the Greater Sunrise unit reservoirs; and

(b) acts done by or in relation to, and matters, circumstances and things affecting, any person who is in the Western Greater Sunrise area for a reason directly or indirectly connected with such exploration or exploitation.

(3) In this section:

Greater Sunrise unit reservoirs has the same meaning as in the *Petroleum (Submerged Lands) Act 1967*.

Western Greater Sunrise area has the same meaning as in the *Petroleum (Submerged Lands) Act 1967*.

8. Petroleum (Timor Sea Treaty) (Consequential Amendments) Acts 2003

An Act to make amendments consequential on the enactment of the Petroleum (Timor Sea Treaty) Act 2003, and for related purposes

[Assented to 2 April 2003]

The Parliament of Australia enacts:

1) Short title

This Act may be cited as the Petroleum (*Timor Sea Treaty*) (Consequential Amendments) Act 2003.

2) Commencement

(1) Each provision of this Act specified in column 1 of the table commences, or is taken to have commenced, on the day or at the time specified in column 2 of the table.

Commencement information		
Column 1	Column 2	Column 3
Provision(s)	Commencement	Date/Details
1. Sections 1 to 4 and anything in this Act not elsewhere covered by this table	The day on which this Act receives the Royal Assent	2 April 2003
2. Schedule 1, items 1 to 52	20 May 2002	20 May 2002
3. Schedule 1, item 53	The day on which this Act receives the Royal Assent	2 April 2003
4. Schedule 1, items 54 to 75	20 May 2002	20 May 2002
5. Schedule 1, items 76 and 77	The day on which this Act receives the Royal Assent	2 April 2003
6. Schedule 1, items 78 to 82	20 May 2002	20 May 2002
7. Schedule 1, item 83	The day on which this Act receives the Royal Assent	2 April 2003

Note: This table relates only to the provisions of this Act as originally passed by the Parliament and assented to. It will not be expanded to deal with provisions inserted in this Act after assent.

(2) Column 3 of the table is for additional information that is not part of this Act. This information may be included in any published version of this Act.

3) Schedule(s)

Each Act that is specified in a Schedule to this Act is amended or repealed as set out in the applicable items in the Schedule concerned, and any other item in a Schedule to this Act has effect according to its terms.

4) Amendment of assessments

Section 170 of the *Income Tax Assessment Act* 1936 does not prevent the amendment of an assessment made before the commencement of this section for the purposes of giving effect to this Act.

Schedule 1　Consequential amendments

Part 1　Amendments

Crimes at Sea Act 2000

1) Section 4 (definition of Area A of the Zone of Cooperation)

Repeal the definition.

2) Section 4 (definition of *East Timor*)

Repeal the definition.

3) Section 4

Insert:

Joint Petroleum Development Area has the same meaning as in the Petroleum (Timor Sea Treaty) Act 2003.

4) Section 4 (definition of *petroleum*)

Repeal the definition, substitute:

petroleum has the same meaning as in the Treaty (within the meaning of the *Petroleum (Timor Sea Treaty) Act 2003*).

5) Subsection 6A (1)

Omit "Area A of the Zone of Cooperation", substitute "the Joint Petroleum Development Area".

Note: The heading to section 6A is altered by omitting "Area A of the Zone of Cooperation" and substituting "the Joint Petroleum Development Area".

6) Subsection 6A (6)

Omit "Area A of the Zone of Cooperation", substitute "the Joint Petroleum Development Area".

7）Subsection 6B（1）

Omit "Area A of the Zone of Cooperation", substitute "the Joint Petroleum Development Area".

8）Subsection 6C（1）

Omit "Area A of the Zone of Cooperation", substitute "the Joint Petroleum Development Area".

Note：The heading to section 6C is altered by omitting "Area A of the Zone of Cooperation" and substituting "the Joint Petroleum Development Area".

9）Subparagraph 6C（2）（b）（i）

Omit "Area A of the Zone of Cooperation", substitute "the Joint Petroleum Development Area".

10）Subparagraph 6C（2）（b）（ii）

Omit "Area A of the Zone of Cooperation", substitute "the Joint Petroleum Development Area".

11）Subparagraph 6C（2）（c）（i）

Omit "Area A of the Zone of Cooperation", substitute "the Joint Petroleum Development Area".

12）Subparagraph 6C（2）（c）（ii）

Omit "Area A of the Zone of Cooperation", substitute "the Joint Petroleum Development Area".

13）Subclause 1(1) of Schedule 1（definition of *Area A of the Zone of Cooperation*）

Repeal the definition.

14）Subclause 1(1) of Schedule 1

Insert：

Joint Petroleum Development Area has the same meaning as in the *Petroleum（Timor Sea Treaty）Act* 2003.

15）Clause 10 of Schedule 1

Omit "Area A of the Zone of Cooperation", substitute "the Joint Petroleum Development Area".

Note：The heading to clause 10 is altered by omitting "Area A of the

Zone of Cooperation" and substituting "the Joint Petroleum Development Area".

16) Paragraph 14(3) (b) of Schedule 1

Repeal the paragraph, substitute:

(b) is not within the Joint Petroleum Development Area;

17) Subparagraph 14(4) (a) (ii) of Schedule 1

Omit "Area A of the Zone of Cooperation", substitute "the Joint Petroleum Development Area".

18) Schedule 1 (legend of the map in Appendix 1)

Omit "Area A of the Zone of Cooperation", substitute "the Joint Petroleum Development Area".

Customs Act 1901

19) Subsection 4 (1) (definition of Area A of the Zone of Cooperation)

Repeal the definition.

20) Subsection 4(1) (definition of *Australian seabed*)

Omit "Area A of the Zone of Cooperation", substitute "the Joint Petroleum Development Area".

21) Subsection 4(1) (definition of *East Timor*)

Repeal the definition.

22) Subsection 4(1)

Insert:

Joint Petroleum Development Area has the same meaning as in the Petroleum (Timor Sea Treaty) Act 2003.

23) Subsection 4 (1) (paragraph (a) of the definition of *place outside Australia*)

Omit "Area A of the Zone of Cooperation", substitute "the Joint Petroleum Development Area".

24) Subsection 4 (1) (paragraph (b) of the definition of *place outside Australia*)

Omit "Area A", substitute "the Joint Petroleum Development Area".

25) Subsection 4(1) (definition of resources installation in Area A)

Repeal the definition.

26) Subsection 4(1)

Insert:

resources installation in the Joint Petroleum Development Area means a resources installation that is attached to the seabed in the Joint Petroleum Development Area.

27) Subsection 4(9A)

Repeal the subsection, substitute:

(9A) If it is necessary to determine whether a resources installation is attached to the seabed in the Joint Petroleum Development Area, subsection (9) has effect as if a reference to the Australian seabed were a reference to the seabed in the Joint Petroleum Development Area.

28) Subsection 58B (2)

Omit "Area A", substitute "the Joint Petroleum Development Area".

29) Subsection 58B (3)

Omit "Area A", substitute "the Joint Petroleum Development Area".

30) Subsection 58B (4)

Omit "Area A", substitute "the Joint Petroleum Development Area".

31) Subsection 58B (5)

Omit "Area A", substitute "the Joint Petroleum Development Area".

32) Section 131AA

Repeal the section, substitute:

131AA Special provisions for goods taken to Joint Petroleum Development Area

(1) Goods taken out of Australia for the purpose of being taken to a resources installation in the Joint Petroleum Development Area and there used for a purpose related to petroleum activities are not liable to any duty of Customs in relation to the taking of the goods out of Australia.

(2) Goods brought into Australia for the purpose of being taken to a resources installation in the Joint Petroleum Development Area and there

used for a purpose related to petroleum activities are not liable to any duty of Customs in relation to the bringing of the goods into Australia.

(3) In this section:

petroleum activities has the same meaning as in the Treaty (within the meaning of the *Petroleum (Timor Sea Treaty) Act 2003*).

Fringe Benefits Tax Assessment Act 1986

33) Subsection 67(12)

Omit "Petroleum (*Timor Gap Zone of Cooperation*) Act 1990", substitute "*Petroleum (Timor Sea Treaty) Act 2003*".

Income Tax Assessment Act 1936

34) Subsection 6(1) (definition of *Timor Gap treaty*)

Repeal the definition.

35) Subsection 6(1)

Insert:

Timor Sea Treaty means the Treaty defined by subsection 5(1) of the Petroleum (Timor Sea Treaty) Act 2003.

36) Paragraph 6AA (4) (e)

Repeal the paragraph, substitute:

(e) *Petroleum Act adjacent area* means:

(i) an area that is an adjacent area for the purposes of the *Petroleum (Submerged Lands) Act 1967*; and

(ii) the Joint Petroleum Development Area within the meaning of the *Petroleum (Timor Sea Treaty) Act 2003*.

37) Subsection 23AG (7) (paragraph (b) of the definition of *double tax agreement*)

Omit "Timor Gap treaty", substitute "Timor Sea Treaty".

38) Subsection 136AA (1)

Insert:

area covered by an international tax sharing treaty has the meaning given by subsection (4).

39) Subsection 136AA (1)

Insert:

international tax sharing treaty:

(a) means an agreement between Australia and another country under which Australia and the other country share tax revenues from activities undertaken in an area identified by or under the agreement; and

(b) does not include an agreement within the meaning of the *International Tax Agreements Act 1953*.

40) At the end of section 136AA

Add:

(4) If, under an international tax sharing treaty, Australia and another country share tax revenues from activities undertaken in an area identified by or under the agreement, that area is referred to in this Division as the *area covered by the international tax sharing treaty*.

41) At the end of section 136AC

Add:

; or (c) a taxpayer:

(i) supplied or acquired property under the agreement in connection with a business; and

(ii) carries on that business in an area covered by an international tax sharing treaty.

42) Paragraph 136AE (4) (a)

Repeal the paragraph, substitute:

(a) a taxpayer (other than a partnership or trustee):

(i) is a resident and carries on a business in a country other than Australia at or through a permanent establishment of the taxpayer in that other country; or

(ii) is a resident and carries on a business in an area covered by an international tax sharing treaty; or

(iii) is a non-resident and carries on a business in Australia at or through a permanent establishment of the taxpayer in Australia; or

(iv) is a non-resident and carries on a business in an area covered by an international tax sharing treaty and also carries on a business somewhere else in Australia at or through a permanent establishment of the taxpayer in Australia; and

43) Paragraph 136AE (4) (e)

Repeal the paragraph, substitute:

(e) in the Commissioner's opinion, the derivation of the income or the incurring of the expenditure is attributable, in whole or in part, to activities carried on by the taxpayer:

(i) at or through the permanent establishment that is referred to in subparagraph (a)(i) or (iii); or

(ii) in the area covered by the international tax sharing treaty that is referred to in paragraph (a)(ii) or (iv);

44) Paragraph 136AE (5) (a)

Repeal the paragraph, substitute:

(a) a taxpayer:

(i) is a partnership and carries on a business in a country other than Australia at or through a permanent establishment of the taxpayer in that other country; or

(ii) is a partnership and carries on a business in an area covered by an international tax sharing treaty; or

(iii) carries on a business in Australia at or through a permanent establishment of the taxpayer in Australia and is a partnership in which any of the partners is a non-resident; or

(iv) carries on a business in an area covered by an international tax sharing treaty and also carries on a business somewhere else in Australia at or through a permanent establishment of the taxpayer in Australia and is a partnership in which any of the partners is a non-resident; and

45) Paragraph 136AE (5) (e)

Repeal the paragraph, substitute:

(e) in the Commissioner's opinion, the derivation of the income or the incurring of the expenditure is attributable, in whole or in part, to activities carried on by the taxpayer:

(i) at or through the permanent establishment that is referred to in subparagraph (a)(i) or (iii); or

(ii) in the area covered by the international tax sharing treaty that is referred to in paragraph (a)(ii) or (iv);

46) Paragraph 136AE (6) (a)

Repeal the paragraph, substitute:

(a) a taxpayer:

(i) is the trustee of a trust estate and carries on a business in a country other than Australia at or through a permanent establishment of the taxpayer in that other country; or

(ii) is the trustee of a trust estate and carries on a business in an area covered by an international tax sharing treaty; or

(iii) carries on a business in Australia at or through a permanent establishment of the taxpayer in Australia and is the trustee of a trust estate of which any of the beneficiaries is a non-resident; or

(iv) carries on a business in an area covered by an international tax sharing treaty and also carries on a business somewhere else in Australia at or through a permanent establishment of the taxpayer in Australia and is the trustee of a trust estate of which any of the beneficiaries is a non-resident; and

47) Paragraph 136AE (6) (e)

Repeal the paragraph, substitute:

(e) in the Commissioner's opinion, the derivation of the income or the incurring of the expenditure is attributable, in whole or in part, to activities carried on by the taxpayer:

(i) at or through the permanent establishment that is referred to in subparagraph (a)(i) or (iii); or

(ii) in the area covered by the international tax sharing treaty that is referred to in paragraph (a)(ii) or (iv);

48) After subsection 136AE (8)

Insert:

(8A) In this section:

(a) a reference to income being derived from a source in Australia is to be read as including a separate reference to income being derived from a source in an area in Australia that is covered by an international tax sharing treaty; and

(b) a reference to expenditure being incurred in deriving income from a source in Australia is to be read as including a separate reference to expenditure being incurred in deriving income from a source in an area in Australia that is covered by an international tax sharing treaty.

Note: This means that the following are the 3 different kinds of sources referred to in this section:

(a) a source in Australia (but not in an area covered by an international tax sharing treaty);

(b) a source in an area in Australia that is covered by an international tax sharing treaty;

(c) a source out of Australia.

49) Subsection 160AF (1)

Repeal the subsection, substitute:

(1) If:

(a) the assessable income of a year of income of a resident taxpayer includes:

(i) income that is foreign income; or

(ii) income, or a profit or gain, that is derived from a source in an area covered by an international tax sharing treaty to the extent to which that income, profit or gain is taxed in Australia; and

(b) the taxpayer has paid foreign tax in respect of that income, profit or gain; and

(c) the taxpayer was personally liable for that tax; the taxpayer is, subject to this Act, entitled to a credit of:

(d) the amount of that foreign tax, reduced in accordance with any relief available to the taxpayer under the law relating to that tax; or

(e) the amount of Australian tax payable in respect of that income, profit or gain;

whichever is the less.

50) Subsection 170(14)

Insert:

international tax sharing treaty has the meaning given by subsection 136AA(1).

51) Subsection 170(14) (definition of *relevant provision*)

Repeal the definition, substitute:

relevant provision means:

(a) paragraph (3) of Article 5, or paragraph (1) of Article 7, of the United Kingdom agreement or a provision of any other double taxation agreement that corresponds with either of those paragraphs; or

(b) paragraph 7, 8 or 9 of Article 5, or Article 7, of the Taxation Code in Annex G to the Timor Sea Treaty or a provision of any other international tax sharing treaty that corresponds with any of those paragraphs or that Article.

52) Subsection 177B (1)

Omit "*Petroleum (Timor Gap Zone of Cooperation) Act* 1990", substitute "*Petroleum (Timor Sa Treaty) Act* 2003".

International Organisations (Privileges and Immunities) Act 1963

53) After section 5A

Insert:

5B Special provisions in relation to Designated Authority

(1) The Designated Authority is an international organisation to which this Act applies.

(2) The Designated Authority ceases to be an international organisation to which this Act applies on the day specified in the regulations.

(3) In this section:

Designated Authority has the same meaning as in the *Petroleum (Timor Sea Treaty) Act* 2003.

Migration Act 1958

54) Subsection 5 (1) (definition of Area A of the Zone of Cooperation)

Repeal the definition.

55) Subsection 5(1) (definition of *Australian seabed*)

Omit "Area A of the Zone of Cooperation", substitute "the Joint Petroleum Development Area".

56) Subsection 5(1)

Insert:

Joint Petroleum Development Area has the same meaning as in the *Petroleum (Timor Sea Treaty) Act* 2003.

Passenger Movement Charge Collection Act 1978

57) Section 3 (definition of Area A of the Zone of Cooperation)

Repeal the definition.

58) Section 3

Insert:

Joint Petroleum Development Area has the same meaning as in the *Petroleum (Timor Sea Treaty) Act* 2003.

59) Section 3 (definition of *petroleum*)

Omit "Timor Gap Treaty", substitute "Timor Sea Treaty".

60) Section 3

Insert:

petroleum activities has the same meaning as in the Timor Sea Treaty.

61) Section 3 (definition of *petroleum operations*)

Repeal the definition.

62) Section 3 (definition of *Timor Gap Treaty*)

Repeal the definition.

63) Section 3

Insert:

Timor Sea Treaty means the Treaty defined by subsection 5(1) of the *Petroleum (Timor Sea Treaty) Act* 2003.

64) Section 3 (definition of *Zone of Cooperation*)

Repeal the definition.

65) Paragraph 5(1)

Omit "Area A of the Zone of Cooperation", substitute "the Joint Petroleum Development Area".

Petroleum (Submerged Lands) Act 1967

66) Subsection 5 (1) (definition of Area A of the Zone of Cooperation)

Repeal the definition.

67) Subsection 5(1)

Insert:

Joint Petroleum Development Area has the same meaning as in the *Petroleum (Timor Sea Treaty) Act* 2003.

68) Paragraph 5A (1A)(c)

Omit "Area A of the Zone of Cooperation", substitute "the Joint Petroleum Development Area".

69) Paragraph 5A (3)(b)

Omit "Area A of the Zone of Cooperation", substitute "the Joint Petroleum Development Area".

Petroleum (Timor Gap Zone of Cooperation) Act 1990

70) The whole of the Act

Repeal the Act.

Quarantine Act 1908

71) Subsection 5 (1) (definition of Area A of the Zone of Cooperation)

Repeal the definition.

72) Subsection 5(1) (definition of *Australian seabed*)

Omit " Area A of the Zone of Cooperation ", substitute "the Joint Petroleum Development Area".

73) Subsection 5(1)

Insert:

Joint Petroleum Development Area has the same meaning as in the *Petroleum (Timor Sea Treaty) Act* 2003.

74) Paragraph 6A (a)

Omit " Area A of the Zone of Cooperation ", substitute "the Joint Petroleum Development Area".

Note: The heading to Section 6A is altered by omitting "Area A of the Zone of Cooperation" and substituting "the Joint Petroleum Development Area".

75) Paragraph 6A (b)

Omit " Area A", substitute "the Joint Petroleum Development Area".

Superannuation Guarantee (Administration) Act 1992

76) After section 4

Insert:

4A Extension to Joint Petroleum Development Area

This Act:

(a) extends to the Joint Petroleum Development Area (within the meaning of the *Petroleum (Timor Sea Treaty) Act* 2003); and

(b) has effect as if that Area were part of Australia.

77) After paragraph 27(1) (c)

Insert：

(ca) salary or wages paid by an employer to an employee who is not a resident of Australia for work done in the Joint Petroleum Development Area (within the meaning of the *Petroleum* (*Timor Sea Treaty*) *Act 2003*);

Taxation Administration Act 1953

78) Subsection 3C (2A)

Repeal the subsection, substitute：

(2A) Subsection (2) does not apply to the extent that the person makes a record of the information, or divulges or communicates the information：

(a) for the purposes of this Act; or

(b) in the performance of the person's duties as an officer; or

(c) for the purposes of complying with an obligation Australia has under an agreement between Australia and another country.

Note：A defendant bears an evidential burden in relation to the matters in this subsection, see subsection 13. 3(3) of the *Criminal Code*.

79) After paragraph 68(3) (b)

Insert：

(ba) the recording or disclosure is for the purposes of complying with an obligation Australia has under an agreement between Australia and another country; or

Workplace Relations Act 1996

80) Section 5A

Repeal the section.

Part 2   Application, saving and transitional provisions

81) Application—items 34 to 52

The amendments made by items 34 to 52 of this Schedule apply in relation to events that occur, and circumstances that arise, on or after 20 May 2002.

82) Continued operation of certain provisions in the *Petroleum (Timor Gap Zone of Cooperation) Act* 1990— item 70

Despite the repeal of the *Petroleum (Timor Gap Zone of Cooperation) Act* 1990 by item 70 of this Schedule, sections 6, 7 and 8, and subsections 9(2), (3) and (4), of that Act have the effect, for the period that:

(a) starts on 20 May 2002; and

(b) ends on the day on which the *Petroleum (Timor Sea Treaty) Act* 2003 receives the Royal Assent;

that they would have had if that Act had not been repealed.

83) Application—items 76 and 77

(1) The amendments made by items 76 and 77 of this Schedule apply in relation to superannuation guarantee shortfalls for the year starting on 1 July 2003 and all later years.

(2) In this item:

superannuation guarantee shortfalls has the same meaning as in the *Superannuation Guarantee (Administration) Act* 1992.

year has the same meaning as in the *Superannuation Guarantee (Administration) Act* 1992.

资料来源: 澳大利亚政府网站 http: //scaleplus. law. gov. au/html/comact/browse/TOCN. htm。

十五、2006 年密克罗尼西亚与马歇尔群岛共同开发案

Treaty between the Federated States of Micronesia and the Republic of the Marshall Islands concerning Maritime Boundaries and Cooperation on Related Matters

Majuro, 5 July 2006

Entry into force: 24 July 2015 by notification, in accordance with article 7

Authentic text: English

Registration with the Secretariat of the United Nations: Micronesia (Federated States of), 4 August 2017

* No UNTS volume number has yet been determined for this record. The Text(s) reproduced below, if attached, are the authentic texts of the agreement /action attachment as submitted for registration and publication to the Secretariat. For ease of reference they were sequentially paginated. Translations, if attached, are not final and are provided for information only.

The sovereign countries of the Federated States of Micronesia and the Republic of the Marshall Islands;

DESIRING to strengthen the bonds of friendship between the two countries;

RECOGNIZING the need to effect a precise and equitable delimitation of the respective maritime areas in which the two States exercise sovereign rights; and

TAKING INTO ACCOUNT the rules and principles of international law as reflected in the 1982 United Nations Convention on the Law of the Sea.

HAVE AGREED AS FOLLOWS:

Article 1   Definitions

In this Treaty —

(a) " Exclusive Economic Zone " means the adjacent waters, including seabed and subsoil, over which each respective Party has sovereign rights and exclusive jurisdiction for the purpose of exploring, protecting, utilizing, exploiting, conserving, regulating, and managing natural resources, whether living or non-living. Supplemental to and without prejudice to the foregoing sentence, the term " Exclusive Economic Zone" shall also include all rights and jurisdiction provided for in the 1982 United Nations Convention on the Law of the Sea to the extent not inconsistent with this Treaty.

(b) "Party" means either the Federated States of Micronesia or the Republic of the Marshall Islands, or both, depending on the context in which the term is used. "Parties" refers to both countries.

Article 2   Maritime Jurisdiction

1. The line of delimitation between the exclusive economic zones and the continental shelves over which each Party respectively exercises sovereign rights in accordance with international law lies seaward of the islands of Kosrae, Pingelap, Mokil, Pohnpei, and Pakin, on the one hand and the island of Ebon, Namidrik, Ujae, and Ujelang on the Other hand, along the geodesics connecting the following points, defined by their coordinates, in the order stated:

(a) commencing at the point of Latitude 10°25′25″ North, Longitude 157°27′50″ East;

(b) running thence south-easterly along the geodesic to the point of Latitude 09°39′44″ North, Longitude 158°10′26″ East;

(c) thence south-easterly along the geodesic to the point of Latitude 08°33′26″ North, Longitude 159°24′13″ East;

(d) thence south-easterly along the geodesic to the point of Latitude 08°18′31″ North, Longitude 160°09′47″ East;

(e) thence south-easterly along the geodesic to the point of Latitude 07°59′10″ North, Longitude 161°00′01″ East;

(f) thence easterly along the geodesic to the point of Latitude 07°51′24″ North, Longitude 162°37′27″ East;

(g) thence north-easterly along the geodesic to the point of Latitude 08°03′31″ North, Longitude 163°04′18″ East;

(h) thence south-easterly along the geodesic to the point of Latitude 07°11′01″ North, Longitude 164°20′22″ East;

(i) thence south-easterly along the geodesic to the point of Latitude 06°17′01″ North, Longitude 165°30′35″ East;

(J) thence south along the geodesic to the point of Latitude 03°33′25″ North, Longitude 165°40′34″ East;

(k) thence south along the geodesic to the point of Latitude 03°11′29″ North, Longitude 165°38′06″ East.

2. The geographical coordinates referred to in this Article are expressed in terms of the World Geodetic System 1984 (WGS84). Where for the purpose of this Agreement it is necessary to determine the position on the surface of the Earth of a point, line or area, that position may be determined by reference to WGS84 in respect of a spheroid having its centre at the centre of the Earth, and a major (equatorial) radius of 6, 378, 137 meters and a flattening of 1/298. 257 223 563.

3. The line described in paragraph 1 of this Article is drawn for illustrative purposes on the map forming Annex 1 to this Agreement.

4. This Agreement shall define the boundary between the zones over which the Parties exercise, or will exercise, jurisdiction or sovereign rights in accordance with international law.

5. Should future surveys indicate significant shifts in the geographic location of islands used as base points in determining the line of

delimitation, technical experts nominated by both parties shall collaborate in recommending revised coordinates of the agreed line, in accordance with the principles used for this agreement.

6. The revised recommended coordinates, determined in accordance with paragraph 4, shall be implemented after agreement in writing by both parties.

Article 3　Dispute Resolution

Any dispute between the two Governments over the interpretation or implementation of this Agreement shall be settled peacefully by consultation and negotiation. Such dispute resolution shall be in accordance with the generally accepted International Law principles for peaceful resolution of Treaty disagreements.

Article 4　Hydrocarbon and Mineral Resources Straddling the Boundary

If any single accumulation or deposit of liquid hydrocarbon, natural gas, or other mineral extends across the maritime boundary line described in paragraph 1 of Article 2, and if one Party by exploiting that accumulation or deposit would withdraw, deplete, or draw down the portion of the accumulation or deposit that is on the other Party's side of the boundary line, then before the accumulation or deposit is exploited, the Parties shall consult with a view toward reaching an agreement on the manner in which the accumulation or deposit may be most effectively exploited and on the equitable sharing of the benefits from such exploitation.

Article 5　Cooperation on Living Resources

As circumstances permit, the Parties shall consult with a view toward cooperation regarding the management, conservation, and utilization of the living resources of their respective Exclusive Economic Zones, with particular regard to highly migratory species, sustainability, and the participation by non-Parties in the exploitation of the living resources of such zones.

Article 6　Protection of the Marine Environment

As circumstances permit, the Parties shall consult with a view toward coordination of their policies, in accordance with international law, with respect to the protection of the marine environment and the conduct of marine research in their respective Exclusive Economic Zones. This includes exploring possibilities for cooperation in the area of maritime enforcement of environmental and fishing laws and regulations.

Article 7　Entry into Force

Each Party shall notify the other of the completion of its constitutional procedures necessary to bring this Agreement into force. The Agreement shall enter into force on the later of those notifications.

Article 8　Treaty Deposit

Upon completion of the constitutional procedures bringing this Agreement into force, each party shall take all the required steps to lodge this Agreement, in particular the coordinates in Article 2, with the appropriate International Bodies.

IN WITNESS WHEREOF, the President of the two Governments, being duly authorized for this purpose, have signed this Agreement.

DONE IN DUPLICATE at Majuro, Republic of the Marshall Islands this 5th day of July 2006

For the Government of the Federated States of Micronesia

8. E. JOSEPH J. URUSEMAL President

For the Government of the Republic of the Marshall Islands

9. E. KESSAI H. NOTE President

资料来源：Treaty between the Federated States of Micronesia and the Republic of the Marshall Islands concerning maritime boundaries and cooperation on related matters（with map），5 July 2006，Federated States of Micronesia— the Republic of the Marshall Islands，U. N. T. S. I-54649（Registration Number），pp. 1-6，https：//treaties. un. org/doc/Publication/UNTS/No% 20Volume/54649/Part/I-54649-08000002804c6ee9. pdf。

十六、2006 年密克罗尼西亚与
帕劳共同开发案

Treaty between the Federated States of Micronesia and the Republic of Paul concerning Maritime Boundaries and Cooperation on Related Matters

The sovereign countries of the Federated States of Micronesia and the Republic of Palau,

Desiring to establish maritime boundaries and to provide for certain other related matters in the maritime zone between the two countries,

Resolving, as good neighbors and in the spirit of cooperation and friendship, to settle permanently the limits of the maritime area within which the Federated States of Micronesia and the Republic of Palau shall respectively exercise sovereign rights with regard to the exploration, management, protection, and exploitation of their respective sea, seabed, and subsoil resources, and

Taking into account the 1982 United Nations Convention on the Law of the Sea to which both the Federated States of Micronesia and the Republic of Palau are a party, and, in particular, Articles 74 and 83 which provide that the delimitation of the continental shelf and Exclusive Economic Zone between States with opposite coasts shall be effected by agreement on the basis of international law in order to achieve an equitable solution,

HEREBY AGREE AS FOLLOWS:

Article 1   Definitions

In this Treaty —

(a) " Exclusive Economic Zone " means the adjacent waters, including seabed and subsoil, over which each respective Party has sovereign and exclusive jurisdiction and rights for the purpose of exploring, protecting, utilizing, exploiting, conserving, regulating, and managing natural resources, whether living or non-living. Supplemental to and without prejudice to the foregoing sentence, the term " Exclusive Economic Zone" shall also include all rights and jurisdiction provided for in the 1982 United Nations Convention on the Law of the Sea (the "Convention") to the extent not inconsistent with this Treaty.

(b) "Party" means either the Federated States of Micronesia or the Republic of Palau, or both, depending on the context in which the term is used. "Parties" refers to both countries.

Article 2   Maritime Jurisdiction

1. The maritime boundary between the area of seabed and subsoil that is adjacent to and appertains to the Federated States of Micronesia and the area of seabed and subsoil that is adjacent to and appertains to the Republic of Palau is set forth in Annex I to this Treaty.

Annex I describes a boundary, which is a series of geodesic line segments of finite length and no breadth, comprised of a series of latitude and longitude coordinate points referenced to the World Geodetic System 1984 (WGS84) with connecting directions between each coordinate point. Each point on the component geodesic line segments (boundary line) is equidistant from the nearest points on the baselines from which the breadth of the territorial seas of each of the two Parties is measured, and at no point is the boundary line greater than 200 nautical miles from the baseline of either Party. The boundary described in Annex 1 is shown on the map incorporated into this Treaty as Annex 2.

2. The maritime boundary line referred to in paragraph 1 of this

Article shall be the boundary of the respective Exclusive Economic Zones of the Federated States of Micronesia and the Republic of Palau. The maritime boundary line shall also be the boundary of the Parties' respective continental shelves, as the term "continental shelf" is defined and used in Part VI of the Convention.

3. Notwithstanding paragraphs 1 and 2 of this Article, nothing in this Treaty shall prejudice each Party's right to claim an extended continental shelf pursuant to Part VI of the Convention and the rules and procedures established by the United Nations Commission on the Limits of the Continental Shelf. Nevertheless, no Party shall claim an extended continental shelf that intrudes into the Exclusive Economic Zone, as delimited by Annex I, of the other Party.

4. The location of the maritime boundary line has been determined by a joint effort between the Federated States of Micronesia and the Republic of Palau based upon a decision by the Parties not to use archipelagic baselines for the specific purpose of determining the location of the maritime boundary line. This agreement does not prejudice the rights of either Party with respect to any future archipelagic claims affecting non-Parties.

Article 3 Hydrocarbon and Mineral Resources Straddling the Boundary

If any single accumulation or deposit of liquid hydrocarbon, natural gas, or other mineral extends across the maritime boundary line described in Annex 1, and if one Party by exploiting that accumulation or deposit would withdraw, deplete, or draw down the portion of the accumulation or deposit that is on the other Party's side of the boundary line, then before the accumulation or deposit is exploited, the Parties shall consult with a view toward reaching an agreement on the manner in which the accumulation or deposit may be most effectively exploited and on the equitable sharing of the benefits from such exploitation.

Article 4　Cooperation on Living Resources

As circumstances permit, the Parties shall consult with a view toward cooperation regarding the management, conservation, and utilization of the living resources of their respective Exclusive Economic Zones, with particular regard to highly migratory species, sustainability, and the participation by non-Parties in the exploitation of the living resources of such zones.

Article 5　Protection of the Marine Environment

As circumstances permit, the Parties shall consult with a view toward coordination of their policies, in accordance with international law, with respect to the protection of the marine environment and the conduct of marine research in their respective Exclusive Economic Zones. This includes exploring possibilities for cooperation in the area of maritime enforcement of environmental and fishing laws and regulations.

Article 6　Settlement of Disputes

Any dispute between the Parties arising out of the interpretation or implementation of this Treaty shall be settled by consultation or negotiation.

Article 7　Consultations

The Parties shall consult, at the request of either, on any matters relating to this Treaty.

Article 8　Annexes

The Annexes to this Treaty shall have full force and effect as integral parts to this Treaty.

Article 9　Ratification

This Treaty is subject to ratification and shall enter into force upon the exchange of the instruments of ratification. Each signatory to this Treaty shall endeavor to complete the ratification of this Treaty without delay.

IN WITNESS WHEREOF, the undersigned being duly authorized have signed this Treaty.

DONE IN DUPLICATE at .... this .... day of .... Two thousand six.

H. E. Joseph J. Urusemal   H. E. Tommy E. Remengesau,

President, Federated State of Micronesia   President, Republic of Palau

FOR THE FEDERATED STATE OF MICRONESIA

FOR THE REPUBLIC OF PALAU

ANNEX 1

FEDERATED STATES OF MICRONESIA REPUBLIC OF PALAU
DESCRIPTION OF BOUNDARY LINE
51 Points in Degrees, Minutes, Seconds
(WGS84 DATUM)

Beginning At	Point	Latitude(North)	Longitude(East)
By Geodesic Line To	900000	4°58′42″	136°59′41″
By Geodesic Line To	900001	5°40′39″	136°45′05″
By Geodesic Line To	900002	5°48′04″	136°42′30″
By Geodesic Line To	900003	5°52′57″	136°40′55″
By Geodesic Line To	900004	5°59′01″	136°38′57″
By Geodesic Line To	900005	6°14′37″	136°33′55″
By Geodesic Line To	900006	6°50′50″	136°22′17″
By Geodesic Line To	900007	6°52′13″	136°21′51″

By Geodesic Line To	900008	6°53′51″	136°21′19″
By Geodesic Line To	900009	7°06′19″	136°17′31″
By Geodesic Line To	900010	7°07′23″	136°17′08″
By Geodesic Line To	900011	7°23′57″	136°11′06″
By Geodesic Line To	900012	7°27′56″	136°09′50″
By Geodesic Line To	900013	7°29′53″	136°09′13″
By Geodesic Line To	900014	7°30′18″	136°09′06″
By Geodesic Line To	900015	7°32′26″	136°08′32″
By Geodesic Line To	900016	7°33′01″	136°08′22″
By Geodesic Line To	900017	7°35′15″	136°07′56″
By Geodesic Line To	900018	7°41′38″	136°06′41″
By Geodesic Line To	900019	7°46′44″	136°05′41″

ANNEX 1

FEDERATED STATES OF MICRONESIA REPUBLIC OF PALAU

Beginning At	Point	Latitude(North)	Longitude(East)
By Geodesic Line To	900020	7°48′18″	136°05′28″
By Geodesic Line To	900021	7°52′13″	136°04′56″
By Geodesic Line To	900022	7°58′16″	136°04′07″
By Geodesic Line To	900023	8°10′14″	136°02′31″
By Geodesic Line To	900024	8°14′23″	136°01′58″
By Geodesic Line To	900025	8°19′52″	136°01′14″

By Geodesic Line To	900026	8°24′35″	136°00′37″
By Geodesic Line To	900027	8°28′48″	136°00′03″
By Geodesic Line To	900028	8°38′03″	135°58′50″
By Geodesic Line To	900029	8°39′42″	135°58′37″
By Geodesic Line To	900030	8°40′31″	135°58′31″
By Geodesic Line To	900031	8°53′49″	135°56′47″
By Geodesic Line To	900032	8°58′09″	135°56′13″
By Geodesic Line To	900033	9°06′14″	135°55′00″
By Geodesic Line To	900034	9°09′29″	135°54′30″
By Geodesic Line To	900035	9°12′28″	135°54′10″
By Geodesic Line To	900036	9°14′06″	135°53′59″
By Geodesic Line To	900037	9°19′50″	135°53′20″
By Geodesic Line To	900038	9°36′18″	135°51′28″
By Geodesic Line To	900039	10°17′53″	135°47′00″
By Geodesic Line To	900040	10°18′54″	135°46′36″
By Geodesic Line To	900041	10°30′15″	135°42′16″

ANNEX 1

FEDERATED STATES OF MICRONESIA REPUBLIC OF PALAU

Beginning At	Point	Latitude(North)	Longitude(East)
By Geodesic Line To	900042	10°41′45″	135°37′53″
By Geodesic Line To	900043	10°47′15″	135°35′46″

By Geodesic Line To	900044	10°50′45″	135°34′25″
By Geodesic Line To	900045	10°52′41″	135°33′40″
By Geodesic Line To	900046	10°54′33″	135°32′57″
By Geodesic Line To	900047	11°02′25″	135°29′49″
By Geodesic Line To	900048	11°18′40″	135°23′20″
By Geodesic Line To	900049	11°27′32″	135°19′37″
By Geodesic Line To	900050	11°29′10″	135°18′56″

资料来源：Treaty between the Federated States of Micronesia and the Republic of Paul concerning Maritime Boundaries and Cooperation on Related Matters ［EB/OL］，http：//www. un. org/Depts/los/LEGISLATIONANDTREATIES/ PDFFILES/FSM-PALAU. pdf。

十七、2006 年法罗群岛、挪威与 冰岛共同开发案

Agreed Minutes on the Delimitation of the Continental Shelf beyond 200 Nautical Miles between the Faroe Islands, Iceland and Norway in the Southern Part of the Banana Hole of the Northeast Atlantic

1. The Minister for Foreign Affairs of the Kingdom of Denmark together with the Prime Minister of the Government of the Faroes, the Minister for Foreign Affairs of Iceland and the Minister of Foreign Affairs of the Kingdom of Norway wish to effect the delimitations of the continental shelf areas beyond 200 nautical miles from the baselines between the Faroe Islands, Iceland, Mainland Norway and Jan Mayen, subject to rights and obligations under the United Nations Convention on the Law of the Sea, hereinafter referred to as "the Convention". This will be done taking into account, inter alia, the functions of the Commission on the Limits of the Continental Shelf established in accordance with Annex II to the Convention, hereinafter referred to as "the Commission".

2. They are in agreement that the bilateral delimitations of the continental shelf will be based on straight geodetic lines connecting the following points, defined in the World Geodetic System 1984 (WGS84):

Iceland/Norway

(A)	67° 36′ 40. 54″ N	6° 38′ 18. 95″ W
(B)	67° 43′ 06. 51″ N	2° 30′ 45. 12″ W

（C）　　66° 49′ 15. 75″ N　　1° 41′ 43. 56″ W

Faroe Islands/Iceland

（C）　　66° 49′ 15. 75″ N　　1° 41′ 43. 56″ W

（F）　　65° 41′ 22. 63″ N　　5° 34′ 42. 22″ W

Faroe Islands /Norway

（C）　　66° 49′ 15. 75″ N　　1° 41′ 43. 56″ W

（D）　　65° 54′ 43. 74″ N　　0° 29′ 13. 23″ W

（E）　　64° 25′ 58. 14″ N　　0° 29′ 19. 30″ W

By way of illustration, these lines and the points listed above have been drawn on the chart appended to these Agreed Minutes (Appendix I).

3. The lines established in paragraph 2 do not restrict the use of relevant information by the States when submitting documentation concerning the outer limits of the continental shelf to the Commission.

4. These Agreed Minutes are based on the shared view that the whole area concerned consists of continuous continental shelf. If, after consideration of national data or other material by the Commission, it is ascertained that any part thereof belongs to "the Area" as defined in Article 1 of the Convention, i. e. that this part does not consist of continental shelf appertaining to any of the coastal States, the coastal State(s) concerned will establish the outer limits of the continental shelf in accordance with Article 76 (8) of the Convention, without this otherwise affecting the lines established in paragraph 2.

5. Norway intends to submit its documentation concerning the outer limits of its continental shelf in the area to the Commission in 2006. Denmark/the Faroe Islands and Iceland intend to submit their respective documentation concerning the outer limits of their continental shelf in the area to the Commission as soon as possible.

6. Each State will, when submitting its documentation concerning the outer limits of its continental shelf in the area, request that the Commission consider it and make its recommendations on this basis, without prejudice to the submission of documentation by the other States at a later stage or to delimitation of the continental shelf between the

three States. The State concerned will in this connection declare that such a request is agreed between the three States.

7. When one State submits documentation to the Commission, the other States will notify the Secretary-General of the United Nations in accordance with the Commission's rules of procedure that they do not object to the Commission considering the documentation and making recommendations on this basis, without prejudice to the submission of documentation by these States at a later stage or to the question of bilateral delimitations of the continental shelf between the three States.

8. If, after consideration by the Commission, one or more of the States has not documented that the area of its continental shelf beyond 200 nautical miles corresponds in size, as a minimum, to the area that falls to the same State according to paragraph 2, the lines established in paragraph 2 will be adjusted. This adjustment will ensure a corresponding reduction of the area that falls to the State concerned and the distribution of the excess area to the remaining State or States that document to the Commission areas of continental shelf more extensive than the areas that follow from paragraph 2.

．

If Denmark/the Faroe Islands fails to document an area of continental shelf beyond 200 nautical miles of at least 27 000 km ^{2} $\rangle$, the excess area will be shared between Iceland (40 per cent) and Norway (60 per cent). ·

If Iceland fails to document an area of continental shelf beyond 200 nautical miles of at least 29 000 km ^{2} $\rangle$, the excess area will be shared between Denmark/the Faroe Islands (40 per cent) and Norway (60 per cent).

If Norway fails to document an area of continental shelf beyond 200 nautical miles of at least 55 528 km ^{2} $\rangle$, the excess area will be shared between Denmark/the Faroe Islands (50 per cent) and Iceland (50 per cent).

If only one of the States is able to document a sufficient area of the continental shelf, the excess area will fall to that State.

No State shall be allocated an area of continental shelf larger than the area it is able to document to the Commission.

Any adjustment of the lines established in paragraph 2 will be made in such a way that it causes the smallest possible departure from their general direction and the number of turning points, primarily by moving point (C).

9. As soon as possible, and no later than three months after the States have concluded the procedure set out in Article 76 (8) of the Convention, the States will meet with a view to simultaneously concluding three parallel bilateral agreements on the final determination of the boundary lines in accordance with these *Agreed Minutes* and their appendices, including the Model Agreement contained in Appendix II. If such a meeting has not been held by the end of 2011, the States will initiate consultations on the further follow-up.

10. The Ministers have agreed that the final delimitations will be effected by the simultaneous entry into force of the three bilateral agreements, following notification that internal requirements have been fulfilled to this end.

11. These Agreed Minutes constitute a joint statement of the Ministers' agreement on the procedure for establishing the delimitations of the continental shelf between the States in the area, subject to fulfilment of their internal requirements.

These *Agreed Minutes* constitute a historic step that reflects the extremely close and good neighbourly relations between Denmark/the Faroe Islands, Iceland and Norway, their common commitment to promoting the international law of the sea and the importance they attach to the United Nations Convention on the Law of the Sea as the legal framework for the peaceful uses of the oceans and seas.

Signed in triplicate at New York on 20 September 2006 in the English language.

The Minister for Foreign Affairs of the Kingdom of Denmark

The Prime Minister of the Government of the Faroes

The Minister for Foreign Affairs of Iceland

The Minister of Foreign Affairs of the Kingdom of Norway

APPENDIX II

MODEL AGREEMENT:

Agreement between the Government of ... [where applicable: and the Government of the Faroes], of the one part, and the Government of ..., of the other part, concerning the delimitation of the continental shelf beyond 200 nautical miles in the area between the Faroe Islands, Iceland, Mainland Norway and Jan Mayen

The Government of ... [where applicable: and the Government of the Faroes], of the one part, and the Government of ..., of the other part,

Desiring to maintain and strengthen the good neighbourly relations between ... and ..., and

Referring to the Agreed Minutes of ··· between Denmark/the Faroe Islands, Iceland and Norway,

Have agreed as follows:

Article 1

Beyond 200 nautical miles from the baselines from which the breadth of the territorial sea of each Party is measured, the boundary line delimiting the continental shelf in the area between ... and ... has been determined as straight lines connecting the following points in the order specified below:

Point 1:

Point 2:

...

...

All straight lines are geodetic lines.

The points listed above are defined by geographical latitude and longitude in accordance with the World Geodetic System 1984 (WGS84).

By way of illustration, the boundary line and the points listed above have been drawn on the chart annexed to this Agreement.

Article 2

If the existence of a mineral deposit in or on the continental shelf of one of the Parties is established and the other Party is of the opinion that the said deposit extends to its continental shelf, the latter Party may notify the former Party accordingly, through submitting the data on which it bases its opinion.

If such an opinion is submitted, the Parties shall initiate discussions on the extent of the deposit and the possibility for exploitation. In the course of these discussions, the Party initiating them shall support its opinion with evidence from geophysical data and/or geological data, including any available drilling data, and both Parties shall make their best efforts to ensure that all relevant information is made available for the purposes of these discussions. If it is established during these discussions that the deposit extends to the continental shelf of both Parties and that the deposit on the continental shelf of the one Party can be exploited wholly or in part from the continental shelf of the other Party, or that the exploitation of the deposit on the continental shelf of the one Party would affect the possibility of exploitation of the deposit on the continental shelf of the other Party, agreement on the apportionment of the deposit between the Parties and on the unitised exploitation shall be reached at the request of one of the Parties, including as to the appointment of a unit operator, the manner in which any such deposit shall be most effectively exploited and the manner in which the proceeds relating thereto shall be apportioned.

The Parties shall make every effort to resolve any disagreement as rapidly as possible. If, however, the Parties fail to agree, they shall jointly consider all of the options for resolving the impasse.

If the Parties fail to agree on unitised exploitation of a transboundary deposit, the disagreement shall be resolved by negotiation. If any such dispute cannot be resolved in this manner or by any other procedure agreed to by the Parties, the dispute shall be submitted, at the request of either Party, to an ad hoc arbitral tribunal composed as follows:

Each Party shall designate one arbitrator, and the two arbitrators so designated shall elect a third arbitrator, who shall be the Chairman. The Chairman shall not be a national of or habitually reside in ... or .... If either Party fails to designate an arbitrator within three months of a request to do so, either Party may request the President of the International Court of Justice to appoint an arbitrator. The same procedure shall apply if, within one month of the designation or appointment of the second arbitrator, the third arbitrator has not been elected. The tribunal shall determine its own procedure, save that all decisions shall be taken, in the absence of unanimity, by a majority vote of the members of the tribunal. The decisions of the tribunal shall be binding upon the Parties.

If the Parties fail to agree on the apportionment of the deposit between themselves, they shall appoint an independent expert to determine the apportionment. The decision of the independent expert shall be binding upon the Parties. The Parties may, however, agree that the deposit shall be reapportioned between themselves according to specified conditions.

Article 3

This Agreement is without prejudice to the respective Parties' views on questions that are not governed by this Agreement, including questions relating to their exercise of sovereign rights or jurisdiction over the seabed and its subsoil.

Article 4

This Agreement enters into force when the Parties have notified each other in writing that the necessary internal procedures have been completed.

Done at ... on the ... day of ... in duplicate in the ... and ...

languages, both/all three texts being equally authentic.

[Place], [Date],

For the Government of ...

For the Government of ...

[Where applicable: For the Government of Denmark and the Government of the Faroes]

资料来源: https://www.regjeringen.no/en/dokumenter/Agreed-Minutes/id446839/。

十八、2007 年特立尼达和多巴哥与委内瑞拉玻利瓦尔共和国共同开发案

Framework Treaty Relating to the Unitisation of Hydrocarbon Reservoirs That Extend Across the Delimitation Line between the Republic of Trinidad and Tobago and the Bolivarian Republic of Venezuela

Caracas, 20 March 2007

Entry into force: 16 August 2010 by the exchange of instruments of ratification, in accordance with article 20

Authentic texts: English and Spanish

Registration with the Secretariat of the United Nations: Trinidad and Tobago, 19 November 2012

The Republic of Trinidad and Tobago and the Bolivarian Republic of Venezuela (hereinafter referred to individually as " the Party " and collectively as "the Parties"),

CONSIDERING that in accordance with Article Ⅶ (Unity of Deposits) of the Treaty on Delimitation of Marine and Submarine Areas of 1990, between Trinidad and Tobago and Venezuela, the Parties, after holding the appropriate technical consultations, have determined that there exist hydrocarbon reservoirs that extend across the Delimitation line, which are exploitable, wholly or in part, from either side of said line.

HAVING REGARD to Article 1 of the Memorandum of Understanding concerning the Procedure for Unitisation of Hydrocarbon Reservoirs that extend across the Delimitation Line between the Republic of Trinidad and Tobago and the Bolivarian Republic of Venezuela signed on August 12, 2003, under which the Parties have undertaken to implement the provisions of Article Ⅶ of the Delimitation Treaty of 1990, and to seek agreement with respect to the manner in which any such hydrocarbon reservoir shall be most effectively exploited.

HAVING REGARD ALSO to the Letter of Intent dated August 12 2003, on enhanced bilateral cooperation between the Republic of Trinidad and Tobago and the Bolivarian Republic of Venezuela which acknowledges their common interest in promoting and contributing to the development of the energy sector of both countries.

CONSIDERING ALSO that the Parties have undertaken to reach agreement on the most effective and efficient manner in which the costs and benefits arising from such exploitations shall be apportioned and to establish the general legal framework for the exploitation of the said hydrocarbon reservoirs.

HEREBY AGREE AS FOLLOWS:

PART 1　GENERAL PROVISIONS

ARTICLE 1　DEFINITIONS

For the purposes of this Treaty the following definitions shall apply:

1. 1 "Delimitation Line" means the maritime boundary between the Republic of Trinidad and Tobago and the Bolivarian Republic of Venezuela as established in Article Il of the "Treaty between the Republic of Trinidad and Tobago and the Republic of Venezuela on the Delimitation of Marine and Submarine Areas" dated 18th April 1990.

1. 2 "Cross-border Hydrocarbon Reservoirs" means hydrocarbon

reservoirs which extend across the Delimitation Line which are exploitable, wholly or in part, from either side of the said line.

1.3 "Hydrocarbons" means crude oil, condensate, natural gas and natural gas liquids that are extracted from the Cross-border Hydrocarbon Reservoirs.

1.4 "Unit Area" means the defined area as agreed by the Parties which includes and encompasses the Cross-border Hydrocarbon Reservoirs to be exploited and developed as a unit.

1.5 "Unitisation Agreements" means the agreements to be executed by the Ministers responsible for the Energy and Hydrocarbon sectors of both Parties for the exploitation and development of Cross-border Hydrocarbon Reservoirs within the Unit Area.

1.6 "Exploration and Production Company" means any company or enterprise to which approval is granted to undertake exploration and production activities according to the laws of the respective Parties.

1.7 "Unit Operating Agreement" means the agreement entered into by the Exploration and Production Companies for the joint exploitation and development of the Cross-border Hydrocarbon Reservoirs within the Unit Area.

1.8 "Unit Operator" means one of the Exploration and Production Companies operating within the Unit Area appointed by the said companies and approved by the Parties to exploit and develop the Cross-border Hydrocarbons Reservoirs.

1.9 "Development Plan" means the plan approved by the Parties that contemplates the planning, exploitation and development of the proven hydrocarbons reserves of the Cross-border Hydrocarbon Reservoirs.

1.10 "Installations" means all platforms and associated facilities that are installed in the Unit Area related to the development of the Cross-border Hydrocarbon Reservoirs.

1.11 "Cross-Boundary Pipelines" means pipelines which extend across the Delimitation Line and which are to be used for the purpose of

418

transporting hydrocarbons from the Cross-border Hydrocarbon Reservoirs within the Unit Area.

ARTICLE 2   SCOPE AND PURPOSE

2.1   This Treaty establishes the general legal framework under which any hydrocarbon reservoir that extends across the Delimitation Line between the Republic of Trinidad and Tobago and the Bolivarian Republic of Venezuela shall be exploited as a unit in the most effective and efficient manner.

2.2   This Treaty also provides for:

(a) the determination and allocation of the volumes of hydrocarbons initially in place as well as the manner in which the costs and benefits arising from such unitised exploitation will be distributed;

(b) the construction, operation and use of Installations related to the unitised exploitation of the Cross-border Hydrocarbon Reservoirs; and

(c) the construction and operation of Cross-Boundary Pipelines.

2.3   Pursuant to this Treaty, the Parties shall conclude, specific Unitisation Agreements for the exploitation and development of Cross-border Hydrocarbon Reservoirs within the Unit Area. Such Unitisation Agreements shall be executed by the Ministers responsible for the energy and hydrocarbon sector in accordance with the laws of each Party.

PART Ⅱ   EXPLOITATION OF THE CROSS-BORDER HYDROCARBON RESERVOIRS AS A UNIT

ARTICLE 3   UNITISED DEVELOPMENT

3.1   PRINCIPLES OF UNITISED EXPLOITATION

The Cross-border Hydrocarbon Reservoirs which extend across the Delimitation Line between the Republic of Trinidad and Tobago and the Bolivarian Republic of Venezuela shall be exploited and developed:

(a) as a single unit in accordance With this Treaty;

(b) in an efficient and effective manner consistent with internationally accepted standards and good petroleum and gas industry practice; and

(c) in compliance with environmental protection and safety laws, regulations and standards.

3.2　DETERMINATION OF UNIT AREA AND ALLOCATION OF HYDROCARBONS INITIALLY IN PLACE

3.2.1　The Parties through the Ministerial Commission upon submission of proposals from the Steering Committee which shall be based upon the recommendation of the Reservoir Technical Working Group shall consult with a view to agreeing：

(a) the identification of the Cross-border Hydrocarbon Reservoirs;

(b) the determination of the limits of the Unit Area;

(c) the estimated volumes of hydrocarbons initially in place of each Cross-border Hydrocarbon reservoir; and

(d) the allocation of the said estimated volumes of hydrocarbons initially in place.

3.2.2　The Parties shall set out in the respective Unitisation Agreement the identification of the Cross-border Hydrocarbon Reservoirs, determination of the limits of the Unit Area, the estimated volumes of the hydrocarbons initially in place and the allocation of those volumes comprising the Cross-border Hydrocarbon Reservoirs.

3.2.3　The Parties shall agree the allocation of the hydrocarbons initially in place of each Cross-border Hydrocarbon Reservoir before unitised exploitation of the reserves commences. Where the Parties are at variance with respect to the allocation, the unitised exploitation may proceed on a provisional basis. Such provisional allocation shall be without prejudice to the position of either Party. Where the Parties agree to an allocation, the agreed allocation shall be substituted retroactively for the provisional allocation as if it were a revision made under Article 3.8.

3. 2. 4   If the Parties are unable to reach agreement on any of the matters referred to in this Article within a reasonable time, the issue shall be settled in accordance with the provision of Article 21.

3. 3   EXPERT OPINION

The Parties may jointly consult experts in the determination of the allocation of the reserves of each Cross-Border Hydrocarbon Reservoir.

3. 4   EXPLORATION AND PRODUCTION COMPANIES

3. 4. 1   The Parties may jointly consult experts in the determination of the allocation of the reserves of each Cross-Border Hydrocarbon Reservoir.

3. 4. 2   Each Party will grant approval in accordance with its respective laws. Each Party shall require its Exploration And Production Companies to enter into agreements including Unit Operating Agreements between themselves and the Exploration And Production Companies of the other Party, regarding the exploitation and development of each Cross Border Hydrocarbon Reservoir in accordance with this Treaty.

3. 4. 3   The Exploration And Production Companies shall be required to submit the agreements referred to at 3. 4. 2 above and any amendments thereto for prior approval by both Parties.

3. 4. 4   Those agreements shall incorporate provisions to reflect that in the event of a conflict between the agreements referred to at Article 3. 4. 2 above and the Treaty, the provisions of this Treaty shall prevail.

3. 4. 5   In the event of the expiration, surrender, assignment, sale, transfer or revocation of any production approval or interest in the production approval granted according to each Party's legislation, the respective Party shall take the necessary steps to ensure the continued production of the Cross-border Hydrocarbon Reservoirs.

3. 5   UNIT OPERATOR

A Unit Operator shall be appointed by agreement between the Exploration and Production Companies, subject to the approval of the Parties, to exploit and develop the Cross-border Hydrocarbon Reservoirs within the Unit Area.

3. 6　DEVELOPMENT PLAN

3. 6. 1　The Unit Operator shall submit the Development Plan for the exploitation and development of the Cross-border Hydrocarbon Reservoirs, which shall be in accordance with the applicable legislation and approvals granted by the Parties. Production from the Cross-border Hydrocarbon Reservoirs shall not commence until the Development Plan is approved by the Parties.

3. 6. 2　The Parties shall ensure that the exploitation of the Cross-border Hydrocarbon Reservoirs is carried out in accordance with the approved Development Plan.

3. 6. 3　The Unit Operator may submit, or be required at any time by either Party to submit, proposals to revise or amend the approved Development Plan. Where one Party requires the Unit Operator to submit proposals, it shall at the same time notify the other Party of such request. All revisions and amendments to the approved Development Plan shall require the prior approval of both Parties.

3. 6. 4　Exploration and Production Companies shall not modify or alter the use of any unit installation as outlined in the approved Development Plan, without the prior approval of the Parties.

3. 7　UNIT AREA ENLARGEMENT

Where as a result of additional data the existence of a new Cross-Border Hydrocarbon Reservoir, which is not located within the Unit Area, is established, the Parties may agree that the Unit Area be enlarged; a provision shall be made in the Unitisation Agreement for the exploitation of such hydrocarbon reservoir.

3. 8　REDETERMINATION

3. 8. 1　The limits of any cross-border hydrocarbon reservoir as well as the total amount of the volumes of hydrocarbon initially in place and the allocation of those volumes shall be reviewed if either Party so requests.

3. 8. 2　Notwithstanding Article 3. 8. 1, the Parties may agree to

include in the Unitisation Agreement a provision limiting the number and timing of redeterminations.

3. 8. 3   Without prejudice to Article 3. 2. 3. , any redetermination shall be effective on and from the first day of the month following the date on which the results of such redetermination become available to, and agreed upon by the Parties.

3. 8. 4   Any redetermination made pursuant to this Article shall be applied retroactively in lieu of the initial determination made pursuant to Article 3. 2. 3.

ARTICLE 4   METERING

4. 1   The metering systems shall be automated, capable of accurately metering the quantity of produced volumes of hydrocarbons from the Cross-border Hydrocarbon Reservoirs and for determining the composition and quality of such hydrocarbons. In addition, the systems shall be capable of separately metering the quantities of hydrocarbons separated offshore, used in field operations, the volume of gas flared or vented, the volumes of hydrocarbons landed onshore as well as the quantities of water discharged as a result of the offshore operation.

4. 2   The Parties shall require the Unit Operator to submit for approval, the proposals showing the manner in which the metering systems are to be designed, installed and operated.

4. 3   The design, installation and operation of the systems as approved by the Parties shall be the responsibility of the Unit Operator. The Parties shall agree on regular calibration of the metering systems.

4. 4   The Unit Operator shall provide the Parties with certified records relating to production from each Cross-border Hydrocarbon Reservoir, the volumes of hydrocarbons extracted offshore, used in field operations, landed onshore as well as the volume of gas flared or vented and the quantities of water discharged.

PART III INTERGOVERNMENTAL COMMISSION AND COMMITTEES FOR THE IMPLEMENTATION OF THIS TREATY

ARTICLE 5

5. 1 INTERGOVERNMENTAL COMMITTEES

A joint Ministerial Commission shall be established to govern the implementation and execution of this Treaty and Other agreements related to this unitisation process. This Commission shall comprise the Ministers responsible for the Energy and Hydrocarbons sector of both Parties and may include two other members of equivalent rank appointed by the respective Governments of each Party.

5. 2 MEETINGS AND DECISIONS OF THE MINISTERIAL COMMISSION

The Ministerial Commission shall meet at least twice a year and as required and agreed by members of the Commission, alternately in Trinidad and Tobago and in Venezuela or as required and agreed by the Commission. The quorum for a valid meeting of the Ministerial Commission shall comprise at least one appointed member of each Party. All decisions of the Ministerial Commission shall be adopted by consensus. Decisions of the Ministerial Commission shall not be valid unless it is recorded in writing and signed by one member of each Party.

5. 3 FUNCTIONS AND POWERS OF THE COMMISSION

The Ministerial Commission shall have overall responsibility for all matters relating to the exploration and exploitation of the Cross-border Hydrocarbons Reservoirs.

5. 4 ADMINISTRATIVE BODY-STEERING COMMITTEE

5. 4. 1 The Ministerial Commission shall establish a Steering Committee for the purpose of facilitating the implementation of this

Treaty.

5.4.2　The Steering Committee shall comprise at least (6) six members, one half to be designated by each of the Ministers responsible for the Energy and Hydrocarbons sector of each Party. The functions of the Steering Committee shall include that of considering matters referred to it by the Ministerial Commission.

5.4.3　The specific functions and powers as well as the procedures governing the operation of the Steering Committee shall be subject to further arrangement as may be agreed by the Ministerial Commission.

5.5　MEETINGS AND DECISIONS

The Steering Committee shall conduct at least one (1) ordinary meeting every two months, and extraordinary meetings as required by either of the Parties. Meetings are to be held alternately in the Republic of Trinidad and Tobago and in the Bolivarian Republic of Venezuela. The decisions of the Steering Committee shall be adopted unanimously.

5.6　WORKING GROUPS AND EXPERTS

5.6.1　The Steering Committee may establish working groups for each Cross-border Hydrocarbon Reservoir in order to implement the provisions of the Treaty. The Steering Committee will determine the priority and the specific content of the activities to be undertaken by the working groups.

5.6.2　The Steering Committee may employ the services of experts from the hydrocarbon industry, preferably from the Republic of Trinidad and Tobago and the Bolivarian Republic of Venezuela to advise on matters to be considered in the process of the implementation of this Treaty.

5.7　CONFIDENTIALITY

Members of the Steering Committee, officers and employees of each Party, shall treat the contents of all data and information produced or received pursuant to this Treaty as confidential, and shall not disclose or publish any such data or information without the authority of both Parties.

PART Ⅳ   APPLICABLE LAW GOVERNING CROSS-BOUNDARY PROJECTS

ARTICLE 6   APPROVALS

6. 1   Subject to fulfilment by the Unit Operator of all requirements of the respective applicable law, the Parties shall facilitate the issuance of approvals relating to the exploitation and development of the Cross-border Hydrocarbon Reservoirs.

6. 2   Copies of all approvals stated above or any amendment thereto granted by one of the Parties shall be made available to the other Party.

ARTICLE 7   FISCAL OBLIGATIONS

7. 1   ROYALTIES

Each Party may only charge royalties and other similar dues in accordance with its laws on the agreed allocation, and on the hydrocarbon volumes produced from each Cross-border Hydrocarbon Reservoir. Exploration and Production Companies shall be required to pay the royalties and other similar dues in accordance with the respective applicable law, as well as the approvals granted and the agreed allocation, notwithstanding the location of the Installations from which the Cross-border Hydrocarbon Reservoir is produced.

7. 2   TAXATION

Profits, gains and capital in respect of the exploitation of the Cross-border Hydrocarbon Reservoirs shall be taxed in accordance with the laws of each Party, and the respective allocation to which they are entitled. Exploration and Production Companies Shall be required to pay their taxes in accordance with the respective applicable law, the approvals granted and the agreed allocation, notwithstanding the location of the Installations from which the Cross-border Hydrocarbon Reservoir is produced.

ARTICLE 8   HEALTH AND SAFETY STANDARDS

8. 1   The Cross-border Hydrocarbon Reservoirs shall be developed in accordance with the respective applicable laws relating to health and safety of the Parties and the applicable internationally accepted health, safety and environmental standards and regulations. The Parties may issue additional guidelines regarding the implementation of the said standards.

8. 2   The Parties shall require their respective Exploration and Production Companies to jointly formulate and implement health and safety policy and procedures to secure the health and safety of all personnel in accordance with national law and international standards and regulations.

8. 3   The Parties shall ensure that the design, construction and maintenance of all Installations, pipelines and other facilities are subject to national laws and international safety and construction standards.

ARTICLE 9   ENVIRONMENTAL MATTERS

9. 1   The Parties shall, jointly and severally, ensure that the exploitation of the Cross-border Hydrocarbon Reservoirs and the operation of any installation or pipeline involved in that exploitation shall not cause or be likely to cause pollution to the marine environment, the coastlines, shore facilities, vessels or fishing gear of either Party.

9. 2   The Parties shall require their respective Exploration and Production Companies to implement the relevant measures and procedures to prevent or remediate pollution of the marine environment, resulting from hydrocarbon activities in the Unit Area, taking into account the respective applicable laws and the relevant international and regional standards, procedures, agreements and recommended practices and guidelines, in particular those promulgated by the Caribbean Environmental Programme of the United Nations Environmental

Programme and the International Maritime Organisation.

9.3　The competent authorities of the Parties shall consult with a view to agreeing to measures and procedures to apply in an emergency.

ARTICLE 10　INSTALLATIONS AND PIPELINES

10.1　COMPLIANCE WITH APPLICABLE LAWS

The Parties shall ensure that all Installations and pipelines are constructed in accordance with the approved Development Plan, the respective laws of either Party as well as internationally accepted standards.

10.2　PIPELINES

The terms and conditions for access to a cross-boundary pipeline, including the setting of transmission tariffs, shall be in accordance with the applicable laws of either Party. Subject to approval by the Parties, the owner of the pipeline shall establish the terms of access for transmission of hydrocarbons through the pipeline. The terms of access shall be reasonable, transparent and non-discriminatory.

10.3　SECURITY

Each Party shall determine the security measures which are to govern the Installations and pipelines under its jurisdiction.

10.4　USE OF INSTALLATIONS AND PIPELINES BY THIRD PARTIES

10.4.1　Either Party may, after consultation and agreement with the other Party and the Exploration and Production Companies, authorise the use of the unit Installations and pipelines within its jurisdiction by third parties for the exploitation of hydrocarbon reservoirs not comprising the Unit Area, subject to the laws of that Party, and provided that such use does not adversely affect the unitised production of the Cross-border Hydrocarbon Reservoirs.

10.4.2　No authorisation referred to in this Article shall be issued, revoked, altered, modified or reissued by one Party without prior consultation and agreement with the other Party.

10.5　DECOMMISSIONING

10.5.1　The Unit Operator shall submit to the Parties for approval a plan including provision for the creation of a fund for the final decommissioning and disposal of Installations, pipelines and other facilities, in the calendar year following commencement of production from the Cross-border Hydrocarbon Reservoirs. A revised decommissioning plan shall be submitted to the Parties for approval every two (2) years.

10.5.2　The Parties shall ensure that the decommissioning of any or all parts of the cross-border Installations, pipelines and other facilities shall be undertaken in accordance with their respective laws and in compliance With internationally accepted standards.

10.5.3　If the decommissioning plan is not approved, the Parties shall notify the Unit Operator of the decision. The Unit Operator shall, in such circumstances, be required to submit a revised plan within a specific time limit as defined by the Parties.

10.5.4　Where the final decommissioning plan is not approved by the Parties, the Parties may prepare or cause to be prepared, for the account of the Unit Operator, a reasonable plan for the decommissioning of unit Installations, pipelines and other facilities.

10.6　PHYSICAL ACCESS AND SAFETY

10.6.1　Subject to the requirements of the laws of the respective Party including those relating to safety, the berthing and landing facilities on each installation shall be accessible to vessels and aircraft authorised by the respective Party for the purposes of activities connected with the exploitation and development of the Cross-border Hydrocarbon Reservoirs and in accordance with any arrangements which may be concluded between the competent authorities.

10.6.2　The Parties shall cooperate with a view to the adoption of relevant safety measures, with respect to Installations, pipelines and any other facilities, including those required in an emergency

ARTICLE 11　CUSTOMS AND IMMIGRATION LAWS

11.1　Each Party shall apply customs, immigration and quarantine laws to persons, equipment and goods entering or leaving its territory.

11. 2　Each Pally shall ensure that persons, equipment and goods do not enter any installation or other facilities, within its territory, without first complying with the respective law.

ARTICLE 12　LOCAL CONTENT

12. 1　In the development of Cross-border Hydrocarbon Reservoirs, the Parties shall ensure that the Exploration and Production Companies comply with the local content policies of both Parties respectively. In the execution of their work programme, Exploration and Production Companies shall maximise the use of goods, services and facilities available from local suppliers, local contractors and local enterprises.

12. 2　In performing all aspects of operations and activities related to exploitation and development of Cross-border Hydrocarbon Reservoirs, Exploration and Production Companies shall, with priority, employ and train or provide suitable and adequate training for local personnel of both Parties.

12. 3　The competent authorities of the Parties shall consult with a view to agreeing on the implementation of this Article.

ARTICLE 13　EXCHANGE OF INFORMATION

Subject to the requirements of the applicable laws of each Party, the Parties will exchange information relating to the exploration and exploitation of the Cross-border Hydrocarbon Reservoirs.

ARTICLE 14　CONFIDENTIALITY

14. 1　Each Party agrees that all information provided directly or indirectly by the other Party shall be Confidential Information and shall be held and protected in strict confidence, except as equired by law and shall not be disclosed by the receiving Party without prior consent of the supplying Party.

14. 2　The term Confidential Information does not include information

that is or comes within the public domain other than through the fault of either Party.

14.3　The confidential information disclosed by one Party shall remain the property of that Party, who may request the return thereof at any time. Upon receipt of such request the other Party shall promptly return to the disclosing party all original confidential information disclosed hereunder and shall ensure that all copies and reproductions thereof in its possessions are destroyed.

14.4　The obligations contained in this Article shall survive for a period of ten（10）years after the termination of the Unitisation Agreements referred to at Article 2.3, unless otherwise agreed by the Parties. Notwithstanding this Article, the Parties may make special provisions for the treatment of sensitive information, in particular seismic data.

PART V　RULES OF PUBLIC INTERNATIONAL LAW

ARTICLE 15　CIVIL AND ADMINISTRATIVE JURISDICTION

15.1　Each Party shall exercise civil and administrative jurisdiction in respect of acts or omissions occurring in that part of the Unit Area over which that Party exercises sovereignty, sovereign rights, or jurisdiction.

15.2　In the exercise of its jurisdiction under paragraph 15.1, the Parties shall give effect to the relevant applicable law and provide legal assistance to and cooperate with the other Party, through arrangements or agreements as appropriate.

ARTICLE 16　CRIMINAL JURISDICTION

16.1　The criminal law of each Party shall apply in respect of acts or omissions occurring in that part of the Unit Area over which that Party exercises sovereignty, sovereign rights or jurisdiction.

16. 2　The Parties shall provide legal assistance and cooperate with each other, including agreements or arrangements as appropriate, for the purposes of enforcement of criminal law under this Article, including the obtaining of evidence and information.

PART VI　FINAL PROVISIONS

ARTICLE 17　MUTUAL CO-OPERATION

The Parties may cooperate where necessary or desirable, in the development of projects and activities to facilitate the monetisation of each Party's hydrocarbon reserves from Cross-border Hydrocarbon Reservoirs in furtherance of national development and regional integration.

ARTICLE 18　SOVEREIGNTY, SOVEREIGN RIGHTS AND JURISDICTION

Nothing in this Treaty shall be interpreted as affecting the sovereignty, sovereign rights or jurisdiction which each Party has over maritime areas appertaining to it in accordance with international law.

ARTICLE 19　OFFICIAL LANGUAGE

All documents relating to the unitisation of the Cross-border Hydrocarbon Reservoirs shall be prepared in both the English and Spanish languages.

ARTICLE 20　ENTRY INTO FORCE

20. 1　This Treaty shall be subject to ratification.

20. 2　This Treaty shall enter into force upon the exchange of the instruments of ratification indicating compliance with the legal formalities required by the constitutional procedures of each Party.

20.3　Each Party shall take such action as is necessary for the purpose of making effective in law the provisions set forth in this Treaty.

20.4　Upon entry into force this Treaty shall be registered with the Secretariat of the United Nations in accordance with Article 102 of the Charter of the United Nations.

ARTICLE 21　DISPUTE RESOLUTION

21.1　The Parties shall encourage the prompt settlement of any dispute arising out of the interpretation or application of this Treaty, through consultation or negotiation by the Steering Committee in the first instance or by the Ministerial Commission.

21.2　Any dispute arising out of the interpretation or application of this Treaty shall be settled amicably by direct consultation or negotiation between the Parties.

ARTICLE 22　AMENDMENTS

This Treaty may be amended by written agreement between the Parties.

ARTICLE 23　DURATION AND TERMINATION

23.1　This Treaty shall remain in force unless terminated by either Party.

23.2　Either Party may denounce this Treaty by written notice through diplomatic channels to the other Party, and the denunciation shall take effect twelve months after the date on which the notice has been received by the other Party.

23.3　Upon termination of this Treaty, the Parties undertake to fulfil any continuing obligation which may have been assumed pursuant to this Treaty or any related agreement, unless otherwise agreed by the Parties.

IN WITNESS WHEREOF the undersigned, being duly authorised thereto by their respective Governments, have signed this Treaty.

DONE in two originals at Caracas this 20th day of March 2007 in the

English and Spanish languages, both texts being equally authoritative.

/Signed/Patrick Manning   /Signed/Hugo Chávez Frias

For the Government of the   For the Government of the

Republic of Trinidad and Tobago   Bolivarian Republic of Venezuela

资料来源：Framework Treaty relating to the unitisation of hydrocarbon reservoirs that extend across the delimitation line between the Republic of Trinidad and Tobago and the Bolivarian Republic of Venezuela. 20 March 2007, Republic of Trinidad and Tobago—the Bolivarian Republic of Venezuela, U. N. T. S. Vol. 2876. pp. 1-24, https：//treaties. un. org/doc/Publication/ UNTS/No%20Volume/50196/Part/I-50196-08000002802bb3a7. pdf。

下篇：与中国有关的海上共同开发的法律文件

一、2000 年中越关于北部湾划界 协定和渔业协定

1.《中华人民共和国和越南社会主义共和国关于两国在北部湾领 海、专属经济区和大陆架的划界协定》

(2000 年 12 月 25 日，北京)

中华人民共和国和越南社会主义共和国(以下简称"缔约双方")，为巩固和发展中越两国和两国人民之间的传统睦邻友好关系，维护和促进北部湾的稳定和发展，在相互尊重独立、主权和领土完整，互不侵犯，互不干涉内政，平等互利和和平共处的原则基础上，本着互谅互让、友好协商和公平合理地解决划分北部湾问题的精神，达成协议如下：

第一条

一、缔约双方根据一九八二年《联合国海洋法公约》，公认的国际法各项原则和国际实践，在充分考虑北部湾所有有关情况的基础上，按照公平原则，通过友好协商，确定了两国在北部湾的领海、专属经济区和大陆架的分界线。

二、在本协定中，"北部湾"系指北面为中国和越南两国陆地领土海岸、东面为中国雷州半岛和海南岛海岸、西面为越南大陆海岸所环抱的半封闭海湾，其南部界限是自地理坐标为北纬 18 度 30 分 19 秒、东经 108 度 41 分 17 秒的中国海南岛莺歌嘴最外缘突出点经越南昏果岛至越南海岸上地理坐标为北纬 16 度 57 分 40 秒、东经 107 度 08 分 42 秒的一点之间的直线连线。

缔约双方确定，上述区域构成本协定的划界范围。

第二条

缔约双方同意，两国在北部湾的领海、专属经济区和大陆架分界线由以下 21 个界点以直线顺次连接确定，其地理坐标如下：

第 1 界点　北纬 21 度 28 分 12.5 秒，东经 108 度 06 分 04.3 秒；

第 2 界点　北纬 21 度 28 分 01.7 秒，东经 108 度 06 分 01.6 秒；

第 3 界点　北纬 21 度 27 分 50.1 秒，东经 108 度 05 分 57.7 秒；

第 4 界点　北纬 21 度 27 分 39.5 秒，东经 108 度 05 分 51.5 秒；

第 5 界点　北纬 21 度 27 分 28.2 秒，东经 108 度 05 分 39.9 秒；

第 6 界点　北纬 21 度 27 分 23.1 秒，东经 108 度 05 分 38.8 秒；

第 7 界点　北纬 21 度 27 分 08.2 秒，东经 108 度 05 分 43.7 秒；

第 8 界点　北纬 21 度 16 分 32 秒，东经 108 度 08 分 05 秒；

第 9 界点　北纬 21 度 12 分 35 秒，东经 108 度 12 分 31 秒；

第 10 界点　北纬 20 度 24 分 05 秒，东经 108 度 22 分 45 秒；

第 11 界点　北纬 19 度 57 分 33 秒，东经 107 度 55 分 47 秒；

第 12 界点　北纬 19 度 39 分 33 秒，东经 107 度 31 分 40 秒；

第 13 界点　北纬 19 度 25 分 26 秒，东经 107 度 21 分 00 秒；

第 14 界点　北纬 19 度 25 分 26 秒，东经 107 度 12 分 43 秒；

第 15 界点　北纬 19 度 16 分 04 秒，东经 107 度 11 分 23 秒；

第 16 界点　北纬 19 度 12 分 55 秒，东经 107 度 09 分 34 秒；

第 17 界点　北纬 18 度 42 分 52 秒，东经 107 度 09 分 34 秒；

第 18 界点　北纬 18 度 13 分 49 秒，东经 107 度 34 分 00 秒；

第 19 界点　北纬 18 度 07 分 08 秒，东经 107 度 37 分 34 秒；

第 20 界点　北纬 18 度 04 分 13 秒，东经 107 度 39 分 09 秒；

第 21 界点　北纬 17 度 47 分 00 秒，东经 107 度 58 分 00 秒。

第三条

一、本协定第二条所规定的第 1 界点至第 9 界点的分界线是两国在北部湾的领海分界线。

二、本条第一款所规定的两国领海分界线沿垂直方向划分两国领海的上空、海床和底土。

三、除非缔约双方另有协议，任何地形变化不改变本条第一款所规定的第 1 界点至第 7 界点的两国领海分界线。

第四条

本协定第二条所规定的第 9 界点至第 21 界点的分界线是两国在北部湾的专属经济区和大陆架的分界线。

第五条

本协定第二条所规定的第 1 界点至第 7 界点的两国领海分界线用黑线标绘在缔约双方于二〇〇〇年共同测制的比例尺为一万分之一的北仑河口专题地图上，第 7 界点至第 21 界点的两国领海、专属经济区和大陆架分界线用黑线标绘在由缔约双方于二〇〇〇年共同测制的比例尺为五十万分之一的北部湾全图上。上述分界线均为大地线。

上述北仑河口专题地图和北部湾全图为本协定的附图。上述地图采用 ITRF-96 坐标系。本协定第二条所规定各界点的地理坐标均系从上述地图上量取。本协定所规定的分界线标绘在本协定附图上，仅用于说明的目的。

第六条

缔约双方应相互尊重按照本协定所确定的两国各自在北部湾的领海、专属经济区和大陆架的主权、主权权利和管辖权。

第七条

如果任何石油、天然气单一地质构造或其他矿藏跨越本协定第二条所规定的分界线，缔约双方应通过友好协商就该构造或矿藏的最有效开发以及公平分享开发收益达成协议。

第八条

缔约双方同意就北部湾生物资源的合理利用和可持续发展以及两国在北部湾专属经济区的生物资源养护、管理和利用的有关合作事项进行协商。

第九条

两国根据本协定对北部湾领海、专属经济区和大陆架分界线的划定对缔约各方有关海洋法方面国际法规则的立场不造成任何影响或妨害。

第十条

缔约双方对本协定的解释或适用所产生的任何争议，应通过友好协商和谈判予以解决。

第十一条

本协定须经缔约双方批准，并自互换批准书之日起生效。批准书在河内互换。

本协定于二〇〇〇年十二月二十五日在北京签订，一式两份，每份都用中文和越文写成，两种文本同等作准。

中华人民共和国　　　　　　越南社会主义共和国
全权代表　　　　　　　　　全权代表
唐家璇　　　　　　　　　　阮怡年
（签　字）　　　　　　　　（签　字）

资料来源：中华人民共和国全国人民代表大会网站，http://www.npc.gov.cn/wxzl/gongbao/2004-08/04/content_5332197.htm。

2.《中华人民共和国政府和越南社会主义共和国政府北部湾渔业合作协定》

（2000 年 12 月 25 日，北京）

中华人民共和国政府和越南社会主义共和国政府(以下简称"缔约双方")，为了维护和发展中越两国和两国人民之间的传统睦邻友好关系，养护和持续利用北部湾协定水域的海洋生物资源，加强两国在北部湾的渔业合作，根据国际法，特别是一九八二年十二月十日《联合国海洋法公约》的有关规定以及二〇〇〇年十二月二十五日签订的《中华人民共和国和越南社会主义共和国关于两国在北部湾领海、专属经济区和大陆架的划界协定》(以下简称"北部湾划界协定")，经友好协商，在相互尊重各自在北部湾的主权、主权权利和管辖权、平等互利的基础上，达成协议如下：

第一部分 总 则

第一条

本协定适用于北部湾两国专属经济区的一部分和两国领海相邻水域的一部分(以下简称"协定水域")。

第二条

缔约双方在相互尊重主权、主权权利和管辖权的基础上，在协定水域进行渔业合作。这种渔业合作不影响两国各自的领海主权和两国各自在专属经济区享有的其他权益。

第二部分 共 同 渔 区

第三条

一、缔约双方同意在北部湾封口线以北、北纬20度以南、距北部湾划界协定所确定的分界线(以下简称"分界线")各自30.5海里的两国各自专属经济区设立共同渔区。

二、共同渔区的具体范围为下列各点顺次用直线连接而围成的水域：

1. 北纬17度23分38秒，东经107度34分43秒之点
2. 北纬18度09分20秒，东经108度20分18秒之点
3. 北纬18度44分25秒，东经107度41分51秒之点
4. 北纬19度08分09秒，东经107度41分51秒之点

5. 北纬 19 度 43 分 00 秒，东经 108 度 20 分 30 秒之点

6. 北纬 20 度 00 分 00 秒，东经 108 度 42 分 32 秒之点

7. 北纬 20 度 00 分 00 秒，东经 107 度 57 分 42 秒之点

8. 北纬 19 度 52 分 34 秒，东经 107 度 57 分 42 秒之点

9. 北纬 19 度 52 分 34 秒，东经 107 度 29 分 00 秒之点

10. 北纬 20 度 00 分 00 秒，东经 107 度 29 分 00 秒之点

11. 北纬 20 度 00 分 00 秒，东经 107 度 07 分 41 秒之点

12. 北纬 19 度 33 分 07 秒，东经 106 度 37 分 17 秒之点

13. 北纬 18 度 40 分 00 秒，东经 106 度 37 分 17 秒之点

14. 北纬 18 度 18 分 58 秒，东经 106 度 53 分 08 秒之点

15. 北纬 18 度 00 分 00 秒，东经 107 度 01 分 55 秒之点

16. 北纬 17 度 23 分 38 秒，东经 107 度 34 分 43 秒之点

第四条

缔约双方本着互利的精神，在共同渔区内进行长期渔业合作。

第五条

缔约双方根据共同渔区的自然环境条件、生物资源特点、可持续发展的需要和环境保护以及对缔约各方渔业活动的影响，共同制订共同渔区生物资源的养护、管理和可持续利用措施。

第六条

缔约双方尊重平等互利的原则，根据在定期联合渔业资源调查结果的基础上所确定的可捕量和对缔约各方渔业活动的影响，以及可持续发展的需要，通过根据本协定第十三条设立的中越北部湾渔业联合委员会每年确定缔约各方在共同渔区内的作业渔船数量。

第七条

一、缔约各方对在共同渔区从事渔业活动的己方渔船实行捕捞许可制度。捕捞许可证须按照中越北部湾渔业联合委员会确定的当年作业渔船数量发放，并将获得许可证的渔船船名号通报缔约另一方。缔约双方有义务对进入共同渔区从事渔业活动的渔民进行教育和培训。

二、凡进入共同渔区从事渔业活动的渔船均须向本国政府授权机关提出申请，并在领取捕捞许可证后，方可进入共同渔区从事渔业活动。缔约双方进入共同渔区从事渔业活动的渔船应按照中越北部湾渔业联合委员会的规定进行标识。

第八条

缔约各方进入共同渔区从事渔业活动的国民和渔船在进行渔业活动时须遵守中越北部湾渔业联合委员会关于渔业资源养护和管理的规定，依照中越北部湾渔业联合委员会的要求正确填写捕捞日志并在规定时间内上交本国政府授权机关。

第九条

一、根据中越北部湾渔业联合委员会在符合共同渔区特点以及符合两国各自关于渔业资源养护和管理的国内法的基础上制订的规定，缔约各方授权机关对进入共同渔区内己方一侧水域的缔约双方国民和渔船进行监督检查。

二、缔约一方授权机关发现缔约另一方国民和渔船在共同渔区内己方一侧水域违反中越北部湾渔业联合委员会的规定时，有权按中越北部湾渔业联合委员会的规定对该违规行为进行处理，并应通过中越北部湾渔业联合委员会商定的途径，将有关情况和处理结果迅速通知缔约另一方。被扣留的渔船和船员，在提出适当的保证书或其他担保后，应迅速获得释放。

三、必要时，缔约双方授权机关可相互配合进行联合监督检查，对在共同渔区内违反中越北部湾渔业联合委员会关于渔业资源养护和管理规定的行为进行处理。

四、缔约各方有权根据各自国内法对未获许可证进入共同渔区内己方一侧水域从事渔业活动或虽获许可证进入共同渔区但从事渔业活动以外不合法活动的渔船进行处罚。

五、缔约各方应为获得许可证进入共同渔区的缔约另一方渔船提供便利。缔约各方授权机关不得滥用职权，妨碍缔约另一方获得许可证的国民和渔船在共同渔区内从事正常渔业活动。缔约一方如发现缔约另一方授权机关未按照中越北部湾渔业联合委员会制订的共同管理措施进行执法，有权要求该授权机关做出解释，必要时，可提交中越北部湾渔业联合委员会予以讨论和解决。

第十条

　　缔约各方在共同渔区己方作业规模框架内，可采取任何一种国际合作或联营方式。所有获许可证在共同渔区内以上述合作或联营方式从事渔业活动的渔船均须遵守中越北部湾渔业联合委员会制订的渔业资源养护和管理的规定，悬挂向其颁发许可证的缔约一方的国旗，按中越北部湾渔业联合委员会的规定进行标识，在共同渔区向其颁发许可证的缔约一方一侧水域从事渔业活动。

第三部分　过渡性安排

第十一条

　　一、缔约各方应对共同渔区以北（自北纬 20 度起算）本国专属经济区内缔约另一方的现有渔业活动做出过渡性安排。自本协定生效之日起，过渡性安排开始实施。缔约另一方应采取措施，逐年削减上述渔业活动。过渡性安排自本协定生效之日起四年内结束。

　　二、关于过渡性安排水域的范围和过渡性安排的管理办法，由缔约双方以补充议定书形式加以规定，该补充议定书为本协定不可分割的组成部分。

　　三、过渡性安排结束后，缔约各方应在相同条件下优先准许缔约另一方在本国专属经济区入渔。

第四部分　小型渔船缓冲区

第十二条

　　一、为避免缔约双方小型渔船误入缔约另一方领海引起纠纷，缔约双方在两国领海相邻部分自分界线第一界点起沿分界线向南延伸 10 海里、距分界线各自3海里的范围内设立小型渔船缓冲区，具体范围为下列各点顺次用直线连接而围成的水域：

1. 北纬21度28分12.5秒，东经108度06分04.3秒之点
2. 北纬21度25分40.7秒，东经108度02分46.1秒之点
3. 北纬21度17分52.1秒，东经108度04分30.3秒之点
4. 北纬21度18分29.0秒，东经108度07分39.0秒之点
5. 北纬21度19分05.7秒，东经108度10分47.8秒之点
6. 北纬21度25分41.7秒，东经108度09分20.0秒之点
7. 北纬21度28分12.5秒，东经108度06分04.3秒之点

二、缔约一方如发现缔约另一方小型渔船进入小型渔船缓冲区己方一侧水域从事渔业活动，可予以警告，并采取必要措施令其离开该水域，但应克制：不扣留，不逮捕，不处罚或使用武力。如发生有关渔业活动的争议，应报告中越北部湾渔业联合委员会予以解决；如发生有关渔业活动以外的争议，由两国各自相关授权机关依照国内法予以解决。

第五部分　中越北部湾渔业联合委员会

第十三条

一、为实施本协定，缔约双方决定设立中越北部湾渔业联合委员会(以下简称"渔委会")。渔委会由两国政府各自任命的一名代表和若干名委员组成。

二、渔委会将对其活动机制作出具体规定。

三、渔委会的职责如下：

(一)协商协定水域渔业资源养护和可持续利用的有关问题，并向两国政府提出建议；

(二)协商两国在协定水域渔业合作的有关事项，并向两国政府提出建议；

(三)根据本协定第五条，制订共同渔区的渔业资源养护和管理规定及其实施办法；

(四)根据本协定第六条，每年确定缔约各方进入共同渔区的作业渔船

数量；

（五）协商和决定与共同渔区有关的其他事项；

（六）根据过渡性安排补充议定书的规定履行其职能；

（七）解决发生在小型渔船缓冲区内的有关渔业活动的争议；

（八）在其职能范围内对渔业纠纷和海损事故的处理进行指导；

（九）对本协定执行情况进行评估并向两国政府报告；

（十）可就本协定、本协定附件和本协定补充议定书的补充和修改向两国政府提出建议；

（十一）对缔约双方共同关注的其他事项进行协商。

四、渔委会的一切建议和决定均须经缔约双方代表一致同意。

五、渔委会每年举行一至二次会议，在两国轮流举行。必要时，经缔约双方同意可举行临时会议。

第六部分　其他条款

第十四条

为确保航行安全，维护海上捕捞作业秩序和安全，并顺利及时处理协定水域海上事故，缔约各方应对本国国民和渔船进行指导、法律教育并采取其他必要措施。

第十五条

一、缔约一方国民和渔船在缔约另一方一侧海域遭遇海难或发生其他紧急事态需要救助时，缔约另一方有义务予以救助和保护，同时迅速将有关情况通报缔约一方的有关部门。

二、缔约一方的国民和渔船因天气恶劣或其他紧急事态需要避难时，可按本协定附件和渔委会的规定，经与缔约另一方有关部门联系，到缔约另一方避难。该国民和渔船在避难期间须遵守缔约另一方的有关法律和法规，并服从缔约另一方有关部门的管理。

第十六条

缔约各方按照一九八二年十二月十日《联合国海洋法公约》的规定确保

缔约另一方渔船的无害通过权和航行便利。

第十七条

一、缔约双方应在协定水域就渔业科学研究和海洋生物资源养护进行合作。

二、缔约各方可在协定水域己方一侧进行国际渔业科研合作。

第七部分 最后条款

第十八条

缔约双方之间对本协定的解释或适用而产生的任何争端，应通过友好协商予以解决。

第十九条

本协定附件和本协定补充议定书为本协定不可分割的组成部分。

第二十条

经协商，缔约双方可对本协定、本协定附件和本协定补充议定书进行补充和修改。

第二十一条

本协定第三条第二款规定的共同渔区的地理坐标和本协定第十二条第一款规定的小型渔船缓冲区的地理坐标均从作为北部湾划界协定附图的北部湾全图和北仑河口专题地图上量取。

第二十二条

一、本协定经缔约双方履行各自国内法律程序后，自两国政府换文商定之日起生效。

二、本协定有效期为十二年，其后自动顺延三年。顺延期满后，继续合作事宜由缔约双方通过协商商定。

本协定于二〇〇〇年十二月二十五日在北京签订，一式两份，每份均用中文和越文写成，两种文本同等作准。

中华人民共和国政府　　　　越南社会主义共和国政府

代　表　　　　　　　　　　代　表

陈耀邦　　　　　　　　　　谢光玉

附件：

关于紧急避难的规定

为实施本协定第十五条第二款的规定：

一、中华人民共和国政府指定的联络部门为农业部南海区渔政渔港监督管理局。越南社会主义共和国政府指定的联络部门为水产部水产资源保护局。

二、紧急避难的联络办法由缔约双方在渔委会上相互通报。

三、紧急避难的联系内容应包括：船名、呼号、当时船位（纬度、经度）、船籍港、总吨位、全长、船长姓名、船员数、避难理由、请求避难的目的地、预计到达时间和联络方法。

资料来源：中华人民共和国外交部网站，http：//www.fmprc.gov.cn/web/ziliao_674904/tytj_674911/tyfg_674913/t556668.shtml。

二、2002 年《南海各方行为宣言》

Declaration on the Conduct of Parties in the South China Sea

The Government of the People's Republic of China and the Governments of the Member States of ASEAN,

REAFFIRMING their determination to consolidate and develop the friendship and cooperation existing between their people and the governments with the view to promoting a 21st century-oriented partnership of good neighbourliness and mutual trust;

COGNIZANT of the need to promote a peaceful, friendly and harmonious environment in the South China Sea between ASEAN and China for the enhancement of peace, stability, economic growth and prosperity in the region;

COMMITTED to enhancing the principles and objectives of the 1997 Joint Statement of the Meeting of President of the People's Republic of China and the Heads of State/Government of the Member States of ASEAN;

DESIRING to enhance favourable conditions for a peaceful and durable solution of differences and disputes among the countries concerned;

HEREBY DECLARE the following:

1. The Parties reaffirm their commitment to the purposes and principles of the Charter of the United Nations, the 1982 UN Convention on the Law of the Sea, the Treaty of Amity and Cooperation in Southeast

Asia, the Five Principles of Peaceful Coexistence, and other universally recognized principles of international law which shall serve as the basic norms governing state-to-state relations;

2. The Parties are committed to exploring ways for building trust and confidence in accordance with the above-mentioned principles and on the basis of equality and mutual respect;

3. The Parties reaffirm their respect for and commitment to the freedom of navigation in and overflight above the South China Sea as provided for by the universally recognized principles of international law, including the 1982 UN Convention on the Law of the Sea;

4. The Parties concerned undertake to resolve their territorial and jurisdictional disputes by peaceful means, without resorting to the threat or use of force, through friendly consultations and negotiations by sovereign states directly concerned, in accordance with universally recognized principles of international law, including the 1982 UN Convention on the Law of the Sea;

5. The Parties undertake to exercise self-restraint in the conduct of activities that would complicate or escalate disputes and affect peace and stability including, among others, refraining from action of inhabiting on the presently uninhabited islands, reefs, shoals, cays and other features and to handle their differences in a constructive manner;

Pending the peaceful settlement of territorial and jurisdictional disputes, the Parties concerned undertake to intensify efforts to seek ways, in the spirit of cooperation and understanding, to build trust and confidence between and among them, including:

a. holding dialogues and exchange of views as appropriate between their defense and military officials;

b. ensuring just and humane treatment of all persons who are either in danger or in distress;

c. notifying, on a voluntary basis, other Parties concerned of any impending joint/combined military exercise; and

d. exchanging, on a voluntary basis, relevant information.

6. Pending a comprehensive and durable settlement of the disputes, the Parties concerned may explore or undertake cooperative activities. These may include the following:

a. marine environmental protection;

b. marine scientific research;

c. safety of navigation and communication at sea;

d. search and rescue operation; and

e. combating transnational crime, including but not limited to trafficking in illicit drugs, piracy and armed robbery at sea, and illegal traffic in arms.

The modalities, scope and locations, in respect of bilateral and multilateral cooperation, should be agreed upon by the Parties concerned prior to their actual implementation.

7. The Parties concerned stand ready to continue their consultations and dialogues concerning relevant issues, through modalities to be agreed by them, including regular consultations on the observance of this Declaration, for the purpose of promoting good neighbourliness and transparency, establishing harmony, mutual understanding and cooperation, and facilitating peaceful resolution of disputes among them;

8. The Parties undertake to respect the provisions of this Declaration and take actions consistent therewith;

9. The Parties encourage other countries to respect the principles contained in this Declaration;

10. The Parties concerned reaffirm that the adoption of a code of conduct in the South China Sea would further promote peace and stability in the region and agree to work, on the basis of consensus, towards the eventual attainment of this objective.

Done on the Fourth Day of November in the Year Two Thousand and Two in Phnom Penh, the Kingdom of Cambodia.

资料来源：中华人民共和国外交部网站，http：//www. fmprc. gov. cn/web/wjb_673085/zzjg_673183/yzs_673193/dqzz_673197/nanhai_67。

《南海各方行为宣言》

中华人民共和国和东盟各成员国政府，重申各方决心巩固和发展各国人民和政府之间业已存在的友谊与合作，以促进面向 21 世纪睦邻互信伙伴关系；

认识到为增进本地区的和平、稳定、经济发展与繁荣，中国和东盟有必要促进南海地区和平、友好与和谐的环境；

承诺促进 1997 年中华人民共和国与东盟成员国国家元首或政府首脑会晤《联合声明》所确立的原则和目标；

希望为和平与永久解决有关国家间的分歧和争议创造有利条件；

谨发表如下宣言：

一、各方重申以《联合国宪章》宗旨和原则、1982 年《联合国海洋法公约》、《东南亚友好合作条约》、和平共处五项原则以及其它公认的国际法原则作为处理国家间关系的基本准则。

二、各方承诺根据上述原则，在平等和相互尊重的基础上，探讨建立信任的途径。

三、各方重申尊重并承诺，包括 1982 年《联合国海洋法公约》在内的公认的国际法原则所规定的在南海的航行及飞越自由。

四、有关各方承诺根据公认的国际法原则，包括 1982 年《联合国海洋法公约》，由直接有关的主权国家通过友好磋商和谈判，以和平方式解决它们的领土和管辖权争议，而不诉诸武力或以武力相威胁。

五、各方承诺保持自我克制，不采取使争议复杂化、扩大化和影响和平与稳定的行动，包括不在现无人居住的岛、礁、滩、沙或其它自然构造上采取居住的行动，并以建设性的方式处理它们的分歧。

在和平解决它们的领土和管辖权争议之前，有关各方承诺本着合作与谅解的精神，努力寻求各种途径建立相互信任，包括：

（一）在各方国防及军队官员之间开展适当的对话和交换意见；

（二）保证对处于危险境地的所有公民予以公正和人道的待遇；

（三）在自愿基础上向其它有关各方通报即将举行的联合军事演习；

（四）在自愿基础上相互通报有关情况。

六、在全面和永久解决争议之前，有关各方可探讨或开展合作，可包括以下领域：

(一)海洋环保；

(二)海洋科学研究；

(三)海上航行和交通安全；

(四)搜寻与救助；

(五)打击跨国犯罪，包括但不限于打击毒品走私、海盗和海上武装抢劫以及军火走私。

在具体实施之前，有关各方应就双边及多边合作的模式、范围和地点取得一致意见。

七、有关各方愿通过各方同意的模式，就有关问题继续进行磋商和对话，包括对遵守本宣言问题举行定期磋商，以增进睦邻友好关系和提高透明度，创造和谐、相互理解与合作，推动以和平方式解决彼此间争议。

八、各方承诺尊重本宣言的条款并采取与宣言相一致的行动。

九、各方鼓励其他国家尊重本宣言所包含的原则。

十、有关各方重申制定南海行为准则将进一步促进本地区和平与稳定，并同意在各方协商一致的基础上，朝最终达成该目标而努力。

本宣言于2002年11月4日在柬埔寨王国金边签署。

资料来源：中华人民共和国外交部网站，http：//www.fmprc.gov.cn/web/ziliao_674904/1179_674909/t4553.shtml。

三、2005年中菲越《在南中国海协议区三方联合海洋地震工作协议》

A Tripartite Agreement for Joint Marine Scientific Research in Certain Areas in the South China Sea By and Among China National Offshore Oil Corporation, Vietnam Oil and Gas Corporation, Philippine National Oil Company

This Agreement is entered into on this ＿＿ day of ＿＿ 2005 by and among China National Offshore Oil Corporation (hereinafter referred to as CNOOC), a company organized and existing under the laws of the People's Republic of China, having its headquarters domiciled in Beijing, and Vietnam Oil and Gas Corporation (hereafter referred to as "Petrol Vietnam"), a company organized and existing under the laws of the Socialist Republic of Vietnam, having its headquarters domiciled in Hanoi and Philippine National Oil Company (hereinafter referred to as "PNOC"), a company organized and existing under the laws of the Republic of the Philippines, having its headquarters domiciled at Fort Bonifacio, Taguig, Metro Manila, as the other part.

CNOOC Petrol Vietnam and PNOC are collectively referred to as "Parties" and individually as "Party".

WITNESSETH: That

WHEREAS, CNOOC is a state-owned oil company of the People's Republic of China;

WHEREAS, Petrol Vietnam is the national oil company of the Socialist Republic of Vietnam;

WHEREAS, PNOC is the national oil company of the Republic of the Philippines;

WHEREAS, the Parties' respective governments have expressed their commitment to pursue peaceful efforts to transform the South China Sea into an area of peace, stability, cooperation and development;

WHEREAS, the Parties shall abide by their respective government's commitment to fully implement the United Nations Convention on the Law of the Sea (UNCLOS) and the ASEAN-China Declaration on the Conduct of Parties in the South China Sea (DOC);

WHEREAS under the authorization of the Chinese Government, CNOOC has the exclusive right to sign this Agreement with PNOC and Petrol Vietnam for a joint marine seismic undertaking within the Agreement Area;

WHEREAS, under the authorization of the Socialist Republic of Vietnam, Petrol Vietnam has the exclusive right to sign this Agreement with CNOOC and PNOC for a joint marine seismic, undertaking within the Agreement Area;

WHEREAS, under the authorization of the Philippine Government, PNOC has the exclusive right to sign this Agreement with CNOOC and Petrol Vietnam for a joint marine seismic undertaking within the Agreement Area;

WHEREAS, the Parties recognize that the signing of this Agreement shall not undermine the basic position held by the Government of each Party on the South China Sea issue;

NOW, THEREFORE, the Parties hereby agree, as follows:

Article 1   The Agreement Term

Unless otherwise agreed upon by the Parties, the term of this Agreement shall be Three (3) years starting from the date of commencement of implementation of the Agreement. The said three-year period is hereinafter referred to as the "Agreement Term".

Article 2   The Agreement Area

The Agreement Area as of the date of signing of this Agreement covers a total area of one hundred forty-two thousand eight hundred and Eighty-six (1420 886) square kilometers as defined and marked out by the geographic location and the coordinates of the connecting points of the boundary lines in the Annex "A" attached hereto.

Article 3   Financing

Each Party shall be responsible for the costs of its own personnel designated for the implementation of this Agreement. Such costs shall include but not be limited to salaries or wages, allowance, expenses for travel and accommodation. However, the expenses incurred for carrying out the activities referred to in Article 4. 1 hereof and any other necessary activities determined by

the Joint Operating Committee referred to in Article 5 hereof to be necessary for the implementation of this Agreement shall be shared by the Parties on equal basis.

Article 4   Seismic Work

4. 1   It is agreed that certain amount of 2D and/or 3D seismic lines shall be collected and processed and certain amount of existing 2D seismic lines shall be reprocessed within the Agreement Term. The seismic work shall be conducted in accordance with the seismic program unanimously approved by the Parties to ensure safety, stability and

protection of the environment in the Agreement Area.

4.2   The actual annual work program and budget within the Agreement Term shall be formulated by the Joint Operating Committee referred to in Article 5 hereof pursuant to the Parties' authorization. The interpretation and evaluation on data should be done by a joint team created by the Parties either in Beijing or Hanoi or Manila.

Article 5   The Joint Operating Committee

5.1   For the proper performance of the joint activity, the Parties shall establish a Joint Operating Committee ("JOC") within thirty (30) days from the date of commencement of the implementation of the Agreement.

5.2   CNOOC, Petrol Vietnam and PNOC shall each appoint three (3) representatives to form the JOC, and each Party shall designate one of its representatives as its chief representative. When a decision is to be made on any proposal, the chief representative from each Parry shall be the spokesman on behalf of such Parry.

5.3   Decisions of the JOC shall be made unanimously through consultation.

5.4   The Parties shall empower the JOC to:

5.4.1   Propose to the Parties a Joint Operating Agreement (JOA) which will provide the terms of reference for the conduct of the joint activity;

5.4.2   Formulate the annual work program and budget;

5.4.3   Discuss and determine the manner of data exchange;

5.4.4   Arrange further joint studies;

5.4.5   Formulate the actual plan for seismic line acquisition;

5.4.6   Sign subcontracts and service contracts for seismic line acquisition and processing; and

5.4.6   Interpret and evaluate the relevant data and submit final evaluation report to the Parties.

5.5   The JOC may discuss and determine relevant job descriptions, work procedures, the establishment of subordinate bodies, methods of cash calls, accounting methods and other necessary rules and regulations within the JOC as the joint activity may require.

5.6　The JOC shall report to the Parties on a timely basis the progress of joint activity and be subject to the directions given by the Parties.

Article 6　Subcontracts and Service Contracts.

6.1　As a general rule, the Parties agree to have effective and equal participation in all activities relevant to the implementation of this Agreement.

6.2　The Parties agree to use vessels of CNOOC's or Petrol Vietnam's or PNOC's affiliates or other party's vessels to conduct the seismic line acquisition provided that the costs are competitive and reasonable. The Parties shall exert best efforts to allow such vessels' of CNOOC's, Petrol Vietnam's or PNOC's affiliates or those of such other parties to use the ports of the Philippines. Vietnam or China, as the case may be, to get necessary supplies.

6.3　The Parties agree to use CNOOC's or Petro Vietnam's or PNOC's affiliates or other parties to process the relevant seismic data.

Article 7　Mutual Assistance

7.1　The Parties shall use reasonable efforts to obtain all the necessary approvals from their respective governments for the implementation of this Agreement.

7.2　A Party shall facilitate each other's and other party's personnel and vessels to enter into relevant areas to conduct joint marine seismic undertaking to get necessary supply and to obtain all the necessary permits on a timely basis.

7.3 With regard to the joint activity, a Party shall, upon the other Party's request, use reasonable efforts to contact and coordinate with its relevant governmental departments.

Article 8   Negotiation Term

In the event the Panics elect to enter into negotiations for signing a more definitive agreement for further cooperation covering all or part of the Agreement Area prior to or at the expiration of the Agreement Term then such negotiations shall take place during the Agreement Term or during the period of ninety (90) days following the date of expiration of the Agreement Term (all of which periods are hereinafter referred to as the "Negotiation Period"). The Negotiation Period shall be reserved for the sole purpose of negotiations among CNOOC. Petrol Vietnam and PNOC During such Negotiation Period, unless otherwise agreed by the Panics, neither Party shall have the right to negotiate an agreement for a marine seismic undertaking or any other agreements with any other part with in the Agreement Area.

After the Parties have decided to pursue a definitive agreement, the Parties will consult with their appropriate authorities on the terms for allowing the participation of other national and international oil companies, including the specific arrangements for their participation.

Article 9   Assignment

9. 1   Except for the retention of CNOOC's management functions, CNOOC shall assign all its rights and obligations under the Agreement to one of its affiliates (it is understood by the Parties that such affiliate shall be CNOOC China Limited). Petrol Vietnam reserves the right to assign all its rights and obligations under the Agreement to one of its affiliates. PNOC shall assign all its rights and obligations under the Agreement to one of its affiliates (it is understood by the Parties that such affiliate shall be PNOC Exploration Corporation). Each of CNOOC, Petrol Vietnam and PNOC shall provide one another with copies of the written agreement for such assignment of all of its rights and obligations.

9. 2   Except for the assignments described in Article 9. 1, no Party shall, assign ail or part of its rights and obligations under the Agreement

to any other *party* without the prior written consent of the other Parties herein.

Article 10 Confidentiality of Information

This Agreement and all relevant documents, information, data and reports with respect to the joint marine seismic undertaking shall be kept confidential during the Agreement Term and within five (5) years after its expiration and shall not be disclosed by a Party to any third party without the written consent of the other Party. However, no consent shall be required when said documents, information, data and reports are disclosed, for the purpose of implementation of this Agreement, to the Parties' respective governments, affiliates or stock exchanges on which a Party's shares are registered.

Article 11   Miscellaneous Provisions

11.1   The Parties shall exert their best efforts to settle amicably through consultation any dispute arising in connection with the performance or interpretation of any provision hereof.

11.2   All the data and information acquired for the fulfillment of the Seismic Work referred to in Article-I hereof and their interpretation shall be jointly owned by the Parties. In the event any Party wishes to see or disclose the above-mentioned data and information after the expiration of the confidentiality term, prior written consent; therefor shall be obtained from the other Parties.

11.3   AH notices and documents by one Party to the other Party shall be delivered by hand or sent by mail, registered airmail or facsimile transmission to the addresses hereunder specified:

For CNOOC:

Cao Yunshi

General Counsel

CNOOC

PO Box 4705, No. 6 Dongzhimenwai Xiaojie

Dongcheng District, Beijing

People's Republic of China

Postcode: 100027

Tel: 008610 84521056

Fax * 008610 84522028

For Petrol Vietnam:

Vietnam Oil and Gas Corporation

22 Ngo Quyen Str,

Hoan Kiem Dist. , Hanoi

Socialist Republic of Vietnam

Postcode: 84-

Tel: (84. 4) 8252526

Fax: (84. 4) 8265942

For PNOC:

Eduardo V. Manalac

President and CEO

PNOC

Building: Energy Center,

Merritt Road, Fort Bonifacio, Taguig,

1634, Metro Manila, Philippines

Tel: +63. 2 840 2236

Fax: +63. 2 840 2138

Each Party may change its address or representative by a written notice to the other Party.

11. 4 The Parties' rights, interest and obligations under the Agreement shall be on equal basis.

11. 5 The Parties commit to observe and follow all laws and regulations, as well as any international obligation, of their respective countries that may have a bearing on this Agreement or any further or subsequent agreements that may be signed by the Parties.

11. 6 After the Agreement is signed, it shall be approved by the Parties respective governments. The later date of such approvals shall be

the effective date of the Agreement. The Parties agree that the first day of the month following the effective date of the Agreement shall be the date of commencement of the implementation of the Agreement.

11.7　The Parties agree to issue a joint press release on the purpose, scope and area of agreement after this Agreement has been signed.

11.8　*The* Agreement shall be written in Chinese, Vietnamese and English languages. In case of divergence in interpretation, the English text shall prevail.

The Agreement is signed on this ＿＿＿＿ day of ＿＿＿＿ 2005 in ＿＿＿＿ by the authorized representatives of the Parties hereunder.

China National Offshore Oil Corporation

　　Signature：

　　Name：Fu Chengyu

　　Title：President

Petrol Vietnam

　　Signature：

　　Name：Tran Ngoc Canh Title：

　　President and CEO

Philippine National Oil Company

　　Signature：

　　Name：Eduardo V. Manaiac

　　Title：President and CEO

四、2008 年《中日东海问题原则共识》

China-Japan Principled Consensus on the East China Sea Issue

(18 June 2008)

Foreign Ministry Spokesperson Jiang Yu announced on June 18 that China and Japan reached a principled consensus on the East China Sea issue through consultation on equal footing.

Ⅰ. COOPERATION BETWEEN CHINA AND JAPAN IN THE EAST CHINA SEA

In order to make the East China Sea, of which the delimitation between China and Japan is yet to be made, a "sea of peace, cooperation and friendship," China and Japan have, in keeping with the common understanding reached by leaders of the two countries in April 2007 and their new common understanding reached in December 2007, agreed through serious consultations that the two sides will conduct cooperation in the transitional period prior to delimitation without prejudicing their respective legal positions. The two sides have taken the first step to this end and will continue to conduct consultations in the future.

II. UNDERSTANDING BETWEEN CHINA AND JAPAN ON JOINT DEVELOPMENT OF THE EAST CHINA SEA

As the first step in the joint development of the East China Sea between China and Japan, the two sides will work on the following:

(a) The block for joint development shall be the area that is bounded by straight lines joining the following points in the order listed:

1. Latitude 29°31′ North, longitude 125°53′30″ East
2. Latitude 29°49′ North, longitude 125°53′30″ East
3. Latitude 30°04′ North, longitude 126°03′45″ East
4. Latitude 30°00′ North, longitude 126°10′23″ East
5. Latitude 30°00′ North, longitude 126°20′00″ East
6. Latitude 29°55′ North, longitude 126°26′00″ East
7. Latitude 29°31′ North, longitude 126°26′00″ East

(b) The two sides will, through joint exploration, select by mutual agreement areas for joint development in the above-mentioned block under the principle of mutual benefit. Specific matters will be decided by the two sides through consultations.

(c) To carry out the above-mentioned joint development, the two sides will work to fulfill their respective domestic procedures and arrive at the necessary bilateral agreement at an early date.

(d) The two sides have agreed to continue consultations for the early realization of joint development in other parts of the East China Sea.

III. UNDERSTANDING ON THE PARTICIPATION OF JAPANESE LEGAL PERSON IN THE DEVELOPMENT OF CHUNXIAO OIL AND GAS FIELD IN ACCORDANCE WITH CHINESE LAWS

Chinese enterprises welcome the participation of Japanese legal person in the development of the existing oil and gas field in Chunxiao in accordance with the relevant laws of China governing cooperation with foreign enterprises in the exploration and exploitation of offshore petroleum resources.

The governments of China and Japan have confirmed this, and will work to reach agreement on the exchange of notes as necessary and exchange them at an early date. The two sides will fulfill their respective domestic procedures as required.

资料来源：中华人民共和国外交部网站，http：//www. fmprc. gov. cn/ web/fyrbt_673021/dhdw_673027/t466568. shtml。

《中日东海问题原则共识》

（2008 年 6 月 18 日）

外交部发言人姜瑜 2008 年 6 月 18 日宣布，中日双方通过平等协商，就东海问题达成原则共识。

一、关于中日在东海的合作

为使中日之间尚未划界的东海成为和平、合作、友好之海，中日双方根据 2007 年 4 月中日两国领导人达成的共识以及 2007 年 12 月中日两国领导人达成的新共识，经过认真磋商，一致同意在实现划界前的过渡期间，在不损害双方法律立场的情况下进行合作。为此，双方迈出了第一步，今后将继续进行磋商。

二、中日关于东海共同开发的谅解

作为中日在东海共同开发的第一步，双方将推进以下步骤：

（一）由以下各坐标点顺序连线围成的区域为双方共同开发区块（附示意图）：

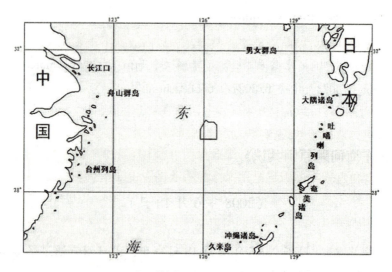

中日共同开发区块示意图

1. 北纬 29°31′，东经 125°53′30″
2. 北纬 29°49′，东经 125°53′30″
3. 北纬 30°04′，东经 126°03′45″
4. 北纬 30°00′，东经 126°10′23″
5. 北纬 30°00′，东经 126°20′00″
6. 北纬 29°55′，东经 126°26′00″
7. 北纬 29°31′，东经 126°26′00″

（二）双方经过联合勘探，本着互惠原则，在上述区块中选择双方一致同意的地点进行共同开发。具体事宜双方通过协商确定。

（三）双方将努力为实施上述开发履行各自的国内手续，尽快达成必要的双边协议。

(四)双方同意,为尽早实现在东海其它海域的共同开发继续磋商。

三、关于日本法人依照中国法律参加春晓油气田开发的谅解

中国企业欢迎日本法人按照中国对外合作开采海洋石油资源的有关法律,参加对春晓现有油气田的开发。

中日两国政府对此予以确认,并努力就进行必要的换文达成一致,尽早缔结。双方为此履行必要的国内手续。

资料来源:中华人民共和国外交部网站,http://www.fmprc.gov.cn/web/fyrbt_673021/dhdw_673027/t466568.shtml。

五、2011 年《落实〈南海各方行为宣言〉指导方针》

Guidelines for the Implementation of the DOC

Reaffirming that the DOC is a milestone document signed between the ASEAN Member States and China, embodying their collective commitment to promoting peace, stability and mutual trust and to ensuring the peaceful resolution of disputes in the South China Sea;

Recognizing also that the full and effective implementation of the DOC will contribute to the deepening of the ASEAN-China Strategic Partnership for Peace and Prosperity;

These Guidelines are to guide the implementation of possible joint cooperative activities, measures and projects as provided for in the DOC.

1. The implementation of the DOC should be carried out in a step-by-step approach in line with the provisions of the DOC.

2. The Parties to the DOC will continue to promote dialogue and consultations in accordance with the spirit of the DOC.

3. The implementation of activities or projects as provided for in the DOC should be clearly identified.

4. The participation in the activities or projects should be carried out on a voluntary basis.

5. Initial activities to be undertaken under the ambit of the DOC should be confidence-building measures.

6. The decision to implement concrete measures or activities of the

DOC should be based on consensus among parties concerned, and lead to the eventual realization of a Code of Conduct.

7. In the implementation of the agreed projects under the DOC, the services of the Experts and Eminent Persons, if deemed necessary, will be sought to provide specific inputs on the projects concerned.

8. Progress of the implementation of the agreed activities and projects under the DOC shall be reported annually to the ASEAN-China Ministerial Meeting (PMC).

资料来源：中华人民共和国外交部网站，http：//www. fmprc. gov. cn/ web/wjb_673085/zzjg_673183/yzs_673193/dqzz_673197/nanhai_6。

《落实〈南海各方行为宣言〉指导方针》

(2011 年 7 月 20 日，巴厘岛)

重申《南海各方行为宣言》是中国同东盟成员国签署的具有里程碑意义的文件，显示了他们共同促进和平稳定和互信以及确保和平解决南海争议的承诺；

认识到全面、有效落实《宣言》将有助于深化中国—东盟面向和平与繁荣的战略伙伴关系；

本指针旨在指导落实《宣言》框架下可能开展的共同合作活动、措施和项目。

一、落实《宣言》应根据《宣言》条款，以循序渐进的方式进行。

二、《宣言》各方将根据《宣言》的精神，继续推动对话和磋商。

三、落实《宣言》框架下的活动或项目应明确确定。

四、参与活动或项目应建立在自愿的基础上。

五、《宣言》范围内最初开展的活动应是建立信任措施。

六、应在有关各方共识的基础上决定实施《宣言》的具体措施或活动，并迈向最终制订"南海行为准则"。

七、在落实《宣言》框架下达成共识的合作项目时，如有需要，将请专家和名人为有关项目提供协助。

八、每年向中国—东盟外长会报告《宣言》范围内达成共识的合作活动或项目的实施进展情况。

资料来源：中华人民共和国外交部网站，http：//www.fmprc.gov.cn/web/wjb_673085/zzjg_673183/yzs_673193/dqzz_673197/nanhai_6。

六、中国与东盟部分国家的联合声明

1. 2013 年《中华人民共和国和文莱达鲁萨兰国联合声明》

（2013 年 10 月 11 日，斯里巴加湾市）

一、应文莱达鲁萨兰国苏丹和国家元首苏丹·哈吉·哈桑纳尔·博尔基亚·穆伊扎丁·瓦达乌拉陛下邀请，中华人民共和国国务院总理李克强阁下于 2013 年 10 月 9 日至 11 日对文莱进行正式访问。李克强总理还出席了 2013 年 10 月 9 日至 10 日在文莱举行的东亚领导人系列会议。

二、访问期间，李克强总理与苏丹陛下举行了会谈，双方在和谐友好的气氛中就双边关系以及共同关心的地区和国际问题深入交换了意见。

三、双方对 1991 年两国建交以来双边关系取得的显著成就表示高兴。两国领导人回顾了中文之间密切的历史和文化联系，对两国长期以来的关系表示肯定。双方重申以 1991 年《中华人民共和国政府和文莱达鲁萨兰国苏丹陛下政府关于两国建立外交关系的谅解备忘录》、1999 年和 2004 年《中华人民共和国与文莱达鲁萨兰国联合公报》、2005 年《中华人民共和国和文莱达鲁萨兰国联合新闻公报》和 2013 年《中华人民共和国和文莱达鲁萨兰国联合声明》中确立的原则和精神为基础，通过各领域合作深化双边关系的政治意愿。

四、双方重申相互尊重主权和领土完整，互不干涉内政。李克强总理赞赏文莱继续坚持一个中国政策，支持两岸关系和平发展与中国和平统一大业。

五、双方认为，中国和文莱互为紧密的合作伙伴，双方为实现共同繁荣与发展密切合作，为地区和平与进步作出贡献。双方鼓励各自官员开拓思路，进一步加强 2013 年 4 月习近平主席和苏丹陛下一致同意建立的中文战略合作关系。

六、双方同意保持双边交往的频度，加强两国外交、政治、经贸等各层级的磋商机制。双方同意进一步加强在经贸、能源、基础设施、农渔业、防务、教育和人文交流等领域的合作。

七、双方对中文在能源领域，特别是中国海洋石油总公司（中国海油）与文莱国家石油公司（文莱国油）之间的现有合作表示满意，对中国海油与文莱国油近期签署关于成立油田服务领域合资公司的协议表示欢迎。双方鼓励各自官员根据 2013 年 4 月 5 日中文联合声明第十条所表述的原则为基础，探讨两国相关企业在其他方面共同勘探和开采海上油气资源。

八、双方注意到 2003 年 9 月两国签署《中华人民共和国国防部与文莱达鲁萨兰国国防部关于军事交流的谅解备忘录》后防务领域取得的积极进展，愿不断加强两军在高层互访、团组往来、人员培训等领域的交流与合作。苏丹陛下欢迎更多的中方防务人员赴文莱皇家国防学院进修。苏丹陛下感谢中方对 2013 年 6 月在文莱举行的第一届东盟防长扩大会议框架下人道主义救援、减灾和军事医学联合演习所作的贡献，以及出席 2013 年 8 月在文莱举行的第二届东盟防长扩大会议。苏丹陛下期待中方出席 2013 年 12 月在文莱举办的文莱国际防务展。

九、双方认为，人员交流以及教育、旅游、文化和体育领域的合作在增进两国人民友谊方面发挥着重要作用。

十、双方欢迎中方志愿者继续在文莱相关机构为文莱汉语教学、体育和医疗科学事业发展作出贡献。

十一、苏丹陛下赞赏中方对文莱担任 2013 年东盟轮值主席国工作的支持，以及为促进本地区和平、稳定、发展与繁荣所作贡献，赞赏中方支持东盟通过自身引领的东盟与中日韩（10+3）、东亚峰会（EAS）和东盟地区论坛（ARF）等机制，在不断演变的区域架构中发挥主导作用。

十二、李克强总理祝贺文莱成功举办第 16 次中国-东盟领导人会议，赞赏中国-东盟对话伙伴关系，特别是 2003 年中国与东盟建立战略伙伴关系以来取得的进展。双方积极评价中国和东盟战略伙伴关系 10 周年系列庆祝活动。苏丹陛下赞赏李克强总理在此次中国-东盟领导人会议上重申中国长期坚持与东盟致力于友谊和伙伴关系的睦邻友好政策。

十三、苏丹陛下赞赏中方提出的打造中国-东盟自贸区"升级版"、设立亚洲基础设施投资银行、启动中国-东盟海上合作基金支持项目等倡议，以加强中国与东盟的经贸、投资、互联互通、海上等领域合作。苏丹陛下同时高度评价中方作为"东盟东部增长区"发展伙伴，加大参与并支持次区域层面经济发展。

十四、双方重申，将继续在亚太经合组织、亚欧会议、联合国和世界贸易组织等其他地区国际场合就共同关心的问题加强磋商。苏丹陛下期待中方明年担任亚太经合组织东道主，赞赏中方为增强世界经济所作出的努力，希望两国继续密切合作，共同促进强劲、可持续和平衡发展。苏丹陛下还对中方支持东盟继续参加二十国集团峰会表示赞赏。

十五、双方强调应由直接有关的主权国家根据包括 1982 年《联合国海洋法公约》在内的公认的国际法原则，通过和平对话和协商解决领土和管辖权争议。双方重申将致力于全面有效落实《南海各方行为宣言》，维护地区和平、稳定和安全，增进互信，加强合作。双方欢迎 2013 年 9 月 15 日在中国苏州举行的落实《南海各方行为宣言》第六次高官会，及在落实《南海各方行为宣言》框架下就"南海行为准则"进行的磋商取得的积极进展，认为应以循序渐进和协商一致的方式稳步推进"南海行为准则"进程。

十六、李克强总理感谢文方在访问期间给予的热情友好接待，期待着苏丹陛下和文莱其他王室成员在不久的将来访问中国。

资料来源：中华人民共和国外交部网站，http：//www.fmprc.gov.cn/web/ziliao_674904/1179_674909/t1087458.shtml。

2. 2013 年《新时期深化中越全面战略合作的联合声明》

（2013 年 10 月 15 日，河内）

一、应越南社会主义共和国政府总理阮晋勇邀请，中华人民共和国国务院总理李克强于 2013 年 10 月 13 日至 15 日对越南社会主义共和国进行正式访问。

访问期间，李克强总理同阮晋勇总理举行会谈，同越共中央总书记阮富仲、国家主席张晋创、国会主席阮生雄举行会见。在真诚友好、相互理解的气氛中，双方就新形势下进一步深化中越全面战略合作、当前国际地区形势及共同关心的问题深入交换意见，达成广泛共识。

二、双方回顾并高度评价中越关系的发展，重申将遵循两国领导人达成的重要共识，在"长期稳定、面向未来、睦邻友好、全面合作"的方针和"好邻居、好朋友、好同志、好伙伴"的精神指引下，发展中越全面战略合作伙伴关系。双方一致认为，在当前国际政治经济形势复杂演变的背景下，加强战略沟通，进一步深化务实合作，妥善处理存在的问题，加强在国际地区事务中的协调配合，推动两国关系长期稳定健康发展，符合两党两国和两国人民的根本利益，有利于地区及世界的和平、稳定与发展。

三、双方高度评价两国高层接触具有不可替代的重要作用，同意继续保持高层接触和互访，从战略高度牢牢把握新时期两国关系发展方向。同时，通过多边场合会晤等多种形式推动高层交往，用好领导人热线电话，就双边关系及共同关心的重大问题深入沟通。

四、双方同意继续用好中越双边合作指导委员会机制，统筹推进各领域互利合作，实施好《落实中越全面战略合作伙伴关系行动计划》，使用好两国外交、国防、经贸、公安、安全、新闻和两党中央对外部门和宣传部门交流合作机制，开好双边合作指导委员会会议、合作打击犯罪会议、经贸合委会会议、两党理论研讨会，做好年度外交磋商、防务安全磋商、党政干部扩大培训等工作，有效使用国防部直通电话，加强对舆论和媒体的正确引导，为增进双方互信，维护两国关系稳定发展作出重要贡献。

五、双方一致认为，中越互为近邻和重要伙伴，均处在经济社会发展的关键阶段，从两国共同需要和利益出发，双方同意在平等互利的基础上，以下述领域为重点进一步深化全面战略合作：

（一）关于陆上合作

双方同意抓紧落实《中越2012-2016年经贸合作五年发展规划》及重点合作项目清单。建立两国基础设施合作工作组，规划并指导具体项目实施。尽快就凭祥-河内高速公路项目实施和融资方案达成一致，争取早日动工建设。双方将积极推进东兴-下龙高速公路项目，中方支持有实力的中国企业按市场原则参与该项目，并愿在力所能及的范围内提供融资支持。双方有关部门将加紧工作，适时启动老街-河内-海防铁路项目可行性研究。

双方同意落实好《关于建设跨境经济合作区的备忘录》，积极研究商签《中越边境贸易协定》(修订版)，为促进两国边境地区合作与繁荣发挥积极作用。

双方同意加强经贸政策协调，落实好《农产品贸易领域合作谅解备忘录》、《关于互设贸易促进机构的协定》，在保持贸易稳定增长的基础上，促进双边贸易平衡增长，争取提前实现2015年双边贸易额600亿美元目标。中方将鼓励中国企业扩大进口越南有竞争力的商品。中方将支持中国企业赴越投资兴业，也愿为更多越南企业来华开拓市场创造更便利条件。越方将为早日建成龙江和海防两个经贸合作区提供便利和协助。双方将加紧施工，推动越中友谊宫项目早日建成。

双方同意进一步深化在农业、科技、教育、文化、体育、旅游、卫生等领域的交流合作。

双方同意继续发挥两国陆地边界联委会作用，认真落实年度工作计划。召开两国口岸合作委员会首次会议，推进陆地边境口岸开放工作，尽快正式开放峒中-横模国家级口岸。推动《德天瀑布地区旅游资源共同开发和保护协定》谈判尽快取得实质进展，尽快启动《北仑河口地区自由航行协定》新一轮谈判并达成一致，早日建成北仑河公路二桥、水口至驮隆中越界河公路二桥等跨境桥梁，为两国边境地区稳定和发展奠定基础。

双方同意进一步加强两国地方特别是边境省(区)的合作，发挥两国地方有关合作机制的作用。

(二)关于金融合作

双方同意加强在金融领域的合作，积极创造条件并鼓励双方金融机构为双边贸易和投资合作项目提供金融服务。在2003年两国央行签署边境贸易双边本币结算协定基础上，继续探讨扩大本币结算范围，促进双边贸易和投资。双方决定建立两国金融合作工作组，提高双方抵御金融风险的能力，维护两国及本地区经济稳定与发展。加强多边协调与配合，共同推进东亚地区财金合作。

(三)关于海上合作

双方同意恪守两党两国领导人共识，认真落实《关于指导解决中越海上问题基本原则协议》，用好中越政府边界谈判机制，坚持通过友好协商和谈判，寻求双方均能接受的基本和长久的解决办法，积极探讨不影响各自立场和主张的过渡性解决办法，包括积极研究和商谈共同开发问题。本着上述精神，双方同意在政府边界谈判代表团框架下成立中越海上共同开发磋商工作组。

双方同意加强对现有谈判磋商机制的指导，加大中越北部湾湾口外海域工作组和海上低敏感领域合作专家工作组工作力度。本着先易后难、循序渐进的原则，稳步推进湾口外海域划界谈判并积极推进该海域的共同开发，年内启动该海域共同考察，落实北部湾湾口外海域工作组谈判任务。尽快实施北部湾海洋和岛屿环境管理合作研究、红河三角洲与长江三角洲全新世沉积演化对比研究等海上低敏感领域合作项目，继续推进在海洋环保、海洋科研、海上搜救、防灾减灾、海上互联互通等领域合作。

双方同意切实管控好海上分歧，不采取使争端复杂化、扩大化的行动，用好两国外交部海上危机管控热线，两国农业部门海上渔业活动突发事件联系热线，及时、妥善处理出现的问题，同时继续积极探讨管控危机的有效措施，维护中越关系大局以及南海和平稳定。

六、双方同意办好第二届中越青年大联欢、中越青年友好会见、中越人民大联欢等活动，为中越友好事业培养更多接班人。双方同意在越建立孔子学院，并加快推动互设文化中心、切实加强中越友好宣传，深化两国民众之间的了解与友谊。

七、越方重申坚定奉行一个中国政策，支持两岸关系和平发展与中国统一大业，坚决反对任何形式的"台独"分裂活动。越南不同台湾发展任何官方关系。中方对此表示赞赏。

八、双方同意加强在联合国、世贸组织、亚太经合组织、亚欧会议、东盟地区论坛、中国-东盟、东盟-中日韩、东亚峰会等多边场合的协调与配合，为维护世界的和平、稳定与繁荣共同努力。

双方高度评价中国-东盟关系发展取得的巨大成就，一致同意以中国-东盟建立战略伙伴关系10周年为契机，进一步增进战略信任，赞赏和欢迎中方关于缔结中国-东盟国家睦邻友好合作条约，升级中国-东盟自贸区，建立亚洲基础设施投资银行的倡议。中国与东盟开展广泛合作，促进东南亚地区和平、稳定、相互尊重和信任非常重要。

双方一致同意，全面有效落实《南海各方行为宣言》，增进互信，推动合作，共同维护南海和平与稳定，按照《南海各方行为宣言》的原则和精神，在协商一致的基础上朝着制定"南海行为准则"而努力。

九、访问期间，双方签署了《关于互设贸易促进机构的协定》、《关于建设跨境经济合作区的备忘录》、《关于成立协助中方在越实施项目联合工作组的备忘录》、《关于共同建设水口-驮隆中越界河公路二桥的协定》及其实施议定书、《关于开展北部湾海洋和岛屿环境管理合作研究的协议》、《关于长江三角洲与红河三角洲全新世沉积演化对比研究项目的协议》、《关于合作设立河内大学孔子学院的协议》及一些经济合作文件。

十、双方对中国国务院总理李克强访越成果表示满意，一致认为此访对推动两国关系发展及各领域务实合作具有重要意义。

资料来源：中华人民共和国外交部网站，http：//www.fmprc.gov.cn/web/ziliao_674904/1179_674909/t1089639.shtml。

3. 2015 年《中越联合声明》

（2015 年 11 月 6 日，河内）

2015 年 11 月 6 日，中华人民共和国和越南社会主义共和国在河内发表《中越联合声明》，联合声明全文如下：

一、应越南共产党中央委员会总书记阮富仲、越南社会主义共和国主席张晋创邀请，中国共产党中央委员会总书记、中华人民共和国主席习近平于 2015 年 11 月 5 日至 6 日对越南进行国事访问。

访问期间，习近平总书记、国家主席分别同阮富仲总书记、张晋创国家主席举行了会谈，并会见了越南政府总理阮晋勇、国会主席阮生雄。两党两国领导人在友好坦诚的气氛中，就进一步深化两党两国关系及共同关心的国际和地区问题深入交换意见，达成了重要共识。

双方一致认为，访问取得了圆满成功，为巩固中越传统友谊、深化全面战略合作、促进本地区乃至世界的和平、稳定与发展作出了重要贡献。

二、双方对两国在符合本国国情的社会主义建设事业中取得的历史性伟大成就感到高兴，同意加强相互交流和借鉴，推动中国改革开放和越南革新事业向前发展，为各自社会主义建设事业注入新活力。

中方衷心祝愿越南共产党 2016 年初成功召开第十二次全国代表大会，相信在越南共产党领导下，越南人民将胜利实现既定目标，把越南建设成为民富、国强、民主、公平、文明的社会主义国家。

越方衷心祝愿并相信中国人民在中国共产党领导下，一定能协调推进全面建成小康社会、全面深化改革、全面依法治国、全面从严治党，胜利实现建成富强民主文明和谐的社会主义现代化国家目标。

三、双方回顾了中越建交 65 年来两党两国关系发展历程，一致认为由毛泽东主席和胡志明主席等老一辈领导人亲手缔造和精心培育的中越友谊是两国人民共同的宝贵财富，双方应共同继承、维护和发扬，落实好"长期稳定、面向未来、睦邻友好、全面合作"方针和"好邻居、好朋友、好同志、好伙伴"精神，牢牢把握中越友好的正确方向，加强战略沟通，增进政治互信，在相互尊重、平等互利基础上推进各领域合作，管控好和妥善处理分歧，推动中越全面战略合作伙伴关系健康稳定发展。

四、双方认为，两党两国高层保持经常接触，对增进政治互信、推动双边关系发展具有重要作用，同意通过双边互访、互派特使、热线电话、年度会晤、多边场合会晤等灵活多样的方式保持高层交往，及时就两党两国关系中的重大问题交换意见。

五、双方认为，中越均处在经济社会发展的重要时期，双方视对方的发展为自身发展的机遇，同意发挥好中越双边合作指导委员会的统筹协调作用，重点推动以下领域合作：

（一）执行好两党合作计划，深化两党中央各部门和地方特别是接壤各省（区）党组织间交流合作，继续办好理论研讨会，实施好此访期间签署的两党干部培训合作计划（2016—2020 年）。积极推进中国全国人大与越南国会、中国全国政协与越南祖国阵线之间的友好交流合作，促进两国民间友好交流。

（二）落实好两国外交部合作议定书，保持两部领导经常交往，继续举办年度外交磋商，加强两部对口司局交流，实施好两部干部培训工作。越方愿为中国在越南岘港设立总领馆提供便利。

（三）保持两军高层交往，用好两军防务安全磋商、边境高层会晤机制和国防部直通电话，加强两军在边防友好交流、人员培训、军事学术研究、海军北部湾联合巡逻和军舰互访等领域交流合作，深化联合国维和及军队党务政治工作方面经验交流。加强两国海警的海上执法合作，共同维护北部湾海域和平稳定，推动中国海警局与越南海警司令部签署合作备忘录。深化执法安全合作，继续办好两国公安部合作打击犯罪会议和中国国家安全部与越南公安部副部级安全战略对话，加强在反恐、禁毒、打击电信诈骗、出入境管理、边境管控、网络安全等领域合作，开展国内安全保卫、联合追逃、非法就业管理方面的经验交流。

（四）加强两国间发展战略对接，推动"一带一路"倡议和"两廊一圈"构想对接，加强在建材、辅助工业、装备制造、电力、可再生能源等领域产能合作。加紧成立工作组，积极商签跨境经济合作区建设共同总体方案，推进中国在越前江省龙江、海防市安阳两个工业园区的建设并积极吸引投资，督促和指导两国企业实施好中资企业在越承包建设的钢铁、化肥等合作项目。

用好中越经贸合委会机制，积极研究续签《中越经贸合作五年发展规划》，加紧修订《中越边贸协定》，推动双边贸易平衡、稳定、可持续发展，努力实现2017年双边贸易额1000亿美元目标。加强在《农产品贸易领域合作谅解备忘录》框架下的合作，鼓励双方企业扩大农产品贸易合作，欢迎两国有关部门和地方探讨设立贸易促进机构。

用好基础设施合作工作组和金融与货币合作工作组，推动有关领域合作不断取得积极进展。实施好河内轻轨二号线（吉灵-河东）项目，加紧制定老街-河内-海防标准轨铁路线路规划，推进云屯-芒街高速公路等基础设施互联互通合作。

深化海关合作，共同打击跨境走私行为，继续探索促进边境口岸通关便利化的合作措施，加强两国边境口岸基础设施建设和管理，提升两国边境口岸开放合作水平。

（五）扩大科技、教育、文化、旅游、新闻等领域合作。用好两国科技合作联委会机制，积极推进技术转移、科学家交流等合作，探讨建立联合实验室。争取于2017年建成越中友谊宫并投入使用，早日在对方国家设立文化中心，办好河内大学孔子学院。加强两国媒体交流，加大对中越友好的宣传力度。继续办好中越青年友好会见、人民论坛等活动，2016年在越举办第三届中越青年大联欢。

六、继续发挥好中越陆地边界联合委员会作用，落实好此访期间签署的《北仑河口自由航行区航行协定》和《合作保护和开发德天瀑布旅游资源协定》，总结两国陆地边界三个管理文件实施五年来的情况。加强两国边境省区合作，促进边境地区发展。

七、双方就海上问题坦诚交换意见，强调恪守两党两国领导人达成的重要共识，认真落实《关于指导解决中越海上问题基本原则协议》，用好中越政府边界谈判机制，坚持通过友好协商和谈判，寻求双方均能接受的基本和长久解决办法，积极探讨不影响各自立场和主张的过渡性解决办法，包括积极研究和商谈共同开发问题。

双方宣布于 2015 年 12 月中旬启动北部湾湾口外海域共同考察海上实地作业，认为这是双方开展海上合作的重要开端。双方将稳步推进北部湾湾口外海域划界谈判并积极推进该海域的共同开发，同意加大湾口外海域工作组谈判力度，继续推进海上共同开发磋商工作组工作，加强低敏感领域合作，宣布启动中越长江三角洲与红河三角洲全新世沉积演化对比合作研究项目。

双方同意共同管控好海上分歧，全面有效落实《南海各方行为宣言》（DOC），推动在协商一致的基础上早日达成"南海行为准则"（COC），不采取使争议复杂化、扩大化的行动，及时妥善处理出现的问题，维护中越关系大局以及南海和平稳定。

八、越方重申坚定奉行一个中国政策，支持两岸关系和平发展与中国统一大业，坚决反对任何形式的"台独"分裂活动。越南不同台湾发展任何官方关系。中方对此表示赞赏。

九、双方同意继续加强在联合国、亚太经合组织、中国-东盟等多边框架内的配合，共同维护与促进世界的和平、繁荣与发展。中方支持越方成功主办 2017 年亚太经合组织领导人非正式会议。

十、访问期间，双方签署了《中国共产党与越南共产党干部培训合作计划(2016-2020 年)》、《中华人民共和国政府与越南社会主义共和国政府关于北仑河口自由航行区航行的协定》、《中华人民共和国政府与越南社会主义共和国政府关于合作保护和开发德天瀑布旅游资源的协定》、《中华人民共和国政府与越南社会主义共和国政府关于互设文化中心的协定》、《中华人民共和国政府与越南社会主义共和国政府关于越南老街-河内-海防标准轨铁路线路规划项目可行性研究换文》、《中华人民共和国国家发展和改革委员会与越南社会主义共和国工业贸易部关于促进产能合作的谅解备忘录》、《中华人民共和国商务部与越南社会主义共和国计划投资部关于越中友谊宫项目优化设计谅解备忘录》、《中国共产党广西壮族自治区委员会与越南共产党广宁省委员会关于建立友好地方组织的交流协议》、《中国共产党云南省委员会与越南共产党老街省委员会关于开展地方党委友好交往协议》等合作文件。

十一、习近平总书记、国家主席对阮富仲总书记、张晋创国家主席以及越南共产党、政府和人民所给予的隆重、热情和友好接待表示衷心感谢。

资料来源：中华人民共和国外交部网站，http：//www. fmprc. gov. cn/web/ziliao_674904/1179_674909/t1312772. shtml。

4. 2016 年《中华人民共和国与菲律宾共和国联合声明》

（2016 年 10 月 21 日，北京）

一、应中华人民共和国主席习近平邀请，菲律宾共和国总统罗德里戈·罗亚·杜特尔特于 2016 年 10 月 18 日至 21 日对中华人民共和国进行了国事访问。

二、访问期间，习近平主席同杜特尔特总统在亲切友好气氛中进行了富有成果的会谈，就双边关系及共同关心的国际和地区问题深入交换了意见。国务院总理李克强、全国人大常委会委员长张德江分别与杜特尔特总统举行了会见。国务院副总理张高丽与杜特尔特总统共同出席了中菲经贸合作论坛开幕式并致辞。

三、双方认为，中菲人民之间传统友谊历史悠久。双方同意两国人民之间的相互理解和友谊至关重要，将共同致力于巩固两国人民之间的传统友谊。

四、双方同意自建交以来中菲关系发展顺利，在诸多合作领域取得显著进展，造福了两国和两国人民。

五、双方同意进一步丰富建立于相互尊重、真诚、平等和互惠互利原则基础上的双边关系，这也有利于本地区的和平、稳定与繁荣。

六、双方重申了 1975 年中菲建交公报及其他文件所包含的原则，其中包括通过和平方式解决争端的原则和菲方恪守一个中国政策。

七、双方重申了两国伙伴关系和对争取有益于两国人民的可持续发展、包容性增长的共同愿望，一致认为此访具有里程碑式意义，将为两国关系注入新动力，给两国人民带来实实在在的好处。双方将携手努力，推动两国致力于和平与发展的战略性合作关系健康稳定发展。

八、双方认为保持高层交往对促进双边关系全面发展具有重要意义。

九、双方欢迎访问期间签署的诸多合作协议和谅解备忘录（见附件）。

十、双方表达了在诸如教育、金融、海关、体育等其他领域签署合作协定和谅解备忘录的意愿。

十一、双方重申现有中菲双边对话机制对增进理解、拓展合作、增强双边关系的重要性，同意恢复两国外交磋商、领事磋商、经贸联委会、防务安全磋商、农业联委会、科技联委会及其他双边对话机制。

十二、双方愿鼓励两国高级别政府团组、地方政府、立法机构、政党、民间组织互访，增进沟通交流。

十三、菲方欢迎中方提议中国驻达沃总领馆将尽快开馆。双方将基于国际实践和互惠原则，并遵循1975年建交公报的原则对双边外交馆舍的最急迫问题优先作出妥善安排。

十四、双方认识到共同行动打击跨国犯罪的必要性，两国相关部门将根据共同认可的安排，加强在打击电信诈骗、网络诈骗、计算机犯罪、毒品贩卖、人口贩卖、濒危野生动植物及其制品走私等跨国犯罪方面的交流合作。

十五、双方反对任何形式的恐怖主义和暴力极端主义，将在包括信息交流、能力建设等方面进行合作，以共同防范和应对恐怖主义和暴力极端主义威胁。

十六、中方理解并支持菲政府致力于打击毒品犯罪的努力。双方认识到毒品问题给两国人民健康、安全和福祉构成严重威胁，同意加强信息共享，在打击毒品犯罪、预防教育、戒毒康复等方面分享知识技术。

十七、为加大禁毒行动力度，双方同意建立专案侦办和情报搜集领域的联合行动机制。菲方感谢中方在人员培训和捐赠毒品查缉检验设备等方面向菲禁毒工作提供援助。

十八、双方承诺根据公认的国际法原则，包括1982年《联合国海洋法公约》，加强两国海警部门间合作，应对南海人道主义、环境问题和海上紧急事件，如海上人员、财产安全问题和维护保护海洋环境等。

十九、双方同意继续探讨商签移管被判刑人条约。

二十、双方同意两军关系是两国关系重要组成部分。为增进互信，双方同意执行好《中菲防务合作谅解备忘录》，加强在人道主义援助、减灾、维和领域的交流合作。

二十一、双方一致认为双边经济合作发展强劲并仍存在增长空间。双方承诺将通过开展《关于加强双边贸易、投资和经济合作的谅解备忘录》框架下的活动发挥互补优势，不断促进贸易、投资和经济合作，加强两国在优先领域的经济关系。

二十二、双方认识到《中菲经贸合作五年发展规划（2011—2016年）》所取得的经济和社会成就，并通过签署《关于编制中菲经济合作发展规划的谅解备忘录》表达续签《发展规划》的承诺。

二十三、双方在减贫领域具有共同意愿，鉴此同意加强减贫实践交流和项目合作。

二十四、双方表达了在包括基础设施投资、基础设施项目建设、工业产能等领域共同开展务实合作的意愿。双方同意共同实施的基础设施合作需服从适当招标程序、透明度，符合两国相关国内法律法规和通行的国际实践。

二十五、双方将在优惠贷款、优惠出口买方信贷、债券、贷款、投资、证券及其他双方同意的如开发性专项贷款等领域加强金融合作。双方愿在亚投行和其他国际和地区银行框架下加强合作。

二十六、双方愿扩大双边贸易和投资本币结算，协调积极推进清迈倡议多边化等区域金融合作和双边本币互换安排。中方欢迎菲央行有意参与中国银行间债券市场。

二十七、双方承诺扩大在包括农业科技和基础设施、农业贸易、灌溉、适应和减缓气候变化、遵循动植物卫生标准等领域的合作。

二十八、双方同意加强在动植物检验检疫方面的合作，菲方欢迎中方宣布恢复相关菲企业对华出口香蕉、菠萝许可，将继续进口符合中方标准的设施包装的热蒸处理芒果。

二十九、双方愿共同努力，推动双方在优质杂交水稻种子、农业基础设施、农业机械、进一步发挥中菲农技中心作用及其他同意的领域的合作。中方承诺支持菲方遵照国内法律提升粮食生产能力、培训农业技术人员、发展农渔业和能力建设的努力。

三十、中方愿积极支持于紧急状态下在东盟与中日韩大米储备机制下向菲提供紧急粮食援助。

三十一、中方愿协助菲建立科研产业体系，帮助菲开展科技培训。双方愿探讨共建技术转移中心、联合实验室和科技资源共享平台的可能性。

三十二、双方认识到过去几年双向游客增长状况，注意到2017年"东盟-中国旅游合作年"的推动势头，同意设立旅游合作增长目标。双方愿鼓励本国公民赴对方国家旅游，探讨航空服务领域可能的增长点，鼓励双方航空公司在中国城市和菲律宾达沃及维萨亚、棉兰老地区城市间开设新航线，助力实现上述旅游合作增长目标。

三十三、双方鼓励两国大学间在研究、创新领域开展实质性交流，加强学术和产学研模式交流合作。中方愿在科学、技术、工程和数学领域对菲增加政府奖学金名额。

三十四、双方同意鼓励中国媒体同菲媒体包括"人民广播公司"开展人员互访、新闻产品互换、设备技术和培训等业务合作。中国新闻主管部门愿同菲总统府新闻部加强交流与合作。

三十五、双方表达了在两国省市间缔结更多友好省市关系的意愿，注意到这种安排将鼓励两国人民间增进了解，释放地方合作潜力。

三十六、双方同意在紧急援助和救灾领域开展合作。

三十七、双方重申推进落实《中菲文化合作协定2015年至2018年执行计划》的重要性，鼓励两国文化机构和团体加强互访。双方愿积极考虑在对方国家设立文化中心。

三十八、双方重视两国人员往来，注意到2017年是菲律宾苏禄苏丹访华600周年，愿举办相关纪念活动。

三十九、双方将探讨在包括信息科技、卫生、海关、研发、教育和其他领域的合作，使两国共同受益。

四十、双方就涉及南海的问题交换了看法。双方重申争议问题不是中菲双边关系的全部。双方就以适当方式处理南海争议的重要性交换了意见。双方重申维护及促进和平稳定、在南海的航行和飞越自由的重要性，根据包括《联合国宪章》和1982年《联合国海洋法公约》在内公认的国际法原则，不诉诸武力或以武力相威胁，由直接有关的主权国家通过友好磋商和谈判，以和平方式解决领土和管辖权争议。

四十一、双方回顾了2002年《南海各方行为宣言》和2016年7月25日于老挝万象通过的中国-东盟外长关于全面有效落实《宣言》的声明。双方承诺全面、有效落实《宣言》，愿共同努力在协商一致基础上早日达成"南海行为准则"。

四十二、双方同意继续商谈建立信任措施，提升互信和信心，并承诺在南海采取行动方面保持自我克制，以免使争议复杂化、扩大化和影响和平与稳定。鉴此，在作为其它机制的补充、不损及其他机制基础上，建立一个双边磋商机制是有益的，双方可就涉及南海的各自当前及其他关切进行定期磋商。双方同意探讨在其他领域开展合作。

四十三、中方支持菲担任 2017 年东盟轮值主席国。双方对过去 25 年来中国-东盟对话关系的发展感到满意，重申对地区架构中坚持东盟中心原则的承诺。中方重申支持东盟一体化、东盟共同体建设和东盟为实现"东盟 2025：携手前行"愿景文件目标所作的努力。

四十四、双方同意进一步加强在联合国、东盟地区论坛、亚太经合组织、亚欧会议、世界贸易组织、联合国气候变化大会及其他地区和国际组织中的合作。

四十五、双方重申恪守《联合国宪章》宗旨中的主权平等、不干涉、不干预原则，强调共同致力于通过在双方均参与的主要人权机制中开展对话合作来保护和增进人权。

四十六、双方支持通过必要和合理的改革加强联合国的作用，并主张推动落实发展问题、维护发展中国家合法权益、加强发展中国家在国际事务中的发言权和代表性，应成为联合国包括安理会改革的重点，不断增强发展中国家在联合国决策过程中的作用。

四十七、杜特尔特总统对中方给予的热情接待表示感谢。杜特尔特总统邀请习近平主席在方便时访问菲律宾，习近平主席愉快地接受了邀请。杜特尔特总统也表示欢迎中方领导人出席 2017 年东亚合作领导人系列会议。

附件：

签署合作文件清单

一、《中国政府和菲律宾政府经济技术合作协定》

二、《中国国家发展改革委和菲律宾国家经济发展署关于开展产能与投资合作的谅解备忘录》

三、《中国国家发展改革委与菲律宾交通部、公共工程与公路部关于交通基础设施合作项目清单的谅解备忘录》

四、《中国商务部和菲律宾贸工部签署关于加强贸易、投资和经济合

作的谅解备忘录》

五、《中国商务部和菲律宾国家经济发展署关于编制中菲经济合作发展规划的谅解备忘录》

六、《中国商务部和菲律宾财政部关于支持开展重大项目可行性研究的谅解备忘录》

七、《中国农业部与菲律宾农业部农业合作行动计划(2017—2019)》

八、《中国国新办和菲律宾总统府新闻部关于新闻、信息交流、培训和其他事宜的备忘录》

九、《中国质检总局和菲律宾农业部关于动植物检验检疫合作谅解备忘录》

十、《中国海警局和菲律宾海岸警卫队关于建立海警海上合作联合委员会的谅解备忘录》

十一、《中国国家旅游局和菲律宾旅游部旅游合作谅解备忘录执行计划(2017—2022)》

十二、《中国公安部禁毒局和菲律宾肃毒局合作议定书》

十三、《中国进出口银行和菲律宾财政部融资合作备忘录》

资料来源：中华人民共和国外交部网站，http：//www.fmprc.gov.cn/web/ziliao_674904/1179_674909/t1407676.shtml。

七、2015 年中国外交部声明《中国东海油气开发活动正当合法》

《中国东海油气开发活动正当合法》

（2015 年 7 月 24 日）

2015 年 7 月 22 日，日本在其外务省网站公布了中国东海油气开发有关情况，并要求中方停止在日方单方面主张的"中间线"中方一侧海域的开发活动。日方的要求毫无道理，中方在东海有关油气开发活动完全正当、合法。

一、中国东海油气开发活动是在无争议的中国管辖海域进行，完全是中国主权权利和管辖权范围内的事情，无可非议。上世纪 70 年代以来，中方一直在上述海域进行油气勘探开发活动，日方多年来从未提出异议。自2004 年以来，日方逐渐改变以往做法，不断对中方正当油气开发活动进行指责和炒作。

二、中日两国在东海尚未进行海域划界，中国不承认日本单方面划出的所谓"中间线"，中国也不认同日本以所谓"中间线"为基础进行海域划界的立场。中国主张 200 海里专属经济区，中国在东海的大陆架自然延伸至冲绳海槽。对于中日东海划界问题，中国愿在包括《联合国海洋法公约》在内的国际法基础上按照公平原则以协议方式进行解决。

三、中方长期以来一直从两国关系大局出发，保持克制，未在争议海域进行油气开发活动，我们主张与日方在不影响各自法律立场的前提下进行共同开发。

四、中日多年来就东海有关问题保持着沟通，双方于 2008 年 6 月达成东海问题原则共识。但日方随后曲解共识，为双方落实原则共识制造障碍。双方2010年7月举行了落实原则共识第一轮政府间磋商，后因日方在东海制造事端致使磋商中断至今。希望日方尽早回归共识、维护共识，为双方重启落实原则共识磋商创造良好的条件和气氛。

五、中方愿同日方在尊重历史事实的基础上，依据国际法，继续通过包括海洋事务高级别磋商机制在内的渠道就东海有关问题进行对话沟通，增进互信，管控分歧，促进合作。这有利于东海的和平稳定，也符合中日两国和两国人民的共同利益。

资料来源：中华人民共和国外交部网站，http：//www.fmprc.gov.cn/web/ziliao_674904/1179_674909/t1283725.shtml。

后　记

　　2016年，社会科学文献出版社出版了我组织翻译的《海上共同开发协定汇编》（汉英对照、上下册）。读者对该书的反应出乎我的意料：不少读者跟我提及该书对于从事有关海上共同开发问题的理论研究和实际工作，具有较为重要的参考价值。于是，我萌生了把这几年在从事海上共同开发问题研究过程中收集的其他相关资料加以整理出版的念头。这就是呈现在读者面前的《海上共同开发协定续编》的由来。

　　本书分上下两篇，上篇为"海上共同开发协定"，下篇是"与中国有关的海上共同开发的法律文件"。

　　本书由杨泽伟主编，具体分工如下：

　　杨泽伟（武汉大学"珞珈杰出学者"、法学博士、二级教授、国家高端智库武汉大学国际法研究所和中国边界与海洋研究院博士生导师、2011"国家领土主权与海洋权益协同创新中心海洋权益的保障与拓展研究创新团队"负责人）：负责本书的策划、统稿工作，并具体收集整理"案例三""下篇：与中国有关的海上共同开发的法律文件"的资料；

　　何海榕（法学博士、海南大学法学院副教授）：负责"案例六"；

　　陈思静（武汉大学国际法研究所博士研究生，国家高端智库武汉大学国际法研究所研究人员）：负责"案例五、七、九、十、十一、十三、十四、十七"；

　　王阳（武汉大学中国边界与海洋研究院博士研究生、2011"国家领土主权与海洋权益协同创新中心研究人员）：负责"案例五、七、九、十三"；

　　梅玉婕（武汉大学中国边界与海洋研究院博士研究生、2011"国家领土主权与海洋权益协同创新中心研究人员）：负责"案例五、七、九、十三"；

　　程时辉（武汉大学中国边界与海洋研究院博士研究生、2011"国家领土主权与海洋权益协同创新中心研究人员）：负责"案例一、二、四、八、十二、十五、十六、十八"。

杨泽伟

2018 年 3 月 27 日